I0878693

Rewriting Buddhism

Rewriting Buddhism

Pali literature and monastic reform in Sri Lanka, 1157–1270

Alastair Gornall

UCLPRESS

First published in 2020 by
UCL Press
University College London
Gower Street
London WC1E 6BT

Available to download free: www.uclpress.co.uk

Text © the author, 2020

The author has asserted his rights under the Copyright, Designs and Patents Act 1988 to be identified as the author of this work.

A CIP catalogue record for this book is available from The British Library.

This book is published under a Creative Commons 4.0 International licence (CC BY 4.0). This licence allows you to share, copy, distribute and transmit the work; to adapt the work and to make commercial use of the work providing attribution is made to the authors (but not in any way that suggests that they endorse you or your use of the work). Attribution should include the following information:

Gornall, Alastair 2020. *Rewriting Buddhism: Pali Literature and Monastic Reform in Sri Lanka, 1157–1270*. London: UCL Press. DOI: https://doi.org/10.14324/111.9781787355156

Further details about Creative Commons licences are available at http://creativecommons.org/licenses/

Any third-party material in this book is published under the book's Creative Commons licence unless indicated otherwise in the credit line to the material. If you would like to re-use any third-party material not covered by the book's Creative Commons licence, you will need to obtain permission directly from the copyright holder.

ISBN: 978-1-78735-517-0 (Hbk)
ISBN: 978-1-78735-516-3 (Pbk)
ISBN: 978-1-78735-515-6 (PDF)
ISBN: 978-1-78735-518-7 (epub)
ISBN: 978-1-78735-519-4 (mobi)
DOI: https://doi.org/10.14324/111.9781787355156

Cover image: A statue of a bodhisattva near the site of the tooth relic temple in Polonnaruva.

For my parents

Contents

List of Maps

List of Tables

List of Figures

Note on the Presentation of Texts and Sources

I have transliterated Pali (P.), Sanskrit (Sk.) and Sinhala (Sin.) texts according to standard scholarly conventions. The translations contained herein are either my own or as cited. For personal and geographical names, I have usually adopted the Pali version of the name along with diacritics. Some names, however, are more familiar in their Sanskrit/Sinhala form, such as 'Parākramabāhu' and 'Daṁbadeṇiya', and in these cases I follow common usage. The one exception is the Cōḻa dynasty, which I refer to using the transliterated Tamil name. I do not transliterate terms such as 'nirvana' and 'Theravada', which have entered the English lexicon.

I use the modern country name 'Sri Lanka' primarily as a toponym designating the geographical island. Where I occasionally refer specifically to a political territory, however, I have opted to use the most common medieval name for the kingdom, namely, Laṅkā, in order to distinguish the fluctuating territorial boundaries of kings during the period with the actual geographical boundaries of the island. On occasion I have also used the modern English name for a Southern Asian place, such as 'Kashmir' rather than 'Kaśmīra', where appropriate.

Wherever possible I cite primary source material with a page number and line number, with the line number indicated in subscript (e.g. 1_2). In general, whenever I directly quote and translate a passage from a primary source, I also provide the Pali, Sanskrit or Sinhala text in the endnotes of each chapter. If the texture of the original language itself is relevant to the topic of discussion, then I also quote it in the main text of the book too. In each chapter the titles of Pali, Sanskrit and Sinhala works are translated in the first instance of their use and, likewise, the regnal dates of each king or queen are cited when they are first mentioned.

Acknowledgements

This book could not have been written without the generous support of a number of institutions and funding bodies. I am grateful to the Faculty of Asian and Middle Eastern Studies, University of Cambridge, and the Rapson Scholarship Committee for supporting my dissertation research; to the School of Languages, Cultures and Linguistics (South Asia Section), School of Oriental and African Studies, University of London, for granting me a Research Associateship; to the Singapore University of Technology and Design for supporting my research with a Start-Up Research Grant; and to the Robert H.N. Ho Family Foundation, for a Research Fellowship in Buddhist Studies (2018–19) that allowed me finally to finish this manuscript. I am also grateful to the British Library, Cambridge University Library, National University of Singapore's ISEAS Library, Peradeniya University's Main Library, the School of Oriental and African Studies Library, and SUTD Library for their valuable assistance and for their permission to use their collections.

The scope and approach of this book owes much to the wonderful teachers I have had over the years. As an undergraduate and master's student at the School of Oriental and African Studies, University of London, I studied Pali with Kate Crosby, who instilled in me the confidence to pursue an academic career and who first introduced me to the literary world of late medieval Sri Lanka, and Sanskrit with Whitney Cox, who encouraged my interest in Sanskrit *śāstra* and generously let me sit in on numerous Sanskrit courses. I completed my doctoral dissertation on traditional Pali grammar at the University of Cambridge under the supervision of Eivind Kahrs, who showed me with constant humour and patience how to uncover human stories even within the most technical Sanskrit and Pali texts. This book also owes much to a number of other teachers, friends and colleagues at SOAS, Cambridge, MIT, Pune and SUTD who have supported my research, in particular, Arthur Bahr, James Buzard, Chong Tow Chong, Giovanni Ciotti, Margaret Cone, Mahesh Deokar, Paolo Di Leo, Michael M.J. Fischer, Chetana and Rajeev Gosavi, Amal Gunasena, Maddalena Italia, Varun Khanna, Alan Kolata, Lim Sun Sun, Francesca Orsini, Pey Kin Leong, Shankar Raman, Aleix Ruiz-Falqués, Andrew Skilton, Vincenzo Vergiani and Paolo Visigalli.

I am deeply indebted to the generosity of the many scholars and friends who took the time to respond with care and attention to drafts of the book and its chapters. Special thanks are due to Petra Kieffer-Pülz and Alan Strathern, true *kalyāṇa-mitta*s, who both read full drafts of the book (at short notice) as well as versions of chapter three and the introduction, respectively. Jeffrey Sundberg read chapter two; Rhema Hokama, Samson Lim, Sandeep Ray, Aleix Ruiz-Falqués and Gabriel Tusinski read chapter four; Rupert Gethin and Aleix Ruiz-Falqués read chapter five; Maria Heim read chapter six; Yigal Bronner read chapter seven; Michael M.J. Fischer, Rhema Hokama, Samson Lim, Zsombor Méder, Paolo Visigalli, and Jonathan Walters read chapter eight; and both Whitney Cox and Alan Strathern provided comments on my book proposal to UCL Press. Enlightening conversations with the participants of a Theravada Civilizations Project workshop in Springfield, Missouri, in particular, Stephen Berkwitz, Steven Collins, Kate Crosby and Charles Hallisey, also helped shape the overall scope of the book. I am profoundly grateful to all for their feedback and I only wish I was more capable of taking full advantage of their insightful comments and criticisms. I should stress, therefore, that all the deficiencies that remain in the work reflect my own shortcomings.

I also wish to express my gratitude to three brilliant scholars who sadly passed away while I was completing this book, all of whom contributed in various ways to its completion. Steven Collins, an inspirational figure throughout my study of Buddhism, opened my eyes to the civilizational history of Pali literature. Lance Cousins, who had an inspiring command of Pali commentarial literature, offered me early guidance in untangling a number of knotty issues related to the Theravada Abhidhamma. Anne Monius, one of the kindest and most intelligent scholars I had the pleasure to meet, supported my work on Pali grammar and poetics and generously read and commented on chapters of my PhD dissertation.

I am fortunate to have had the love and support of a wonderful family. My parents, Richard and Morag Gornall; my grandparents, Peter and Elizabeth Edwards and Ronald and Annette Gornall; my brother, Robert Gornall; my sister, Ailsa Davis; and my parents-in-law, Rumman and Naveed Faruqi, have all been such an important presence in my life. I especially thank my beautiful wife, Samar Faruqi, who was a constant source of encouragement, and my son, Zaki, who made the last few years writing this book such a joyful time. I dedicate this book to my parents who raised me to love learning.

Map 1. Laṅkā and neighbouring kingdoms, c. 900–1300.

Map 2. Sri Lanka in the twelfth and thirteenth centuries.

1
Introduction: Themes and Theories

Throughout history Buddhists have held vastly different views about the language in which the Buddha taught. For some he possessed a supernatural ability to speak in any language he wished.[1] Others claimed by contrast that the Buddha never taught anything at all.[2] Theravada Buddhist scholar-monks, however, believe that the Buddha taught in only one language, Pali, or 'the language of Magadha' (*magadhabhāsā*), as it is known by the tradition, and that he produced a body of teachings, the Tipiṭaka ('three baskets'), so large that, after his death, it took his disciples seven months to recite and compile it.[3] When we speak of 'Pali literature' it is perhaps understandable that many people will think of the Tipiṭaka or 'Pali canon', as it is often referred to in Western academic writings. And yet for almost 2,000 years the monastic community, the Saṅgha, has continued to use Pali as a privileged language for commenting on and elaborating upon the Buddha's doctrine, the Dhamma.

One of the most important commentators in Buddhist history was a fourth or fifth-century South Indian scholar fittingly known as Buddhaghosa or 'voice of the Buddha' who wrote a number of definitive works in Sri Lanka elucidating and developing upon the Buddha's ideas. Tradition has it that Buddhaghosa based his commentaries on Sinhala translations of earlier Pali works that were brought to Sri Lanka by a monk named Mahinda, the eldest son of emperor Aśoka. A late Burmese biography of Buddhaghosa states that, when these first Sinhala commentaries were piled up, they reached the height of seven 'medium-sized' elephants.[4] Throughout the first millennium the Pali tradition continued to grow; scholars added new commentaries, some composed explanations of older commentaries, and others occupied themselves by writing histories of the Buddhist tradition and their monastic lineage.[5]

Then something radically changed. From around the tenth century there was a massive explosion in the number and types of works composed in Pali. This period of literary efflorescence reached its peak in the twelfth and thirteenth centuries, specifically between the years 1157–1270. To give a rough estimate, it is likely that out of all the known Pali works composed in Sri Lanka and South India, more than a third were composed during this long century.[6] The number of works preserved from this era attests not only to the relative magnitude of literary production but also to the fact that these works have long been preserved as key authorities for the Theravada Buddhist tradition throughout Southern Asia.

For the new Pali texts that emerged during this period were taken by scholar-monks from Sri Lanka to Southeast Asian kingdoms from the twelfth century onwards and they thus became an important resource in the development of early modern Theravada Buddhism.[7]

I refer to this long century, spanning 1157–1270, as Sri Lanka's 'reform era', since the period was marked by three important monastic reforms held in 1165, c. 1232–6 and 1266 during the reigns of Parākramabāhu I (1157–86),[8] Vijayabāhu III (1232–6) and Parākramabāhu II (1236–70) respectively. These reforms responded to what was perceived to be an age of religious decline and attempted to purify and unify the monastic community, which before 1165 was traditionally said to have been divided into three fraternities, but that in reality was likely even more fragmented than this formulaic enumeration suggests.[9] The idea of a 'reform era' does not mean, however, that the reform process began or ended with the reigns of these three kings, when in fact moves towards unifying the Saṅgha are apparent in the decades before 1165, in particular during the reign of Vijayabāhu I (1055–1110), and also between 1165 and 1232, when the monastic community emerged as a more coherent and autonomous entity better able to regulate itself. Despite the turmoil of the decades after Parākramabāhu I's reign, the process of reform, characterized by constant attempts to reconcile the different factions of the Saṅgha and unify them under a single administrative structure, continued even during times of minimal royal intervention, patronage and protection.

This book is the first intellectual history of what was the most culturally productive period in Sri Lanka's premodern era.[10] It is less concerned with cataloguing the doctrinal positions of the reform-era Saṅgha than with describing broader changes in the monastic community's religious orientation as expressed primarily in the Pali literature composed during the reforms and in the role played by these works in facilitating the reform process. It argues that the intensive production of Pali literature during this era was fundamentally a consequence of the Saṅgha's emerging political autonomy and that scholar-monks composed works in Pali, in particular philological works, commentaries, anthologies and poems, as a means of framing the increasingly chaotic political landscape of their time within an organizational plane, in which they could navigate their changing social and economic conditions.[11]

Pali specifically, rather than Sinhala, was the privileged medium for creating this ordered, conceptual space for three main reasons.[12] First, scholar monks viewed Pali as authoritative both because it was the language of the Buddha and because it was thought to have magical properties that made it uniquely capable of expressing reality. Second, reform-era scholars, increasingly conscious of Pali's relationship with the other literary languages of South Asia, also began to view Pali as a sui generis, independent language that, unlike all other languages in South Asia, was underived from Sanskrit. As such Pali was considered to be 'pure' (*suddha*) and we can hypothesize that underlying ideas of moral and linguistic purity, in part, also meant that reform-era works were preferably composed in Pali before being translated and disseminated more widely in what were perceived to be derivative languages like Sinhala. Finally, as a transregional medium, Pali was the choice language for conveying the Saṅgha's new, unified monastic identity to the increasingly cosmopolitan monastic community at home; to non-Sinhala speaking communities abroad, in particular those in the Tamil South; as well as to the royal court, which from the eleventh century onwards was dominated by foreign rulers and factions such as the Kāliṅgas and the Pāṇḍyas from Northeast and Southeast India respectively.[13]

1.1. Three Orientations of Reform-era Literature

The forces of reform governing the unification of the monastic community are, in many respects, mirrored in the changing form of the Pali literature produced during this period. The new Pali works and textual genres that emerged out of the reforms all reflect, in various degrees, the desire to fight the forces of doctrinal degeneration and social fragmentation. This desire emerges in the literature of the long century in a number of ways but which, for analytical purposes, we can group together under three interrelated orientations, namely (1) an increasing concern for the degeneration of the Dhamma, social-moral order and cosmos; (2) a desire to recover and protect the perceived essential meaning of the Buddha's teachings through new forms of scholastic enquiry; and (3) an urgent need among elites to accrue vast amounts of merit through devotion to the Buddha, facilitated, in particular, by new aesthetic literary techniques better able to inculcate such devotional sentiments.

The first of these orientations provides much of the context for understanding the development of the other two. The monastic writings of the reform era are haunted by a sense of urgency to counter the perceived decline of their Buddhist tradition. In 993 the South Indian Cōḻa king Rājarāja Cōḻa I (985–1012) invaded Sri Lanka and moved its capital to Poḷonnaruva, resulting over the century of Cōḻa rule in the gradual collapse of the old sacred capital of Anurādhapura. The post-Cōḻa political environment was marked, furthermore, by frequent, transregional wars for the throne between rival foreign factions. These events aligned with ideas about the precipitous decline of the Dhamma. The Buddha's Dhamma, it is said, would last 5,000 years and over time the possibility of liberation would diminish.[14] Faced with social upheaval, monks depict their age as one in which disorder prevails in the interpretation of texts, in the production of literature and in the behaviour of monks. Authors explicitly state that they codified the rules of language, wrote new works and revised old ones with the idea that they were creating order out of what was perceived to be chaos.

These attempts to unify the sprawling Pali textual tradition were based, in part, on the traditional belief that preserving the Dhamma would postpone this inevitable decline. What was innovative about the exegetical approaches of reform-era works, the book argues, is that they adopted new textual models from the Sanskrit tradition while also subtly shifting their attitude concerning the nature of the Dhamma. Scholar-monks of the era, in contrast to earlier commentators, such as Buddhaghosa, began to think of the Dhamma principally as the meaning of the Buddha's teachings rather than its wording and they place emphasis on distilling and condensing the 'essence' (*sāra*) of this meaning through philological work. The concern for the essence of the Dhamma, rather than simply its literal form, accompanied the development of new modes of scriptural analysis, including new types of grammar, anthology and handbook commentary all of which claimed to recover or protect some essential part of their scriptural heritage that in some way had been obscured by previous scholarly approaches.

The need to protect and preserve their tradition in the face of religious decline was accompanied by a desire to intervene in the circumstances they faced. The eschatological concerns of the scholar-monks of the era shifted their attention to more immanent religious goals – transforming their lives within Saṃsāra rather than obtaining nirvana – since transcendence was perceived to be increasingly difficult to achieve. Central to this shift was a need to develop better karmic conditions for the survival of their religious tradition. The attention of elites thus turned to enhancing the accrual of merit through devotional practices, in particular the cultivation of favourable emotions in the worship of the Buddha and his relics. New forms of Pali literature too played an important role in supporting this emotionally charged soteriology, and scholar-monks, for the first time, composed devotional poems designed to inspire transformative sentiments in their audience. In writing these works, monks disregarded centuries of scepticism about the moral value of ornate poetry and relied on Sanskrit aesthetics and Sanskritic literary models as a resource for their new literature.

1.2. Theoretical Considerations

A close reading of the texts produced in the reform era allows us to critique and re-examine more generally a number of important themes and concepts frequently used in the civilizational history of Theravada Buddhism. The book challenges ideas about Buddhism in Sri Lanka as an essentially conservative tradition preserving Buddhism in its earliest form, it rethinks the social role of Pali literature as an '*imaginaire*' or 'databank' and lastly it critiques the pervasive characterization of the relationship between the Saṅgha and the royal court in terms of a symbiosis of social functions.

(a) An Island unto Itself?

Island cultures, it is said, can be viewed in two ways, either as 'continental islands', that is, those 'accidental, derived islands' that at some point drifted away from the mainland, and 'oceanic islands', the 'originary, essential islands' that spontaneously arose from the sea.[15] These two physical processes mirror the way in which medieval Buddhism in Sri Lanka has been discussed in much academic writing. Early colonialists and Orientalists, for instance, often regarded Buddhism in Sri Lanka and its Pali canon, in particular, as representative of 'original' or 'early' Buddhism.[16] There was an assumption that the island of Sri Lanka had protected the Buddha's teachings from the same fate as its Indian counterpart, which according to R.C. Childers (1838–1876) had fallen over time into 'an extraordinary state of corruption and travesty'.[17]

Related is the commonly held view of Theravada Buddhism in Sri Lanka as an essentially conservative tradition that stubbornly resisted the cultural influence of the wider region.[18] The Theravada Buddhist tradition in Sri Lanka is, of course, conservative in that it strove to preserve the Buddha's teachings in a literal form, though, as we will see, these practices of conservation were themselves subject to change. What is problematic is the idea of a generalized conservative mentality, almost akin to a political attitude, in opposition to 'liberal' Buddhists elsewhere, that has often meant that scholars have viewed Buddhism on the island, in particular during the 'traditional period' of the middle ages, as without innovation.[19] In light of the intellectual vigour of the reform era, it is remarkable that Sri Lanka's foundational national history, the *University of Ceylon History of Ceylon*, dismisses the period as follows: 'This literature does not reveal that there has been much original thinking in the domains of metaphysics, philosophy or doctrine. The Pāli language, in fact, had ceased to be an instrument of original thought long before our period.'[20]

When scholars have recognized the innovations of the Pali literature of the reform era, there has been the opposite tendency to view it as inauthentic, both in relation to canonical language and to the Sanskrit literary tradition. With respect to late medieval Pali poetry, A.K. Warder in particular noted that 'scholars have often spoken, with something like scorn, of "Sanskritised" Pali in works like these, as if their style of composition is not really legitimate or natural'.[21] We can partly explain this attitude as a by-product of the way Orientalists privileged Pali canonical writings as the authentic representation of Buddhism over those of the later tradition. It re-emerges in the late colonial writings of Sri Lankan scholars too, who sometimes recapitulated the same idea, albeit now imbued with a sense of authentic national identity. G.P. Malalasekera in his *The Pāli Literature of Ceylon*, for instance, linked the influence of Sanskrit during the reform era with the presence of Tamil 'colonists' and wrote of Sanskrit as a contaminating influence on Pali.[22] At the same time one can detect an intellectual chauvinism among Sanskrit scholars and historians of India too who habitually ignore Sri Lanka as a participant in the cultural history of South Asia. To his credit, P.L. Vaidya, editor of numerous Buddhist Sanskrit works, put this usually informal bias into writing and, with respect to later Pali literature, once wrote that, 'save for the lively commentarial literature, it is but a poor imitation of the corresponding works in Sanskrit literature'.[23]

The island model then presents us with a false dichotomy: either medieval Theravada Buddhism in Sri Lanka was conservative and culturally isolated, or it was derivative and provincial. A combination of these approaches has resulted in the extraordinary fact that the full intellectual significance of this era has been largely overlooked in modern academic writing. This book challenges both positions by demonstrating firstly that Theravada Buddhism in Sri Lanka was always intimately connected with the history and culture of the Indian subcontinent but that the contours of its engagement appear differently depending on the texts and genre one is looking at. In addition, we will see in the six case studies that the Pali literature of this long century was not simply a mere imitation of continental literary traditions, but rather that it played a genuine and authentic role in Sri Lanka's changing religious and political life.

(b) The Pali Imaginaire: A View from Nowhere?[24]

The Orientalist view of the Pali canon as original or ideal Buddhism further led some early scholars to view the culture of later Buddhist societies, more generally, as a vulgarization and deviation from the perceived purity and pristine teachings of the Buddha. For almost half a century anthropologists in particular have challenged this approach and have instead analysed contemporary Buddhist societies on their own terms, viewing the historical developments of the tradition as 'continuities' and 'transformations' rather than deviations.[25] And yet, while scholars no longer make a moral distinction between the Buddhism of Pali literature and contemporary forms of Buddhist life, the dichotomy between the ideal Pali canon and 'living' Buddhism – which was originally the product of an Orientalist concern for origins – lives on, in many respects, even in the works of the foremost critics of this view.

Pali texts in some way or another are still used, for instance, as a point of reference for contextualizing local forms of Buddhist belief and practice. While nobody speaks any more of 'original Buddhism', the Pali canon and Pali literature in general often form the constituent part of what is signified by more innocuous, but in some cases no less suspect, analytical categories, such as the 'doctrinal', 'orthodox' and 'normative'.[26] These concepts are then used as a structural framework to think about the specificities of religion in a particular time and place, sometimes referred to as 'practical', 'popular' or 'local'. Distinctions such as these are, to some extent, a necessary outcome of establishing 'Theravada Buddhism', both in its universality and particularity, as a coherent, historical and social object of academic enquiry. One unintended consequence of this analytical dichotomy, however, is that, in many cases, what is regarded as 'doctrinal', 'orthodox' and 'normative' is treated as if it transcends history.

This is the case even in one of the most sophisticated models for thinking about the social function of Pali literature in Buddhist civilizational history. In his erudite and expansive work, *Nirvana and other Buddhist Felicities*, Steven Collins coined the felicitous expression 'the Pali *imaginaire*', which he defined as 'a discursive, textual world available to the imagination of elites, and gradually others, in the premodern agrarian societies of Southern Asia'.[27] It was an ideology, he argues, that primarily established the hegemony of a dominant class comprising the royal court and the Buddhist monastic community and that further served to naturalize its extraction of tribute from the agrarian populace. Collins presents the Pali *imaginaire* as a stable system, preserved by scholar-monks, enmeshed and intertwined within the societies and cultures of what we might *ex post facto* call the Theravada world. It played this role throughout what Collins refers to as 'the long middle ages', an agrarian, pre-industrial period that he argues lasted from the third century BCE to the nineteenth century.[28]

There is much to admire in the notion of the Pali *imaginaire* as an analytical category, that is, as a way of thinking about the historical influence of 'the mental universe created by and within Pali texts'.[29] The concept, however, has limitations when one tries to historicize the Pali intellectual tradition itself. This is because Collins, due to the admirably broad historical scope of his book, adopts an analytical dualism in which he strategically separates Pali texts as a 'cultural system', from what he refers to as 'socio-cultural life', with the former possessing an 'a priori and a posteriori coherence'.[30] He states that:

> there is sufficient coherence in the Pali *imaginaire* – at least in the grand matters of time, death, happiness and wisdom with which this book has been concerned – to treat it as a Cultural System in abstraction from its (greater or lesser) imbrication and enmeshment in the Socio-Cultural life of countless millions of people in Southern Asia over countless generations.[31]

Collins thus approaches the Pali tradition as an intellectual resource independent of the historical Buddhist tradition in which it played an important cultural part. He perhaps overlooks, then, the role of Pali texts themselves as agents of social and cultural change.

While Collins stresses that he treats the Pali *imaginaire* as autonomous in this way only for *analytical* utility, he imbues his analytical category with an ontological coherence by connecting it to real economic conditions, explaining that the *imaginaire*'s constancy and longevity derives from the general stability of the agrarian society of the Middle Ages. Any analysis of the possible dynamic interplay between the 'cultural system' and 'socio-cultural life' is largely curtailed, therefore, first by his deterministic view of material conditions and second by an exceedingly long definition of the Middle Ages. Peter Skilling in a recent, useful critique has questioned this overly stable depiction of premodern Pali textual culture and the very notion of a long 'traditional period', stating 'I do not see any exceptional degree of stability or cohesion – there is continuity, there is rupture, there is reformation, and there is reformulation, none of which avoid or inhibit change and reinvention.'[32] Skilling still subscribes, however, to a similar analytical dichotomy that places Pali textual culture as a 'databank', 'a fount of ideas, a system or network of references and co-ordinates', and states that these 'key ideological components are, so to speak, downloaded through sermons and through liturgy, through social etiquettes and hierarchies, through legal enactments and educational patterns, and through architecture and the visual and plastic arts'.[33]

In critiquing the Pali *imaginaire* I do not wish to challenge the general premise that culture plays a role in structuring agency. Rather, I think it is necessary, if we are to recover the historical agency of the authors of Pali texts, to no longer objectively conflate the analytical category of a 'cultural system', that is, the structuring ideas of a society, with existing texts in a particular language. This is important, first, so that we do not confuse analytical utility with ontological reality and second, so that we can view the ideas of Pali texts, where suitable, either as cultural structures – part of the system – or as part of 'socio-cultural life', that is, as a key expression of agency in history that allowed individuals to actively and purposefully change and reshape their already existing circumstances. This book emphasizes the latter role of Pali texts in the intellectual history of Buddhism in Sri Lanka. It is perhaps better, in this regard, then, to think of these works as something like a matrix (*mātikā*) rather than *imaginaire*; an orientating point of origin that was created to inspire new thoughts, feelings and actions.

(c) Saṅgha, State and Compound Kingship

The economic and intellectual stability that scholars have seen in premodern Theravada Buddhist societies also pervades ideas about the historical relationship between 'Saṅgha and state'. Frequently invoked to describe all types of premodern Buddhist societies is R.A.L.H. Gunawardana's description of monastic and court relations in early medieval Sri Lanka as an 'antagonistic symbiosis'.[34]

Gunawardana's useful ecological metaphor reveals an essentially functionalist approach to this relationship, where the state is thought to have provided the necessary coercive power to protect the Saṅgha and, in return, the Saṅgha offered religious ideology and legitimation in support of the state. In its foundations, then, Gunawardana's notion of symbiosis is clearly inspired by earlier sociological models, such as those of Georges Dumézil and Louis Dumont.[35] Gunawardana notes, however, that this symbiosis of functions became steadily antagonistic in the early medieval period due to the fact that the Saṅgha was developing into an increasingly autonomous legal and fiscal entity.[36] In his felicitous expression, then, Gunawardana manages to capture not only the historical interdependence between the two institutions but also the often conflictual nature of their relationship.

Gunawardana did not necessarily intend for his expression to be a definitive characterization of the relationship between Saṅgha and state, however. Rather, he coined the expression specifically to describe early medieval Sri Lanka in contrast to Walpola Rahula's characterization of the early

Saṅgha-state relationship as purely symbiotic and A.M. Hocart's view that the Saṅgha effectively functioned as a 'court and kingdom in miniature'.[37]

It is worth turning to A.M. Hocart (1883–1939) in more detail for our late medieval context since he offered a more nuanced understanding of the relationship between institution and function. Hocart developed a theory of 'dual kingship' in which he argues that society is structured by complementary 'terrestrial' and 'spiritual' functions.[38] While predicated on a similar notion of natural symbiosis, Hocart differs from Gunawardana in that he did not regard function and institution (Hocart's 'organization') as necessarily contiguous. He stresses that this 'dichotomy need not produce a pair' and that the duality of functions can manifest in any institutional pattern, whether, one, two or many institutions.[39] When observing the societies of India and Sri Lanka, Hocart observed, in this regard, that:

> the Church and the State are one in India. The head of this Church-State is the king … The king's state is reproduced in miniature by his vassals; a farmer has his court, consisting of the personages most essential to the ritual, and so present even in the smallest community, the barber, the washerman, the drummers and so forth. The temple and the palace are indistinguishable, for the king represents the gods. Therefore, there is only one word in Sinhalese and in Tamil for both. The god in his temple has his court like the king in his palace; smiths, carpenters, potters all work for him.[40]

A.M. Hocart could not have known at the time that what he observed in Sri Lanka had a specific historical genesis. Based, in particular, on the work of Ronald Inden, we can now describe the politics of late medieval Sri Lanka more accurately as one based on political models that developed in India between the eighth and twelfth centuries. Inden describes the medieval Indian imperial formation as a 'society of kings' structured by a 'scale of kingships', that is, a hierarchy of rulers based on encompassing spheres of lordship, from village chieftains at the bottom to the emperor, or 'king of kings' at its worldly apex. Above him, still, Inden describes a higher transcendent king, usually a deity, such as Viṣṇu or Śiva, but also, the Jina too, who bestowed lordship upon the emperor. This formation was not structured by a balance of religious and political functions *between institutions* but rather – and here we see the influence of Hocart's more fluid view of social function – Inden describes political power as 'compound kingship', 'the manifestation of divine and human wills relative to one another in a complex agent'.[41] Each of the political actors, then, in this scale of kingship, is a compound king and maintains a diminishing sphere of both temporal and spiritual power.

This book shows that beginning in reform-era Sri Lanka we see monks claiming a similar position for the Buddha as sovereign over the temporal and spiritual worlds and depicting the ruling monarch as the Buddha's inferior vassal. What is less clear in Inden's work, however, is where religious specialists, such as Buddhist monks, fit within such a scale of kingship. Inspired by Hocart's analysis of the sociological position of the Saṅgha, the book argues that the monastic elite in the twelfth and thirteenth centuries increasingly styled itself as an independent royal court led by a king-like figure, the so-called 'grandmaster' (*mahāsāmi*), with an administrative structure that resembled a political actor. Monastic elites presented themselves, rather than the king and his court, under the Buddha at the apex of Laṅkā's long chain of lordship and believed that the superior rights enjoyed by the Buddha should extend first to them before the king. The relationship then between the Saṅgha and the royal court was no longer one of an antagonistic symbiosis but rather a hierarchy of compound kingship, in which, at least from the monastic perspective, the Buddha and monastic elites possessed temporal and spiritual rights superior to the ruling king and nobility.[42]

1.3. Chaos, Order and Emotion

This book is divided into three parts, 'chaos', 'order' and 'emotion'. In part one, we explore the historical context of the first of our overarching themes, namely that the cultural efflorescence that took place in the twelfth and thirteenth centuries was in part a response to social and political disorder. The term 'chaos' is not used to denote a complete breakdown of order but rather reflects the multiple, competing orders that ruptured the stable social structures of the previous millennium.

In the first chapter we will explore the prehistory of the reform era in the two centuries before the reform and unification of the Saṅgha in 1165. The chapter focuses in particular on the Cōḻa invasion and rule of Sri Lanka in the tenth century and the role it played in the rise of new centres of monastic power, changes in the cultural make-up of the royal family in Sri Lanka, and the increasing authority of Sanskrit textual models within the Saṅgha's literary culture. In the second chapter we will then situate the production of Pali literature itself within the immediate context of the monastic reforms that took place in the era. The chapter outlines in broad terms the connection between reform-era Pali texts, the Saṅgha's developing institutional autonomy and the localization of politics on the island.

The following two sections of the book are divided according to the two other intellectual orientations that shaped the reform era, namely a desire to enframe and protect the essential meaning of the Buddha's teachings and to accrue transformative merit through devotion to the Buddha. In part two, 'Order', we will discuss the connection between social and political disorder, monastic perceptions of religious decline and the emergence of new types of grammar, commentary and anthology.

Chapter three discusses the prominence of grammar or *vyākaraṇa* in reform-era intellectual culture. It focuses on the new grammar of Moggallāna and its perceived role as the first line of defence in stemming religious decline. Moggallāna adopted Sanskrit grammatical models and philosophies of language that allowed the Saṅgha to think about their scriptures in new ways. In chapter four, we turn to Sumaṅgala's reform-era handbook commentaries and highlight the development of a new scholastic formalism in these works, based in part on the pedagogical needs of the reform-era school system. These formal changes were accompanied by a reappraisal of the authority of handbooks and the nature of scriptural language. Chapter five focuses on the composition of new anthologies, in particular, Siddhattha's *Sārasaṅgaha*, 'Compendium of the essence'. It explores how Siddhattha used new philological techniques to curate his scriptural heritage into practical models for pursuing religious goals relevant to his chaotic era, in particular the pursuit of buddhahood through devotional practices.

In part three, 'Emotion', we explore in more detail the renewed emphasis on religious devotion to the Buddha, in particular relic worship, in the reform era, its role in instantiating a new social order presided over by monastic elites, and how these changes in orientation reflected and were supported by the development of independent works of Pali *kāvya* or poetry, including histories of the Buddha's relics and Buddha biographies.

Chapter six focuses on the development of Pali poetics (*alaṅkāra*) in the reform era and investigates how literary theorists abandoned their scepticism about the religious value of ornate poetry and instead came to view literary eloquence in devotional poetry as a moral virtue. In chapter seven, we then turn to how Pali *kāvya* worked in practice. One relic history, the *Dāṭhāvaṃsa* or 'History of the tooth', the chapter argues, was used to establish devotional relationships with the reform-era's shifting elites and to instantiate relic shrines and the monastic leadership above the royal court at the pinnacle of a new devotional and political hierarchy. Chapter eight concerns a similar development in the composition of ornate Buddha biographies. It explores in particular how one Buddha biography, the *Jinālaṅkāra* or 'Ornament of the Conqueror', managed the aesthetic experiences and religious ambitions of its audience so as to support, rather than destabilize, monastic power.

The final chapter brings together the different intellectual strands discussed in the book, namely the creative influence of perceived religious decline, the desire to protect the Buddha's teachings through new scholastic forms, and the perceived need to accrue transformative merit through devotion to the Buddha, as expressed in particular in new forms of Pali poetry. It then explores how Pali literary production changed in Sri Lanka in the two centuries after the reform era and reassesses the way in which reform-era monastic lineages were transmitted to Southeast Asia, in particular to the Pagan empire in what is now Burma.

Notes

1. See Wallace, 2018. Mahayana literature and some early Pali texts before Buddhaghosa also interpret the so-called 'analytical knowledge of language' (*niruttipaṭisambhidā*, Sk. *niruktipratisaṃvid*) as the ability of an enlightened being to convey the Dhamma in any language necessary. See *Mahāyānasūtrālaṅkārasvavṛtti* of Asaṅga, 18.34; *Peṭakopadesa*, 33$_{,21-4}$.
2. See, for instance, a passage from the *Tathāgatācintyaguhyanirdeśasūtra*, translated and quoted in Lopez, 1993, 48–9.
3. See *Vinaya* II, 139$_{,13-16}$; *Samantapāsādikā* VI, 1214$_{,16-19}$. Bond, 1982, 19. There has been much recent debate about the analytical validity of the term 'Theravada' in academic discourse since it was never used by the tradition itself prior to modernity. See, for instance, Skilling *et al.* (eds) 2012. I continue to use the term 'Theravada' since I am wary of adopting a nominalist stance where the lack of a single, shared identity marker among these monks – though there are some contenders, such as Mahāvihāravāsi and Vibhajjavādi – is taken as evidence that such a monastic circle did not exist, for the monks and monasteries of this book certainly had: (1) common authoritative religious texts; (2) similar ritual practices; (3) a shared corporate memory; and (4) were often administratively linked. When I use the term in this book, I am referring specifically either to one or more of the three *nikāya*s in pre-reform Sri Lanka and South India and, then, in the reform era, usually to the Mahāvihāran monastic lineage as it emerged in Sri Lanka after the reforms themselves. I also often use the term 'Buddhism' to refer to the same lineage in cases where the context is clear.
4. *Buddhaghosuppatti* of Mahāmaṅgala, 60$_{,24-9}$.
5. See Gornall and Ruiz-Falqués, 2019.
6. Taking as guides: Franke, 1902; Von Hinüber, 1996; Subhūti, 1876.
7. See chapter nine.
8. The dates given after the names of kings and queens, unless otherwise specified, refer to the duration of their reigns. On the regnal dates of reform-era kings and queens, see chapter three.
9. See chapter two.
10. There are a number of useful social, economic and political histories that, at least in part, cover the reform era. Book-length studies include, for instance, Ariyapala, 1956; Bechert, 1966; De Silva, 1981; De Silva, 1997; Dhammavisuddhi, 1970; Gunawardana, 1979; Ilangasinha, 1992; Liyanagamage, 1968; Panabokke, 1993; Ray, ed. 1959–60.
11. Throughout this book I have found useful Whitney Cox's recent work on politics in premodern South India. See Cox, 2016, esp. 16–21. I borrow the concept of an 'organizational plane' from Deleuze and Guattari, 1994. I have found helpful their distinction between the chaotic conceptual world as a whole, the 'virtuality', and the local conceptual orders immanent within this virtuality that help agents think and act. For an earlier, looser adaptation of similar Deleuzian ideas in the interpretation of the Sri Lankan 'Suniyama' ritual, see Kapferer, 1997. I have also found particularly inspiring Alan Strathern's recent monumental study on religious and political change in premodernity, especially his second chapter. See Strathern, 2019.
12. Here, see chapter two.
13. On this, see the discussions in chapters one and four.
14. A number of other works have drawn a connection between cultural production and eschatological expectations. See, in particular, Blackburn, 2001, 80–6; Blackburn, 2017; Frasch, 2014; Frasch, 2017.
15. Deleuze, 2004.
16. See, for instance, Hallisey, 1995.

17. Childers, 1875, xii.
18. Gombrich, 1988, 22–3. See also the criticisms in Blackburn, 2001, 5–9.
19. See, for instance, Paranavitana, 1960, 566–70.
20. Paranavitana, 1960, 577.
21. Warder, 1981, 204.
22. Malalasekera, 1994, 148; 163; 168.
23. Vaidya, 1946, 479.
24. I borrow the description of Pali texts as a 'view from nowhere' from a critical appraisal of this position in Choompolpaisal, 2008.
25. Tambiah, 1984, 7–8. On the methodological divide between anthropologists and philologists, see Crosby, 2008a.
26. See, for instance, Spiro, 1982.
27. Collins, 1998, 1–117, esp. 18. This book owes a great deal to the works and advice of Steven Collins. In testament to his generosity as a teacher and intellectual spirit, I am particularly grateful to him for encouraging me to engage more critically with his work.
28. Here following Le Goff, 1988.
29. Collins, 1998, 41.
30. Here relying on Archer, 1988.
31. Collins, 1998, 570.
32. Skilling, 2012, 336. For similar criticisms of Jacques Le Goff, see Savy, 2014.
33. Skilling, 2012, 345–6.
34. The expression is employed by Steven Collins, for instance, to describe premodern Buddhist civilizations in general. See Collins, 1998, 1–40. It has been adopted in comparative studies of premodern religion too.
35. See Dumézil, 1958; Dumont, 1999. Also, Rahula, 1956.
36. Gunawardana, 1979, 343–4; Gunawardana, 1976.
37. Gunawardana, 1979, 344, citing Hocart, 1968, 68.
38. Hocart, 1970, 162–79. Hocart recognized that this dichotomy was an analytical distinction rather than a natural one, stating that 'the divorce of temporal and spiritual is unnatural; for both are rules of living, and there cannot be two sets of rules' (176).
39. Hocart, 1970, 289. He earlier in the work distinguishes the fluctuating functions of persons or organizations in contrast with the more stable functions of what he calls 'personages', that is, characters or representations of persons. He writes, for instance, that 'we thus see how vain it is to try and define the terms "priest", "king" in fact any titles. You cannot define what is in a constant state of flux; priest passes into king, especially law-king, such as the Dalai Lama and the Pope, and king may be assimilated to priest.' See Hocart, 1970, 200.
40. Hocart, 1968, 67–8.
41. Inden, 2000, 213–62. See also Inden, 1981. Victor Lieberman has similarly spoken of a 'model', developed in Gupta India, of 'multiple, nested sovereignties and attenuated zones of influence' that 'provided a template for all later South Asian – and Indic Southeast Asian – states.' See Lieberman, 2009, 640, cited also in Strathern, 2009, 824.
42. This is not to say that this phase of 'compound kingship' cannot be thought of as a development on the antagonistic symbiosis of the early medieval period. It is simply that we need to view symbiosis as defining the relationship between functions (in this case, of a single institution) and not between institutions, since function and institution were no longer identifiably contiguous in the reform era. Rather, the relationship was now largely competitive and hierarchical, with co-operation induced through the powers of persuasion rather than met as a result of social needs. See also the extended discussion in the notes on part four of chapter eight.

Part I
Chaos

2
Before 1165 and All That

Scholar-monks composed new Pali texts in the reform era as a creative response to perceived religious decline and it was the very upending of traditional order in the preceding two centuries that provided these monks not only with the motivation but also the resources to bring about a resurgence of their tradition. Early attempts to explain this era of literary efflorescence focused narrowly only on the causal role of political stability and patronage during the events of the reforms themselves. Declaring this period to be Sri Lanka's 'Augustan age', for instance, G.P. Malalasekera in his influential *The Pāli Literature of Ceylon* emphasized Parākramabāhu I's role (1157–86) in determining the cultural character of the era. He wrote that, 'with this perfect internal tranquillity, undisturbed by oppression, encouraged in their activities by the great and devout interest taken by the head of the State himself, and working amidst congenial and beautiful surroundings, there arose during this period a band of scholars, who made this epoch the Augustan age of Ceylon literature'.[1]

There is no doubt that the reforms of Parākramabāhu I were a crucial moment in the monastic community's cultural resurgence and we will explore the nature of these reforms in the following chapter. To understand more fully the relationship between culture and society during the reform era, however, it is worth expanding the scope of our analysis beyond the momentary stability of the events themselves to examine how such reforms could not have occurred without the social and political turmoil that surrounded them. What, in particular, had changed on the island to allow the Saṅgha to finally achieve unity for the first time in well over 1,000 years? It is impossible to single out any one reason for this development, for, as Buddhaghosa wisely once wrote about causality, 'conditions ... give rise to phenomena ... only when they are not independent of each other or deficient with respect to each other'.[2]

That said, three interrelated changes in the tenth and eleventh centuries in particular stand out as important, namely the invasions of the South Indian Cōḻa kings Rājarāja (985–1012) and Rājendra I (1012–44), the fragmentation of the royal family as a result of its pursuit of a new, exogamous marriage strategy alongside growing monastic involvement in dynastic politics, and lastly changing attitudes to Sanskrit literature as a model for composing Pali and Sinhala works. Each of these factors, which roughly correspond to changes in the island's economic, social and intellectual resources, played an important role in both disrupting the old cultural order and in setting the stage for the emergence of new forms of religious life.

2.1. The Cōḻas, Monastic Property and the Rise of the Forest Monks

The millennium that preceded the reform era in Sri Lanka was characterized by contained conflict. It was marked by constant upheaval caused by endless dynastic and succession disputes that importantly, however, did not present an existential threat to the general patterns of social and political life.[3] The dynastic struggles of the first millennium were often local and centred on a rivalry between two competing branches of the royal family, the Lambakaṇṇa, who ruled in Anurādhapura until 428 CE and then again after 614 CE, and the Moriya, who ruled with only a slight interruption between 455 and 614 CE.[4] One distinct feature of the monarchy in Sri Lanka in particular in the second Lambakaṇṇa dynasty after 614 CE was the general preference for an endogamous marriage strategy, that is, for marrying in the family. Thomas Trautmann has observed that:

> to a much greater extent than elsewhere in South Asia, the Ceylonese throne may be described as the joint property of an extended family, and the monarch as its trustee. The family itself was large, but its boundaries were fairly well defined. It did not need to favor the other families occupying the inferior offices of state by marrying their daughters, since its own members filled those offices, supplied brides and gave support; nor did it have to choose brides from a wide array of neighboring states which, as an island, Ceylon lacks. On the whole the attempt to keep the property in the family was remarkably successful, and the Ceylonese monarchy had a degree of continuity not to be found in the Sub-continent.[5]

The history of the Saṅgha during the same period displays a similar tension between constant shifts in power and a general trend towards institutional continuity. From early on in its history the Saṅgha in Sri Lanka too was riven with rivalries and was ultimately split into three main fraternities or *nikāya*s, the Mahāvihāra, Abhayagirivihāra and Jetavanavihāra, for most of the Middle Ages. The Abhayagiri split from the Mahāvihāra during the reign of king Vaṭṭagāmaṇi Abhaya (89–77 BCE) and a further schism in the Mahāvihāra occurred in the reign of Mahāsena (274–301) from which the Jetavana arose.[6] Throughout the first millennium these three fraternities competed for the patronage of the royal family, who variously favoured one fraternity over the other two. The Saṅgha as a whole was successful in maintaining its wealth and property and, for much of the first millennium, monarchs respected the continued rights of a monastery over previously donated lands. R.A.L.H. Gunawardana observed, in this regard, that 'apart from instances of plunder of the wealth accumulated in monasteries by kings at war, no attempt to confiscate the land granted to monasteries is evident until the end of the period of the Anurādhapura kingdom'.[7]

At the end of the first millennium all of this changed. Sri Lanka became intimately embroiled in a struggle with the three great powers of South India, the Pāṇḍyas, Pallavas and Cōḻa.[8] It began when Sena II (853–887) invaded Pāṇḍya country in revenge for the Pāṇḍya sacking of Anurādhapura in around 840, killing the monarch and forming a new alliance with the king's son who he placed on the throne.[9] Then came the fall of the Pallavas when in 897 a Cōḻa feudatory, crowned as Āditya I (871–907), defeated and killed his Pallava overlord Aparājita (879–97) in battle and annexed the Pallava heartland of Toṇḍaimaṇḍalam.[10]

The rapid end to Pallava rule led to a hasty reorganization of the political status quo that had existed in the orbit of the old power. The Laṅkan monarchy, in particular, pursued a dangerous strategy of maintaining alliances with the Cōḻa's neighbouring enemies. The alliance with the Pāṇḍyas led Kassapa V (914–23) to send an army in support of Rājasiṃha II (900–20) against the Cōḻas and to give the latter's son asylum in Sri Lanka after the defeat of their combined forces. The Cōḻa king Parāntaka (907–55) was intent on invading Sri Lanka in order to capture the Pāṇḍya regalia, briefly succeeding in the reign of Udaya IV (946–54), who is remembered by monastic historians as a lazy drunk.[11] It was Parāntaka's later successors, Rājarāja and his son Rājendra, however, who were able to firmly establish Cōḻa rule on the island. The Cōḻas chose Poḷonnaruva in the east as their principal base instead of the old capital of Anurādhapura and maintained settlements around Poḷonnaruva and various port towns that acted as staging posts for incursions into the south of the island.[12]

It has been suggested that the Cōḻa invasions brought about cultural change due to imperialism or even some ethno-religious rivalry.[13] There is little evidence, however, that the Cōḻas harboured much cultural ambition in their rule. In terms of literary influence, the Cōḻa rulers only left a few inscriptions often connected with the patronage of Śaiva temples.[14] It was rather the wider South Indian elite – courtiers, warlords, artisans and merchant guilds – and also later kings who were responsible for the majority of Tamil inscriptions produced on the island, most of which can be dated to long after Cōḻa rule had ended. An inscription dating to the reign of Vijayabāhu I (1055–1110), for instance, entrusting the protection of the tooth relic of the Buddha to the Vēlaikkāra mercenary company, begins with a Sanskrit verse and eulogizes Vijayabāhu in literary Tamil.[15] Most of the religious patronage connected with the Cōḻas came from the new mercantile communities who supported the construction of Śaiva temples and also some Buddhist monasteries around Poḷonnaruva, port towns and other commercial centres.[16] If this religious patronage did result in the production of Tamil literature, no work prior to the fifteenth century has survived.[17]

Monastic histories viewed the Cōḻa invasions as primarily an economic loss. The late-medieval *Cūḷavaṃsa* ('Little history') states that 'by violently breaking open the relic chambers of all three fraternities in the undivided land of Laṅkā with their numerous, valuable golden images and thus taking the vitality (*oja*) out of all the monasteries here and there, demons seized the heart (*sāra*) of Laṅkā'.[18] The emphasis on the widespread looting and destruction of monasteries and relic sites found in such monastic accounts was possibly more of a literary embellishment than reality.[19] Keir Strickland in a recent archaeological study, for instance, has concluded that there is very little evidence at Anurādhapura for any of the mass devastation of the Sacred City mentioned in monastic histories.[20]

Strickland confirms, though, that the civilization around the old sacred capital of Anurādhapura did indeed collapse by the eleventh century. It seems that more damaging than the sacking of monasteries was that the Cōḻas recentred their administration and economic infrastructure around Poḷonnaruva, redirecting long-distance trade routes away from the west to the northeast. According to Strickland, 'we see the reorganisation of trade routes away from Anurādhapura, the disappearance from Anurādhapura of craft specialists, of manufacturing, of the elite, of monumental construction, effectively the loss of all the characteristics of an urbanised complex society, all the characteristics of a centralised economy'.[21] The economic shock was compounded by the fact that Vijayabāhu I, having overthrown the Cōḻas in 1070, maintained Poḷonnaruva as his administrative base.[22]

Cōḻa rule was also likely more harmful to monastic interests than any prior incursion on the island due to the fact that in the preceding centuries the monastic community had transformed into a powerful landowner. From around the late eighth century inscriptions record a large number of royal donations to the Saṅgha of land and immunities, in particular exemption from taxation. Recent analysis of Christopher Davis suggests a steady rise in such donations, peaking in the ninth and tenth centuries.[23] The Saṅgha benefited from the alienation of land by taxing its inhabitants, using their labour, or extracting their surplus produce.[24] As R.A.L.H. Gunawardana notes:

> by about the ninth century, monasteries had come to own, apart from movable possessions, a vast extent of property in estates, irrigation works and even salterns, some of them situated at considerable distance from the owning institution.[25]

The Saṅgha maintained its rights through a variety of methods. In the cases where the original donor continued to manage the estate, the donor oversaw the continued transference of appropriate income from the estate to the Saṅgha. In instances where the Saṅgha had full proprietary rights over the land, it employed coercive strategies to maintain control such as restricting the water supply to unco-operative tenant farmers or confiscating their tools, which the monastery owned.[26] While it is unclear if the Cōḻas forcibly deprived the Saṅgha of its land rights, the economic shift east would have drastically reduced its income centred on Anurādhapura and its hinterland.

It is in the context of this unprecedented economic change that we can perhaps understand the curious rise to prominence of a group of forest monks based in Diṁbulāgala, a hilltop monastery situated roughly twenty kilometres from Poḷonnaruva. Most significantly, Parākramabāhu I selected these monks, led by a certain Kassapa, to oversee the reform and unification of the Saṅgha in 1165. The highest ranks of the Saṅgha after the reforms continued to be dominated by monks from this forest fraternity. It was a certain Medhaṅkara, another forest monk from Diṁbulāgala, who led the monastic reforms of Parākramabāhu II in 1266. Explanations of the meteoric rise of what prior to the Cōḻa invasions was a peripheral monastic outpost have tended to rely on Weberian theories about the revolutionary potential of charismatic leaders.[27] It was the 'ascetic charisma' of forest fraternities, R.A.L.H. Gunawardana has argued, that enabled them to secure popularity in the eyes of the laity.[28] There is clearly some truth to this in that the forest monks of the reform era do play up their ascetic credentials in their claims for authority. We can speculate that what actually brought these forest monks into power in the first place, however, was their fortuitous economic position in Poḷonnaruva's hinterland.

We learn from an inscription of Sundarī or Sundaramahādevī, the Kāliṅga dowager-queen of Vikramabāhu I (1111–32), for instance, that more than five hundred monks were living at Diṁbulāgala prior to the reforms, indicating that the hilltop monastery had thrived after the Cōḻa invasions.[29] The monastery had likely benefited from the new trade routes and was now better connected with the northeast Indian mainland than the old centres in the west of the island. H.C.P. Bell noted that even in 1917 Diṁbulāgala was a 'beacon-hill', 'by which mariners skirting the Eastern coast of Ceylon are greatly assured of their position'.[30] While historians have debated the extent to which the reforms of 1165 actually amounted to a victory of the Mahāvihāra over the Jetavana and Abhayagiri, few have questioned how much continuity there was between the post-Cōḻa Mahāvihāra and what had been before.[31] There is an argument to be made that the reformed monastic community after 1165 was the product of a unique strand of Mahāvihāran thought and practice found at this hilltop site.

2.2. Stranger Queens, Civil War and Buddhist Politics

When the Cōḻas overthrew the Pallavas in 897, there was no guarantee that they would become the hegemonic power in the region that they did. In fact, in the century before their conquest of Sri Lanka beginning in 993, there were occasions when the Laṅkan court asserted its independence from the Cōḻas and fended off a number of attempts to bring the island under their suzerainty.[32] And yet, paradoxically, the court's very attempt to assert its independence from its neighbours contributed to its rapid fragmentation from the eleventh century onwards. This was in part because rulers, for the first time, intensified marriage alliances with kingdoms rivalling the Cōḻas, creating rival factions within the royal family.

Nearly all the foreign queens who married into the Laṅkan royal family from the tenth century onwards were from the kingdom of Kaliṅga, situated on India's eastern coast just south of Bengal in what is now Orissa, though later marriages with the South Indian Pāṇḍyas and other northern lineages further complicate the picture. We find frequent mention of Kāliṅga royalty present in the Laṅkan court from the reign of Kassapa IV (898–914) onwards.[33] Mahinda IV (956–72) was the first to marry a Kāliṅga princess, who may have been mother of his son Mahinda V (982–1029).[34] The author of the *Cūḷavaṃsa* thought the event unusual enough to write that 'even though there existed a lineage of *kṣatriya*s in Laṅkā, the ruler of men had fetched a princess born in the lineage of the Wheel-Turning king of Kāliṅga and made her his principal queen'.[35] Her brother also had a daughter Lokitā who then became the wife of Kassapa VI (known as 'Vikramabāhu', 1029–40).[36]

Vijayabāhu I strengthened ties with the Kāliṅgas and took a Kāliṅga princess, Tilokasundarī, as his queen or *mahesī* to ensure 'the longevity of his own lineage', according to the *Cūḷavaṃsa*.[37] He had three of his queen's kinsmen, Madhukaṇṇava, Bhīmarāja and Balakkāra, brought from Sīhapura in

Kaliṅga country and established at his court.[38] Vijayabāhu and Tilokasundarī had a son, Vikramabāhu I, and, for the purpose of continuing their line, arranged his marriage to a Kāliṅga princess, Sundarī or Sundaramahādevī, the younger sister of these three Kāliṅga princes.[39]

It was in the reign of Vijayabāhu I that the monarchy's ties to India became more complex. During Cōḻa rule there appears to have been a number of foreign dignitaries in the kingdom of Rohaṇa in the South of Sri Lanka, most notably a certain Jagatipāla, who is described in the *Cūḷavaṃsa* as a prince of the solar dynasty hailing from 'Ayojjhā' (Sk. Ayodhyā) in northern India. In a power struggle over control of the South, the Cōḻas killed Jagatipāla and captured his queen and daughter, Līlāvatī.[40] In the reign of Vijayabāhu I both queen and daughter escaped to Sri Lanka and the monarch took Līlāvatī as one of his queens.[41] Vijayabāhu further sent his sister, Mittā, to marry a Pāṇḍya prince, whose offspring identified as Pāṇḍyas and as scions of the lunar dynasty, opposing the Kāliṅga side of the royal family.[42]

After the death of Vijayabāhu I, rightful succession was meant to pass to his brother Jayabāhu I (1110–11), followed by Vijayabāhu's son Vikramabāhu I.[43] Vikramabāhu's right to the throne, however, was soon challenged by Mittā's three sons, Vīrabāhu (also known as Māṇābharaṇa), Kittisirimegha and Sirivallabha, who plotted with Jayabāhu to install Vīrabāhu instead as his successor. This led to a bloody civil war between the two factions resulting in Vikramabāhu I nominally ascending the throne at Poḷonnaruva and the three brothers along with the elderly Jayabāhu ruling regions outside of the capital.[44] Matters were not helped by the fact that Vikramabāhu while fighting his half-brothers also had to contend with an invasion of the island by a north Indian prince, Vīradeva, who temporarily captured Poḷonnaruva before being finally slain on a muddy highway somewhere near the capital.[45] The Saṅgha it seems opposed Vikramabāhu's usurpation of Jayabāhu's throne and never officially consecrated him as king. The monastic community suffered greatly during this period of war and monastic historians remember the warring brothers with contempt, singling out Vikramabāhu in particular for stealing monastic property in order to support his military exploits:

> King Vikramabāhu seized the maintenance villages belonging to the Buddha and so forth and gave them to his attendants. In Poḷonnaruva he gave over many monasteries distinguished with relics for foreign soldiers to live in. Gems, pearls and the like that had been given by the faithful as offerings to the alms-bowl relic and precious tooth relic; the sandalwood, the aloes, the camphor, and the many images of gold and the like too; those he plundered and forcefully took away as he pleased.[46]

This civil war encouraged further social and political fragmentation. The people of the different regions stopped paying dues (*kara*) to these different kings and, according to the *Cūḷavaṃsa*, 'ignoring the ruler, they resorted to banditry, and lived impudently (lit. 'raised up', i.e. independently) each in their own territory'.[47]

This newly fragmented social and political order continued into the reign of Vikramabāhu's son and nominal successor, Gajabāhu II (1132–53). Gajabāhu never sat securely on the throne and his reign was constantly threatened by familiar rival factions. His biggest threat was a young Parākramabāhu, ruler of the province of Māyāraṭṭha. Parākramabāhu was of mixed Kāliṅga and Pāṇḍya ancestry since his mother, Ratanāvalī, was the daughter of Vijayabāhu and the Kāliṅga Tilokasundarī, and his father was Vīrabāhu, the eldest son of Mittā, who had unsuccessfully attempted to install himself as Jayabāhu I's successor. Another contender for the throne was Mānābharaṇa, ruler of Rohaṇa in the South. He too had a heritage reflective of the court's rival factions since he was the son of Sirivallabha, the youngest of Mittā's three sons, and Sugalā, who was the great-granddaughter of the North Indian prince Jagatipāla, through Vijayabāhu's marriage to Līlāvatī.

Eyeing the throne, Parākramabāhu steadily amassed a large army and finally attacked Gajabāhu in Poḷonnaruva. According to the *Cūḷavaṃsa*, he justified his challenge to the Kāliṅga king on religious grounds since Gajabāhu 'had fetched princes holding evil beliefs from abroad and had thus filled Rājaraṭṭha with enemies (lit. thorns)'.[48] It was the monastic community, however, who stepped in and brokered a peace deal between Gajabāhu and Parākramabāhu in which the latter was effectively recognized as Gajabāhu's legitimate successor.[49] But upon Gajabāhu's death in 1153 his ministers reneged on the treaty and brought to the throne Parākramabāhu's cousin, Mānābharaṇa, ruler of Rohaṇa. Parākramabāhu's forces attacked Mānābharaṇa and forced him to flee south for refuge, where he died. His mother Sugalā hid the Buddha's tooth and bowl relics in Rohaṇa and, in pursuit, Parākramabāhu violently subdued the province and brought both Sugalā and the relics back to Poḷonnaruva.[50] While Parākramabāhu's twenty-nine-year reign ushered in relative peace on the island, old enmities between royal factions re-emerged upon his death and sixteen rulers, allied variously to Kāliṅga and Pāṇḍya factions, took the throne in the fifty years before the reign of Parākramabāhu II (1236–70).

The increasingly cosmopolitan nature of the royal court changed political discourse on the island too. Kassapa IV in 904 CE claimed for the first time in a royal inscription that he as monarch descended from the Indian Okkāka or Ikṣvāku (Sk.) lineage of kings. Rulers from Kassapa IV onwards frequently assert their supremacy within this transregional royal lineage at the beginning of their inscriptions in royal eulogies or *praśasti*s often modelled on continental Sanskrit forms.[51] The Sinhala of the royal court, then, took on many of the characteristics of what Sheldon Pollock has called a 'cosmopolitan vernacular', localizing for the court's audience on the island transregional, Sanskritic conceptions of kingship and power.[52] Mahinda IV, for instance, regularly claimed in his inscriptions to be 'descended from the royal line of King Okkāka, who abounds in a multitude of illustrious, boundless and transcendental virtues' and that he 'had made other Kṣatriya families of the entire Jambudvīpa (India) his vassals'.[53]

At the same time we also begin to see in the monastic writings of the era detailed discussions about the connection between the Okkāka royal line and the Buddha's own genealogy.[54] A contemporary Pali commentary on the *Mahāvaṃsa* 'Great history' that was perhaps in dialogue with Mahinda IV's political project, for instance, claimed that the Śākya branch of the Okkāka lineage, which it argues was the superior branch of the solar dynasty, solely survived in Sri Lanka since the royal family on the island descended from Paṇḍukābhaya, the mythic king of Laṅkā, who was a grandson of Amitodana, the Buddha's paternal uncle, and whose Kāliṅga wife was also a grandchild of Amitodana.[55] (In introducing within this narrative a Kāliṅga queen, who is pointedly also descended from the Buddha, it is tempting to see here as well an attempt to accommodate Mahinda IV's unusual Kāliṅga marriage within expectations about the religious identity of the island's rulers.)

There are occasions in the tenth century where we find mirrored in the inscriptions of the monarchs of the era this explicitly Buddhist form of political identity, where kings connect their Okkāka genealogy to the Śākya clan of the Buddha. The few inscriptions that do echo monastic expectations of royal identity are always addressed to monastic elites.[56] We can perhaps explain the explicit religious inflection occasionally given to these rulers' Okkāka ancestry as a sign of more local political constraints where kings chose to mirror monastic expectations of kingship, at least partly, we can imagine, in deference to the very real power of the monasteries they patronized. This is evident in the very first inscription to evoke the Śākya clan in a *praśasti*, namely, Kassapa V's regulatory inscription at the Abhayagirivihāra in Anurādhapura in 920, where he responds to an incident in which his officials had given away oxen from a service village belonging to the monastery. Kassapa V reminds the monks of his benevolence to them, formally reconfirms the villages owned by the monastery and establishes a number of other freedoms and protections, while also – perhaps in return for siding with the monastery – assigning new rules for monastic behaviour and practice.[57]

In periods of royal power and relative stability, as we find in the early tenth century, we can easily overlook the political necessity of such diplomacy. It is only when the island descended into civil war, with some rulers attempting to deprive monasteries of their land, that we begin to see the actual contingency underlying relations between the court and monastic community. In such a fragmented social and political environment, ignoring monastic power could have disastrous consequences, as the fate of one of Vijayabāhu's foreign queens attests. According to the *Cūḷavaṃsa*, either Tilokasundarī or Līlāvatī made the error of seizing property belonging to the monastic community and, in a theatrical show of deference, the king 'had her led by the neck and evicted from the city'.[58]

And yet it is also in the inscriptions of the foreign queens of the era that we find some of the most creative religious politics ever produced on the island.[59] Perhaps the greatest politician of the age, at least in terms of monastic relations, was the Kāliṅga queen Sundarī, wife of Vikramabāhu I. Her diplomatic interventions were particularly crucial since, as mentioned, her husband was largely despised by the Saṅgha. In one unprecedentedly deferential inscription, Sundarī actually begins her record with a short *praśasti* in Pali eulogizing a powerful monk, Ānanda, who she describes as a 'banner raised aloft in the land of Laṅkā'.[60] Never before had Pali been used as a language of inscriptional encomium and nor had a member of the royal family treated the monastic community as a political overlord by placing a praise poem to a monk before the traditional eulogy to the monarch.

Another impressive political statement is her inscription at Diṁbulāgala, discussed above, where Sundarī records the construction of a road between two caves at the hilltop monastery.[61] In a masterful political move, she donated to the 'cave of the sun' (*hiru-maha-leṇa*) – the name of which evokes her 'solar' royal lineage – 'statues, stūpas and *bodhi* trees' and renamed it 'Kāliṅga' cave (*kāliṅgu-leṇa*) after her own clan. Sundarī further describes herself in the inscription's opening eulogy 'as descended from the Solar dynasty which belongs to the lineage of Suddhodana, the Buddha's father, that has sprung from the royal race of Okkāka'. She does not mention king Paṇḍukābhaya, grandson of the Buddha's paternal uncle, perhaps because, as Kaliṅga-born, she was technically not part of this branch of the Śākyas, and instead, echoing the commentary on the *Mahāvaṃsa*, connects her Kāliṅga lineage directly with Suddhodana himself.[62] She further uniquely dates the inscription (c. 1136) not to the reign of her deceased, unpopular husband, but from the date of the coronation of king Jayabāhu I who, as mentioned, was the last king before the civil war consecrated by the monastic community.[63]

Her skilful Buddhist politics, without precedent in earlier inscriptions, were likely intended to win favour for her son Gajabāhu and it seems to have helped when, faced with imminent death at the hands of Parākramabāhu's forces, the Saṅgha intervened on Gajabāhu's behalf and brokered a peace deal between him and Parākramabāhu, ultimately saving the king's life. The war and in-fighting among the long line of pretenders to the throne prior to the reign of Parākramabāhu I, then, had turned the Saṅgha into an important political entity in its own right, introducing as a result more localized, religious forms of political discourse.

2.3. The Complex Prehistory of Reform-era Sanskrit

The adoption of Sanskrit literary models in the royal inscriptions of the tenth century was part of a growing engagement with Sanskrit court culture – centred on poetry or *kāvya* and its ancillary philological disciplines such as grammar and poetics – both within the Laṅkan court and the Mahāvihāra prior to the reforms. Kassapa V, for instance, likely composed the first treatise on Sinhala poetics, based on Sanskrit models, and a number of scholar-monks composed Sanskrit grammatical works too.[64] Both the court and monastery relied upon similar intellectual resources, notably the Sanskrit works of Buddhist monks with ties to northeast India.

The most influential scholar of the pre-reform era was undoubtedly Ratnamati or Ratnaśrījñāna. Ratnamati was one of a number of monks from Sri Lanka who travelled in this period between the island and northeast India, especially to the sacred site of Bodh Gayā.[65] In a recent pioneering study Dragomir Dimitrov has plausibly argued that this scholar-monk composed, among other works, a Sanskrit commentary on Candragomin's *Cāndravyākaraṇa* ('Grammar of Candragomin'), a work of grammatical philosophy, the *Śabdārthacintā* ('Reflections on words and their meanings'), as well as a Sanskrit commentary on Daṇḍin's *Kāvyādarśa* ('Mirror of literature', c. eighth century).[66] It was possibly under this scholar's influence that Kassapa V composed his work on Sinhala poetics, the *Siyabaslakara* ('Literary ornaments for our own language'), with Ratnamati writing its Sinhala commentary (*sannaya*) soon after.[67] As we will see in later chapters, Ratnamati's Sanskrit works on poetics and grammar served as models for new forms of Pali philology in the reform era too.

It is difficult to say with any certainty why a scholar-monk such as Ratnamati suddenly became an important authority for both the royal court and the Mahāvihāra from the tenth century onwards. For there had long been scholars from Sri Lanka present in northeast India. There is a tradition in a seventeenth-century Tibetan history, for instance, that in the reign of king Dhammapāla (775–812) a contingent of Sinhalese monks at Bodh Gayā, likely allied to the Mahāvihāra, joined with certain monks from Sindh in actively opposing Tantric practices there.[68] Some of the monks who travelled must have become highly educated. We learn from the same history too that a scholar-monk from Sri Lanka, Jayabhadra, even rose to the position of abbot at Vikramaśīla in the middle third of the ninth century.[69] Ratnamati's peculiar rise to prominence may be explained, as Dragomir Dimitrov has argued, by the fact that he was simply a rare and brilliant individual. Or perhaps also his influence was a sign of a shift in the Mahāvihāra's own attitude to Sanskrit.

It seems that Mahāvihāran monks in Sri Lanka began to engage with courtly forms of Sanskrit prior to the reforms. Kassapa, the leading hierarch at Diṁbulāgala, had the library and resources there to write a grammatical handbook for the Sanskrit *Cāndravyākaraṇa*, probably at some point before the reforms of 1165 took place.[70] Such scholarship, while not identifiably religious, cannot easily be explained as service to the royal court either, since there is no evidence it was undertaken for any king or minister. We can speculate that perhaps scholar-monks had started to produce such works for their own sake, adopting forms of culture suitably expressive of their status in the political landscape.[71] That the Sanskrit learning usually associated with court culture was now a sign of status and prestige for the reform-era Mahāvihāra is reflected in the changing scholarly ideal of the period.[72] In one of his works, for instance, a reform leader, Sāriputta, is compared favourably with great Sanskrit grammarians and poets, such as, Pāṇini and Kālidāsa.[73]

The history of reform-era Sanskrit is further complicated by the fact that the monastic literary culture of the period was influenced not only by courtly forms of Sanskrit but also Buddhist Sanskrit works associated with the Mahayana and Tantric traditions. From the tenth century, for instance, we begin to see in Pali and Sinhala works a more conspicuous engagement with themes and ideas usually associated with the literary cultures of these other Buddhist traditions.[74] While we can speculate that the scholar-monks of the reform era engaged with these ideas as part of a larger cultural package that had entered the Saṅgha through the travels of monks such as Ratnamati, we should keep in mind that the study of Buddhist Sanskrit works among the monks of the three fraternities in Sri Lanka had a much longer history too, in particular during the period of Pallava dominance in the seventh and eighth centuries.

Pallava kings encouraged Buddhist intellectual centres, such as the district of Kāñcī, to flourish on the periphery of their empire.[75] These centres acted as diplomatic nodes in a complex religious, trade and political network, including Sri Lanka, the Pālas in northeast India, Śrī Vijaya (modern-day Sumatra) and the Tang court in China.[76] The Pallavas in the early eighth century, for instance, sent a number of ambassadors to the Tang court and even built a Buddhist monastery for the Chinese emperor in Nāgapaṭṭana.[77] Sri Lanka, it seems, was an important centre of relics and Tantric learning at the time. Thanks to Jeffrey Sundberg and Rolf Giebel, we know of scholar-monks such as Vajrabodhi (d. 743) who travelled with merchants to Sri Lanka via the Pallava court to worship the island's relics, in particular the Buddha's tooth relic at the Abhayagirivihāra, en route to Śrī Vijaya and then China.[78] Travelling the other way, we find Chinese monks, such as Amoghavajra (705–744), who also stayed at the Abhayagirivihāra in search of Tantric texts.[79]

Of the three monastic fraternities in Sri Lanka, then, the Abhayagirivihāra was most connected to this 'esoteric Buddhist network'.[80] Contemporary accounts from Chinese travellers to South Asia note that the Abhayagiri engaged in Tantric and Mahayana practices. A seventh-century Chinese monk-explorer, Xuanzang (602–664) learned on his travels in India that the monks of the Abhayagiri in Sri Lanka studied the Mahayana whereas those of the Mahāvihāra rejected it.[81] In a number of articles Jeffrey Sundberg has argued that king Mānavamma (684–718) and his descendants, who had all spent years exiled in the Pallava court, were great patrons of the Abhayagirivihāra and supported its esoteric Buddhist practices.[82] According to the *Cūḷavaṃsa*, Mānavamma even ordained as a monk in the Abhayagiri order and his brother 'Māna' ruled in his stead.[83] These monarchs of Laṅkā with Pallava associations oversaw institutional changes in the Abhayagiri, establishing, in particular, a number of *pariveṇa*s or 'schools' within the fraternity, such as the Uttaromūla, which became the custodian of the Buddha's tooth relic.[84]

The Mahāvihāra's longstanding opposition to Buddhist Sanskrit literary culture began to shift subtly during the period of Pallava dominance too. The late Lance Cousins has revealed that Mahāvihāran monks at the time, most notably a certain Jotipāla (possibly from the seventh century), composed Sanskrit works seemingly in debate with other Buddhist counterparts.[85] The Mahāvihāra's attitude to Buddhist Sanskrit likely further changed in the ninth century when Sena II and his successors shifted their patronage from the Abhayagirivihāra to the Mahāvihāra.[86] Having supplanted their old adversary, the Mahāvihāra began to resemble the Abhayagiri in a number ways. It adopted some of its ritual practices, such as enshrining scriptures in reliquaries,[87] it took on similar social functions, such as consecrating kings,[88] and it also began to develop its own network of powerful schools or *pariveṇa*s. We can speculate, then, that this emerging continuity between the two fraternities prior to the reforms, whether due to an affinity or rivalry, likely extended to their attitude about studying the Sanskrit works of other Buddhists too.[89]

2.4. Summary

The world faced by the beleaguered monastic factions who gathered together in 1165 with the idea of uniting for the first time in more than a thousand years was radically different from the one experienced only two hundred years earlier in 956, when Mahinda IV had come to occupy the throne. Then, the monarchy in Sri Lanka asserted its independence from its neighbours and unprecedentedly favoured the Mahāvihāra over the other two fraternities. And yet within a few years everything collapsed. Cōḻa rule in Poḷonnaruva decimated Anurādhapura's economy and resulted in the abandonment of the old capital as anything more than a ceremonial site. The marriage practices of the kings of Laṅkā during their brief freedom from suzerainty led, perhaps paradoxically, to the fragmentation of the traditional royal family and to a greater monastic involvement in politics. Wars of succession between rival factions allied to other royalty in India raged either side of Parākramabāhu I's reign, again to the detriment of the Saṅgha's prosperity. At the same time, the absorption of the island into continental dynastic politics was mirrored culturally in the adoption of continental, Sanskrit textual forms, both by the royal court and monastic elites. These new forms of expression not only reflected stronger ties with India but also changing attitudes among the elites of the Mahāvihāra to court culture as well as to the Sanskrit literary cultures of other Buddhists.

Notes

1. Malalasekera, 1994, 178. Also, Wijesekera, 1973, 102–9.
2. *Visuddhimagga* of Buddhaghosa, 444,$_{1-3}$.
3. De Silva, 1981, 17.
4. De Silva, 1981, 18.
5. Trautmann, 1973, 180.
6. Bareau, 1955, 205–43; Gunawardana, 1979, 7–51; Rahula, 1956, 78–111. There is no definitive proof, however, that these schisms immediately resulted in the emergence of a separate *nikāya*. See, for instance, Kieffer-Pülz, 1999a, 72–3.
7. Gunawardana, 1979, 67. On the sacking of monasteries to fund wars, see Liyanagamage, 2001a, 57.
8. De Silva, 1981, 17–26.
9. Walters, 2000, 134; Sundberg, 2018, 342, n. 442.
10. Nilakanta Sastri, 1935, 135–6; 1958, 168.
11. *Cūḷavaṃsa* 53.40. Jeffrey Sundberg has noted that Parāntaka in his inscriptions actually describes himself as 'taker of Īḻam', that is, as conqueror of Sri Lanka, years before his invasion in the reign of Udaya IV. See Sundberg, 2018, 434, n. 597, citing Nilakanta Sastri, 1935, 435. It is difficult to determine, however, how far these early boasts were statements of fact or simply expressions of intent.
12. De Silva, 1981, 24–6; Spencer, 1976, 409. See also, Pathmanathan, 1978, 33–61; Nilakanta Sastri, 1960, 413–14; Wijayatuṅga, 1965, 69–70.
13. See, for instance, Bechert, 1976, 30; 2005, 36; Malalasekera, 1994, 168.
14. *South Indian Inscriptions* IV, nos. 1388; 1392; 1393; Gunasingam, 1974; Indrapala, 1971a; 1978.
15. *Epigraphia Zeylanica* III, 242–55.
16. Indrapala, 1971b; Pathmanathan, 1978, 66–83; 1976; 1982b; 1984.
17. Henry, 2017, 84–90.

18. *Cūḷavaṃsa* 55.20–1:
nikāyattitaye dhātugabbhe laṅkātale 'khile
mahārahe suvaṇṇādipaṭibimbe ca 'nappake
bhinditvā sahasā sabbe vihāre ca tahiṃ tahiṃ
yathojohārino yakkhā laṅkāyaṃ sāram aggahuṃ.
Chapters 37–79 of the *Cūḷavaṃsa* are often considered to be the work of a single scholar-monk Dhammakitti in the thirteenth century. Sirima Wickramasinghe, however, argued convincingly that Dhammakitti likely composed only the section dealing with Parākramabāhu's reign. See Wickramasinghe, 1958, 8–33.
19. Davis, 1993. Vijayabāhu I's repairs in Anurādhapura are mainly mentioned in the context of decay rather than destruction, for instance. He only refers to damage caused by the Cōḻas in relation to the Thūpārāma and relic shrines in Mahāgāma, that is, modern-day Hambantota in the far South of Sri Lanka. See *Cūḷavaṃsa* 60.56–63.
20. Strickland, 2017, 150–3; 2011, 302–9.
21. Strickland, 2017, 161; 2011, 331.
22. It has been plausibly suggested that a transfer of power from Anurādhapura to Poḷonnaruva had begun earlier as a result of the Pāṇḍya invasion of 840. See Sundberg, 2018, 213, n. 268. Even so, the evidence suggests that the economy and population of Anurādhapura continued to grow until the eleventh century, that is, until Cōḻa rule. See Strickland, 2017, 87; 113; 138; 2011, 196; 243; 286.
23. Davis, 2013, 269–318, esp. 308; 2017. Due to the loss of much of the inscriptional record prior to this period, it is difficult to properly assess the relative significance of this perceived increase in land grants. The gaps in the inscriptional record may be due to the fact that kings seem to have removed the inscriptions of their predecessors which their own edicts superseded, sometimes using the older rock inscriptions as building materials. See Sundberg, 2018, 194, n. 242.
24. Gunawardana, 1979, 57–67.
25. Gunawardana, 1971, 19.
26. Gunawardana, 1979, 57; 1971, 20.
27. On the few mentions of Diṁbulāgala in pre-reform literature, see Nicholas, 1963, 40.
28. Gunawardana, 1979, 46–7; 316; 349–50. See also Blackburn, 1999b, 361.
29. *Epigraphia Zeylanica* II, 184–9; 194–202 (= *Inscriptions of Ceylon* 6, no. 8.1). Vikramabāhu I is sometimes referred to as Vikramabāhu II since Kassapa VI was also known as 'Vikramabāhu'. See Pathmanathan, 1993.
30. Bell, 1917.
31. Bechert, 1993; Gunawardana, 1979, 282–337.
32. Walters, 2000, 132–46. Jeffrey Sundberg has critiqued Walters for overestimating the power of the monarchy during the tenth century. See Sundberg, 2018, 429. I would contend, however, that, while it was perhaps not a dominant, transregional power, the monarchy was certainly resisting suzerainty, much to the frustration of neighbouring kingdoms.
33. *Epigraphia Zeylanica* V.III, 340; *Epigraphia Zeylanica* I, 161, cited in Walters, 2000, 135. See also from the reign of Kassapa IV: *Inscriptions of Ceylon* 5.1, nos. 69.18; 72.21; 78.27; 79.28; 83.32.
34. Note, however, that S. Paranavitana has incorrectly argued that Mahinda V identified as Kāliṅga due to his reading of an inscription he attributed to the king. See *Epigraphia Zeylanica* IV, 59–67. Sirimal Ranawella has contested this reading and rather dates the inscription to the reign of Udaya III. See *Inscriptions of Ceylon* 5.2, no. 37.3.
35. *Cūḷavaṃsa* 54. 9–10ab:
vijjamāne pi laṅkāyaṃ khattiyānaṃ narādhipo
kāliṅgacakkavattissa vaṃse jātaṃ kumārikaṃ
ānāpetvāna taṃ aggamahesiṃ attano akā.
See also Sirisena, 1971, esp. 12.
36. Geiger, interpreting *Cūḷavaṃsa* 57.27–9, has argued that Kassapa VI's son Moggallāna was also the father of Vijayabāhu I. See Geiger and Rickmers, 1998, 195, n. 3. But see Ranawella, *Inscriptions of Ceylon 6*, xxiv–xxvi.
37. *Cūḷavaṃsa* 59.30.
38. *Cūḷavaṃsa* 59.46–8.
39. *Cūḷavaṃsa* 59.49.
40. *Cūḷavaṃsa* 56.13–15.
41. *Cūḷavaṃsa* 59.23–5. Vikramabāhu would later take his father and Līlāvatī's granddaughter, also named Līlāvatī, as his second queen.
42. *Cūḷavaṃsa* 59.41.
43. See Geiger and Rickmers, 1998, 225, n. 1.
44. See the description in *Cūḷavaṃsa* 61.

45. *Cūḷavaṃsa* 61.46.
46. *Cūḷavaṃsa* 61.54–7
uddharitvāna buddhādisantake bhogagāmake
so vikkamabhujo rājā sevakesu samappayi.
pulatthinagare nekavihāre dhātumaṇḍite
so va desantarīyānaṃ bhaṭānaṃ vasituṃ dadi.
saddhehi pattadhātussa dāṭhādhātuvarassa ca
pūjanatthāya dinnāni maṇimuttādikāni ca
candanāgarukappūraṃ suvaṇṇādimayā bahū
paṭimāyo ca acchijja yathākāmaṃ vayaṃ nayi. Trans. adapted from Geiger and Rickmers, 1998, 230.
47. *Cūḷavaṃsa* 61.71:
rājāṇaṃ agaṇentā te gatā dāmarikattanaṃ
sakaṃ sakaṃ va visayaṃ āvasiṃsu samuddhatā.
Trans. adapted from Geiger and Rickmers, 1998, 231.
48. *Cūḷavaṃsa* 70.53–4ab:
tadā desantarā rājakumāre pāpadiṭṭhino
gajabāhumahīpālo ānāpiya sakaṇṭakaṃ
rājaraṭṭhaṃ akāsī ti suṇitvāna narissaro …
Trans. adapted from Geiger and Rickmers, 1998, 291. Pathmanathan has speculated that Gajabāhu was in fact Hindu, based on his reading of the Tamil history of the temple of Koṇesvaram, the seventeenth-century (?) *Koṇēcar Kalveṭṭu*. See Pathmanathan, 1987, 58–60. Also, Henry, 2017, 115–26.
49. *Epigraphia Zeylanica* IV, 1–8.
50. *Cūḷavaṃsa* 70–2; Liyanagamage, 1968, 34–8.
51. For the first such inscription, see *Inscriptions of Ceylon* 5.1, no. 67.16.
52. Pollock, 2006, 26. On the Sinhala *praśasti*, see Berkwitz, 2016; Hallisey, 2003, 698–9.
53. *Inscriptions of Ceylon* 5.2, no. 62.1. I have added the information in parentheses to Ranawella's translation.
54. Walters, 2000, 125–32. For earlier accounts of the *Okkāka* lineage, see *Dīpavaṃsa* 10; *Mahāvaṃsa* of Mahānāma, 9.1–28. I differ from Walters in that I do not view this genealogy as necessarily working in service of the imperial aims of the court.
55. Walters, 2000, 129.
56. The inscriptions that refer to the Śākyas, Paṇḍukābhaya or Suddhodana in the tenth century are as follows:

Ruler	Dates	Issuer	Inscription	Audience	Purpose
Kassapa V	914–23	Kassapa V	IC 5.1, no. 104.14	Monastic	Monastic regulations
		Ādipāda Mahinda	IC 5.1, no. 110.20	Monastic	Immunities
Dappula IV	924–35	Lämäni Mahiṅdu	IC 5.2, no. 10.10	Monastic	Immunities
		Mahapā Udā	IC 5.2, no. 18.18	Monastic	Immunities
		Dappula IV	IC 5.2, no. 19.19	Monastic	Immunities
		Mahapā Udā	IC 5.2, no. 29.29	Monastic	Immunities
Udaya III	935–8	Udaya III	IC 5.2, no. 37.3	Monastic	Immunities
Sena III	938–46	Sena III	IC 5.2, no. 40.3	Monastic	Monastic regulations
Mahinda IV	982–1029	Mahinda IV	IC 5.2, no. 65.4	Monastic	Rules for maintenance
		Mahinda IV	IC 5.3, no. 26	Monastic	Hospital regulations

57. *Inscriptions of Ceylon* 5.1, no. 104.14 (= *Epigraphia Zeylanica* I, 41–57). On this inscription, see Sundberg, 2018, 355–82.
58. *Cūḷavaṃsa* 60.54–5, cited in Gunawardana, 1979, 209.
59. On the queens of the era, see Seneviratne, 1969; Schrijvers, 1986.
60. *Epigraphia Zeylanica* IV, 67–72 (= *Inscriptions of Ceylon* 6, no. 7.2). Junko Matsumura has identified this Ānanda with the teacher of Buddhappiya, author of the *Rūpasiddhi*. See Matsumura, 1999, 158.
61. *Epigraphia Zeylanica* II, 184–9; 194–202 (= *Inscriptions of Ceylon* 6, no. 8.1).
62. It is of course possible that this was simply a convention. In fact, *Inscriptions of Ceylon* 5.3, no. 26 also connects Mahinda IV's genealogy directly to Suddhodana and does not mention king Paṇḍukābhaya either.
63. See Paranavitana's discussion on this point in *Epigraphia Zeylanica* II, 200–2. Also, Kiribamune, 1976.
64. Dimitrov, 2016, 105–23. See also Hallisey, 2003; Pollock, 2006, 386–7. The Sanskrit works that likely predate the reforms include Dharmakīrti's *Rūpāvatāra*, Kassapa's *Bālāvabodhana* and Sāriputta's *Cāndrapañcikālaṅkāra*. Another possibility is Buddhanāga's *Pātrīkaraṇaṭīkā*, a commentary on a grammatical handbook, Guṇākara's *Pātrīkaraṇa*, though we can only be sure that it was composed before 1458 since it is quoted in Śrī Rāhula's *Moggallānapañcikāpradīpaya*. On these works, see also Bechert, 1987, 5–16.
65. Frasch, 1998, 69–72.
66. Dimitrov, 2016, 51–74; 565–96; 599–706. For a critical overview of Dimitrov's arguments concerning the works he attributes to Ratnamati, see Gornall, 2017. In this book, I follow Dimitrov in taking Ratnamati and Ratnaśrījñāna to be the same individual, though I am also aware that this cannot be conclusively proved.
67. Dimitrov, 2016, 105–22.
68. Chimpa and Chattopadhyaya, trans. 1990, 279.
69. To be precise, he was the third *vajrācārya*. See Chimpa and Chattopadhyaya, trans. 1990, 325. The historian Tāranātha wrote his work in 1608 supposedly using three Sanskrit sources. On the date and identity of this monk, see Sundberg and Giebel, 2011, 207, n. 137.
70. Bechert, 2005, 142.
71. While there is no doubt a historical connection, then, as Sheldon Pollock has skilfully elucidated, between such courtly forms of Sanskrit and political power, it is necessary to disentangle political function from the institution of the court and to acknowledge that the monastery was an equally important site of cultural change. Sheldon Pollock discusses the Buddhist monastery as a site for the production of Sanskrit court literature in an earlier article, but really only as an exception that proves the rule. See Pollock, 2003, esp. 114–121. On sites of literary production outside the court, see Cox, 2017, 156. On monastic political autonomy in India, see Davidson, 2002, esp. 167–8.
72. See also Hallisey, 2003, 707–12.
73. *Abhidharmārthasaṅgrahasannaya* of Sāriputta, 257_{27-30}.
74. See, for instance, Bechert, 2005, 59–90; Dimitrov, 2016; Gunawardana, 1979, 322–7; Kieffer-Pülz, 2013, 129–31.
75. Schalk, 2002, 378–429.
76. Sen, 2003, 224.
77. Sundberg and Giebel, 2011, 143–5.
78. Sundberg and Giebel, 2011, 134–40.
79. Sundberg and Giebel, 2011, 145; 149; 186, n. 72.
80. See Acri, 2016. On the Abhayagiri's transregional connections, see De Casparis, 1961; Sundberg, 2004.
81. Bechert, 1977; Deeg, 2012, 152. On the Abhayagiri and Sanskrit literary culture, see, most recently, Chandawimala, 2016. The Abhayagiri also maintained a rich tradition of studying the Pali canon and composing Pali works. See Cousins, 2012.
82. See, in particular, Sundberg, 2014; 2017.
83. *Cūḷavaṃsa* 57.4–27, discussed in Sundberg, 2017, 204–18. This passage has also been analysed as an origin story for the position of 'grandmaster' (*mahāsāmi*) in the Saṅgha's hierarchy. See Gornall, 2013, 37–40; Rohanadeera, 1985, 33–5.
84. Sundberg, 2017, 213–18.
85. Cousins, 2013; 2016. See also chapter six.
86. See Walters, 2000, 132–41.
87. On the 'cult of the book' in late medieval Sri Lanka, see chapter six.
88. Walters, 2000, 130; 134–5.
89. The reform-era Saṅgha, for instance, seems to have tolerated monks studying the works of other religious traditions. See Gornall, 2014a, 524–5.

3
The Reform Era and its Pali Literature

When the Cōḻas ruled Sri Lanka and brought about the gradual collapse of Anurādhapura, they set in motion a complex chain of events that upended life on the island. If the early post-Cōḻa era appears confusing to us today, it must have been utterly bewildering for those who were buffeted by what no doubt seemed like an uncontrollable wave of disasters. Importantly, however, this misfortune did not distinguish between the three fraternities within the monastic community. Faced for the first time with an apparent existential threat, the old sectarian politics of Anurādhapura began to fall away. Smaller monastic groupings emerged alongside the traditional *nikāya* divisions and at least some elite monks decided to unify under the banner of the Mahāvihāra, leading to the dissolution of the Abhayagiri and Jetavana fraternities.[1] It took almost one hundred years after Cōḻa rule, however, for these elites to gather together at a council overseen by Parākramabāhu I (1157–86) and fight against the often intangible forces of perceived religious decline through the composition of new Pali texts.

This scholarship differed from earlier heydays not only in terms of the quantity and types of works composed but also in its sharp focus on monastic reform. Surveys of the Pali textual tradition rarely distinguish these works from earlier monastic scholarship and pay little attention to issues of periodization, simply treating Pali literature as 'everything that is written in Pali'.[2] When its literature is historicized it is usually from a linguistic standpoint. From this perspective, the Pali language can be understood as a partly Sanskritized patchwork of a variety of Middle-Indic dialects.[3] These dialects from various regions of India developed and intertwined to form the language of the Tipiṭaka and then that language changed through increasing Sanskritization into the language of canonical commentary and medieval literature.[4] This is certainly an important part of the story. A less understood aspect, however, concerns the formal changes in genre and style that occurred in Theravada monastic literary culture over time and the place of these developments in the wider history of Buddhism.

Few scholars have given any serious attention to this history. Heinz Bechert stands out as one of the earliest and most insightful scholars to combine philology and social and political history in the study of Pali, Sanskrit and Sinhalese literature in Sri Lanka.[5] More recently, the late Steven Collins pioneered studies of Pali literature within the broader civilizational history of Theravada Buddhism.[6] Collins was the first to question, in particular, why monks during the reform era started to compose independent works of poetry or *kāvya* in Pali in a 'consciously high-literate, Sanskritized manner' when previously they had concerned themselves almost exclusively with writing commentaries on the Pali canon and histories of their religious tradition. Collins referred to this question as 'the *problem* of literature in Pali'.[7] To a large extent, this book is an extended answer to Collins's question, though this chapter will establish that the problem may be far larger than Collins first thought. For it was not only a Sanskritized Pali poetry that emerged during this period but also, as we will see, new forms of philology, including grammar and poetics, pedagogical handbooks and new types of commentary.

Collins speculated that this new Pali literature, while formally innovative, continued to share with older Pali texts the same general purpose of providing societal elites a cultural coherence on which their rule and status depended. These texts were, he speculated, 'an element in the rhetorical, theatrical constitution of civilization-bearing state-systems: symbolic capital contributing to the prestige of both the *maṇḍala*-organizing king and his clients'.[8] If we were only to speak about the court-centred polities of early medieval Sri Lanka or the charter states of Southeast Asia, there may be some sense, due to the concentration of wealth in the court and the monastery's dependence on it, to speak of Saṅgha and state as part of a single community and to think about Buddhist textual culture in terms of the cultural cohesion it brought to this elite. And yet, as we have seen, the old order had entirely changed after Cōḻa rule. Political power on the island had fragmented and the monastic community had been increasingly drawn into dynastic politics as a political actor in its own right.

The Pali literature of the reform era, then, necessarily performed a different type of labour from that produced in the pre-Cōḻa period. This chapter attempts to draw a contrast between the reform era and what came before and also between the differing aims of Pali texts within the monastic reforms, in particular their role in maintaining the autonomous order of the monastic community and in establishing new forms of patronage among a shifting elite. These posited aims of Pali literature are inextricably linked with how we view the reforms as historical phenomena too. This chapter further explores the nature of the royal reforms and argues that the reform process did not turn Buddhism into a kind of imperial religion, as is often argued, but

Table 3.1: The reigns of the kings and queens of Laṅkā, 1157–1270[9]

Regnal Dates	Monarch
1157–86	Parākramabāhu I
1186–7	Vijayabāhu II
1187 (*five days*)	Mahinda VI
1187–96	Niśśaṅka Malla
1196	Vikramabāhu II
1196–7	Coḍagaṅga
1197–1200	Līlāvatī
1200–2	Sāhassa Malla
1202–8	Kalyāṇavatī
1208–9	Dharmāśoka
1209	Anīkaṅga, Mahādipāda
1209–10	Līlāvatī
1210–11	Lokeśvara
1211–12	Līlāvatī
1212–15	Parākrama Paṇḍu
1215–36	Māgha (Kāliṅga Vijayabāhu)
1232–6	Vijayabāhu III
1236–70	Parākramabāhu II

rather that, even when the process was overseen by powerful rulers, such as, Parākramabāhu I, it primarily enabled the monastic community to regulate itself and better survive as a political entity more autonomous than before.

3.1. A Short Sketch of Pre-reform Pali and its Literature

Before we can discuss the reforms and the literature they produced it is necessary to sketch out a short history of the Pali tradition prior to this period. The Theravada Buddhist tradition divides the teachings of the Buddha into three (*ti-*) baskets (*piṭaka*), namely, the monastic rules (Vinaya), his religious discourses (Sutta), and the so-called 'supreme teachings' (Abhidhamma), systematic presentations of the ideas contained in the Suttas. While the contents of many of the texts of the Pali canon may date at least in oral form to the early centuries after the Buddha's death, the process of arranging, systematizing and authorizing the texts of the Tipiṭaka as we now have it probably occurred over a much longer period.[10] A key part of this process was the development of exegetical literature on canonical texts. Some of the earliest commentaries and manuals of textual exegesis, namely the *Suttavibhaṅga* ('Analysis of the [*Pātimokkha*] discourse'), *Niddesa* ('Exposition'), *Nettipakaraṇa* ('Guide') and *Peṭakopadesa* ('Piṭaka disclosure'), were composed in Pali possibly at the turn of the Common Era.[11] It is perhaps to the same early post-Aśokan period that we witness the beginning of Pali historiography as represented by the *Cariyāpiṭaka* ('Basket of conduct'), *Buddhavaṃsa* ('History of the buddhas') and *Apadāna* ('Legends').[12]

Monastic literature for much of the first millennium continued to be divided into these two genres: histories (*vaṃsa*) of Buddhism in Sri Lanka and the far more numerous commentaries and subcommentaries on the Pali canon. Nearly all of the works we possess from the era are the products of the Mahāvihāra, since it was this fraternity's textual tradition that formed the basis of the 1165 reforms. Foremost of the early commentators was the fourth or fifth-century exegete Buddhaghosa who, according to tradition, wrote Pali commentaries on the five Nikāyas of the Suttapiṭaka, two commentaries on the Vinaya, commentaries on the seven books of the Abhidhamma, and a comprehensive summary of Buddhist practice, the *Visuddhimagga* ('Path of purification').[13] Modern scholars have rightly cast doubt on a number of the works attributed to Buddhaghosa and often only view the *Visuddhimagga* and the commentaries on the first four Nikāyas as his own.[14]

Before 'Buddhaghosa' composed his works, an anonymous scholar or scholars authored the *Dīpavaṃsa* ('History of the island'), a history of Buddhism in Sri Lanka and possibly the first Pali work ever composed on the island.[15] Following Buddhaghosa's works, a scholar monk known as Mahānāma also composed another history of Buddhism, the *Mahāvaṃsa* ('Great history'), improving upon the language of the *Dīpavaṃsa* and siding more specifically with the Mahāvihāra sect.[16] A number of other commentators succeeded Buddhaghosa prior to the reform era, including Buddhadatta, who composed some of the first handbooks on the Abhidhamma and Vinaya in around the fifth century, Ānanda, who wrote commentaries on Buddhaghosa's Abhidhamma works in the sixth century, and Dhammapāla who, as well as writing commentaries on books of the *Khuddaka Nikāya*, composed a number of Pali subcommentaries at some point before the twelfth century.[17]

It is in these early commentaries that we see develop distinct ideas about Pali as a sacred language. At least since Buddhaghosa, Pali was thought to be the only language in which the Buddha spoke, the 'language of Magadha' (*Magadhabhāsā*), and the language of the earliest commentaries that were brought to Sri Lanka by Aśoka's son Mahinda. To write in Pali, then, was to connect one's work with the universal authority of the Buddha and his immediate disciples. In Buddhaghosa's *Visuddhimagga* and also in the Abhidhamma commentaries, we further find descriptions of Pali as a magical language.[18] It is there that the commentator explains, for instance, that Pali is the *sabhāvan-irutti* or 'essence-language' because it is spoken throughout the cosmos by animals, hungry ghosts, humans and gods and that it is the default language of a child brought up without human contact. Echoing similar Brahmanical claims for Sanskrit, the commentator states that Pali is unchanging unlike the other languages of the world that are subject to the ravages of time and that, for the adept, its meaning immediately manifests as soon as it is heard, without intellectual reflection. He determines too that one can obtain an analytical knowledge (*paṭisambhidā*) of scripture only when it is studied in Pali and not when it is translated.[19]

Many, if not the majority, of commentators, including Buddhaghosa, Buddhadatta and Dhammapāla, were likely of South Indian origin and another main reason Pali was cultivated as a commentarial language was to allow communication within the wider circle of scholar-monks in South India and Sri Lanka.[20] In the preamble to the commentary on the Vinaya, for instance, the author writes that he specifically wrote his commentary in what he refers to as a language 'imitative of the style of canonical texts' and not in Sinhala for the benefit also of those on the 'other island' (*dīpantara*) or the Indian mainland.[21] The scholar monks of the period tended to divide their world into two islands: 'Lion island' (*sīhaḷadīpa*) or Sri Lanka and 'Plum island' (*jambudīpa*), India.[22] In transcending Lion island, then, Pali commentaries became a frame of reference through which a transregional Buddhist community could be created, one that would persist fairly unaltered until the reform era when we see the emergence of separate, sectarian identities in Cōḻa India and Sri Lanka.[23]

The literary activity of the first millennium has usually been connected with periods in which the Mahāvihāra was favoured by the ruling monarch. G.P. Malalasekera put it most succinctly when he wrote with respect to early commentarial activity in Pali that, 'material prosperity is the handmaid of literary development, as of all artistic work'.[24] The idea that literary production was necessarily predicated on royal support and stable kingship reflects a longstanding assumption in histories of Buddhism that the court and monastery were interdependent parts of a social whole or even a proto-nation state. If the royal court was stable and prosperous, so the logic goes, the monastic community had the resources and necessary peace of mind to engage in scholarly work. For Walpola Rahula, for instance, the Buddhist tradition and the Saṅgha, in particular, was a 'fully-fledged state department' and Buddhist monasteries were 'centres of national culture'.[25] R.A.L.H. Gunawardana, while setting aside tropes of nationhood, spoke instead of an 'antagonistic symbiosis' between court and monastery and viewed the two institutions as functionally interdependent, if sometimes disputatious, parts of a single social whole, with monks providing ideological support for the ruling monarch in return for protection and patronage. Gunawardana's more sophisticated model also forms the sociological basis of Steven Collins's Pali *imaginaire* too.[26]

The reality, with respect to textual production in particular, is more difficult to determine due to a lack of historical information in most early Pali texts. Monastic historians certainly viewed the changing fate of their fraternity in dynastic terms, according to the successive reigns of the island's moral and immoral kings. They regarded Buddhaghosa's commentaries, for instance, as a product of the resurgence of the Mahāvihāra under the patronage of king Mahānāma (406–28).[27] The *Dīpavaṃsa* too may have been composed, at least partly, for king Sirimeghavaṇṇa (301–28) in order to regain patronage for the Mahāvihāra, which the king's father Mahāsena (274–301) had neglected in favour of the Abhayagiri.[28] We can also tentatively connect certain South Indian exegetical works with periodic support for the Mahāvihāra in the region. Buddhadatta, the author of early Pali handbooks, states in his *Vinayavinicchaya* ('Exegesis on the Discipline') that he wrote his work in Cōḻa country during the reign of a certain Accutavikkanta of the 'Kalambha' dynasty.[29] He was likely referring to the Kaḷabhras, a minor South Indian clan who perhaps favoured Buddhists or Jains in their patronage.[30] The majority of first millennium Pali works, however, provide little insight into the politics of their production and we can only speculate about how far royal patronage actually determined monastic literary activity.

Table 3.2: A hypothetical chronology of Pali works composed in South India and Sri Lanka, 300–900 CE[31]

Text	Author	Date
Commentaries/Subcommentaries on Canonical Texts		
Sumaṅgalavilāsinī	Buddhaghosa	370–450
Papañcasūdanī	Buddhaghosa	370–450
Sāratthappakāsinī	Buddhaghosa	370–450
Manorathapūraṇī	Buddhaghosa	370–450
Atthasālinī	Anon.	370–450
Sammohavinodanī	Anon.	370–450
Pañcappakaraṇaṭṭhakathā	Anon.	370–450
Samantapāsādikā	Anon.	386/427
Kaṅkhāvitaraṇī	Anon.	after 386/427
Jātakatthavaṇṇanā	Anon.	after 450
Dhammapadaṭṭhakathā	Anon.	after 450

(Continued)

Table 3.2: (Continued)

Text	Author	Date
Paramatthajotikā I	Anon.	after 450
Paramatthajotikā II	Anon.	after 450
Dhammasaṅgaṇimūlaṭīkā	Ānanda	500–600
Vibhaṅgamūlaṭīkā	Ānanda	500–600
Pañcappakaraṇamūlaṭīkā	Ānanda	500–600
Saddhammapakāsinī	Mahānāma	559
Paramatthadīpanī I	Dhammapāla	after 700
Paramatthadīpanī II	Dhammapāla	after 700
Paramatthadīpanī III	Dhammapāla	after 700
Paramatthadīpanī IV	Dhammapāla	after 700
Paramatthadīpanī V	Dhammapāla	after 700
Paramatthadīpanī VI	Dhammapāla	after 700
Paramatthadīpanī VII	Dhammapāla	after 700
Līnatthappakāsinī	Dhammapāla	after 700
Līnatthavaṇṇanā I	Dhammapāla	after 700
Paramatthamañjūsā	Dhammapāla	after 700
Nettiaṭṭhakathā	Dhammapāla	after 700
Līnatthavaṇṇanā II	Dhammapāla	after 700
Saddhammapajjotikā	Upasena	877
Histories		
Dīpavaṃsa	Anon.	300–400
Mahāvaṃsa	Mahānāma	400–500
Handbooks		
Visuddhimagga	Buddhaghosa	370–450
Khuddasikkhā	Dhammasiri	after 386/427
Vinayavinicchaya	Buddhadatta	450–600
Uttaravinicchaya	Buddhadatta	450–600
Abhidhammāvatāra	Buddhadatta	450–600
Rūpārūpavibhāga	Buddhadatta	450–600
Saccasaṅkhepa	Anon.	after 500
Mūlasikkhā	Mahāsāmi	before 1200
Philological works		
Kaccāyanavyākaraṇa	Kaccāyana	600–700
Kaccāyanavutti	Saṅghanandi	after 700

3.2. An Era of Reform, Unification and Education

The reign of Parākramabāhu I, characterized by its attempt at centralized, charter state politics, appears on the surface like a good example of this ideal Saṅgha-state model. And yet, as we have seen, his reign was something of an anomaly when compared with the general political trajectory towards the fragmentation and localization of power.[32] 'Parākramabāhu I's empire', Keith Taylor perceptively noted, 'though not an example of political fragmentation, was only possible by the destruction of the traditional order and the welding together of the resulting fragments through sheer physical force'.[33] Parākramabāhu's rise was born of this chaos and the political turmoil after his reign was, to some degree, the natural continuation of the centrifugal political patterns prior to his ascension to the throne. We should be wary, then, of understanding the comparisons in monastic histories between his 1165 reforms and the third council (*saṅgīti*) held in the reign of the emperor Aśoka too literally.[34] For the Aśokan model, in which a Buddhist emperor acts as the 'crux of order in society', was by 1165 an abstraction or ceremonial ideal with little correspondence to the general political reality of the era.[35]

Heinz Bechert was the first to refer aptly to the events of 1165 as '*sāsana* reforms' and it is through the lens of 'reform' that similar royal councils have been viewed subsequently.[36] There is no equivalent to the word 'reform' either as a movement or as an event in the monastic writing of the era. The actual activity of reform is usually described as a 'purification' (*visuddhi, visodhana*) of the religion or *sāsana*. The 'purity' of the tradition, at least in royal edicts, was always primarily associated with monastic behaviour and the formal rules of monastic discipline. This meant in the 1165 reforms purging the order of most of the monks who did not conform to Mahāvihāran standards of discipline.[37] Doctrinal coherence was an important aspect of reforms but it was dealt with within the Saṅgha and not by royal intervention. Buddhist monastic reforms also often included, at least rhetorically, a unification (*samagga*) of antagonistic monastic factions.[38] The unification of the remaining monastic groups in 1165, for instance, enabled the Saṅgha to claim that they had restored the religion to an original, pristine state, 'as it had been in Buddha's time'.[39]

The dual reform processes of purification and unification were viewed cosmologically as postponing the inevitable disappearance of the *sāsana*. In the royal edict issued after the 1165 reforms, it is said that while Parākramabāhu I 'was enjoying the delight of kingship with a display of abundant virtues, he witnessed sons of noble families of the Buddhist persuasion on the road to hell'.[40] He then evokes in the edict a prophecy, which first emerges in fourth- or fifth-century commentaries, that the Buddhist tradition would survive five thousand years after the Buddha's death and hoped that, as a result of his effort, the unified monastic community would not disappear prematurely.[41] Reference continues to be made to this prophecy in the 1266 Daṁbadeṇiya edict too, and later in the ordinance Parākramabāhu II specifically connects the perceived decline of the Buddhist tradition with the monastic neglect of the study of their sacred scriptures. Monks are thus encouraged to 'study the Tipiṭaka together with the commentaries from virtuous teachers and thereby become very learned'.[42]

The 1165 reforms and those like them that followed both in Sri Lanka and Southeast Asia have been interpreted as evidence that the Saṅgha had been further integrated into the state.[43] The schematic nature of much of this analysis, however, obscures what was a varied and highly complex phenomenon. Even if we limit ourselves to our 'reform era', there are marked differences, for instance, between the 'imperial' nature of the reforms of Parākramabāhu I and II in 1165 and 1266 respectively. One might think of the 1165 reforms as imperial in nature, on the basis that it was the king himself who oversaw the events and who used his coercive power to expel troublesome factions from the order, that it is said he personally selected monks from the monastery of Diṁbulāgala, led by the elder Kassapa, to undertake the reforms and that monks were invited from regions bound by the territory of his kingdom. That said, there is also no evidence that Parākramabāhu I played any role in formulating the rules promulgated in the edict or in supporting the appointment of monks to administrative positions. In fact, he appears to encourage the Saṅgha to regulate itself, stating, 'devoting themselves diligently to the two tasks of scriptural study and contemplation, may the Saṅgha protect the *sāsana* by the administration of admonitions (*avavāda*) and decrees (*śāsana*)'.[44] In terms of motive, Parākramabāhu simply cites the pain he felt as a Buddhist emperor, a *cakravartin*, in seeing the religion in an impure state, though economic interest in reclaiming ownership of the land that formerly belonged to expelled monks may have been an underlying factor.[45]

The reforms of Vijayabāhu III around 1232 and Parākramabāhu II in 1266 differ for a number of reasons. We will speak of both together since the edict Vijayabāhu issued was lost and what we know about his reforms comes from Parākramabāhu's Daṁbadeṇiya edict, which subsumed and supplanted the former's proclamations. The Daṁbadeṇiya edict describes the Saṅgha's administrative structure as akin to a royal court. There it is stated, for instance, that the Saṅgha was led by a *mahāsāmi* 'grandmaster' who was assisted by two *mahātheras* or 'great elders' representing both forest monks (*araññavāsi*) and village monks (*gāmavāsi*). Under these *mahātheras* were placed the heads of eight fraternities (*āyatana*), followed by the heads of various schools (*pariveṇa*).[46]

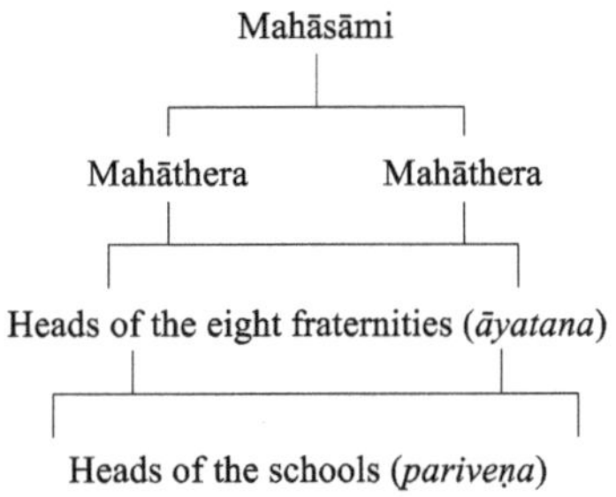

Figure 3.1 The hierarchy of the Saṅgha as depicted in the Daṁbadeṇiya edict[47]

Unlike the 1165 reforms it is stated that both the king and the Saṅgha needed to consent to the appointment of the leaders of the eight fraternities as well as the heads of monastic schools (*pariveṇa*). The two *mahāthera*s needed the approval of the Saṅgha to be appointed but were only required to 'venerate' the king prior to taking up their position. The 'grandmaster' was succeeded after his death by one of these *mahāthera*s seemingly without need for either royal or monastic approval.[48] If we view royal involvement in the appointment of senior religious figures as characteristic of an imperial religion – as it has been, for example, in the study of 'the imperial church systems' in northern Europe – then the 1266 reforms could be seen as more imperial than 1165.[49] And yet, we should also note that, unlike 1165, Parākramabāhu II's reforms were not clearly defined by his kingdom's territory – he invited Cōḷa monks, for instance, from outside of his kingdom as part of his reforms – and that as a relatively weak ruler his territorial control was slight and his jurisdictional reach must have been limited.[50]

These reforms facilitated monastic literary production not only because of royal patronage but also because textual study constituted the Saṅgha's new institutional and conceptual order. The qualifications needed to rise in the Saṅgha's administration related to a monk's moral purity as well as his familial lineage but by far the most important was his level of education.[51] The 1266 edict, for instance, presents traditional forms of monastic education in a six-tiered hierarchy: (1) the lay candidate for ordination; (2) the novice; (3) higher ordination; (4) one free from pupillary dependence (*nissayamutta*); (5) an elder (*thera*); and (6) great elder (*mahāthera*) – each involving increasingly difficult forms of textual study with senior monks.[52] It is in the context of this formal educational system that we can partly understand the intensity of literary activity during the reform era. New texts, in particular Pali handbooks and handbook commentaries, sifted and sorted the doctrine and discipline – sometimes experimenting with new pedagogical techniques from the Sanskrit tradition – in order to unify Buddhist thought and practice and disseminate it within the reformed Saṅgha. As part of the 1165 reforms or soon after, we see that a prominent monk, Sāriputta, who would go on to become leader of the Saṅgha, composed three new works on the monastic discipline, namely, a subcommentary on the Vinaya, a new Vinaya handbook and a commentary for this handbook, as well as a subcommentary on the *Aṅguttara Nikāya*.[53]

The curriculum set out in the detailed 1266 edict reveals distinct roles played by Pali and Sinhala texts in monastic education.[54] The studies of novice monks focused largely on Sinhala texts, especially handbooks on monastic discipline, such as the *Heraṇasikha* ('Rules for novices') and *Sikhavalaṅda* ('Illustration of the rules').[55] There was some emphasis in the early stages of education, even for candidates for ordination, on memorizing protective (*paritta*) Pali texts. The monastic discipline only began to be studied more intensely in Pali after higher ordination and, even then, it was mainly through handbooks, such as the *Mūlasikkhā* ('Basic training'). The highest levels of study within the monastic hierarchy, however, were exclusively in Pali. When monks trained to be free from pupillary dependence (*nissayamutta*) they were expected to study Vinaya handbooks, such as the *Khuddasikkhā* ('Minor rules'), Pali commentaries (*ṭīkā*) presumably on handbooks, canonical Vinaya texts such as the *Pātimokkha* and its Pali commentary, the *Kaṅkhāvitaraṇī* ('Overcoming doubts'), as well as Pali grammatical texts. The edict is less specific about the curriculum for the position of 'elder' (*thera*), though we know it included Pali commentaries (*ṭīkā*) as well as various parts of the canonical Vinaya. Monastic candidates for the high position of 'great elder' (*mahāthera*) were further encouraged to master the 'Tipiṭaka together with its commentaries'.

It is clear from the Daṁbadeṇiya edict that Pali was not simply a transregional medium but the principal means of organizing the Buddhist tradition, both on a conceptual level and in terms of social hierarchy. The expanding use of Pali in service of the reforms was accompanied by a new assessment of the nature of Pali as a literary language in a number of Pali treatises on grammar and poetics modelled on Sanskrit works. Within these texts Pali is explicitly placed for the first time alongside and in contrast with the classical Indian division of literary languages into Sanskrit, Prakrit, Apabhraṃśa and Paiśācī, with the latter three viewed as subordinate to Sanskrit. Pali is never placed within this framework and, instead, is simply situated as an independent, singular language sharing the same literariness as these languages but without figuring as a language derived from Sanskrit.[56] The scholar-monk Saṅgharakkhita stresses this independence by referring to Pali or Māgadha as *suddha-* or 'pure' Māgadha. He states that the prefix *suddha-* means that this language and those who know it are free from the impurity or obscurity (*kālusiya*) of Sanskrit and the other languages.[57]

There is a danger in focusing on these edicts – viewing monastic reforms simply as 'events' – that we lose sight of the real social contours of the era.[58] Immediately prior to the reign of Parākramabāhu I and the fifty years that followed it there was no discernible stability in the royal court as the island witnessed an endless stream of monarchs due to wars of succession, as we discussed in chapter one. One would think based on the 'imperial' model that a Saṅgha left rudderless without a dependable monarch would have similarly fragmented. And yet all the historical evidence we have points to the contrary. It seems that prior to the reign of Parākramabāhu I the Saṅgha was by its own volition agitating for unity and that, after the reforms, it continued to develop its administrative structure.[59]

It is only after 1165 that the position of 'grandmaster' (*mahāsāmi*) emerges as a title for the leader of the Saṅgha.[60] A system of inheriting the position after the grandmaster's death also seems to have been established far earlier than the 1266 edict. In fact, the succession of grandmasters during the period occurred, at least on the surface, without interruption and followed regular, pupillary succession without exception. After the 1165 reforms, for instance, we find Sāriputta as the first official 'grandmaster', followed by his pupil Moggallāna, his pupil Saṅgharakkhita in 1232, and then his pupil Medhaṅkara, who led the reforms in 1266.[61] The monastic elite was remarkably stable when compared with the sixteen kings from different lineages that took the throne between Parākramabāhu I and II. This is not to say that monks were happy about being left without a stable king as reference point – changing political conditions could not remove centuries of viewing a single, central monarch as the primary benefactor and protector of the religion – rather it is that the Saṅgha's administrative autonomy meant that a stable core of elites could withstand such political chaos.

That the reforms should be regarded more as a process than a single event is reflected in the fact that monks wrote new works long after the councils took place but with them still in mind. Thanks to the remarkable work of Petra Kieffer-Pülz in dating many reform-era texts, in particular those composed after the reign of Parākramabāhu I, it is now possible to show that prominent monks continued to write even during times that fell outside periods of strong Buddhist kingship. We now know, for instance, that the scholar monk Vācissara, pupil of Sāriputta, composed commentaries on Buddhadatta's Vinaya handbooks at some point between 1210 and 1245.[62] Another pupil of Sāriputta and Moggallāna, Saṅgharakkhita, wrote the *Subodhālaṅkāra* ('Lucid poetics'), the first work on Pali poetics, the *Vuttodaya* ('Exposition of metres'), the first treatise on Pali metrics, and also a handbook on Pali syntax, the *Sambandhacintā* ('Reflections on syntactic relationships'), at some point between 1186 and 1232.[63] Despite writing long after the reforms of 1165, both authors reference these events as part of their shared 'corporate memory'.[64] Authors of this period often compose eulogies in memory of their teacher, Sāriputta, who had likely already passed away, as a means of reaffirming their bonds to the reformed Saṅgha and the continuing process of reform. Writing after 1232, Saṅgharakkhita (or one of his acolytes) praised Sāriputta as follows:

> By composing subcommentaries, such as that for the Vinaya, he, a priceless necklace among the wise (lit. having an unrivalled ornament-like throat), created *order*, desiring the conqueror's (i.e. the Buddha's) religion to be pure. Victorious on earth was this grandmaster, my heroic teacher, Sāriputta ('son of Sārī'), who pursued peace, possessed no trifling intellect, and who deserves utmost respect.[65]

Such fidelity and devotion between guru and pupil, reinforced by a structured educational system, must have placed the monastic community at a strategic advantage when compared with the now unstable kinship practices of the court.

In the space of a few decades then, depending on one's perspective, the process of reform involved events in which monastic elites and royal court co-operated closely as well as years of political instability where those same elites had to function without any long-term, reliable source of central patronage. In many ways the very fact that the degree of royal involvement in monastic reform fluctuated during the period reveals that royal oversight was not the main factor or, at least, a necessary condition for the production of literature in aid of the reforms. Rather, one could argue that what was common to both periods of stability and turmoil was the newly centralized, hierarchical structure of the Saṅgha itself. It was this reluctant autonomy, more akin to the Benedictine monasteries of Cluny than any 'imperial church', that best explains how the Saṅgha managed to unify and how it continued the process of reform in between the events of 1165, 1232–6 and 1266.[66]

3.3. Monastic Literature and the Localization of Politics

The emergence of a fragmented political landscape also meant that the Saṅgha throughout the period was negotiating an increasingly complex patronage network of *petits nobles* governing smaller political domains, including, warlords[67], merchants, minor royals, monastic nobles and lay functionaries[68] who had become progressively powerful through the maintenance of the Saṅgha's extensive wealth and lands.[69] This form of negotiation differed from the politics of the first millennium not only in terms of the diversity of patrons able to support the Saṅgha with largesse, in particular by building monasteries, but due to the explicitly personal relationships authors had with these individuals.[70] The works of Saṅgharakkhita and Vācissara, studied by Petra Kieffer-Pülz, are again a useful case study in this regard. Saṅgharakkhita, for instance, writes in the colophon of his grammatical commentary that he lived in a monastery built by a warlord named 'Subha', who he praises as 'endowed with qualities such as strength, wisdom and compassion'.[71] He then, in the second part of the colophon, which we discussed above, goes on to eulogize the intellectual achievements of his teacher, Sāriputta, and the political prowess of a monarch who we may identify with Vijayabāhu III. Similarly, Vācissara in the colophon to his commentary on a Vinaya handbook praises five individuals who helped initiate his work, including three monks, two of whom were from Cōḻa country in South India, a lay disciple and a merchant named 'Bhāṇu'.[72]

It is made explicit in reform-era works for the first time that both educational and kinship ties with the laity played important roles in establishing bonds of textual patronage. Vācissara in the colophon to an exposition on an Abhidhamma handbook praises at length one of his lay students, Dhammakitti. It appears from his colophon that, in the middle of writing his commentary, his student, having built a monastery, invited him there to complete the work and provided him with 4,000 books to do so.[73] The earliest explicit example of lay involvement in the patronage of a work, other than by the king himself, took place a decade or two earlier in the composition of a Pali grammatical handbook by a monk Piyadassi, probably in the early years after the reign of Parākramabāhu I. The unusual colophon to the grammar demonstrates how personal relationships could shape the composition of Pali works:

> Having composed the *Padasādhana* ('Forming words'), which I undertook for the benefit of others, may this world through that merit accomplish (*sādhetu*) the unchanging goal (*pada*).
>
> With purity as a support, Moggallāna [Piyadassi's teacher] rose up having perfected his virtues. As an exemplar, he serves the Saṅgha of exemplary monks. Dwelling in the beautiful town of Anurādha, he is a lotus among bees and a standard for his own pure family. Filled with faith,[74] he reveres the Buddha at each and every step, burns asunder all evil enemies with the fires of a continuous and unbroken asceticism, and is like a gold cup containing the lion's perfume[75] called the true Dhamma. He is skilled in the different, deficient views of philosophers, a master of the wife that is language, and a compassionate teacher who follows tradition with intelligence.

> Trained in grammar and the like by the renowned elder Moggallāna at his feet like a parakeet caught in a cage, the monk named Piyadassi wisely composed this work for the attainment of happiness, having been spoken to by his kind maternal uncle named Kappiṇa who is like a nuptial mark (*tilaka*) on the forehead of the wife-like Ramhā monastery, which offers the finest enjoyments (*upabhoga*), has full breasts/water containers (*payodhara*), is free of anger/jungle (*vana*), and is servile/has servants (*sevikā*).[76]

The colophon, it seems, was composed in two parts. Piyadassi only wrote the opening verse where he plays on the title of his grammar, *Padasādhana*, which can either mean forming words grammatically or attaining nirvana. The second part consists of an ornate, Sanskritic praise of Moggallāna, Piyadassi's teacher. The final verse of the colophon, which appears to have been added at some point before the fifteenth century, further reveals that Piyadassi's maternal uncle, Kappiṇa, who was the chieftain of a maintenance village connected to the Ramhā monastery, requested Piyadassi to compose the grammar. This village was likely situated in Rohaṇa near the old provincial capital of Mahānāgakula.

With respect to the final part of the colophon, the fifteenth-century commentary on this passage explains that in this verse the uncle likens himself and his village to a husband and wife.[77] It seems to me, however, that the verse compares the uncle to a decoration adorning the wife-like village and that it is actually to Piyadassi that the village is being offered as a spouse, with the uncle acting as symbolic evidence of the union between monk and village. The offer is framed as a marriage in sensual language, with the village's material requisites described in terms that can also refer to an ideal wife's physical beauty and subordinate disposition.

The colophon, in this regard, memorializes both Piyadassi's educational and familial ties in highly stylized Sanskritic poetry, celebrating asceticism and sensuality with seemingly no recognition of any potential incompatibility. The colophon also reveals that it was thought possible that a head of a maintenance village would have the financial means to sponsor a grammatical work, an expensive affair if one considers the costs of housing the monk, scholarly ritual and ceremony, procuring and copying books and producing writing material, in particular the elaborate process of actually making the palm leaves suitable for inscribing.

The continued production of literature among monastics in periods where patronage from a single, powerful royal court was either intermittent or completely lacking has proved puzzling. 'One would wonder', M. Sri Rammandala once wrote, 'whether any kind of movement either for the development of education in the country or for the material or the spiritual welfare of the Island could ever have been fostered during this turbulent epoch'.[78] The evidence we have suggests, however, that the fragmentation of power on the island, while viewed negatively by the monks themselves, may not actually have been as deleterious to Buddhist literary culture as imagined. In fact, the formation of multiple centres of power produced multiple sources of patronage and it is a testament to the acumen of the monastic elites that they quickly adapted to the local and personal politics of the age.

At least as important as material patronage was also the monastic community's own sense of itself as a political actor who, in writing Pali texts, could shape its social relationships, bound by religious identity, education, kinship and perceived karmic ties. We have already discussed in the previous chapter how the monastic community was drawn further into dynastic politics as a result of the instability of Cōḻa rule and that the ruling elite occasionally addressed monks in their inscriptions as political actors, sometimes in almost royal terms. After the reforms these scholar-monks began to write back, composing new Pali texts, especially literary works modelled on Sanskrit poetry, as a means of creating devotional subjects out of the new elites that had emerged during the period. A senior monk known as Dhammakitti, for instance, seemingly allied with a warlord, Parakkama, who was grooming a young Pāṇḍya prince from South India for the throne of Laṅkā, composed a history of the Buddha's tooth relic, the *Dāṭhāvaṃsa* ('History of the tooth'), in which he reframes the genealogy of the Pāṇḍya royal family within the karmic history of Buddhism as a means of cultivating the prince into a patron favourable to the monastic community.[79]

The desire to establish new ties of patronage in an unstable, localized political situation also led, perhaps paradoxically, to monks travelling abroad and establishing ties with *petits nobles* outside of the island too. A good example of this is the *Upāsakajanālaṅkāra* ('Ornament of lay followers'), a Buddhist manual for the laity, composed by Ānanda, a forest monk from Sri Lanka, likely at some point during the reign of Māgha.[80] We learn that he had left Sri Lanka to Pāṇḍya country during this period of upheaval and that he wrote his manual under the patronage of a certain Coḷagaṅga, who is referred to as a 'feudatory chieftain of a forest tract' (*vaññosāmantabhūmipa*). Displaying sensitivity to local politics, Ānanda adapts the form of his manual according to what he refers to as the wishes of his newly Buddhist (*abhinavasādhujana*) audience.[81] Though it is clear his main motivation was to satisfy his immediate readers, Ānanda maintained close ties with Sri Lanka and monks there had access to his work soon after it was composed.[82] When some authors, then, still claimed to be writing in Pali for those from Sri Lanka and India – partly in imitation of the early commentators – we can hypothesize that they often primarily meant their local, cosmopolitan audience and that any further dissemination was a secondary consideration.[83]

Even when scholar-monks did compose works with elite monastic institutions in South India in mind, they did so under new, regionally defined identities as an indirect consequence of the 1165 reforms. Having sought unity and political autonomy in the midst of the fragmented nature of politics in reform-era Sri Lanka, the Saṅgha's identity had become locally bounded in that it began to be viewed, first by those outside of the island, as a separate, independent monastic lineage. Scholar-monks from Sri Lanka living in South India first started to identify as 'Sīhaḷa' and, likewise, monks in Sri Lanka occasionally spoke of those living in the South Indian Cōḻa kingdom as 'Coḷiya' too.[84] The emergence of separate, locally-defined identities within a lineage that prior to the twelfth century had been regarded as part of the same monastic circle led to intensified, occasionally adversarial communication between the two communities, which was formalized in the renewed composition of Pali texts addressing controversial issues of doctrine and discipline. After Sāriputta wrote his subcommentary on the Vinaya, a certain Coḷiya Kassapa composed another subcommentary, often challenging Sāriputta's interpretations.[85] We should note, however, that the separation of the identities of the two communities was primarily political rather than linguistic or ethnic. It has been plausibly suggested that Coḷiya Kassapa was actually a Sinhalese monk who had relocated to a South Indian monastery.[86]

In light of the local character of the reform era it may be surprising, then, that this period in Sri Lanka's history is often framed as the moment in which Theravada Buddhism or at least Sīhaḷa monastic lineages became transregional and 'spread' to Burma and Thailand. This type of teleological reading of the twelfth and thirteenth centuries, however, focusing on the period as a staging post *towards* the spread of Buddhism in Southeast Asia, can obscure the historical reality of the period.[87] The elite scholar-monks of the reform era hardly ever mention Southeast Asia and their world was still very much a dichotomous one, split between Plum island and Lion island, India and Sri Lanka.[88] The revival of Pali then was not at this point connected to the 'spread of Buddhism' but was indirectly linked in so far as the political chaos and new, local politics on the island meant that some ambitious monks traced their capillary personal relationships further afield to find patronage, including to Southeast Asia.[89] For the most part, this movement did not produce 'networks' in the sense of continuous ties – we only know of most of these monks due to Southeast Asian chronicles and inscriptions – and at this stage there was little in the way of intellectual exchange between the regions. Rather these new lineages in Southeast Asia can be better regarded as 'filiations', that is, offspring who maintained a certain familial identity and a shared tradition of historical memories but who, for much of their early existence, acted independently without continuous contact or oversight.[90]

Table 3.3: A hypothetical chronology of Pali works composed in South India and Sri Lanka, 900–1500 CE[91]

Text	Author	Date
Commentaries/Subcommentaries on Canonical Texts and Histories		
Visuddhajanavilāsinī	Anon.	Unknown
Amatarasadhārā	Upatissa	900–1000
Madhuratthappakāsinī	Upatissa?	900–1000
Vaṃsatthappakāsinī	Upatissa?	900–1000
Vajirabuddhiṭīkā	Vajirabuddhi	900–1000
Kaṅkhāvitaraṇīporāṇaṭīkā	Anon.	after 900–1000 (after Vajirabuddhiṭīkā)
Sāratthadīpanī	Sāriputta	1165–86
Sāratthamañjūsā	Sāriputta	1165–86
Vinayatthamañjūsā	Buddhanāga	1165–86 (after Sāratthadīpanī)
Mohavicchedanī	Kassapa	1165–1300
Vimativinodanī	Kassapa	1165–1300
Handbooks, Anthologies and Compendia		
Nāmarūpasamāsa	Khema	Unknown
Abhidhammatthasaṅgaha	Anuruddha	before 1200
Paramatthavinicchaya	Anuruddha	before 1200
Nāmarūpapariccheda	Anuruddha	before 1200
Suttasaṅgaha	Anon.	before 1200
Vinayasaṅkhepaṭṭhakathā	Anon.	1100–1300
Vinayasaṅgaha	Sāriputta	1165–86
Upāsakajanālaṅkāra	Ānanda	1215–32
Sīmālaṅkārasaṅgaha	Vācissara	1225–50
Sārasaṅgaha	Siddhattha	1250–1300
Bhesajjamañjūsā	Anon.	1267
Commentaries/Subcommentaries on Handbooks, Anthologies and Compendia		
Abhidhammāvatārapurāṇaṭīkā	Anon.	before 1165
Vinayasaṅgahapurāṇaṭīkā	Sāriputta	1165–86

(*Continued*)

Table 3.3 (Continued)

Text	Author	Date
Abhidhammatthavibhāvinī	Sumaṅgala	1165–1232
Abhidhammāvatāravikāsinī	Sumaṅgala	1165–1232
Khuddasikkhāpurāṇaṭīkā	Anon.	1175–1250
Līnatthappakāsinī	Vācissara	1210–45
Sāratthasālinī	Vācissara	1210–45
Vinayasāratthasandīpanī	Vācissara	1210–45
Mūlasikkhāpurāṇaṭīkā	Anon.	after 1232
Sumaṅgalappasādanī	Saṅgharakkhita	after 1232
Philological Texts		
Mukhamattadīpanī	Vimalabuddhi	900–1100
Rūpasiddhi	Buddhappiya	1008–1165
Moggallānavyākaraṇa	Moggallāna	1165–86
Moggallānavutti	Moggallāna	1165–86
Moggallānapañcikā	Moggallāna	1165–86
Abhidhānappadīpikā	Moggallāna (II)	1186–1232
Padasādhana	Piyadassi	1186–1232
Sambandhacintā	Saṅgharakkhita	1186–1232
Subodhālaṅkāra	Saṅgharakkhita	1186–1232
Vuttodaya	Saṅgharakkhita	1186–1232
Yogavinicchaya	Saṅgharakkhita	1186–1232
Sāratthavilāsinī	Saṅgharakkhita	after 1232
Subodhālaṅkāraṭīkā	Saṅgharakkhita	after 1232
Payogasiddhi	Medhaṅkara	1272–84
Bālāvatāra	Dhammakitti	1350–1400
Buddhippasādanī	Śrī Rāhula	1468–76
Literary Texts		
Telakaṭāhagāthā	Anon.	Unknown
Sīhaḷavatthuppakaraṇa	Dhammanandi	Unknown
Anāgatavaṃsa	Upatissa?	900–1000
Mahābodhivaṃsa	Upatissa	900–1000
Naḷātadhātuvaṃsa	Anon.	900–1100
Sahassavatthuppakaraṇa	Raṭṭhapāla	900–1236
Jinālaṅkāra	Buddharakkhita	1156/7
Saddhammopāyana	Ānanda	before 1165
Cūḷavaṃsa (part)	Dhammakitti	after 1186
Pajjamadhu	Buddhappiya	1200–1300

(*Continued*)

Table 3.3 (Continued)

Text	Author	Date
Dāṭhāvaṃsa	Dhammakitti	1211/12
Mahānāgakulasandesa	Nāgasena	1211–56
Thūpavaṃsa	Vācissara	1236–50
Hatthavanagallavihāravaṃsa	Anon.	1236–66
Jinacarita	Medhaṅkara	1236–70
Rasavāhinī	Vedeha	1236–70
Samantakūṭavaṇṇanā	Vedeha	1236–70
Sāratthasamuccaya	Anon.	after 1266
Janānurāgacarita	Dhammakitti I	1300–50
Pāramīsataka	Dhammakitti I	1300–50
Jinabodhāvalī	Dhammakitti II	1350–1400

3.4. Summary

The reform-era Saṅgha, then, was primarily inward looking. The explosion in the production of Pali literature was in part due to the need to unify the discipline and doctrine on the island, to constitute the Saṅgha's new hierarchy and achieve status within it in accordance with new scholarly ideals, to establish and maintain ties with a more diffuse and localized patronage network and finally to draw disciplinary distinctions between themselves and those in India or the 'other island', as they traditionally referred to it. This radically different context for Pali literary production contributed to large changes in genre and style. Compared with the Pali works produced prior to the Cōḻa ascendancy, which largely focused on canonical commentaries (tab. 3.2), the period after around 900 CE and in particular during the reform era, 1157–1270, witnessed a rapid diversification of Pali works including the renewed composition of handbooks, numerous handbook commentaries, a large amount of grammatical literature as well as some works on poetics and finally new literary works that rewrote the Buddhist history of the island (tab. 3.3).

In the following two sections of this book we will now build upon this skeletal outline by turning away from the question of what happened to rather how it happened, in particular the way in which scholar-monks of the age reacted to and experienced this unprecedented change and turmoil. Part two, in particular, focuses on how scholar-monks viewed their exegetical activities as a battle against this perceived religious decline. They composed new works of grammar, experimented with more systematic forms of commentary and also, for the first time, started to produce anthologies of canonical and commentarial literature. This project of organizational philology was united by the shared reform goal of protecting and framing their scriptures within new, systematic forms of scholastic enquiry. This process, we will see, was not purely descriptive but also creative in that these new approaches changed the very way scholar-monks thought about their scriptural tradition, its language and authority.

Notes

1. R.A.L.H. Gunawardana has argued that there was a unification of eight sub-groups, *mūla* or *āyatana*, that he suggests had supplanted the traditional division of the three *nikāyas*. Monastic elites from these eight fraternities, however, did unify under the umbrella of the Mahāvihāra. See Gunawardana, 1979, 282–337. Heinz Bechert questioned the degree to which these eight groups had in fact supplanted the three *nikāyas* within the Saṅgha's structure. See Bechert, 1993. It is the case, for instance, that these *mūlas* still maintained at least a nominal affiliation with one of the three fraternities. See, in this regard, Panabokke, 1993, 179.
2. Collins, 2003, 650, fn. 1, citing Norman, 1983, ix.
3. Norman, 1997, 59–76; Von Hinüber, 1982.
4. For example, Norman, 1983, 2–7.
5. For instance, Bechert, 1966.
6. See Collins, 1998.
7. Collins, 2003, 649–50.
8. Collins, 2003, 682–3.
9. Regnal dates are from De Silva, 1981, 565–73. I have also included the reign of Mahinda VI. On Mahinda VI, see Liyanagamage, 1968, 45–6. Thanks to the recent epigraphical work of G.S. Ranawella, we can now more accurately date the official coronation of Parākramabāhu I to 1157 and not 1153, as previously thought. See Ranawella, *Inscriptions of Ceylon* 6, xxvi–vii.
10. Wynne, 2005.
11. Von Hinüber, 1996, §§22–7; §§116–18; §§158–71.
12. Walters, 1997.
13. Norman, 1983, 121.
14. Von Hinüber, 1996, §207.
15. Von Hinüber, 1996, §183. R.A.L.H. Gunawardana has suggested that nuns could have written the *Dīpavaṃsa*. See Gunawardana, 1988.
16. Von Hinüber, 1996, §185.
17. Gornall and Ruiz-Falqués, 2019, 422–3.
18. *Sammohavinodanī*, 387$_{,4}$ – 388$_{,16}$; *Visuddhimagga* of Buddhaghosa, 373$_{,27-34}$.
19. See also Collins, 2003, 46–53; Crosby, 2004; 2013, 82–4; Von Hinüber, 1994. The qualification '*sabhāva-*' may also refer to the language's capacity to capture the essence of reality. See, for instance, *Vibhaṅgamūlaṭīkā* of Ānanda, 191$_{,16-17}$: dhammaniruttābhilāpe ti ettha dhammasaddo sabhāvavācako ti katvā āha yā sabhāvaniruttī ti.
20. On this circle, Cousins, 2001; Gethin, 2012.
21. *Samantapāsādikā* I, 2$_{,7-14}$. Also, Crosby, 2004.
22. See, for instance, *Dīghanikāyaṭīkā* of Dhammapāla I, 20$_{,10-12}$.
23. Collins, 2003, 52–3. On the translation of *jambudvīpa*, see Wujastyk, 2004.
24. Malalasekera, 1994, 104.
25. Rahula, 1956, 62–77.
26. See introduction.
27. *Cūḷavaṃsa* 37.215–46. On problems with dating this commentary to the reign of Mahānāma, however, see Kieffer-Pülz, 1992, 162–7.

28. Walters, 1999, 331–7. There is also a tradition that king Dhātusena (455–73) ordered 'a redaction of the Buddhist canon and a revision of *Dīpavaṃsa*', with the latter possibly referring to the composition of the *Mahāvaṃsa*. See Walters, 1997, 120, citing *Cūḷavaṃsa* 38.43–59.
29. *Vinayavinicchaya* of Buddhadatta, vv. 3166–82.
30. Buddhadatta, 1945; Nilakanta Sastri, 1935, 120–1. Valérie Gillet has persuasively argued, however, that the 'Kaḷabhra' dynasty was not a dominant power in South India between the third and sixth centuries, as has been thought. See Gillet, 2014, esp. 298–9.
31. This chronology is based on information provided in Gornall and Ruiz-Falqués, 2019; Von Hinüber, 1996; Kieffer-Pülz, 2015c; Pind, 1997, 523–7.
32. See Strathern, 2009, 827–8.
33. Taylor, 1976, 258.
34. *Cūḷavaṃsa* 78.6; *Epigraphia Zeylanica* II, 274. On Aśoka as a model for kings in Sri Lanka, see Lingat, 1989; Tambiah, 1976, 54–72; 168.
35. In this regard, see also Hallisey, 1991.
36. For instance, Bechert, 1965; 1970; 1974.
37. *Cūḷavaṃsa* 78.20–7.
38. *Epigraphia Zeylanica* II, 275. The edict issued after the 1266 reform, which incorporated the edict of 1232–6, makes no mention of any unification of the Saṅgha. We know from the *Cūḷavaṃsa*, however, that the 1266 reforms involved a reconciliation between the Cōḻa and Sīhaḷa monastic communities. The *Pūjāvaliya* also adds that the 1232 reforms included a similar reconciliation between factions in the Saṅgha too but gives little detail. See *Cūḷavaṃsa* 78.5; 84.7–10; *Pūjāvaliya* of Mayūrapāda, $733_{,9}$; $736_{,1}$; $740_{,28-32}$; *Nikāyasaṅgrahaya* of Devarakṣita Dharmakīrti, $19_{,28-9}$; $20_{,33}$. The term *samagga* in an early Buddhist context refers to legal unanimity and it seems to maintain this sense for medieval historians in Sri Lanka. See Von Hinüber, 1969, 124.
39. *Cūḷavaṃsa* 78.27.
40. *Epigraphia Zeylanica* II, 274.
41. *Epigraphia Zeylanica* II, 274. On these two processes, see Gunawardana, 1979, 319.
42. Ratnapāla, 1971, 146.
43. For instance, Bechert, 1973, 87.
44. *Epigraphia Zeylanica* II, 275. The text in parentheses is my own addition. Compare this with Niśśaṅkamalla, who specifically states that *he* protects the religion by means of admonitions (*avavāda*). See *Epigraphia Zeylanica* II, 96–8.
45. *Epigraphia Zeylanica* II, 274. Michael Aung Thwin has interpreted monastic reforms as a royal mechanism to reappropriate land from the Saṅgha 'in a legal and socially acceptable manner'. See Aung Thwin, 1979, on Sri Lanka esp., 686–8. That Parākramabāhu I had such motivations in mind is not unlikely since, as R.A.L.H. Gunawardana noted, the king did not return to the Saṅgha lands that had been confiscated during the civil war prior to his ascension to the throne. See Gunawardana, 1979, 94. For criticisms of Aung Thwin's analysis, see Lieberman, 1981; Frasch, 1996, 237–44.
46. Ratnapāla, 1971, 147. We can make the conjecture that the two *mahāthera*s here mentioned correspond both in their role and function with the courtly positions of *apa* (heir presumptive) and *mahapa* (heir apparent) who were ideally charged with administrating the regions of Rohaṇa and Māyāraṭṭha, respectively.
47. Adapted from Phadnis, 1976, 78.
48. See also, Bechert, 1966, 211. Royal involvement in the appointment of the heads of *āyatana*s continued into the early fifteenth century. See Ilangasinha, 1992, 69–70.
49. For a useful critique of the notion of an 'imperial' Church in medieval Europe, see Reuter, 1982. We should keep in mind too that the relative importance of royal ecclesiastical appointments in defining 'imperial religion' in a European context is largely due the importance of this issue in the 'investiture controversy', which led after the Concordat of Worms in 1122 to a restriction on royal oversight in the appointment of bishops.
50. *Cūḷavaṃsa* 84.10; *Pūjāvaliya* of Mayūrapāda, $740_{,28-32}$. On the reality of Parākramabāhu II's relatively weak rule, see Liyanagamage, 1968, 133–59.
51. On caste as a determining factor in monastic rank, see Ratnapāla, 1971, 141; 147; Liyanagamage, 2001b, 169–216.
52. Dhammavisuddhi, 1970, 247–315.
53. Crosby, 2006; Kieffer-Pülz, 2013, 22; 2017a; Pecenko, 1997.
54. Ratnapāla, 1971, 142–7.
55. It is only in the Poḷonnaruva edict that the *Sikhavalaňda* is mentioned in the context of a novice's education but I infer that it was studied at the time of the Daṁbadeṇiya edict too since its commentary,

Sikhavalaṅdavinisa, is required to be studied by monks after higher ordination. See Ratnapāla, 1971, 143. While handbooks dominated monastic education, the Tipiṭaka still played an important role as the final source of religious authority. See, for instance, Kieffer-Pülz, 2016–17.

56. *Moggallānapañcikā* of Moggallāna, 3,$_{33-5}$; *Moggallānapañcikāṭīkā* of Saṅgharakkhita, 14,$_{22-5}$; *Subodhālaṅkāramahāsāmiṭīkā* of Saṅgharakkhita, 28,$_{27}$–29,$_{10}$ (≈ *Ratnaśrīṭīkā* on *Kāvyādarśa* 1.33). Andrew Ollett has dubbed this classical arrangement of literary languages headed by Sanskrit as 'the language order of premodern India'. See Ollett, 2017.
57. *Subodhālaṅkāramahāsāmiṭīkā* of Saṅgharakkhita, 7,$_{12-27}$, quoted and translated in chapter seven. Similarly, Sāriputta in his Vinaya subcommentary criticizes those who mix Pali with other languages. See chapter five.
58. Similarly, Vanderputten, 2013, 1–13.
59. Gunawardana, 1979, 321–9.
60. But before 1185, see Rohanadeera, 1985, 30.
61. On the evolution of the position of *mahāsāmi*, see Rohanadeera, 1985; 1996.
62. Kieffer-Pülz, 2018, 197.
63. Kieffer-Pülz, 2017b.
64. On 'corporate memories of reform', see Vanderputten, 2013, 14–30.
65. *Moggallānapañcikāṭīkā* of Saṅgharakkhita, 285,$_{24-7}$:
    ṭīkāyo vinayādinaṃ viracayī yo kaṇṭhabhūsāparo
    viññūnaṃ jinasāsanāmalamatī so 'kāsi cānākulaṃ.
    santosakkamano-m-anomakamano sabbhāvanīyo mahā-
    sāmī me gurupuṅgavo vijayate sārīsuto 'yaṃ bhuvi.
    For ease of comprehension, I have separated the glide -m- in *pāda* A of the second verse, which the Burmese edition leaves unmarked. See also, Kieffer-Pülz, 2017b, 28–31.
66. For instance, Rosenwein, 1982, esp. 30–56; 101–12. Strathern has noted too the general capacity of 'transcendentalist clerisies' in premodernity to maintain organizational power during periods of social and political turmoil. See Strathern, 2019, 140–1.
67. I use the term 'warlord' here to loosely translate *senāpati* or *yuddhapati* often rendered as 'general' since it is not clear that these figures were subsumed within any particular state bureaucracy.
68. It has been plausibly suggested, for instance, that a new group of nobles, the *gaṇavāsi* (Sin. *gaṇaväsi*), emerged at the end of the Anurādhapura period and that this lineage was intimately tied to the lay management of monastic property. See Ilangasinha, 1992, 85–6.
69. On this localization, see Liyanagamage, 1968; Perera, 1960–1; de Silva, 1981, 81–96; Taylor, 1976. Also, Indrapala, 1970; Indrapala (ed), 1971c; Pathmanathan, 1972.
70. On similar feudal developments in Europe, see Bloch, 1961.
71. Kieffer-Pülz, 2017b, 28.
72. Kieffer-Pülz, 2018, 195.
73. Kieffer-Pülz, 2018, 209–10.
74. The *Padasādhanasannaya* glosses *saddhālunā* as *śraddhābahulavū*, 'one who has lots of faith'. See *Padasādhanasannaya* of Ānanda, 197,$_{32}$.
75. On *sīhatela* or *sīhavasā*, literally, 'lion's oil/perfume', see Norman, 1993, 161–2.
76. *Padasādhana* of Piyadassi, 197,$_{5}$–198,$_{8}$:
    paratthāya mayā laddhaṃ katvāna padasādhanaṃ
    puññena tena loko 'yaṃ sādhetu padam accutaṃ.
    suddhāsayena parisuddhaguṇoditena
    sārena sārayatisaṅghanisevitena
    ramme 'nurādhanagare vasatambujena
    vidvālinaṃ nijavisuddhakuladdhajena
    mānentena tathāgataṃ paṭipadāyogena saddhālunā
    niccākhaṇḍataponalehi nikhilappāpārisantāpinā
    saddhammavhayasīhatelaṭhitiyā cāmīkaratthālinā
    nānāvādikudiṭṭhibhedapaṭunā vāṇivadhūsāminā
    satthānaṃ karuṇāvatā gatavatā pāramparaṃ dhīmatā
    therenātumapādapañjaragato yo saddasatthādisu
    moggallāyanavissuten' iha suvacchāpo vinīto yathā
    so 'kāsī piyadassi nāma yati 'daṃ byattaṃ sukhappattiyā.
    vutto 'va vuttam (*corr.* uttam°) upabhoginiyā sakāya pinappayodharavanāpagasevikāya,
    ramhāvihāravadhuyā tilakātulena santena kappiṇasamavhayamātulena.
77. *Buddhippasādanī* of Śrī Rāhula, 133,$_{24}$–134,$_{9}$.

78. Rammandala, 1954, 38. Similarly, see Dhammapala, 2003, 35.
79. See chapter seven.
80. Liyanagamage, 2001a; Kieffer-Pülz, 2015a.
81. Agostini, 2015, xi–xiv.
82. It is quoted, for instance, in the *Sārasaṅgaha*. See Neri, 2015, 345. See also chapter five.
83. On Tamil monks in Sri Lanka, see Gunawardana, 1979, 47–8. Tilman Frasch has argued similarly that Pali was used in Burma, in part, to communicate with the increasingly diverse monastic community at home. See Frasch, 2017, 72.
84. See, for instance, Liyanagamage, 2001a; Monius, 2001, 123–5. It is difficult to say when monks started using these labels as forms of identification. It is certainly present in Vācissara's *Sīmālaṅkārasaṅgaha*. See Kieffer-Pülz, 2020.
85. Dhammaratana, 1997; Kieffer-Pülz, 2005.
86. Crosby and Skilton, 1999, 176.
87. S. Paranavitana invented fantastical and fictitious accounts of Sri Lanka's relations with Southeast Asia in the twelfth and thirteenth centuries. For thorough critiques of his theories, see Gunawardana, 1967; Indrapala, 1967; Kiribamune, 1970; Nilakanta Sastri, 1962; Sirisena, 1971.
88. In fact, the *Abhidhānappadīpikā*, when adapting the *Amarakośa*'s geographical vocabulary, includes Sri Lanka in *Jambudvīpa* and lists twenty regions in this realm, none of which are Southeast Asian. See *Abhidhānappadīpikā* of Moggallāna, vv. 184–5.
89. On relations with Burma, specifically, see chapter ten.
90. I borrow the concept of monastic 'filiations' from Tellenbach, 1993, 109.
91. In addition to the sources mentioned for table 3.2, this chronology is based on information provided in Barnett, 1905; Dimitrov, 2016, 157–450; Kieffer-Pülz and Peters, 2002; Kieffer-Pülz, 2015a; 2018; Kitsudo, 2015; Liyanaratne, 1983, Wickramasinghe, 1958, 8–33. With respect to Buddhappiya's *Rūpasiddhi*, it must have been composed before 1165 since Moggallāna refers to it in his grammatical works. Buddhappiya also must have composed his grammar after his monastery, the *Cūḍāmaṇivarmavihāra*, was founded in 1005/6. See *Epigraphia Indica* 22, no. 34.

Part II
Order

4
Scholarly Foundations: Moggallāna's Grammar

The scholar-monks of the reform era approached the composition of literature with a mindset that was akin to a form of technological determinism or, better still, philological determinism. For they viewed the state of their scriptures and the degree to which the monastic community adhered to those texts as the principal cause of the social and political upheaval in which they had found themselves. At the same time, they believed that by better preserving their scriptures and, in particular, by improving their understanding of them through further exegetical work they could actively change these conditions. This was nothing new, of course, and reflected longstanding Buddhist beliefs about the interdependence between the moral character of a particular historical era and the state of the Buddha's teachings.[1] What seems to have changed or at least come to a head during the reform era was the attitude of scholar-monks towards implementing new philological technologies in preserving and protecting the coherence of their religious literature.[2] One such technology introduced after the 1165 reforms was a new system of Pali grammar, the *Moggallānavyākaraṇa* ('Grammar of Moggallāna'), modelled on older, derivational grammars in the Sanskrit tradition. This grammar introduced new approaches to language that helped change how monks thought about and approached their sacred texts.

The term *vyākaraṇa* or 'grammar' as it is most often translated in English refers to the discipline of analysing (lit. dividing) language into its constituent parts, such as nouns, verbs, roots, bases and suffixes.[3] The post-seventh-century commentator Dhammapāla, echoing older Brahmanical interpretations in the Sanskrit tradition, defines *vyākaraṇa* as 'the means by which one analyses (*byākaroti*) and explains (*byācikkhati*) different words and their meanings'.[4] There is a longstanding connection between Hinduism and the oldest Sanskrit grammatical works, namely, Pāṇini's *Aṣṭādhyāyī* ('Eight lectures', early to mid-fourth century BCE), Kātyāyana's *vārttika*s or 'annotations' on the *Aṣṭādhyāyī*, and Patañjali's *Mahābhāṣya* ('Great commentary', mid-second century BCE), the oldest surviving exposition of Pāṇini's grammar that is ostensibly a commentary on Kātyāyana's annotations.[5] At least since Patañjali, Hindu grammarians have viewed *vyākaraṇa* as the first and foremost of the so-called *vedāṅga*s, that is, the six disciplines or limbs (*aṅga*) that help preserve the Vedas and Vedic ritual.[6] Early in its history, however, the discipline spread outside of the Vedic sphere and transitioned from being a technology of liturgy to also one of literature. Sheldon Pollock has described in detail how grammar developed into a prestigious discipline within the literary culture of the royal court; kings patronized grammatical scholarship, competed with rival courts in the grammatical works they produced, and their knowledge of grammar was praised as an integral part of just rule.[7] For much of its history, then, grammar was an ecumenical science used by priests and poets alike and 'a support shared by all', in the words of the fifth-century grammarian Bhartṛhari.[8]

The comparable role grammar played in Buddhist intellectual life from an early period has received relatively little attention. Buddhist Sanskrit grammarians reinterpreted the religious origins of *vyākaraṇa* and viewed Pāṇini as a Buddhist inspired by the Bodhisattva Avalokiteśvara.[9] Grammar was used to interpret Buddhist Sanskrit scriptures, though Buddhists writing in Sanskrit did not view the discipline of grammar as exclusively an exegetical tool. Rather scholar-monks also saw grammar as a useful weapon in debates with other religious competitors and, as a result, categorized the discipline as an 'external' (Sk. *vāhya*) knowledge due to the fact it was directed 'outwards', towards others.[10] They further considered grammar, more broadly, to be part of a buddha's omniscient knowledge and thus as an important object of study for one who aspired to achieve the state of buddhahood.[11] Towards the end of the first millennium, like their Brahmanical contemporaries, Buddhist grammarians further composed grammatical works, occasionally for royal patrons, but also, we can speculate, for their own intellectual and political ends.[12]

Pali grammar became an important scholarly discipline for the Theravada Buddhist tradition in the second half of the first millennium.[13] Prior to that, early commentators such as Buddhaghosa relied upon Sanskrit grammars, such as Pāṇini's *Aṣṭādhyāyī*, in the interpretation of Pali scripture.[14] The earliest known Pali grammar, the *Kaccāyanavyākaraṇa* ('Grammar of Kaccāyana'), was likely composed in around the seventh century, though a number of Pali grammarians from the tenth century onwards believed that the work was composed by the Buddha's disciple Mahā Kaccāyana.[15] While Pali grammatical works were more singularly rooted in the exegesis of scripture than the Sanskrit grammars of their Buddhist counterparts, in the reform era we begin to see a transition from purely exegetical approaches to language to those that were more analytical in nature.

Pali *vyākaraṇa* never became a courtly discipline in reform-era Sri Lanka, though it did develop associations with political power within the

Saṅgha's own monastic hierarchy.[16] During the reform era, for instance, all the monks to hold the high office of 'grandmaster' were grammarians.[17] The forest-monk and Sanskrit grammarian, Diṁbulāgala Kassapa, held the position of leader of the Saṅgha during the 1165 reforms, though he was not referred to as grandmaster.[18] Sāriputta, his pupil, was the first to be acknowledged officially with this title and early in his career authored a Sanskrit grammatical commentary, the *Cāndrapañcikālaṅkāra* ('Ornament to the extensive commentary on Candra's grammar').[19] Our Pali grammarian Moggallāna subsequently attained the position of grandmaster, presumably after Sāriputta's death.[20] Saṅgharakkhita then ascended to the role in the reign of Vijayabāhu III (1232–6), administered monastic reforms and composed a commentary on Moggallāna's grammar during his tenure too.[21] His pupil, Medhaṅkara, author of a grammatical handbook, the *Payogasiddhi* ('Practical construction'), and a member of the Diṁbulāgala forest fraternity, succeeded him in turn and led further monastic reforms during the reign of Parākramabāhu II in 1266.[22]

Despite its important place in Buddhist intellectual culture, grammar has been almost entirely overlooked in the academic study of Buddhism.[23] One possible reason for this is that Pali *vyākaraṇa* and Sanskrit *vyākaraṇa*, in particular, have generally been studied within the fields of philology and linguistics. Commonly understood as a poor imitation of its Sanskrit counterpart, traditional Pali grammar has languished among what the historian of science Otto Neugebauer famously defended as 'wretched subjects', that is, premodern scientific disciplines viewed as debased or flawed.[24] Wilhelm Geiger (1882–1945), for instance, lamented the 'slavish imitation' of Pali grammars on the Sanskrit grammatical tradition and their 'artificial' grammatical constructions not found in any attested canonical literature.[25] This chapter aims to unmoor the study of traditional Pali grammar from the empiricist character of such assessments by exploring from a social and historical perspective why grammar was thought to be so important for the reform era, how it shaped new ways of thinking about language and literature, and also what it can tell us about the monastic community's engagement with Sanskrit literary culture.[26]

4.1. The Changing Purpose of Grammar

When in around the seventh century a scholar-monk known as Kaccāyana composed the first Pali grammar for the language of scripture his work soon inspired a number of commentaries and other independent grammars, most of which are no longer extant.[27] Among these early works, still available are Vimalabuddhi's *Mukhamattadīpanī* ('Straightforward illuminator'), an influential tenth or eleventh-century commentary, and the grammar's eleventh or early twelfth-century handbook, Cōḻa Buddhappiya's *Rūpasiddhi* ('Construction of [word] forms').[28] Writing at the Thūpārāma in the old capital of Anurādhapura in the aftermath of the unification of the Saṅgha in 1165, the scholar-monk Moggallāna brought the dominance of the *Kaccāyana* grammatical tradition in Sri Lanka to an abrupt end with the composition of a new grammatical system consisting of a set of rules, the *Moggallānavyākaraṇa*, a paraphrase on those rules, the *Moggallānavutti*, and an extensive commentary, the *Moggallānapañcikā*. Moggallāna in his colophon to the *Moggallānapañcikā* explicitly connects the composition of this new grammatical system with the monastic reforms that had taken place in the years before.[29] That a new grammar was considered to be a necessary outcome of the 1165 reforms raises the question about the role the discipline was thought to play in the unification and purification of the Saṅgha.

The early grammarians presented Pali grammar as essentially a tool used for the exegesis of the Buddha's discourses. The author of the *Kaccāyanavyākaraṇa*, for instance, writes at the outset of his work that he composed his grammar in order to 'understand well the right meaning of the discourses of the Teacher'.[30] Centuries later, Vimalabuddhi adds in his *Mukhamattadīpanī* that studying grammar has a further incidental (*anusaṅgika*) purpose. A monk who understands grammar, he states, lives according to the meaning of scripture and as a result becomes joyful in the knowledge that he is behaving appropriately. This joy leads to other calming emotions, such as satisfaction (*pīti*) and happiness (*sukha*), which help produce a composed mind that can achieve spiritual insights.[31] Here Vimalabuddhi evokes a longstanding causal connection in Buddhist thought between studying authoritative scripture (*pariyatti*), good practice (*paṭipatti*) and the attainment of spiritual insight (*paṭivedha*), and places the study of grammar as its foundation.

In his own discussion on the purpose of the discipline, Moggallāna similarly presents grammar as the foundation of the same causal sequence of spiritual development: grammatical knowledge, followed by scriptural knowledge, followed by good practice and culminating in spiritual insight. His discussion differs, however, in two main ways. Moggallāna first speaks of the loss of one's status within the Saṅgha's hierarchy as a result of not knowing grammar. He stresses that an individual who does not know grammar cannot become a teacher of others or lead legal rites within the Saṅgha. He further differs from older grammarians in explicitly justifying the study of the discipline in terms of the need to counter religious decline. There he argues that without grammar, scripture would completely disappear, followed by practice and then finally by insight:

> For one who is ignorant of grammar is not skilled in the doctrine and discipline, and since he is not skilled in them he is not able to practise

> according to the Dhamma. In losing his practice he partakes only in the suffering of cyclic existence and is not able to become a support (i.e. a teacher) for the faithful renunciates, the noble sons. For only those who know grammar are able to train noble sons in the doctrine and discipline, having checked the wording according to the meaning and the meaning according to the wording, and are able to complete this or that legal act (*kamma*) among the disciplinary acts, such as the probation ritual (*parivāsa*), having recited the legal formulae (*kammavācā*) in accordance with it (i.e. the discipline). No other can do this. He who does not know grammar, moreover, and who does not practise accordingly eliminates also the three-fold true Dhamma. To explain:
>
> He who does not know grammar destroys scripture, which is only based on it (i.e. grammar). Then when this is destroyed, practice, which is based on scripture, is destroyed. And then realization, which is based on practice, is also destroyed. For the Bhagavan has said this: 'Monks, these two conditions lead to the confusion and destruction of the true Dhamma. What two? An incorrectly placed expression and the misunderstanding of meaning. If an expression is misplaced, monks, the meaning in turn is liable to be misunderstood. These two conditions, monks, lead to the confusion and destruction of the true Dhamma.'[32] This is the fault in not knowing grammar.[33]

Moggallāna likely raised the issues of education and legal rites here due to the fact that grammar in the reform-era curriculum was a testing ground for monks who aspired to leading positions in the monastic community's educational hierarchy. The Daṁbadeṇiya edict of Parākramabāhu II highlights a Vinaya regulation that after higher ordination a monk could undertake a five-year period of study with a teacher in order to be declared 'independent' (Sin. *niśrayamukta*), that is, he could move freely without permission.[34] The highest course of study as part of its curriculum was delivered by a leading monk (*nāyaka*) and included the study of grammatical texts. Once these texts were memorized the monk was examined on them and finally released from dependence on his teacher, with the request that he would occasionally recite these works in front of the monastic community from time to time.[35] Grammar was studied widely, then, since knowledge of the subject was also a means by which a monk could achieve independence and a high rank within the Saṅgha.[36]

Moggallāna's emphasis on religious decline may reflect the wider eschatological concerns motivating these monastic reforms.[37] Descriptions of the reforms that took place in 1165, c. 1232 and 1266 all emphasize a perceived deterioration in the monastic tradition, as discussed in chapter two, and it seems likely that these eschatological considerations also informed Moggallāna's view of grammar as the first line of defence in delaying the destruction of Buddhism. That Moggallāna had such eschatological concerns in mind when writing his grammar is supported by its earliest interpreter, Saṅgharakkhita, who wrote a commentary to his teacher's work in the third quarter of the thirteenth century. There, in elaborating on this passage, he specifically evokes the source of this eschatological prophecy, Buddhaghosa's fourth- or fifth-century *Aṅguttara Nikāya* commentary, where the commentator describes in detail how, over a five-thousand-year period after the Buddha's death, there would be the gradual disappearance of 'five aspects' of the Buddhist tradition, namely realization, practice, scripture, signs of monasticism such as robes, and the Buddha's relics.[38] Saṅgharakkhita connects Moggallāna's discussion of religious decline with this passage by quoting the following three verses that Buddhaghosa appends to his prophecy:

> As far as the Suttantas remain and the Vinaya shines
> they illuminate the entire world as when the sun has arisen.
> When the Suttantas are no more and the Vinaya has been lost
> there will be darkness in the world as when the sun has set.
> When the Suttanta is being preserved, practice is preserved.
> Steadfast in practice, the wise do not lose their freedom from bondage.[39]

Saṅgharakkhita creatively reframes Buddhaghosa's short poem here by placing before these verses his own opening couplet that presents the study of language, that is, grammatical practice, as the basis of scriptural knowledge. He writes:

> One who would study the three baskets without having studied language
> stumbles on each word (at every step) like a blind elephant in a forest.[40]

Saṅgharakkhita thus connects Moggallāna's initial discussions about religious decline with traditional eschatological theory. The association in Saṅgharakkhita's mind between grammar and eschatology suggests that he too saw grammar not only as the foundation of one's personal spiritual development but, from a civilizational perspective, also as the basis for protecting the world from impending darkness. In this regard we can speculate that the very real, exegetical connection between understanding the rules of the Pali language and studying its literature had, in the minds of some scholar-monks of the era, become generalized into an ideal connection, where the study of grammar took on a magical or apotropaic role in forestalling the impending disappearance of the religion.[41]

4.2. The Information Order of Reform-era Grammarians

Reform-era grammarians differed from their predecessors not only in their aims but also in their radical rejection of tradition, dispensing with the older Kaccāyana grammar and adopting and better adapting new models of grammatical analysis from other Sanskrit grammars. This new orientation owed much to the wider reforming mentality of the era, characterized by the need to stem religious decline, but also to the availability of new intellectual resources, described in chapter two, that allowed scholars to rethink the ways in which they were taking care of their sacred language and scriptures. The sources Moggallāna used to create a new organizational framework for his sacred language provide an insight into his 'information order', that is, the historical 'knowledge flows' through which his work was produced.[42]

Moggallāna wrote his eponymous grammar at the Thūpārāma in the southwest of Anurādhapura, nestled equidistantly between the main monasteries of the three fraternities, the Mahāvihāra, Abhayagiri and Jetavana.[43] Prior to the Cōḻa invasions, the Thūpārāma's affiliation with any one particular fraternity was contested and evidence suggests that it maintained an administrative autonomy in the sectarian landscape of the old capital.[44] The location of the Thūpārāma was deemed particularly sacred since it housed the Buddha's collar-bone relic and it was thought to occupy the same abstract topological space in Anurādhapura as the site of the Buddha's passing in the ancient Indian town of Kuśinārа.[45]

Moggallāna's sources reflect the wider changes in Sri Lanka's religious and political alliances discussed in chapter two. His grammar reveals, for instance, strong intellectual ties with the scholarly communities of northeast India, in particular the Bengal region, as well as an increasing rivalry with Cōḻa scholar-monks in South India. While most of the Sanskrit works Moggallāna used betray no religious affiliation, based on the little information we know about the authors of these works it seems that his sources were largely Buddhist and monastic.

Moggallāna's main opponent and representative of the older *Kaccāyana* grammatical tradition was the South Indian scholar-monk Buddhappiya. Buddhappiya presided as head monk over two monasteries in Nāgapaṭṭana, modern day Nagapattinam, namely the Bālādityavihāra and Cūḍāmaṇivarmavihāra, and perhaps led his own reforms of the monastic community in Cōḻa country prior to those that took place in Sri Lanka in 1165, resulting in a schism in what monks had regarded as their shared 'circle of influence' (*maṇḍala*).[46] The latter monastery, in particular, is historically significant since it was built by the ruler of Śrīvijaya, Māravijayottuṅgavarman, of the Śailendra dynasty in 1005/6 and continued to receive endowments from Cōḻa kings throughout the eleventh and twelfth centuries.[47]

We can speculate that Buddhappiya's close ties with the Cōḻa court may have contributed to the split that took place between the monastic orders in South India and Sri Lanka. This schism manifests itself intellectually throughout Moggallāna's grammar but it is worth highlighting two main points of linguistic controversy. First, Moggallāna directly argues against Buddhappiya in his very first rule in claiming that Pali has forty-three sounds, including short *e* and *o*, in its syllabary rather than the forty-one enumerated by the *Kaccāyana* tradition.[48] Second, Moggallāna, again partly in opposition to Buddhappiya, radically reduces the scope of the Pali dative case. He argues that *Kaccāyana* grammarians were overly influenced by Sanskrit grammars in ascribing many of the functions they do to the dative. He instead argues that most of these functions should be subsumed under an expanded Pali genitive case.[49]

In terms of Sanskrit sources, Moggallāna modelled his grammar on the *Cāndravyākaraṇa* ('Grammar of Candragomin'), a work that was composed by Candragomin, who, according to late Tibetan tradition, was a Buddhist layman and resident at the monastery of Nālandā in northeast India.[50] Possibly written in the fifth century his work is second only to Pāṇini's *Aṣṭādhyāyī* in its influence on South Asia's indigenous grammatical traditions.[51] A Buddhist monk called Dharmadāsa composed a paraphrase (*vṛtti*) for the *Cāndravyākaraṇa* possibly in the late fifth or sixth century and Moggallāna also nearly always follows his explanations when writing his own paraphrase on rules borrowed from the *Cāndra* grammar.[52] Moggallāna's use of the *Cāndra* tradition of Sanskrit grammar was mediated by two Sanskrit commentaries composed by scholar-monks from Sri Lanka prior to the reforms. A prolific tenth-century scholar known as Ratnamati, discussed in chapter two, composed an influential commentary, the *Cāndrapañcikā* ('Extensive commentary on Candra's grammar'), on Dharmadāsa's paraphrase.[53] This work, in turn, was commented upon by Sāriputta in a work known as the *Cāndrapañcikālaṅkāra*.[54]

Both Ratnamati and Sāriputta may have had personal ties with the monastic communities of northeast India. Dragomir Dimitrov has recently argued that it was this same Ratnamati, using the name Ratnaśrījñāna, who composed an inscription at the sacred site of Bodh Gayā as well as a commentary on Daṇḍin's *Kāvyādarśa* ('Mirror of literature') in northeast India.[55] Sāriputta's Sanskrit commentary was lost in Sri Lanka and is only known about through quotations in other reform-era works. Dimitrov, however, has published a facsimile edition of a manuscript of a commentary on Ratnamati's work entitled the *Candrālaṅkāra*, which was copied in 1116 at the Somapura Mahāvihāra, a monastery located near the modern-day village of Paharpur in Bangladesh, and identifies this work with Sāriputta's lost commentary.[56] Recorded quotations from Sāriputta's commentary in works from Sri Lanka unfortunately fall outside the material covered in this fragmentary manuscript and so this attribution, while possible, cannot as yet be confirmed. If the work is indeed Sāriputta's then the early date of the manuscript would suggest that the island's monastic community likely had close contact with this monastery in Bengal.

One of the keenest observers of Moggallāna's source material was the fifteenth-century polymath Śrī Rāhula. He was the head monk of the academy of Toṭagamuva, the personal tutor of king Parākramabāhu VI (1411–66) and a distant relative of Sāriputta. In 1458 he composed the *Moggallānapañcikāpradīpaya* ('Lamp on Moggallāna's extensive commentary'), a Sinhala commentary on the *Moggallānapañcikā*, and later also a commentary on Piyadassi's grammatical handbook.[57] In this latter work Śrī Rāhula confirms that Moggallāna knew the *Cāndra* grammar, its paraphrase by Dharmadāsa and its commentaries composed by Ratnamati and Sāriputta. He also notes, furthermore, that Moggallāna had mastered many other Sanskrit grammars, including Pāṇini's *Aṣṭādhyāyī*, its paraphrase, Jayāditya's *Kāśikāvṛtti* ('Benares paraphrase') and a commentary, Jinendrabuddhi's *Kāśikāvṛttipañcikā* ('Extensive commentary on the Benares paraphrase') as well as the *Kātantravyākaraṇa* ('Little grammar') with its paraphrase and commentary by Durghasiṃha and Trilocanadāsa respectively.[58] These other commentaries that Śrī Rāhula states Moggallāna used, namely, Jinendrabuddhi's seventh-century *Kāśikāvṛttipañcikā* and Trilocanadāsa's eleventh-century (?) *Kātantrapañcikā* ('Extensive commentary on the Little grammar') are both traditionally associated with the Buddhist monastic intellectual culture of northeast India.[59]

Śrī Rāhula's Sinhala commentary is useful in and of itself in ascertaining a reliable picture of the full scope of Sanskrit source material available to the monks of the reform era. His work is renowned in Sri Lanka for the sheer breadth of texts he had at his disposal in his library at Toṭagamuva in 1458. The commentary thus provides a snapshot of the Sanskrit knowledge preserved in Sri Lanka in the middle of the fifteenth century. Śrī Dharmārāma, who edited Śrī Rāhula's 'Lamp' in 1886, lists fifty-nine quoted works in his introduction.[60] Almost half of these works were Sanskrit philological texts, principally grammars and lexica (see Table 4.1).

The diversity of Śrī Rāhula's source material is quite astounding, all the more so since much of this knowledge was lost in Sri Lanka in the subsequent centuries of colonial rule.[61] What is interesting from the perspective of the reform era's intellectual history, specifically, is the concentration of sources from the tenth to twelfth centuries and the focus on the region of Bengal. This connection seems to have persisted even after the 1165 reforms since Śrī Rāhula cites Sena dynasty works, such as Puruṣottamadeva's *Bhāṣāvṛtti*

Table 4.1: A hypothetical chronology of Śrī Rāhula's Sanskrit grammatical and lexicographical sources[62]

	Title	Author	Date	Provenance
1	Aṣṭādhyāyī	Pāṇini	300–400 BC	N.W. India
2	Vārttika	Kātyāyana	300–400 BC	S. India
3	Mahābhāṣya	Patañjali	200–100 BC	N.W. India
4	Kātantravyākaraṇa	Śarvavarman	100–200	S. India
5	Cāndravyākaraṇa	Candragomin	100–200	S. India
6	Amarakośa	Amarasiṃha	500–600	Unknown
7	Kāśikāvṛtti	Jayāditya	600–700	Kashmir
8	Kāśikāvṛttipañcikā	Jinendrabuddhi	after 700	Bengal
9	Śākaṭāyanavyākaraṇa	Pālyakīrti	800–900	W. India
10	Rūpāvatāra	Dharmakīrti	900–1000	Sri Lanka
11	Halāyudhakośa	Halāyudha	900–1000	W. India
12	Cāndrapañcikā	Ratnamati	900–1000	Sri Lanka
13	Śabdārthacintā	Ratnamati/ Ratnaśrījñāna	900–1000	N.E. India
14	Bhāgavṛtti	Vimalamati	900–1000	Bengal
15	Vopālitakośa	Vopālita	900–1000	Unknown
16	Bhāṣyapradīpa	Kaiyaṭa	1000–1100	Kashmir
17	Anunyāsa	Indumitra	1000–1100	Bengal
18	Kavikāmadhenu	Subhūticandra	1000–1100	Bengal
19	Kātantrapañcikā	Trilocanadāsa	1000–1100	Bengal
20	Bhāgavṛttipañcikā	Śrīdhara	before 1100	Bengal
21	Cāndrapañcikālaṅkāra	Sāriputta	before 1165	Sri Lanka
22	Pātrīkaraṇaṭīkā	Buddhanāga	1100–1300	Sri Lanka
23	Viśvaprakāśa	Maheśvarakavi	1111/12	Unknown
24	Vaijayantīkośa	Yādavaprakāśa	1100–1200	S. India
25	Trikāṇḍaśeṣa	Puruṣottamadeva	1100–1200	Bengal
26	Bhāṣāvṛtti	Puruṣottamadeva	1179–1209	Bengal
27	Sārasvatavyākaraṇa	Anubhūtisvarūpa	1200–1400	Unknown

('Commentary on language'), which was composed at some point during the reign of king Lakṣmaṇasena (1179–1206).[63]

While there was likely an ornamental, stylistic purpose in citing such a diverse array of works, it seems on occasion too that Śrī Rāhula used his Sanskrit archive to provide historical explanations for Moggallāna's more unusual linguistic observations. By way of example, in his paraphrase on rule 4.80 Moggallāna explains that the word *vaṇṇa* (caste, class, complexion; Sk. *varṇa*) means 'celibate ascetic' (Sk. *brahmacārin*) when combined with a possessive suffix *–ī* (i.e. *vaṇṇī*, Sk. *varṇin*).[64] This sense is not attested in the Pali canon and would likely be unfamiliar to the average monastic reader. In an extraordinary demonstration of his learning, Śrī Rāhula quotes an explanation of the term *brahmacārin* from Śrīdhara's eleventh-century (?) *Bhāgavṛttipañcikā* ('Extensive commentary on the *Bhāgavṛtti*'), followed by a definition of the Sanskrit *varṇin* in the sense of 'ascetic' from Puruṣottamadeva's twelfth-century *Trikāṇḍaśeṣa* ('Appendix to the three chapters [of the *Amarakośa*]'), and then turns to the opening verse from Bhāravi's sixth-century court epic, the *Kirātārjunīya* ('On Kirāta and Arjuna'), where the word is used in the same sense.[65]

There is not a single reason for this sudden engagement with a wide range of Sanskrit grammatical literature associated with the Bengal region. As discussed in chapter two, the rise of the Cōḻas in South India led to a strengthening of ties between Laṅkā and the Cōḻa empire's adversaries, in particular the kingdoms of northeast India. It is possible too that increased trade and mobility between Sri Lanka and northeast India – perhaps along the new trade routes established during Cōḻa rule – may have further facilitated the exchange of monks and Buddhist knowledge.[66] Finally, we can also speculate that another factor contributing to the movement of texts outside of northeast India in the twelfth century specifically was the weakening of Pāla rule in Bengal, the rise of the Senas, who more openly favoured Hindu groups, and the imminent threat of the Turkic invasions of northern India.[67]

4.3. Moggallāna's New Philology and the Creation of Order

Contact between Sri Lanka and Bengal cannot in and of itself explain cultural change, however. Why did scholar-monks decide to take up these Sanskrit texts and use them as a model for their own grammatical works? Descriptions of scholarly practice from the reform era suggest that monks thought new textual practices would establish a better order for their sacred language and scriptures and thus help stem the decline of their community and society. This connection is reflected in the common metaphors authors use to describe the effects of both their new textual practices and the process of reform. Authors frequently employ the terms *ākula* 'confused' and its negation *anākula* or *nirākula* 'unconfused', in particular, to compare the disordered nature of their textual tradition and the behaviour of monks prior to the reforms with the order of their texts and community after the reforms.[68] In the colophon of his paraphrase, for instance, Moggallāna juxtaposes the 'ordered' nature of his work with the 'order' brought about in the previously 'disordered' Saṅgha by the reforms of Parākramabāhu I in 1165.[69] His student, Saṅgharakkhita, further favourably contrasts Moggallāna's grammar with the perceived disorder of the older Pali grammatical tradition.[70]

In using the *Cāndravyākaraṇa* as a model for his grammar, Moggallāna radically differentiated his system from the style of earlier Pali grammatical texts. Moggallāna adopts a similar means of grammatical description to the *Cāndra* grammar in that he composed his main work using short aphorisms or *sūtra*s connected by the principle of ellipsis (Sk. *anuvṛtti*), whereby the whole or part of one *sūtra* may be used to make sense of another. The *sūtra* genre had a long history in Sanskrit writing, with brevity and economy praised as the principal virtue of scholarly discourse. (There is a Sanskrit maxim that compares the happiness at shortening an aphorism to the birth of a son.)[71] In Sri Lanka, this form of writing, while not unknown, was not widely studied or used in Pali and Sinhala texts prior to the reform era.[72] The older *Kaccāyana* grammar, for instance, was modelled on the Sanskrit *Kātantravyākaraṇa*, a work more concerned with the simplicity of descriptive detail than with the brevity of its analytical model.[73]

To understand how such aphorisms work, take, for example, a series of rules in Moggallāna's grammar, which he has adapted from the *Cāndra* grammar, prescribing some of the functions of the fifth or 'ablative' case (see Table 4.2).

These statements below may be quite meaningless for most readers of this book who are unfamiliar with traditional Sanskrit grammar. But if we look beyond the strange style and technical terminology the basic mechanisms at work are quite simple.

Table 4.2: A comparison of rules in the Moggallāna and Cāndra grammars

Moggallāna grammar	Cāndra grammar
2.28 *pañcamy avadhismā*[74] The fifth case [occurs after a nominal stem] that is a limiting point (*avadhi*).	**2.1.81** *avadheḥ pañcamī* The fifth case occurs [after a nominal stem] that is a limiting point (*avadhi*).
2.31 *rite dutiyā ca* **[#2.28** *pañcamī*] The second case and [the fifth case occur after a nominal stem co-occurring with] *rite* 'apart'.	**2.1.84** *ṛte dvitīyā ca* **[#2.1.81** *pañcamī*] The second case and [the fifth case occur after a nominal stem co-occurring with] *ṛte* 'apart'.
2.32 *vināññatra tatiyā ca* **[#2.29** *pañcamī* **#2.31** *dutiyā ca*] The third case, [the fifth case and the second case occur after a nominal stem co-occurring with] *vinā* 'without' and *aññatra* 'except'.	**2.1.85** *vinā tṛtīyā ca* **[#2.1.81** *pañcamī* **#2.1.84** *dvitīyā ca*] The third case, [the fifth case and the second case occur after a nominal stem co-occurring with] *vinā* 'without'.

First, rule 2.28 begins Moggallāna's discussion of the fifth or ablative case and consists of two words. Literally it means, 'fifth, after limiting point'. To understand what is meant here we must supply an implicit verb 'to be' – which I translate as 'occurs' – and also understand that the 'limiting point' refers to the word denoting the point from which an action occurs. In the sentence, 'he flies from London to Singapore', for instance, London acts as the limiting point for the act of flying and thus in English takes the ablative preposition 'from'. In the Pali sentence *gāmasmā āgacchatu* ('let him come from the village') the village (*gāma*) acts as the limiting point for the act of movement and thus takes the fifth case suffix *–smā*.[75] The rule thus prescribes the fifth case after a noun that denotes such a limiting point.

If we skip over a few rules and turn to 2.31 and 2.32 we can further see the principle of ellipsis at work. Rule 2.31 consists of three words and literally means 'without, and the second'. Here we must also include the word 'fifth' from 2.28 to understand that both the fifth ('ablative') *and* the second ('accusative') cases occur after a noun alongside the word 'apart' (*rite*). For example, one can use the fifth case and say *rite dhammā* 'apart from the doctrine' or the second and say *rite dhammaṃ*. More than one word can be introduced through this mechanism of ellipsis too. In 2.32 which literally means 'without, except, and the third' we must understand that the fifth, second *and* third cases occur after a noun alongside the words 'without' (*vinā*) and 'except' (*aññatra*). One can say, for instance, *vinā dhammā* 'without the doctrine', using the fifth case, or *vinā dhammaṃ* and *vinā dhammena*, using the second and third cases respectively, without altering the meaning of the expression.

Moggallāna was the first grammarian to produce a faultless piece of technical writing of this style in Pali and he acknowledges in the opening to his commentary that not everyone in the Saṅgha would be familiar with it.[76] When commenting on the very first rule of his grammar he writes that 'this statement might be meaningless – some kind of speech of a mad man or such like'. He introduces this possibility only to demur, of course, and adds: 'or it may be meaningful like the [Buddha's] statement: "mind is the forerunner of all things"'.[77] Grammatical aphorisms are meaningful, he states, because the meaning of each aphorism should be sought in its paraphrase or *vutti* (Sk. *vṛtti*).

Most works of grammar composed using *sūtras* are accompanied by a paraphrase that rewrites the rules in plain language making all the implied information explicit. As mentioned, a Buddhist monk called Dharmadāsa composed a paraphrase for the *Cāndra* grammar possibly in the late fifth or sixth century and Moggallāna nearly always follows his explanations when writing his own paraphrase. Take the paraphrases in both works on the rules 2.32 and 2.1.85, which we have just discussed above:

Table 4.3: A comparison of Moggallānavutti 2.32 and Cāndravṛtti 2.1.85

Moggallāna **paraphrase on 2.32**	*Cāndra* **paraphrase on 2.1.85**
vināññatrasaddehi yoge nāmasmā tatiyā ca hoti dutiyāpañcamiyo ca. (1) vinā vātena, (2) vinā vātaṃ, (3) vinā vātasmā, (4) *aññatra ekena piṇḍapātanīhārakena*, (5) aññatra dhammaṃ, (6) aññatra dhammā. The third case, as well as the second and fifth cases, occur after a nominal stem when co-occurring with the words *vinā* 'without' and *aññatra* 'except'. [For example:] (1) without wind (*vātena*), (2) without wind (*vātaṃ*), (3) without wind (*vātasmā*), (4) *except the one who brings alms-food* (*Dīgha Nikāya* II 237$_{,31}$), (5) except the Dhamma (*dhammaṃ*), (6) except the Dhamma (*dhammā*).	**vināśabdena yoge tṛtīyāpañcamyau bhavato dvitīyā ca.** (1) vinā vātena, (2) vinā vātāt, (3) vinā vātam. The third and fifth cases occur, as well as the second, when co-occurring with the word *vinā* 'without'. [For example:] (1) without wind (*vātena*), (2) without wind (*vātāt*), (3) without wind (*vātam*).

After restating the meaning of the *sūtra*s in simple prose each paraphrase usually introduces a series of practical examples. Dharmadāsa's example here 'without wind' (*vinā vātena*) alludes to possible sentences such as 'the tree fell without a gust of wind'.[78] Moggallāna does not follow his Sanskrit sources blindly, however, and is sensitive in adapting Sanskrit grammatical theory to the Pali language. He introduces the word *aññatra* 'except' into the rule, for instance, in order to cover the particularities of his scriptural language and includes a canonical quotation in support: 'I must not be approached by anyone *except the one who brings the alms-food*.'[79] This sentence is taken from the *Mahāgovinda Sutta*, an account of the Buddha's past life as a young Brahmin royal steward, Mahāgovinda, who undertakes a meditative retreat in order to visit the heavens and see the gods.

It is important to understand that the act of placing Pali within such an organizational framework was not simply a descriptive practice of a modern, linguistic kind. Rather, it was inherently creative in that such grammatical analysis established the idea of Pali as an object of knowledge and associated it with scholarly and monastic virtues: economy, regularity and orderliness. These ideas could then be generalized for scripture in its entirety, since the 'canon' described by these grammars was not the actual canon but rather select phrases, 'symbols of grammatical knowledgeability', that had circulated among scholars as a synecdoche for the Pali canon as a whole.[80] As an access discipline for any monk wishing to ascend the monastic hierarchy and study Pali scriptures, grammar must have served for many as one of the first ways they engaged in any scholarly fashion with their sacred texts and thus, with respect to the literary value of their scriptures, grammar could be said to have shaped ideas about the Pali canon as much as it described it.

Moggallāna further takes care to place his canonical sentences among stock grammatical examples from the Sanskrit tradition, such as the example 'without wind' mentioned above. Since they are unmarked only a careful reader would be able to distinguish the canonical quotations from the non-canonical. This ambiguity encourages the reader, furthermore, to imagine the Pali language as grammatically complete, despite the fact that certain grammatical expressions, as Wilhelm Geiger lamented, may be unattested in the canon. Far from being a methodological flaw, we can view this treatment of Pali as an attempt to go beyond the purely exegetical character of the *Kaccāyana* grammar and to represent the boundless, expressive capacity of the Pali language as a whole. It is Moggallāna's interest in investigating the workings of Pali as a language beyond simply establishing the meaning of scriptural sentences that further distinguished his approach from his predecessors, and it is to this issue we will now turn.

4.4. From Exegetical to Analytical Approaches to Language

A certain exegetical pragmatism characterized the way early commentators and grammarians used *vyākaraṇa* to analyse scriptural language. For the commentators in particular, grammar was only thought about insofar as it could help resolve linguistic problems in the interpretation of the canon and as such their grammatical analysis often reveals a willingness to bend the scope of the Sanskrit grammars they used to suit their exegetical needs. The *Kaccāyana* grammar represented a large improvement on the analysis of the commentators but even it confused rudimentary principles of Sanskrit grammar and slowly lost much of its coherence due to the additions and clarifications of later grammarians who prioritized exegetical comprehensiveness over the integrity of the metarules of the discipline.

We see in Moggallāna's works and those of his students an interest in the analysis of language as an object of knowledge outside of the narrow confines of exegetical utility. The impetus for this change appears to have been a number of Sanskrit philological works composed by the tenth-century Sri Lankan monk Ratnamati, in particular his *Cāndrapañcikā*, a commentary on Dharmadāsa's *Cāndravṛtti*, and his *Śabdārthacintā* ('Reflections on words and meanings'), a work of grammatical philosophy. Dragomir Dimitrov and Mahesh Deokar have recently revealed the large extent to which the *Cāndrapañcikā* served as the model for much of Moggallāna's own autocommentary, the *Moggallānapañcikā*.[81] Dimitrov has noted Ratnamati's deep interest in grammatical philosophy in both his *Cāndrapañcikā* and *Śabdārthacintā* and has shown that his ideas about the metaphysics of semantics (*artha*) particularly influenced Moggallāna and his students.[82]

The ability to isolate semantics as an object of philosophical analysis can be understood as a by-product of the derivational nature of most Sanskrit grammars, where meaning conditions the introduction of affixes.[83] In the Pāṇinian and *Cāndra* grammatical traditions, for instance, there are implicit analytical distinctions between what we can think about as semantics, syntax, morphology and phonology, with no one-to-one correspondence between them, that is to say these traditions can explain how one and the same meaning may be represented by different syntactic roles, which then can be represented by different cases, and which, in turn, can be represented by different case-endings. Moggallāna throughout his grammar and commentaries assumes similar analytical distinctions in the derivational process.

To understand the distinction between these differing domains, take, for example, the sentences (1) *puruso rukkhaṃ chindati* ('the man cuts the tree') and (2) *purusena rukkho chijjati* ('the tree is cut by the man'). To form these sentences derivational grammars begin with a common semantic base: the man is the doer, the tree is the object and cutting is the present action. At a syntactic level, these can correspond – either through operational rules or according to convention (*vivakṣā*) – to an agent, an accusative and either an active or passive verb.[84] In terms of morphology, the first case reflects the agent and second case denotes the accusative, whereas in the passive, the third case denotes the agent and the first case reflects the accusative.[85] Finally, the grammarians assign the relevant suffixes corresponding to these cases. For a skeletal framework outlining these analytical distinctions, see Table 4.4.[86]

Distinguishing these different levels and allowing for variation between them enables precision and consistency in grammatical analysis. Take, for instance, a canonical sentence Moggallāna analyses in his discussion of the accusative: 'the body will lie on the ground' (*kāyo paṭhavim adhisessati*). This sentence comes from a verse in the *Dhammapada*: 'Not long alas, and it will lie this body, here upon the earth. Discarded, void of consciousness, useless as a rotten log.'[87] In this sentence the ground *paṭhaviṃ* is in the second case and is syntactically an accusative (lit. *the body lies the ground), though it has the sense of the *locus* of lying down. Moggallāna observes that the second case is used 'as there is the desire to speak of the accusative (*kamma*) in the sense of

Table 4.4: The derivation of passive and active sentences in the Moggallāna system

Sentence 1: *puruso rukkhaṃ chindati* 'the man cuts the tree'

1. Semantic level	*purusa* $^{\text{*doer}}$	*rukkha* ^{object}	√*chid* $^{\text{present time, doer}}$
2. Abstract syntactic level	*purusa* $^{\text{agent}(\textit{kattu})}$	*rukkha* $^{\text{accusative}(\textit{kamma})}$	√*chid* $^{\text{present tense, active (}\textit{vattamāna, kattari}\text{)}}$
3. Morphological level	*purusa* + *Si* $^{\text{1st case, singular}}$	*rukkha* + *aṃ* $^{\text{2nd case, singular}}$	*chid* + *La* + *ti* $^{\text{3rd person, singular}}$
4. Phonological level	*purusa* + *o*	*rukkha* + *aṃ*	*chind* + *a* + *ti*
	puruso 'the man'	*rukkhaṃ* 'the tree'	*chindati* 'cuts'

Sentence 2: *purusena rukkho chijjati* 'the tree is cut by the man'

1. Semantic level	*purusa* ^{doer}	*rukkha* $^{\text{*object}}$	√*chid* $^{\text{present time, object}}$
2. Abstract syntactic level	*purusa* $^{\text{agent}(\textit{kattu})}$	*rukkha* $^{\text{accusative}(\textit{kamma})}$	√*chid* $^{\text{present tense, passive (}\textit{vattamāna, kamme}\text{)}}$
3. Morphological level	*purusa* + *nā* $^{\text{3rd case, singular}}$	*rukkha* + *Si* $^{\text{1st case, singular}}$	*chid* + *Kya* + *ti* $^{\text{3rd person, singular}}$
4. Phonological level	*purusa* + *ena*	*rukkha* + *o*	*chid* + *ya* + *ti*
	purusena 'by the man'	*rukkho* 'the tree'	*chijjati* 'is cut'

the locus'.[88] Here Moggallāna analytically distinguishes between morphology ('the second case'), syntax ('the accusative') and semantics ('locus') and flexibly prescribes an accusative in the sense of locus of an action rather than in the sense of the object of an action, as is most common.

There is far more going on in this analysis than merely an exegetical need to understand the sentence. In the 2,000-year history of reading the *Dhammapada* there appears to have been little confusion about what this verse meant. The earliest Pali commentators argued that the second case of *paṭhavī* was governed by *adhi–*, and treated *adhi* as an indeclinable particle rather than the preposition of the verb.[89] Buddhappiya in his *Rūpasiddhi* follows the commentators and uses this example to illustrate the use of the second case with certain indeclinable particles.[90] He complicates matters, however, in that later in his grammar he again cursorily refers to the same example under a different grammatical rule appointing 'the second case in the sense of the third or seventh cases'.[91] Moggallāna, it seems, demanded a higher degree of consistency in the analysis of language based on a systematic application of a single grammatical model.[92] In light of our discussion above about the changing purpose of grammar, we can hypothesize that this degree of rigour was ultimately motivated by a need to protect Buddhism, underpinned by a belief in an ontological connection between the order of sacred language and that of society.

The results of the reform era's grammatical turn can be compared, albeit anachronistically, with the way the rather differing scientific aims of modern linguistics transformed the analysis of European languages. Compare, for example, the history of interpreting English phrases, such as 'to walk the streets', as in Shakespeare's *Twelfth Night*: 'I do not without danger walk these streets'.[93] The earliest interpreters of such expressions simply inferred that there had been the elision of a preposition 'through' or 'in' before 'these streets'. Even the first modern linguists, such as Otto Jespersen, merely appealed to the 'vague' and 'indistinct character' of the English object when explaining why 'walk' takes a direct object here. It is only relatively recently, however, that linguists have thought in a similar way to interpret 'streets' as a 'locative object', where the object has a locative sense.[94]

This desire to describe the order of language at its most fundamental level extended to a philosophical investigation of the deeper semantic structures underpinning the Pali language. Moggallāna borrowed from the Sanskrit commentary of his predecessor, Ratnamati, a theory of five unvarying 'meaning elements' (*padattha*) that words can possibly signify, namely the sense of the word itself (*sakattha*), a universal (*jāti*), a quality (*guṇa*), a particular (*dabba*) or an activity (*kriyā*).[95] Following their Sanskrit counterparts, reform-era Pali grammarians were interested in how the ontological relationship between these elements formed the semantic basis of syntax.[96] This relationship was

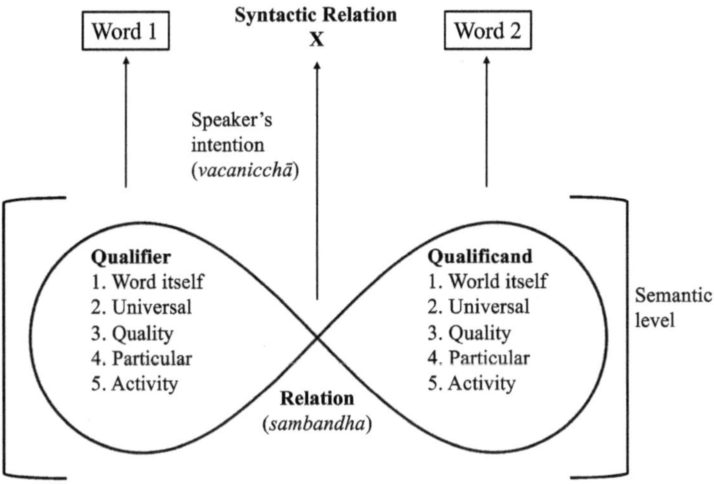

Figure 4.1 The five 'meaning-elements' underpinning linguistic usage

thought of as one of dependency, where elements were described either as qualified (*visessa*) by other elements or as doing the qualifying (*visesana*). In the expression 'the white cloth', for instance, the cloth is a particular (*dabba*) characterized or qualified by a quality (*guṇa*), namely the colour white, and it is this real semantic connection that underpins the syntactic relationship between the words 'white' and 'cloth'.

This form of analysis extended to whole sentences. Take, for instance, the Pali sentence *kaṭe nisīdati devadatto* ('Devadatta sits on the mat') that Moggallāna refers to as an example to illustrate the locative case.[97] Here we have three 'meaning elements', namely, two particulars, Devadatta and the mat, and an activity, sitting. What is happening metaphysically? Reform-era grammarians would say, following their Sanskrit sources, that a particular, the mat, supports another particular, Devadatta, in whom subsists an activity of sitting.[98] This kind of thinking informs Moggallāna's original definition of a locus as 'a support for an activity, in so far as it supports either the agent or object, which is the [ultimate] locus of the activity.'[99] There was a widespread adoption of this type of metaphysical analysis among reform-era grammarians. The first grammar of Sinhala, for example, the late thirteenth-century *Sidat Saṅgarāva* ('Handbook of sound and meaning'), contains a chapter on the meaning elements and analyses Sinhala syntax in a similar way.[100]

The more philosophical orientation of reform-era grammarians is no better illustrated than by Saṅgharakkhita's *Sambandhacintā* ('Reflections on syntactic relationships') the first treatise composed in Sri Lanka on the philosophy of Pali syntax.[101] Saṅgharakkhita begins his work with a lengthy discussion on the five 'meaning elements', how they relate to each other and how they can be spoken of using words in a syntactically coherent sentence.[102] This work demonstrates that scholars were now thinking about Pali primarily in terms of a real, semantic level and only secondarily in terms of the variable distribution of syntactic categories, morphology and phonology. It is simply due to a speaker's intention, he states, that one can speak of the same underlying meaning elements in multiple possible ways. One can say variously 'the pot cooks', 'he cooks in the pot' or 'he cooks with the pot', for example, about the same ontological event.[103] His commentator, Gotama, uses theatre as one of his analogies to describe how the same meaning element can adopt various syntactic roles in speech. He states that a meaning element, just like a single actor, has the capacity (*śakti*) to adopt the costume of the characters of Rāma or Rāvaṇa, that is, it can adopt different syntactic functions and can be spoken of in terms of these functions just as the same actor can be referred to as either 'Rāma' or 'Rāvaṇa'.[104]

This form of analysis will not strike those familiar with Sanskrit grammar as unusual and there is scope for a more fulsome appraisal of this philosophical development than I have been able to give here. What is important from a historical perspective, however, is that scholar-monks were thinking about their sacred language with deep semantic structures rather than phonetics as a starting point and that their approach was increasingly analytical rather than simply exegetical. Taken in light of the way scholar-monks described grammatical practice in the reform era, it seems likely that monks were so concerned about establishing a strong grammatical foundation for the Buddhist tradition that they sought order not only in the organized style of Sanskrit grammars but also in contemporary philosophical views on the deep semantic structures underpinning linguistic usage. The philosophy of language can be seen in this regard as part of the wider cultural work of grammar, namely providing an organizational plane on which the monastic community's sacred canon and language could be established as an ordered and coherent object, bringing into being, as a result, an orderly monastic community and in turn a favourable social and political climate.

4.5. Summary

Scholar-monks of the reform era wrote in Pali primarily to stem the premature decline of their religious tradition. As the acknowledged foundation and access discipline for scriptural study, grammar was seen as playing a pivotal role as the first line of defence against the degeneration of Buddhism. During the reform era in particular, characterized by social and political upheaval and confusion, sensitivity to traditional ideas of religious decline were heightened. In an unprecedented intellectual feat, scholar-monks decided to abandon their old grammatical tradition – much like many abandoned the old sacred capital of Anurādhapura after the Cōḻa invasions – and started anew with a different system of rules, the *Moggallāna-vyākaraṇa*, that would form the basis of philological activity in the centuries to come. In seeking to explain their age of confusion, scholar-monks blamed their older textual practices and sought out new forms of textual order, presumably as a way of pushing back against the harsh political conditions they had endured prior to 1165 and subsequently after Parākramabāhu I's demise in 1186. The framework for this new order was found in the Sanskrit texts that had become available due to intensified contact with monastic centres in northeast India. These new intellectual resources combined with the reform mentality to produce an improved, analytical system of grammar, one that was not only based on understanding Buddhist scriptures and the Pali language but was focused too on establishing linguistic order at its most deep and fundamental level.

Notes

1. Nattier, 1991, 133–44.
2. On grammar as a 'technology of transformation' in the context of *borān kammaṭṭhāna*, see Crosby, 2013, 70–82.
3. Visigalli, 2014, 25–50.
4. *Majjhimanikāyaṭīkā* of Dhammapāla III, $167_{,3\text{–}4}$: taṃ taṃ saddaṃ tadatthañ ca byākaroti byācikkhati etenā ti byākaraṇaṃ saddasatthaṃ (= *Dīghanikāyaṭīkā* of Dhammapāla I, $380_{,4\text{–}6}$).
5. Cardona, 1976, 261–8.
6. *Mahābhāṣya* of Patañjali I, $1_{,19}$. Also, *Vākyapadīya* of Bhartṛhari 1.11.
7. Pollock, 2006, 162–84. Also, Inden, 2000, 40.
8. See *Mahābhāṣyadīpikā* of Bhartṛhari, $28_{,11}$: na hīdaṃ śāstraṃ kasyacid ekasya sahāyabhūtaṃ, sarvasādhāraṇam.
9. Deshpande, 1997.
10. *Mahāyānasūtrālaṅkārasvavṛtti* on *Mahāyānasūtrālaṅkāra* 11.60. The Pali tradition occasionally refers to Sanskrit grammar as *bāhira* 'external' too but this seems to denote the extracanonical status of these texts. See, for instance, *Moggallānapañcikā* of Moggallāna on 2.35, $72_{,22}$; *Moggallānapañcikāṭīkā* of Saṅgharakkhita on 2.33 (35), $113_{,9}$. Also, Gunawardana, 1979, 160, n. 152.
11. See, for instance, Ruegg, 1995, 101.
12. Śaraṇadeva, for instance, composed the *Durghaṭavṛtti* in 1173/4 and can possibly be identified with a poet, Śaraṇa, in the court of king Lakṣmaṇasena (1179–1209). King Lakṣmaṇasena was also the patron of Puruṣottamadeva, author of the *Bhāṣāvṛtti*, who may have been a Buddhist too. See Wielińska-Soltwedel, 2006, esp. 39; 51–3.
13. See Subhūti, 1876, i–c; Franke, 1902; Pind, 2012; Gornall and Gunasena, 2018.
14. Pind, 1989; 1990; Gornall, 2011. There is an older tradition of grammatical analysis in the commentaries, though it is likely that this was inherited from ancient commentarial sources. See Pind, 2012, 61–7.
15. Pind, 2012, 71.

16. The only evidence that kings studied Pali grammar comes from the late thirteenth, early fourteenth-century *Daṁbadeṇiasna*, a history of the reign of Parākramabāhu II, where it is said that the monarch studied both the *Moggallāna* and *Kaccāyana* systems of grammar. See Meddegama, trans. 2011, 102. Parākramabāhu I too was supposedly 'skilled' in Pali and studied grammar, though we do not know whether it was Sanskrit or Pali grammar. See *Abhidhānappadīpikā* of Moggallāna, $182_{,4}$; *Cūḷavaṃsa* 64.2–5.
17. See chapter three.
18. Sāriputta may have been a forest monk prior to ascending to this role. See Liyanagamage, 1968, 92, n. 4; Kieffer-Pülz, 2018, 203, n. 42.
19. Dimitrov, 2010, 25–49.
20. See *Moggallānapañcikāṭīkā* of Saṅgharakkhita, $7_{,18-19}$: *mahāsāmiṭṭhānantarapattiṃ ... vibhāveti.*
21. Kieffer-Pülz, 2017b, 31–4.
22. Ratnapāla, 1971, 140; Kieffer-Pülz, 2017b, 39–40.
23. One notable exception is Ruiz-Falqués, 2017b.
24. Neugebauer, 1951. Neugebauer's article is a succinct defence of research into 'pseudo' sciences such as astrology in response to George Sarton's review of E.S. Drower's 1949 *The Book of the Zodiac* (Sarton, 1950), in which he described the book as a 'wretched collection of omens, debased astrology, and miscellaneous nonsense' (374).
25. Geiger, 1943, 50. Also, Bechert, 1978a, 5.
26. My approach here is indebted to the works of Eivind Kahrs, esp. Kahrs, 1998.
27. Pind, 2012.
28. Pind, 2012, 117–20; Franke, 1902, 23; 25–9; Subhūti, 1876, ix–x; xxi–xxiii. On the date of the *Rūpasiddhi*, see chapter three.
29. *Moggallānapañcikā* of Moggallāna, $380_{,8-19}$.
30. *Kaccāyanavyākaraṇa* of Kaccāyana, $1_{,3-4}$: satthussa tassa vacanatthavaraṃ suboddhuṃ vakkhāmi suttahitaṃ ettha susandhikappaṃ.
31. *Mukhamattadīpanī* of Vimalabuddhi, $6_{,4-9}$.
32. *Aṅguttara Nikāya* I, $58_{,37}$–$59_{,4}$. Also, *Nettipakaraṇa*, $21_{,12-14}$.
33. *Moggallānapañcikā* of Moggallāna, $4_{,4-21}$:
aviññātasaddalakkhaṇo hi dhammavinayesu kusalo na hoti. tesu vākusalattā (*corr.* cākusalattā) yathādhammaṃ paṭipajjitum asakkonto paṭipattiṃ virādhetvā saṃsāradukkhass' eva bhāgī hoti. na ca saddhāpabbajitānaṃ kulaputtānaṃ patiṭṭhā bhavituṃ sakko ti. saddalakkhaṇaññū yeva hi atthānurūpaṃ vyañjanaṃ vyañjanānurūpaṃ atthaṃ sallakkhetvā dhammavinayesu kulaputte sikkhāpetuṃ parivāsādisu ca vinayakammesu tadanurūpaṃ kammavācaṃ katvā taṃ taṃ kammaṃ nittharituṃ sakko ti nāñño. ajānanto pana saddalakkhaṇam ayathāpaṭipajjamāno tividham pi saddhammaṃ antaradhāpeti. tathāhi so saddalakkhaṇam ajānanto tammūlikantā va pariyattiṃ nāseti. tāya ca nāsitāya pariyattimūlikā (paṭipatti) paṭipattimūliko ca paṭivedho nāsito va hoti. vuttaṃ h'etaṃ bhagavatā: "dve 'me bhikkhave dhammā saddhammassa sammosāya antaradhānāya saṃvattanti. katame dve? dunnikkhittañ ca padavyañjanaṃ attho ca dunnīto. dunnikkhittassa bhikkhave padavyañjanassa attho 'pi dunnayo hoti. ime kho bhikkhave dve dhammā saddhammassa sammosāya antaradhānāya saṃvattantī" ti. ayaṃ saddalakkhaṇassa ajānane doso.
34. See chapter three.
35. Ratnapāla, 1971, 144.
36. Many grammatical handbooks define their intended readership explicitly as young monks. See, for instance, the titles of the *Bālāvabodhana* of Kassapa and *Bālāvatāra* of Dhammakitti, as well as the opening comments in the *Rūpasiddhi* of Buddhappiya, 1, and the *Padasādhana* of Piyadassi, $2_{,1}$.
37. On the applicability of the term 'eschatology' in connection with traditional Buddhist theories of religious and cosmic decline, see Apple, 2010.
38. *Manorathapūraṇī* of Buddhaghosa I, $87_{,1}$–$93_{,26}$. See Clark, 2018; Endo, 2013, 123–42.
39. *Manorathapūraṇī* of Buddhaghosa I, $93_{,9-15}$ (= *Moggallānapañcikāṭīkā* of Saṅgharakkhita, $16_{,15-26}$):
yāva tiṭṭhanti suttantā vinayo yāva dippati
tāva dakkhinti ālokaṃ suriye abbh' uṭṭhite yathā.
suttantesu asantesu pammuṭṭhe vinayamhi ca
tamo bhavissati loke suriye attaṅgate yathā.
suttante rakkhite sante paṭipatti hoti rakkhitā
paṭipattiyaṃ ṭhito dhīro yogakkhemā na dhaṃsati.
40. *Moggallānapañcikāṭīkā* of Saṅgharakkhita, $16_{,5-6}$ (= *Kavidappaṇanīti* v. 143):
yo niruttiṃ na sikkheyya sikkhanto piṭakattayaṃ
pade pade vikaṅkheyya vane andhagajo yathā.

41. Tambiah, 1990, 45.
42. I borrow the expression ‘information order’ from Schaffer, 2008.
43. *Padasādhana* of Piyadassi, $197_{,9}$; *Buddhippasādanī* of Śrī Rāhula, $132_{,14}$.
44. Gunawardana, 1979, 9–10.
45. *Sāratthappakāsinī* of Buddhaghosa I, $222_{,24\text{–}9}$.
46. Gornall, 2014a, 519–25.
47. *Epigraphia Indica* 22, nos. 34–5.
48. Gornall, 2014a.
49. Moggallāna offers a number of arguments in support of bringing many of the functions ascribed to the dative in the *Kaccāyana* tradition under the genitive. First, he observes simply that in Pali the dative and genitive cases are almost phonologically identical. Second, he states that Sanskrit grammars, such as Vimalamati’s *Bhāgavṛtti*, consider that all *upapada* cases – that is, the use of a case to syntactically connect two words rather than a word and an action – are to be regarded as exceptions to the sixth case. As such, due to the phonological identity of the fourth and sixth cases in Pali all *upapada* conditions traditionally assigned to the fourth can seamlessly be moved to the sixth. Lastly, he argues that many of the *kāraka* conditions traditionally assigned to the dative are, in fact, *upapada* conditions and can, therefore, for the same reason, be subsumed within the sixth case. See *Moggallānapañcikā* of Moggallāna on 2.27, $56_{,27}$–$57_{,4}$.
50. See Franke, 1902; 1902–3a; 1902–3b. More recently, Deokar, 2008; 2017; Dimitrov, 2016, 599–706; Gornall, 2013, 68–136.
51. Oberlies, 1989, 11–14.
52. Oberlies, 1989, 14; Vergiani, 2011.
53. Dimitrov, 2016, 599–706; Deokar, 2017.
54. See Dimitrov, 2010, 31–8.
55. See chapter two.
56. Dimitrov, 2010, 31–47.
57. On Śrī Rāhula’s works, see Godakumbura, 1955, 152–4; 191–5; 316–17.
58. *Buddhippasādanī* of Śrī Rāhula, $6_{,3\text{–}14}$.
59. On Jinendrabuddhi, see most recently Wielińska-Soltwedel, 2006, 9–11. Far less is known about Trilocanadāsa. A citation of the work in Niścalakara’s *Ratnaprabhā* seems to point to a Bengali origin and eleventh-century floruit. See Bhattacharyya, 1947, 142–3. There is an admittedly unproven assumption that he is identical with a commentator of the same name on the *Amarakośa*. See Dasgupta, 1935. Śrī Rāhula’s observations on Moggallāna’s diverse source material are supported by Saṅgharakkhita, Moggallāna’s earliest commentator, who names and quotes a number of these works when analysing Moggallāna’s discussions.
60. Śrī Dharmārāma, ed. 1896, xix–xxi.
61. In compiling this table, I have relied on the following sources: Bechert, 1987; Bhattacharyya, 1947; Bronner, 2012; Cardona, 1974; Dimitrov, 2016; Scharfe, 1977; Sternbach, 1978; 1980; Vogel, 1979; Wielińska-Soltwedel, 2006; Zachariae, 1897.
62. The rediscovery of Śrī Rāhula’s works supported a revival in monastic education in the nineteenth century. See Blackburn, 2010, 63.
63. On Puruṣottamadeva, see Wielińska-Soltwedel, 2006, 38–42.
64. *Moggallānavutti* of Moggallāna on 4.80 *daṇḍāditvikaī vā*, $237_{,4}$.
65. *Moggallānapañcikāpradīpaya* of Śrī Rāhula, $137_{,25}$–$138_{,6}$. Śrī Rāhula is attentive to local variations in the interpretation of the Pali canon too, quoting Sinhala commentaries as well as lost Tamil exegetical works. With respect to the word *deṇḍimā* ‘drum’ in the *dvandva* or copulative compound *saṅkhadeṇḍimam* ‘conch and drum’, for instance, he notes that the Sinhala glossary on the *Ummagga Jātaka* defines *deṇḍimā* as a ‘lap drum’ (Sin. *ikiḷi-bera*) whereas the Tamil glossary, which is no longer extant, defines it as a ‘kettle drum’ (Tam. *paṭaha*). See *Moggallānapañcikāpradīpaya* of Śrī Rāhula, $114_{,28\text{–}9}$; also $115_{,26}$, giving a second quote of a Tamil glossary.
66. On increased monastic mobility as a result of changing trade conditions between 1000–1500, see Blackburn, 2015, esp. 239–47.
67. Frasch, 1998, 77.
68. See the incipit of the *Sāratthadīpanī* of Sāriputta I, translated in chapter five. See also the incipits of *Vinayasaṅgaha* of Sāriputta, *Vimativinodanī* of Kassapa, *Mohavicchedanī* of Kassapa, *Rasavāhinī* of Vedeha, *Thūpavaṃsa* of Vācissara, and the colophon of the *Vinayatthamañjūsā* of Buddhanāga.
69. *Moggallānavutti* of Moggallāna, $380_{,8\text{–}19}$.
70. *Moggallānapañcikāṭīkā* of Saṅgharakkhita, $9_{,1\text{–}4}$, on *Moggallānapañcikā* of Moggallāna, $1_{,22}$.
71. *Paribhāṣenduśekhara* of Nāgojī Bhaṭṭa I, no. 122. But see the caution of Cardona, 1969, 41, n. 91.
72. On the *sūtra* as a genre of ‘Brahmanical technical writing’, see Bronkhorst, 2010.

73. Scharfe, 1977, 162–3; also, Ruiz-Falqués, 2017b.
74. Technically in each of these *suttas* the word *nāmasmā* 'after a nominal stem' should be introduced from rule 2.1. To simplify matters and to aid comparison I have left it out here. See Gornall, 2013, 101–10.
75. *Moggallānavutti* of Moggallāna, $62_{,2}$; *Moggallānapañcikā* of Moggallāna, $62_{,21-9}$.
76. The *Kaccāyanavyākaraṇa* did attempt it to some extent but with limited success. As Émile Senart wrote almost a century-and-a-half ago with respect to the grammar: 'Nous avons visiblement affaire à une collection d'observations grammaticales bien plus qu'à une grammaire méthodique, où chaque mot serait pesé et les limites naturelles de chaque règle seraient nettement définies.' See Senart, 1871, 94. For counterarguments to some of Senart's observations, see Ruiz-Falqués, 2017a.
77. *Moggallānapañcikā* of Moggallāna, $5_{,24-7}$: idaṃ vacanam anatthakaṃ vā siyā yathā kiñci ummattakādivākyaṃ sātthakaṃ vā yathā "manopubbaṅgamā dhammā" ti ādi vākyaṃ. na tāva anatthakaṃ, vuttiyaṃ vuttena atthena sātthakattā. vakkhamānattham ev' idaṃ suttaṃ.
78. The *Kāśikāvṛtti* quotes from the *Harivaṃsa* 51.29 when discussing the equivalent rule in the *Aṣṭādhyāyī*, A.2.3.32: vinā vātaṃ vinā varṣaṃ vidyutprapatanaṃ vinā, vinā hastikṛtān doṣān kenemau pātitau drumau.
79. *Dīgha Nikāya* II, $237_{,31-2}$: n'amhi kenaci upasaṅkamitabbo aññatra ekena bhattābhihārena (*Moggallānavutti*, piṇḍapātanīhārakena).
80. Here, borrowing from Chin, 2008, 17.
81. Dimitrov, 2016, 599–622; Deokar, 2017.
82. Dimitrov, 2016, 565–96; 632–49.
83. See Kiparsky and Staal, 1969. There has been debate as to the actual semantic, syntactic and morphological 'levels' present in Pāṇini's grammar. See most recently, Scharf, 2009. On *Cāndra* and *Moggallāna*, see Gornall, 2014b.
84. See, for instance, Joshi and Roodbergen, eds. and trans. 1975, xvi. It is important to note that the *Cāndra* system – and thus also the *Moggallāna* system – does not formally map semantic characterizations onto abstract syntactic categories by means of operational rules and rather informally establishes the connection as part of social convention (Sk. *vivakṣā*, P. *vivakkhā*), often indicated in the paraphrase to its *sūtras*. *Cāndra* and *Moggallāna* are thus less complicated than the *Aṣṭādhyāyī* and, to some extent, also the *Kaccāyanavyākaraṇa*, which does try and maintain similar operational 'levels' to Pāṇini and its model grammar, the *Kātantravyākaraṇa*. Both the *Cāndra* and *Moggallāna* traditions still deal with these conceptual differences, however, in their discussions of rules and the *Moggallāna*, in particular, handles these analytical distinctions with greater sophistication than the *Kaccāyana*, despite lacking the equivalent operational rules. Since the technicalities here fall outside the aims of this chapter, I have consciously chosen to present a simplified account for readers of this book. For more detail, see Gornall, 2014b.
85. It is actually more complicated than this. Both Sanskrit and Pali grammarians state that the sense of agent or object is conveyed by the verbal ending. The word in the first case tells us who or what the agent or object is but the first case does not denote agency or objectivity itself. This allows for grammarians to explain instances where the identity of the agent is left unexpressed in a sentence. One can say *sa pacati* 'he cooks' or simply *pacati* 'he cooks', for instance, without a change in meaning. See Cardona, 1974, 246–9.
86. Adapted from Kahrs, 1992, 10–14; 1998, 50–4.
87. *Dhammapada* 41, trans. Khantipālo, trans. 1980, 26.
88. *Moggallānavutti* of Moggallāna on 2.2, $38_{,2-3}$ also cited in Gornall, 2014b, 103.
89. *Dhammapadaṭṭhakathā* I on v. 41, $320_{,17-19}$.
90. *Rūpasiddhi* of Buddhappiya, $439_{,4}$ (after *sūtra* 281 = *Kaccāyanavyākaraṇa* 235).
91. *Rūpasiddhi* of Buddhappiya, $531_{,5}$ (*sūtra* 287, B^{e}290 = *Kaccāyanavyākaraṇa* 309).
92. Moggallāna explicitly acknowledges that his analysis is based on *Aṣṭādhyāyī* 1.4.46 *adhiśīṅsthāsāṃ karma*. See *Moggallānapañcikā* of Moggallāna on 2.2, $40_{,24-6}$.
93. See *Twelfth Night, or What You Will*, Act 3, Scene 3.
94. Jespersen, 1965, 238. On 'locative objects' and other similar examples, see Quirk *et al.*, 1985, 749.
95. See, for instance, *Moggallānapañcikā* of Moggallāna on 5.44, $280_{,19}$– $281_{,10}$ = *Cāndravyākaraṇapañjikā* of Ratnamati on C.1.3.7, ed. and compared in Dimitrov, 2016, 632–3. See also *Moggallānapañcikā* of Moggallāna on 2.1, $36_{,21}$–$37_{,16}$ = *Nyāsa* of Jinendrabuddhi on A.1.4.21, $275_{,5-21}$.
96. See, in particular, *Sambandhacintā* of Saṅgharakkhita, v. 4.
97. *Moggallānavutti* of Moggallāna on 2.34, $71_{,11}$. The example is actually 'he sits on the mat' (*kaṭe nisīdati*). I have added the name 'Devadatta' for the purpose of clarity.
98. See, for instance, Cardona, 1974, 246–51.

99. *Moggallānavutti* of Moggallāna on 2.34, 71,$_{9-10}$: kriyādhārabhūtakattukammānaṃ dhāraṇena yo kriyāyādhāro tasmiṃ kārake nāmasmā sattamī hoti. Compare also *Rūpasiddhi* of Buddhappiya, 633,$_{1-3}$ (*sūtra* 309, B^{e}320 = *Kaccāyanavyākaraṇa* 280): kattukammasamavetānaṃ nisajjapacanādikriyānaṃ patiṭṭhānaṭṭhena yo ādhāro, taṃ kārakaṃ okāsasaññaṃ hoti.
100. *Sidat Saṅgarā* of Vedeha I.2, 16–19.
101. On the earlier (early twelfth century?) Burmese work, Dhammasenāpati's *Kārikā*, see Ruiz-Falqués, 2017b, 65–87. Dragomir Dimitrov and Mahesh A. Deokar are currently editing this work and have discovered that it is largely a translation of Ratnamati/Ratnaśrījñāna's *Śabdārthacintā*. There is no evidence that this work was known in Sri Lanka during the reform era, however.
102. *Sambandhacintā* of Saṅgharakkhita, 3–18. On *śabdapravṛttinimitta*, see Aussant, 2009, 55–68.
103. *Moggallānapañcikā* of Moggallāna on 5.44, 280,$_{19}$–281,$_{10}$. See also *Sambandhacintā* of Saṅgharakkhita, 45,$_{1-4}$; 46,$_{1-3}$; *Moggallānavutti* of Moggallāna on 2.2, 39,$_{1-3}$, where the examples used refer to various ways of saying 'lightning strikes' (*valāhakā vijjotate*).
104. *Sambandhacintāsannaya* of Gotama, 46,$_{25}$–47,$_{9}$.

5
Buddhist Scholasticism: Sumaṅgala's Commentaries

The systematic approach to scriptural language found in reform-era grammatical texts was further developed in the large number of commentaries on doctrinal handbooks produced during the period. These new commentaries, composed explicitly as part of a continuing process of monastic unification, demonstrated a panoptic control over the previous exegetical tradition and often attempted to reconcile the differing views found within these older works. This process was combined with a pervasive belief among exegetes that their new hermeneutic techniques allowed them to recover the 'essential' (*sāra*), even primordial, meaning of the works they were commenting on. The increasingly systematic structure of these commentaries was equally informed by the development of more formal educational curricula and hierarchies within the reformed monastic community and it is not unreasonable, in this regard, to speak of this development as the beginning of scholasticism in Sri Lanka.[1]

There have been few attempts to describe how commentarial style developed in the Pali commentarial tradition throughout its long history, and for good reason. Even if we were to limit the scope of our analysis to the commentaries traditionally ascribed to Buddhaghosa, the sheer diversity of commentarial methods employed in these works makes it difficult to make any substantive generalization about an early commentarial style let alone how this style developed over time.[2] The difficulty is compounded by the fact that the Pali Buddhist tradition itself provides little in the way of an emic framework through which we can begin to understand the complex relationship between commentary, exegetical style and genre, for instance. Scholar monks of the reform era tend to define the three most common words for 'commentary', namely, *aṭṭhakathā*, *ṭīkā* and *saṃvaṇṇanā* (also *vaṇṇanā*), in almost identical terms, often simply as that by which meaning (*attha*) is related ***kathīyati*** <*aṭṭha****kathā***), explained (***ṭikīyati*** <***ṭīk****ā*) or communicated (***saṃvaṇṇīyati***

<***saṃvaṇṇanā***), despite the fact that in practice the term *aṭṭhakathā* is generally reserved for commentaries on canonical literature, *ṭīkā* often refers to a commentary on the *aṭṭhakathā*s, that is, a subcommentary, and *saṃvaṇṇanā*, while frequently used synonymously with *aṭṭhakathā* or *ṭīkā*, can refer to a more elaborate and discursive commentary.[3] Nevertheless, much reform-era commentarial writing, particularly on handbooks, can be distinguished by its more economical and systematic construction, which was likely the result of the adaptation of Sanskritic commentarial methods.[4]

Reform-era commentators on handbooks not only adopted new forms of exegesis but also used their powers of synthesis to innovate doctrinally. The ability of commentators to reshape doctrine has often been overlooked largely because the authors themselves were very conscious to present their work as a continuation or a recovery of tradition rather than something new. The emphasis on preservation rather than innovation within the Pali tradition has on occasion led to the open frustration of intellectual historians and philologists. Erich Frauwallner once remarked about this conservative tendency in the Abhidhamma tradition, specifically, that:

> This degeneration was probably at its worst in the Pali school, which confined itself exclusively to the transmitted doctrinal material and never really developed any original thought of its own. The compulsion always to say the same things while expressing them in a different form helped to promote these methodological excesses and aberrations.[5]

There is no doubt that commentators were generally conservative in that they respected tradition and were ever fearful of being viewed as schismatics. At the same time, if we move beyond their conservative rhetoric, we can begin to see these assertions for what they are: claims for authority that often mask the hidden politics and struggle over the development of doctrine. This is no more apparent than in reform-era literature where the task of adjudicating between the disparate views of the monastic factions that survived the reforms of 1165 led to subtle but significant shifts in doctrine. In this chapter we will continue to explore, in this regard, how scholar-monks began to think differently about Pali as a language and focus, in particular, on how Abhidhamma scholars entertained a conceptual understanding of language, one that acknowledged a separate reality for scripture beyond its exact wording.

The chapter focuses primarily on commentaries on Abhidhamma handbooks, that is, manuals of Buddhist metaphysics, composed by the scholar-monk Sumaṅgala. Sumaṅgala was one of the most prominent intellectuals in the aftermath of the 1165 reforms. He was a pupil of Sāriputta, the first grandmaster, and resided in the Nandi school (*pariveṇa*) at the Jetavana monastery in Poḷonnaruva.[6] Sumaṅgala composed two handbook commentaries: one on Buddhadatta's fifth- or sixth-century *Abhidhammāvatāra* ('Entrance into the Supreme doctrine') and another on Anuruddha's post-sixth-century *Abhidhammatthasaṅgaha* ('Compendium of the meaning of the Supreme doctrine').[7] The renewed systematic study of handbooks as part of the reforms meant that the composition of commentaries on these works became an educational and political necessity, in that clear, systematic explanations were needed to facilitate learning and spread effectively the doctrinal views of the monastic leadership throughout the Saṅgha. In doing so, these new commentaries were better able to innovate in their argumentative methods in contrast to reform-era commentaries on the Pali canon itself, which more closely followed older commentarial styles and techniques.

5.1. The Authority of Commentaries and Handbooks

Scholar-monks in the Theravada tradition have long viewed Pali commentaries on the canon as the pre-eminent, authoritative means of understanding the Buddha's discourses. There is an apparently unique tradition among the exegetes of the Mahāvihāra, for instance, that commentaries on the canon were composed and recited in the three monastic councils held in the centuries after the Buddha's death, with the third occurring under the aegis of the emperor Aśoka.[8] Writing in the preamble to his works, Buddhaghosa explains that these Pali commentaries were brought to Sri Lanka by Aśoka's son, Mahinda, and that they were then translated into Sinhala. Buddhaghosa claimed that, in using these Sinhala commentaries as sources for his new Pali commentaries, he was in effect restoring this exegetical tradition back to its original state.[9] In relating a similar story, the author of the *Samantapāsādikā* ('Completely pleasing') goes further and states that he follows a tradition based on the opinions of the 'sons' of the Buddha, that is, his direct disciples, who understood the Buddha's teachings in the same way (*tath' eva*) as the Buddha taught them.[10]

If there was any doubt, then, the author of the *Samantapāsādikā* makes it clear that the tradition's commentaries explain the Buddha's teachings without deviating from the views of those who first heard those discourses at the teacher's feet. The reform-era commentator Sāriputta takes up this statement in the *Samantapāsādikā* and explains moreover that the commentarial tradition can be thought of as beginning with the Buddha himself. He writes:

> There is not a word of scripture that the Bhagavan has not explained. He has given the meaning for all of them. One should understand, then, that the perfectly enlightened one taught even the method of explaining the

> meaning of the three baskets. For a commentary is simply the miscellaneous teaching that the Bhagavan established here and there.[11]

Sāriputta was not the first to refer to the commentaries as the Buddha's 'miscellaneous teachings' (*pakiṇṇakadesanā*). We find such a description of the commentaries in Dhammapāla's autocommentary on the *Nettipakaraṇa* ('Guide'), for instance. There, however, Sāriputta's predecessor raises the designation only to argue precisely that commentaries should *not* be attributed to the Buddha.

> Even if a commentary is the miscellaneous teaching of the Bhagavan established here and there, it is called 'the doctrine of teachers' (*ācariyavāda*) since the compilers of the Dhamma, who had recited the three baskets, that is, the Buddha's discourses, were the first to establish its wording in conformity with his explanations of its meaning.[12]

Sāriputta, then, subtly differs from Dhammapāla in that he never qualifies his statement in the same way by referring to the orthodox view that commentaries are secondary authorities, since their wording (*vācā*) was established by teachers, not the Buddha. He rather ignores their formal origin and instead states that the commentaries were initiated by the Buddha since it was he who established their meaning.

There was a slight shift in the way handbooks were thought about in the reform era too. Traditionally scholar-monks distinguished between commentaries (*aṭṭhakathā*) and subcommentaries (*ṭīkā*) on the one hand, and handbooks (*saṅgaha*) on the other, with the latter categorized separately as 'books' (*pakaraṇa*).[13] This ambiguous category of the 'book' can refer to any work that falls outside of the domain of the Pali canon and the commentaries that deal with its exegesis.[14] In the reform era, however, handbooks began to be discussed as if they were exegetical works. Sumaṅgala writes in his commentary on Buddhadatta's *Abhidhammāvatāra*, for instance, that the exegetical practice of summarizing (*samāsa*) refers to explaining (*katheti*) a work according to its meaning (*attha*) while condensing its wording (*sadda*).[15] Sumaṅgala treats the *Abhidhammāvatāra*, then, not simply as a primer but as an explanation of the meaning of the Abhidhamma that has less regard for the literal form of the text on which it is commenting.[16] The inherent flexibility in this exegetical approach is reflected in the way Sumaṅgala describes Buddhadatta's practical distillation of the Abhidhamma as taking the meaning of the text and turning it into a ball (*piṇḍana*).[17]

The late thirteenth-century *Pūjāvaliya* ('Garland of offerings') too reportedly refers to the *Abhidhammāvatāra* as an *aṭṭhakathā*, indicating that the work was now formally thought of under the category of commentary rather than 'book'.[18] Scriptural meaning, it seems, as in the grammatical tradition, could now be treated as a domain that was analytically separate from scriptural wording and as something that could be reworked and reproduced in new textual forms, with these works being treated as having the same authoritative status as commentaries.

The titles of reform-era commentaries, in this regard, stand out for their frequent reference to a posited 'essential meaning' (*sārattha*) as the object of their exegesis.[19] The earliest of these, Sāriputta's subcommentary on the Vinaya, is referred to as the *Sāratthadīpanī* or 'Illuminator of essential meaning'. The use of the expression 'essential meaning' is not unique to the reform period; Buddhaghosa's commentary on the *Saṃyutta Nikāya* is similarly named the *Sāratthappakāsinī* ('Illustrator of essential meaning'). What is unusual in the reform era is the pervasive use of the term to explicitly distinguish the object of exegesis from the commentarial practices of previous scholars. In the preamble to these works their authors often speak of this 'essential meaning' as a stable, almost fixed entity that they believed had been obscured by commentarial proliferation in the preceding centuries. Take the opening to Sāriputta's *Sāratthadīpanī*:

> I will compose an exposition of the concealed, essential meaning (*sārattha*) of the Vinaya's commentary that is easy to understand, is complete and unconfused. Though predecessors (*porāṇa*) gave an explanation of the hidden meaning, they did not convey that meaning in its entirety to monks in all cases. Among the many glossaries, some in some places are written in the Sinhala language, which, by nature, is difficult to understand. Someone also wrote a certain [glossary] mixed with other languages, even though it was undertaken in the Māgadha language. Precisely there, the burden of unessential (*asāra*) learning (*gantha*, lit. books) is often apparent, and confusion is created even when actually it (the Vinaya commentary) is easy to understand. How then can those who live in various regions understand the meaning [of the Vinaya commentary] in its entirety with this kind of incomplete [glossary]? I will compose, therefore, an unconfused, complete exegesis, without using another language and by extracting the essence (*sāra*) throughout.[20]

Sāriputta here contrasts his own exposition of the 'essential meaning' of the Vinaya commentary with older types of subcommentary. First, he criticizes his predecessors who focused on explaining the 'hidden meaning' but who did not manage to convey adequately the whole sense of the commentary. He then turns to existing Sinhala glossaries on the *Samantapāsādikā*, the so-called *gaṇṭhipada*s, and argues that the fact they are written in Sinhala makes them difficult to understand. (It is also possible to interpret his statement here as meaning that Sinhala is a form of expression (*nirutti*) through which essences (*sabhāva*), i.e. 'reality', are difficult to comprehend.)

Sāriputta then mentions a certain glossary in Pali that was 'mixed' with other languages. It has been argued that he may be referring here, in particular, to an older Vinaya subcommentary, the *Vajirabuddhiṭīkā* ('Diamond-mind subcommentary', c. tenth century).[21] The work cites a number of Sanskrit texts (the 'unessential books') in Pali translation, which, it seems, scholars like Sāriputta viewed as obstacles to the universal intelligibility of the commentary.[22] We get a sense from Sāriputta's preamble, then, that he believed that his Pali exegesis was in some way better able to recover a complete, clear and concise meaning that had been obscured by older exegetical methods, vernacular expositions and Sanskritic commentaries.

A related literary virtue that is praised highly in reform-era commentaries is brevity or summarizing (*samāsa*). Scholar-monks often connect the recovery of the essential meaning of the text they are discussing with the need to condense older, diverse exegetical material. There are obvious, real connections between the intellectual need for condensation and the reform process of creating a single monastic community based on a unified discipline and doctrine.[23] Vācissara, for instance, composed a Pali commentary on Buddhadatta's *Vinayavinicchaya* ('Exegesis on the Discipline') sometime between 1225 and 1250. In his opening preamble he heaps great praise on the leading scholar Sāriputta and the reforms that took place in the reign of Parākramabāhu I (1157–86) more than fifty years earlier and specifically connects the brevity of his work with the process of establishing a new, doctrinal orthodoxy. He writes that:

> I shall explain the essence of the meaning of that [text], … by avoiding the defect of the views of other monastic fraternities, having made concise the extremely extensive style (of the older commentaries), by elucidating meaning not made explicit and by not deviating from the order of the text, and also by extracting the essence from other books.[24]

This 'essential meaning' (*sārattha*) then was not only identified by its completeness, its apparent totality, but also by its utility, that is, as the most expedient form of representing the Pali scriptural tradition.

Finally, for reform-era commentators, we should add that the social implications of writing commentaries also went far beyond their instrumental purpose in organizing the doctrine and discipline of the Saṅgha. It should be unnecessary to mention were it not so rarely discussed that all literary activity was part of a universal system of karma or moral causation. Monks were fully aware that virtuous intentions behind preserving the Buddha's teachings had the capacity through the merit (*puñña*) accrued to transform their lives both as individuals and as a community.

Another disciple of Sāriputta, Buddhanāga, who composed a subcommentary on the *Kaṅkhāvitaraṇī* ('Overcoming doubts') between 1165 and 1186, writes in his colophon, for instance, that his commentary was produced with a mind of merit (*puññamana*) and lists a series of diverse transformations that he hoped would occur as a result of his meritorious intentions. He wished that the merit accrued would help all living beings find happiness and achieve heaven or nirvana, that this merit would enable his readers specifically to study his commentary with ease and also achieve nirvana, that there would always be rainfall at the right time, that kings would rule justly and that living beings would cultivate merit in performing virtuous acts, such as giving (*dāna*).[25]

Other meritorious results of literary activity may be anticipated far in the future. Sumaṅgala, for instance, writes touchingly at the end of his commentary on Anuruddha's *Abhidhammatthasaṅgaha* that he hoped, due to the scholarly efforts of his guru Sāriputta, to be reborn in the presence of the future Buddha, Metteyya, and to be reunited there again with his teacher who will explain Metteyya's teachings.[26]

5.2. The Grammatization of Commentaries

There are close associations in the reform era between elite scholar monks and monastic schools known as *pariveṇa*.[27] It is in the context of the more formal school system of the period that we can best understand the changes in commentarial style. Many reform-era commentaries in particular adopt increasingly systematic methods of exegesis based on formal lists (*mātikā*) of exegetical procedures.[28] These lists are occasionally mentioned in earlier Pali commentaries, though their programmatic use has a much longer history in the Buddhist Sanskrit tradition and it is no coincidence that many of the schemas quoted in Pali texts are likely adaptations of Sanskrit originals, from works such as Vasubandhu's *Vyākhyāyukti* ('Art of explanation').[29]

Such lists differ and are variously five-fold, six-fold and eight-fold in their classification, though they all follow a similar pattern that can be divided into three components. First, a commentator should establish the context (*sambandha*, *samuṭṭhāna*, *upogghāṭa*) of the root text, that is, the work he is commenting on. This is often accompanied by an analysis of the overall purpose (*payojana*) of the work. In the second component, a commentator should parse the words in the text (*pada*), discuss their meaning (*padattha*) and also provide a philological analysis of them (*padaviggaha*, °*vibhāga*). Sometimes, this analysis is preceded by a series of summaries either of the root text as a whole or its different sections (*padapiṇḍa*) and may also be appended with a discussion of how the sections of the root text are arranged (*anusandhi*). In the third and final component, a commentator should raise objections (*codanā*) with respect to the commentarial analysis conducted and then refute those objections (*parihāra*).[30]

Early commentators viewed these lists as procedures for commenting on a work or text as a whole, in accordance, we can speculate, with the prescriptions of Buddhist Sanskrit exegetical guides.[31] Reform-era commentators, however, often innovatively employ each of these techniques in a systematic fashion for single passages and even single words. The first evidence of such a systematic and repetitive use of these techniques occurs in Vimalabuddhi's *Mukhamattadīpanī* ('Straightforward illuminator'), a tenth-century commentary on the *Kaccāyana* grammar and its paraphrase (*vutti*). Later redactors describe Vimalabuddhi's commentarial method as six-fold, namely: (1) context (*sambandha*); (2) the words (*pada*); (3) the meaning of words (*padattha*); (4) the analysis of words (*padaviggaha*); (5) objections (*codanā*); and (6) their refutation (*parihāra*).[32] Vimalabuddhi, however, often also includes a comment explaining the sequence of rules (*anusandhi*), after the section on word analysis.

The application of these techniques in Vimalabuddhi's work represents a great innovation in Buddhist intellectual history since he uses what is essentially a framework for commenting on Buddhist scripture as a whole in order to analyse grammatical aphorisms (*sūtra*s). This means that for each and every rule in the *Kaccāyanavyākaraṇa*, Vimalabuddhi establishes the rule's context, its words, the meaning of the words, an analysis of the words, objections and their refutation. He often frames his exegesis, in particular, at the beginning of his work, within a scholastic context and refers to the students (*sissa*) to whom his commentary was addressed. There may be some parallels between this excessive 'hypercommentary' and similar developments in the Sanskrit tradition, though any tentative comparison is undermined by the lack of a systematic study of the development of commentarial style in Sanskrit.[33] Take, for example, his analysis of the grammatical rule *sarā sare lopaṃ* (*Kaccāyana* 12, 'vowels before a vowel are to be elided'), which governs the elision of a vowel when two vowels come into contact (i.e. *loka* + *aggo* → *lokaggo*):

1. context	**(1) sarā sare lopaṃ** ‘vowels before a vowel are to be elided’: for what purpose does he (Kaccāyana) say this? [He says this] for the purpose of eliding the preceding vowel, when there is a conjunction [of vowels].
2. words	**(2) sarā**: this is one word; **sare**: this is one; **lopaṃ**: this is one; this rule has three words.
3. meaning	**(3)** The meaning [of the rule] is that ‘vowels undergo elision before a vowel’.
4. analysis[34]	**(4)** And in this [rule], **sarā** is defined as the agent, **sāre** is the cause, and **lopaṃ** is the grammatical operation. ‘They shine’ (*sara*nti), therefore they are **sarā**. Elision (*lutti*) is **lopo**.
5. sequence	**(5)** He states this [rule] here because *sandhi* rules for vowels are to be given first, since it is vowels that are appointed first [in the syllabary].
6. objection	**(6)** And in this [rule], he mentions **sare** ‘before a vowel’ and does not say *saresu* ‘before vowels’ for the purpose of indicating that [the operation should occur] only one [vowel] at a time. Yet if this is the case, why does [the author] say **sarā** ‘vowels’ and not *saro* ‘vowel’?
7. reply	**(7)** [He says **sarā**] for the purpose of indicating that the elision occurs even for one, two or four vowels [simultaneously]. For instance, in [the rule] *sakhāto gass’e vā* (*Kaccāyana* 113, ‘Optionally, *a*, *ā*, *i*, *ī*, and *e* replace *ga* [voc. sg.] after the word *sakhā* “friend”’), *e* has been separated into *a*, *ā*, *i*, *ī*, and *e* and is understood to be a copulative (*dvanda*) compound, in keeping with the governing rule *nāmānaṃ samāso yuttattho* (*Kaccāyana* 318, ‘A compound of words has a unified sense’) and *nāmānaṃ samuccayo dvando* (*Kaccāyana* 331, ‘An aggregation of words is a *dvanda* compound’); and [as a *dvanda*] there is no need to use the word *ca* since ‘one does not use [speech forms] whose object (*ṭṭhāna*) has already been denoted’. One should understand, then, that in the case of *a*, *ā*, *i*, *ī*, and *e*, there is the elision of the other vowels due to the following *e* sound.[35]

Similar forms of punctilious exegesis begin to emerge in subsequent Sinhala commentaries or *sannaya* on grammars too.[36] The Sinhala commentary on Buddhappiya’s *Rūpasiddhi* (‘Construction of [word] forms’), for instance, one of the earliest known Sinhala *sannaya*s, incorporates many of the developed exegetical features employed in the *Mukhamattadīpanī*.[37] We also begin to find in the reform era equivalent forms of commentary outside of the grammatical sphere too as represented by works such as Sāriputta’s Sinhala commentary on the *Abhidhammatthasaṅgaha*.

This ‘grammatization’ of Sinhala commentaries, to borrow a term from Sylvain Auroux, was accompanied by a parallel development in many reform-era Pali handbook commentaries, not least because a number of these Pali works were translated from Sinhala antecedents.[38] This is the case with Sumaṅgala's *Abhidhammatthasaṅgaha* commentary, which is largely a Pali rendering of Sāriputta's Sinhala commentary on the same work. Sumaṅgala never explicitly states that his work is a translation, though he hints at the ease at which he composed his exposition in the final verse of his colophon, stating, to quote R.P. Wijeratne and Rupert Gethin's rendering, that 'this commentary has been completed in twenty-four days, may beings' good-aspirations be as quickly realised'.[39]

The works of Sāriputta and Sumaṅgala will often first provide the reason (*sambandha*) Anuruddha introduces a particular statement or verse. Sāriputta then always moves on to provide a word-by-word analysis of the meaning of the passage under discussion, though Sumaṅgala often omits this in his translation. A separate section in which the commentators provide a more detailed grammatical or etymological analysis of certain words then usually follows. The order and content of these two sections reflects a division between 'word meaning' (*padattha*) and 'word analysis' (*padaviggaha*) similar to the one Vimalabuddhi employs in his *Mukhamattadīpanī*. Likewise, after conducting an analysis of key words, they usually introduce possible objections followed by answers to these objections. Sāriputta and his student translator, Sumaṅgala, then, follow similarly formal exegetical procedures to those employed by Vimalabuddhi and continue to apply these principles sequentially on a narrow scope, whether on single words, sentences or verses.

Take, for example, Sāriputta and Sumaṅgala's discussion of the first sentence of *Abhidhammatthasaṅgaha* 2.8 in which compassion (*karuṇā*) and sympathetic joy (*muditā*) are defined as 'the illimitables' (*appamaññā*):

> **Compassion and sympathetic joy, furthermore, are called 'the illimitables'.** Along with the faculty of wisdom these twenty-five mentalities are all together termed 'the beautifuls'.[40]

Sāriputta begins his Sinhala commentary with an analysis of the meaning of the words in the first sentence, though Sumaṅgala does not include this section in his translation:

1. meaning	(1) **compassion and sympathetic joy, furthermore: compassion** is that which removes the suffering of living beings who are suffering; **sympathetic joy** is having sympathetic joy with respect to the happiness of living beings who are happy; both these two **furthermore**; **called 'the illimitables'**: they are named 'illimitable' since they encompass illimitable living beings.[41]

The rest of the commentary in both Sāriputta and Sumaṅgala's works continues as follows, consisting of exegesis dedicated to word analysis, an objection and finally a reply.[42]

2. analysis	**(2) Compassion** (*karuṇā*) is that which makes (*karoti*), produces, upset in the hearts of good people in response to the suffering of others; or it is that which scatters (*kirati*), disperses, others' suffering; or it is that which kills (*kiṇāti*), harms, it; or it is that which is scattered (*kiriyati*), spread, among those who suffer. It is the characteristic of the state of desiring to remove the suffering of others, for whether one removes others' suffering or not by means of it (i.e. the desire), it certainly exists in that manner. **Sympathetic joy** is that by means of which they rejoice. It is characterized by sympathetic joy in the success of others. As they have measureless beings as their cognitive object they are **illimitables**.
3. objection	**(3)** But will he (i.e. Anuruddha) not state that there are 'four illimitables' (§9.9)? So why are only two mentioned here?
4. reply	**(4)** Because friendliness (*mettā*) and equanimity (*upekkhā*) are taken with lack of hatred and balance [respectively]. For lack of hatred that occurs as the wish for beings' welfare is called friendliness, and balance that occurs as the allaying of disliking or liking them is called equanimity. Therefore, predecessors (i.e. Buddhadatta) have said: Since friendliness is taken with not harming, and equanimity with balance, so neither are included [here]. (*Abhidhammāvatāra*, v. 70)

These more systematic forms of commentary provided a means by which the tradition could better control the interpretation of texts. The balance here, for instance, between internal word analysis and the externalized, dialogic structure of the objection and its rebuttal helps establish the endo- and exo-consistency of philosophical terminology.[43] The commentators use grammar and semantic analysis (Sk. *nirvacana*) to capture the internal particularity or *visesa*, as Dhammapāla calls it, of philosophical terms according to the weave of their linguistic fabric.[44] These terms are then placed in relation to other philosophical terms or other instances where the same term is used in a different philosophical framework. The commentators raise, for instance, the issue of the standard four-fold list of illimitables known as the *brahmavihāras* or 'divine abidings', which include friendliness (*mettā*) and equanimity (*upekkhā*), discussed by Anuruddha in his chapter on meditative practice (*kammaṭṭhāna*). They ask why Anuruddha in his handbook does not include these other two states in his list of illimitables in his chapter on mentalities (*cetasika*). They respond that the mentalities of friendliness and equanimity are in fact mentioned elsewhere in the chapter under the designations of lack of hatred (*adosa*) and balance (*tatramajjhattatā*) and quote the *Abhidhammāvatāra* in support.[45] This objection and its rebuttal, then, allows the author to draw out connections beyond the root text to establish a coherent matrix of meaning within Pali Buddhist thought as a whole.

While there is less uniformity in the systematic application of these techniques among other reform-era Pali commentaries on handbooks, there is certainly a general trend towards such structured forms of exegesis. Sumaṅgala's other commentary on the *Abhidhammāvatāra*, which may not be a translation from a Sinhala commentary, very often exhibits similar strategies in its analysis to his commentary on the *Abhidhammatthasaṅgaha*. He often begins his analysis by providing the context (*sambandha*) for individual verses in the *Abhidhammāvatāra*. In doing so, he sometimes refers to an objection that he thinks was 'hidden' (*antolīna*) in Buddhadatta's mind (*manasi*) or heart (*hadaye*) at the time of composition.[46] These forays in the psychology of authorial intention serve to create parallel structures in the root text and the commentary that enable a closer reading of the two works together, with the latter extending and elaborating on the answers of the former. He then follows a standard order of exegesis and glosses the meaning of words, gives a detailed grammatical and semantic analysis of them and frequently raises a number of possible objections and responses, often as part of what Deven Patel aptly calls a 'staged curiosity', that is, a strategic mechanism through which he can address rudimentary questions in the systematization of Buddhist terminology.[47]

5.3. Language, Concepts and Reality

In employing new exegetical techniques to recover the essence (*sāra*) of their tradition, reform-era scholar-monks emphasized their continuity with the past authorities of the Mahāvihāra. This rhetoric hides a more complex reality and the factions who came together after 1165 held views on doctrinal matters that diverged both from each other and from the early commentators. In an effort to find unity within the new Mahāvihāra, the commentaries composed in the reform era often mediate between these different doctrinal positions.[48] Both Sumaṅgala and Sāriputta in their works, for instance, display skill in weaving conflicting doctrinal strands into a coherent whole. The second half of this chapter, in this regard, offers a new hypothesis that reform-era monks entertained views on the ontological nature of their scriptural language different from those held in the past. Specifically, they increasingly thought of their scriptural language as a mental object rather than as speech.

Before addressing this important shift in intellectual orientation directly, however, it is necessary to frame it within the much longer history of the development of Abhidhamma thought concerning: (1) the ontological status of concepts; and (2) the status of language as a concept.[49] The canonical Abhidhamma as represented by works such as the *Dhammasaṅgaṇi* ('Enumeration of dhammas') and the *Vibhaṅga* ('Analysis') provides a systematic arrangement of the ultimate elements of physical and mental reality (*dhammas*) and a framework for understanding their causal relationship.[50] The eighty-two types of dhamma in the Pali tradition are divided into two groups. Eighty-one are classified as 'conditioned' (*saṅkhata*), that is, they arise, persist and cease due to causes, while only one nirvana is 'unconditioned' (*asaṅkhata*) and sits outside of causality. Concepts (*paññatti*) or ideas, such as 'I' or 'my', have no place in this system since they were not thought to ultimately exist.

One short work in the Abhidhamma basket, however, the *Puggalapaññatti* ('Designation of human types'), does provide a detailed account of the various ways personhood (*puggala*) can be conceptualized and its early commentary more fully elaborates upon the nature of concepts in the Abhidhamma.[51] There the commentator semantically analyses the word *paññatti* and establishes that it refers both to the concepts that can be designated (*paññāpetabba*) by words as well as to the words themselves that designate (*paññāpana*) concepts. In his opening the commentator then proceeds to provide a detailed taxonomy of different types of designations based on whether they signify unreal concepts or real dhammas. Designations (*paññatti*), such as 'form' (*rūpa*), that denote real dhammas, for instance, are said to be 'designations of what is real' (*vijjamāna-paññatti*) and those that denote unreal concepts (*paññatti*), such as 'I', are 'designations of what does is not real' (*avijjamāna-paññatti*).[52]

The formal ontological status of concepts develops in the Abhidhamma handbooks of the fifth- or sixth-century scholar-monk Buddhadatta. Buddhadatta introduces into his *Abhidhammāvatāra* a chapter on concepts or *paññatti*s that follows his analysis of conditioned and unconditioned dhammas. Opening this chapter, he asks, 'is only this much knowable, or is there

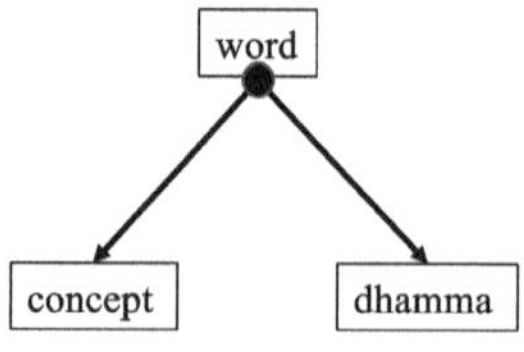

Figure 5.1 Words designate unreal concepts or real dhammas

something else that exists (*atthi*)?' He replies that, 'a concept indeed exists'.[53] Implicit in his question, it seems, is the suggestion that concepts are existing entities that are neither conditioned nor unconditioned. Buddhadatta argues, for instance, that while concepts derive from real dhammas they are different in that they are not subject to 'rise and fall' (*uppāda-vaya*).[54] Later scholars explain that as timeless phenomena concepts are not 'conditioned' like other real entities nor are they 'unconditioned' like nirvana since they still have dhammas as their cause.[55] To put it in simpler terms, we can say, for instance, that while the materiality (*rūpa*) of a chair is conditioned and subject to change, the concept of chair, though dependent on that materiality, may independently persist and thus have a separate, quasi-real status.

Buddhadatta attempts to ground his views on the ontological status of concepts as a third category of existent, one neither conditioned nor unconditioned, in scripture by interpreting a passage from the *Dhammasaṅgaṇi* in a way that would include concepts in its classification of existing things. The passage in question takes three terms used to denote language, namely *adhivacana* 'articulation', *nirutti* 'expression' and *paññatti* 'designation', and describes them identically using a series of equivalent linguistic terms. Here, for instance, is the treatment of *paññatti*:[56]

> 1308. What dhammas are *paññatti*? That label (*saṅkhā*), category (*samaññā*), designation (*paññatti*), discourse (*vohāra*), name (*nāma*), appellation (*nāmakamma*), naming (*nāmadheyya*), expression (*nirutti*), phrasing (*vyañjana*), utterance (*abhilāpa*) of this or that dhamma; These dhammas are *paññatti*. All dhammas have a way of designation.[57]

Separated from its traditional exegesis this passage appears to simply distinguish between dhammas and the spoken words that denote them, which are also viewed as dhammas, perhaps because they are by nature sounds (*sadda*).[58] And yet the fourth or fifth-century *Dhammasaṅgaṇi* commentator provides a semantic analysis of each of the terms in this list in a way that left room for ambiguity. He defines the first four terms here, beginning with *saṅkhā* 'label', for instance, as 'words' in the sense that they are what is stated (e.g. *saṅkhāyati*). He remarks with respect to *saṅkhā*:

> **saṅkhā** 'a label' is what is stated (*saṅkhāyati*), [i.e.] it means 'what is spoken'. 'What' is spoken? 'I', 'my', 'other', 'for another', 'living being', 'being', 'person', 'individual', 'man', 'youth', 'Tissa', 'Datta', 'bed', 'seat', 'mat', 'pillow', 'monastery', 'chamber', 'door' and 'window'. Thus, [the meaning] is spoken through many forms (*ākāra*).[59]

It is possible, however, as later subcommentators cautioned, to interpret the commentary here as defining the first four terms in the list, beginning with *saṅkhā*, as referring to the actual *concept* 'I' denoted by a word rather than the word 'I' that is uttered.[60] This would mean that the *Dhammasaṅgaṇi* in this passage rather categorizes as existent entities not only physical words but also concepts too. This is how Buddhadatta understood the passage:[61]

> Here, **saṅkhā** 'a label' is what is stated (*saṅkhāyati*), [i.e.] it means 'what is spoken'. 'What' is it that is spoken? 'I', 'my', 'other', 'for another', 'bed' and 'seat'. What is spoken by many forms (*ākāra*) is **saṅkhā**. What is categorized is **samaññā**. What is designated is **paññatti**. What is uttered is **vohāra**. 'What' is it that is uttered? 'I', 'my', 'other', 'for another', 'bed' and 'seat'. Thus, first they are referred to as **paññatti** since they are what is to be designated (*paññāpetabba*). For 'I', which relies on dhammas, form (*rūpa*) and the like, [i.e.] depends on them and takes them as a cause, is different from them (*na evaṃvidhā*), since those dhammas, form and the like, arise (*uppāda*) and cease (*vaya*). The meaning is that it is this [concept] I, formed entirely by social convention, which is spoken of and designated as 'I', that is the **paññatti** ('what is designated'). Then, to introduce a **paññatti** which designates (*paññāpana*), it (the *Dhammasaṅgaṇi*) states **nāma** and **nāmakamma**, etc. (i.e. the remaining terms in §§1306–1308). There, **nāma** is what designates this or that dhamma – 'this has such a name' – and therefore is referred to as a **paññatti** ('designation'). [The terms] **nāmakamma**, etc. are simply its synonyms. This is named **paññatti** since it designates (*paññāpana*).[62]

Buddhadatta thus argues that the ten terms for language listed in the *Dhammasaṅgaṇi* can be divided into two groups. The first four, beginning with *saṅkhā* 'label', refer to what is to be designated (*paññāpetabba*) – that is, existing concepts that are dependent on dhammas, but are free from rise and fall – and the remaining six, beginning with *nāma* 'name', refer to what designates (*paññāpana*) either dhammas or concepts. All terms are subsumed under the category of *paññatti* but are divided by its two possible meanings; either a concept or a designation. As the 'shadow of something real', Buddhadatta fits concepts as knowable entities within the *Dhammasaṅgaṇi*'s description of existence and, having done so, continues in his chapter to present a taxonomy of concepts similar to that found in the *Puggalapaññatti* commentary.[63]

We also find a second innovation in Buddhadatta's chapter on concepts, namely that he further differs from even the *Puggalapaññatti* commentary in that he defines *paññatti* in the sense of designation (*paññāpana*) and *paññatti* in the sense of what is to be designated (*paññāpetabba*) *both* as mental objects. That is, he explicitly treats designating *paññatti*s too as mental objects distinct from the sounds of words. He states, for instance, in admittedly technical language that:

> Either way (i.e. whether designating something real or not), furthermore, this [designating *paññatti*] is cognized by an impulse consciousness **at the mind-door**, which has grasped a previous convention immediately **after** the impulse (*javana*) at **the ear-door**. It is by means of this that the impulse consciousness at the mind-door, having grasped the previous convention, makes known [the meaning].[64]

Writing sometime after the sixth century, Anuruddha in his Abhidhamma manuals adopts a similar ontology of concepts and also cites the *Dhammasaṅgaṇi* to support the existence of these two types of concept, that is, designating and designated concepts, though employs new terminology to analytically separate them.[65] He clearly distinguishes, for instance, between designated concepts derived from dhammas, which he calls *upādāpaññatti* 'dependent concepts' or *atthapaññatti* 'meaning concepts', and the concepts that signify these conceptual referents as *nāmapaññatti* 'naming concepts'.[66] Importantly, both types of *paññatti*, the naming *paññatti* and meaning *paññatti*, are explicitly conceptual in nature, that is, they are mental objects. Anuruddha summarizes the processes of cognition and the role played by the naming concept, in particular, as follows:

> It is in conformity with this [naming concept] – which is the objective field of the mind-door that arises immediately after the occurrence of an ear-consciousness process in the wake of the sound of speech – that meanings are afterwards discerned. A concept such as this is to be understood as created by ordinary convention (*lokasaṅketa*).[67]

The handbook tradition's creative reading of the *Dhammasaṅgaṇi* was at odds with the doctrinal interpretations of the subcommentators on the Abhidhamma,

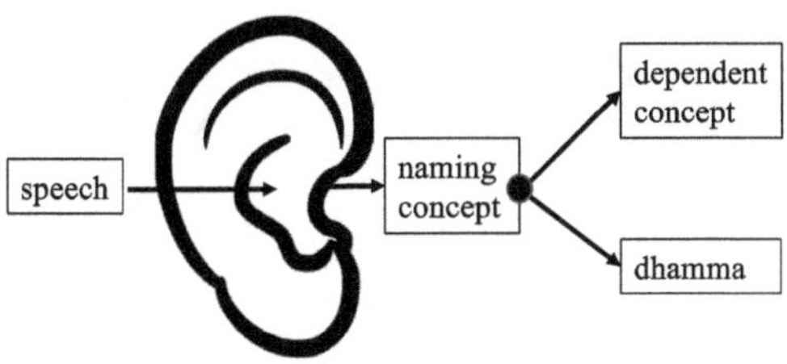

Figure 5.2 A simplified diagram of linguistic cognition in the handbooks

however, who simply viewed all these terms, *saṅkhā* 'label', etc., as referring to speech (*vacana*). A sixth-century scholar-monk Ānanda and his post-seventh-century successor Dhammapāla directly criticize this ontological classification of concepts and its perceived canonical justification in *Dhammasaṅgaṇi* §§1306–8.[68] Ānanda, for instance, writes:

> Teachers state here, however, that, 'the four words **saṅkhā, samaññā, paññatti** and **vohāra** are referred to as *paññatti* since they are what is to be designated. The other [words are referred to as *paññatti*] since they are what designates. And here the former is a dependent concept (*upādāpaññatti*), which lacks the function of rising and falling, and is established by ordinary convention. The latter is a naming concept (*nāmapaññatti*) – grasped by a stream of consciousness at the mind door that manifests immediately after a stream of consciousness at the ear door, having grasped a previous convention – through which the former concept (i.e. the dependent concept) and form (*rūpa*) etc. are made known.'[69]

Ānanda frames his criticism of this standpoint as a 'rejection of the existence (*atthitā*) of what is other than conditioned (*saṅkhata*) and unconditioned (*asaṅkhata*)' in an apparent challenge to the classification of concepts as a third category of existing entity.[70] Ānanda views designated concepts simply as perceptions (*saññā*) of what is unreal and, therefore, ultimately as conditioned (*saṅkhata*) mental objects. While this perception exists, the conceptualized object of cognition is not afforded a separate status as an existent entity too, as it is in the handbooks.[71] He also refutes his opponents' interpretation of *Dhammasaṅgaṇi* §§1306–8 for a number of reasons, most of which are philological.[72] He argues against the existence of naming concepts (*nāmapaññatti*), specifically, on more philosophical grounds and contends that if such a conceptualization of language is needed to establish a conventional association between a word and its meaning, then similarly to form an association between that concept and a word another concept would be needed, and so on, leading to infinite regress.[73] He concludes that *paññatti*, as a category encompassing all the linguistic terms introduced in *Dhammasaṅgaṇi* §§1306–8, should be understood simply as speech (*vacana*) since this conforms with what is said in the canon and its commentaries.[74]

It is a testament to the renewed attention to the Abhidhamma handbooks in the reform era that this disagreement about the ontological status of concepts and the existence, in particular, of naming concepts (*nāmapaññatti*) has gone unrecognized in Western scholarship. In his commentary on the *Abhidhammāvatāra*, Sumaṅgala develops Buddhadatta's *paññatti* theory

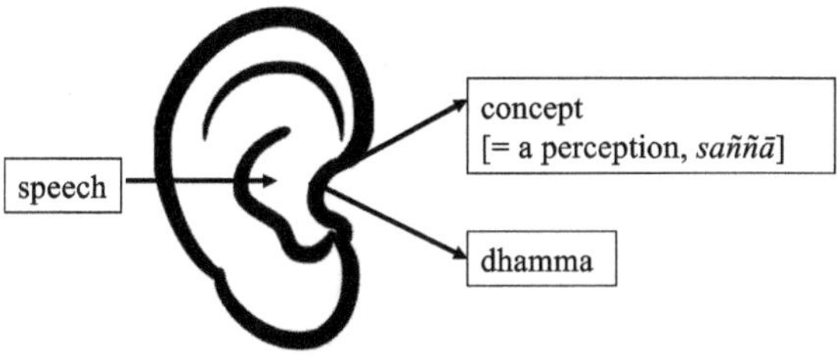

Figure 5.3 A simplified diagram of Ānanda's view of linguistic cognition

by bringing it into harmony with Anuruddha's manuals and also by subtly accommodating some of the criticisms of the subcommentators. In his analysis of Buddhadatta's chapter on *paññatti*, specifically, Sumaṅgala follows Buddhadatta's ontological classification of concepts, though he takes care to admit that this *paññatti* theory is based on an interpretation of the *Dhammasaṅgaṇi* that is only accepted among teachers (*ācariyānaṃ icchitattā*), with the implication being that these views, as Ānanda argues, cannot be supported by the commentaries.[75] Sumaṅgala throughout his analysis brings in aspects of Anuruddha's presentation of *paññatti* theory in order to establish coherence between the handbooks. He uses Anuruddha's terminology to gloss what Buddhadatta describes as *paññatti*s to be designated (*paññāpetabba*) and those that designate (*paññāpana*):

> Here, by **paññāpetabbato** [he means] a **paññatti** [in the sense of] 'what is designated' (*paññāpīyati*), [i.e.] 'what is made known by a means' (*pakārena ñāpiyati*). Thus, as it denotes the object of an action (*kammasādhana*) it is called the 'dependent concept' (*upādāpaññatti*), which becomes the meaning concept (*atthapaññatti*) (i.e. the referent of a designation). By **paññāpanato** [he means] a **paññatti** [in the sense of] 'what designates' (*paññāpeti*), [i.e.] 'what makes known by a means' (*pakārena ñāpeti*). Thus, as it denotes the agent of an action (*kattusādhana*), understand that it is a naming concept (*nāmapaññatti*), which becomes the signifier of it [i.e., of the meaning concept].[76]

Sumaṅgala further develops in his commentary on the precise cognitive stage in which the naming concept arises, breaking down the cognitive process into minute phases of so-called 'cognitive impulses' or *javana*s. He states, following Sāriputta's Sinhala commentary on the *Abhidhammatthasaṅgaha*, that when one hears the word 'pot' (*ghaṭo*), each of the sounds *gha* and *ṭo* are cognized over two 'courses of impulse' (*javanavāra*) each. These are gathered as a whole word (*saddasamudāya*) in another impulse moment, after which the corresponding 'naming concept' (*nāmapaññatti*) immediately arises in the next impulse moment.[77] Sumaṅgala uniquely states in his commentary on the *Abhidhammatthasaṅgaha* too that this 'naming concept' is in fact formed of a string of syllables (*akkharāvalībhūta*).[78] He presents the 'naming concept', then, simply as an immediate, conceptual copy of a word's sounds. We can speculate that in emphasizing the extremely close cognitive connection between a word and the naming concept Sumaṅgala was possibly attempting to reconcile those who believed that a designation (*paññatti*) was speech and those who thought that it was a concept, something ideal rather than physical.

5.4. Rethinking the Nature of Scripture

When reading extremely complex debates such as these it is hard to know exactly what was at stake for these scholar-monks. Why did it matter if concepts were treated as existents and if language was thought of primarily as such a conceptual entity rather than as sound? Clearly there were issues here about Abhidhamma ontology and fidelity to the Pali canon and its commentaries. The arguments of Ānanda were principally philological and they largely support the view of language as sound, in particular, on the basis that it conforms with what is said in scripture. Ānanda cites canonical statements, such as, '[the Buddha's] discourse (*vohāra*) penetrates the worldly ear', to prove that words such as *vohāra* refer to physical sounds rather than something conceptual. In his own commentary on Ānanda's discussion, however, Dhammapāla describes how those who understood *vohāra* 'discourse' to be a mental concept rather than a physical sound interpreted such canonical passages:

> **Discourse penetrates the worldly ear:** understand that in [expressions] such as this, as it is the sound that is heard, **discourse** etc., which are the cognitive objects (*visaya*) of that [sound], are spoken of figuratively as that which penetrates [the ear] and as that which is audible. Or rather, only sound is meant here in so far as it is concomitant (*sahacāritā*) with **discourse,** etc. For it is not possible to say that everywhere the *teaching* exists with a single form (*ekarasa*).[79] For instance, in some places it is said, *sukhā dukkhā* (pleasant and unpleasant) [or] *sukhā pi vedanā dukkhā* (also pleasant and unpleasant feelings); *dukkhā sukhā* (unpleasant and pleasant) [or] *dukkhā pi sukhā* (also unpleasant and pleasant [feelings]).[80] Thus (i.e. for this reason), also the two-fold concept (i.e. meaning and naming concept), as described, is spoken of in the commentary as the meaning of the [*Dhammasaṅgaṇi*] passage (§§1306–1308)

beginning 'articulation' (*adhivacana*). This is the exegesis of those who accept a particular knowable [entity] separate from what is conditioned and unconditioned.[81]

It seems that those who adhered to a conceptual understanding of language, interpreted certain statements in the canon explicitly referring to the Buddha's speech as figurative rather than literal. The second remark here concerning textual variation is also telling for it reveals an awareness among monks that the wording of their scriptures, possibly as found in manuscripts, was not consistent and indicates that, as a result, some sought uniformity rather in a conceptual understanding of language. It appears, then, that looming behind this debate was a wider concern among scholar-monks about what their scriptures actually were.

Sumaṅgala makes this connection explicit in his commentary on the *Abhidhammāvatāra* when explaining at length the term *sabhāvanirutti* or 'natural expression' that was used since Buddhaghosa to describe scriptural language.[82] In doing so Sumaṅgala introduces a debate on the nature of scriptural language first found in the commentary on another canonical Abhidhamma text, the *Vibhaṅga*, that is intimately related with the controversy about 'concepts' in the interpretation of the *Dhammasaṅgaṇi*:

> **Natural expression:** the unchanging expression. The unchanging expression is referred to as the language of Magadha, an unwavering discourse, which has a fixed relationship in all times in making known this or that meaning. For it has a fixed relationship [with meaning] in all times, whereas other languages change over time. The teachers, however, state that 'in fact (*atthato*), this [language] is a "naming concept" (*nāmapaññatti*)'. For they say: 'the expression, the language of Magadha, is in fact a naming figuration (*nāmasammuti*).'[83]

Sumaṅgala begins his analysis here by presenting a definition of scriptural language first found in the commentary on the *Vibhaṅga* on the religious attainment known as the 'analysis of scripture' (*niruttipaṭisambhidā*), where the commentator famously describes the language as an unchanging, magical form of expression naturally spoken throughout the cosmos by humans and gods.[84] Sumaṅgala then introduces a definition of the 'natural expression' that he ascribes to certain 'teachers'. These teachers, he writes, claim that the 'natural expression' is in reality a 'naming concept' (*nāmapaññatti*), that is to say, it is primarily conceptual in nature.[85] Sumaṅgala then quotes the first line of a verse from a Sanskrit Abhidharma manual that the late L.S. Cousins has found quoted in Parākramabāhu II's (1236–70) Sinhala commentary on the

Visuddhimagga ('Path of purification').[86] The Sanskrit original of this verse also contains reference to the opposing view of commentators like Ānanda and Dhammapāla that scriptural language is, in essence, the sound of a text:[87]

niruktir māgadhī bhāṣā sā cārthān nāmasaṃvṛtiḥ
keci dhvāna iti prāhur vijñaptyākārasaṃyutaḥ.

> The expression, the Māgadhī language, is in fact a naming figuration. Some proclaim that it is sound connected with a form of information.[88]

Sumaṅgala understood the expression 'naming figuration' (*nāmasaṃvṛti*) here as synonymous with his 'naming concept' (*nāmapaññatti*) as developed in the handbooks. The Sinhala commentary on the *Visuddhimagga* attributes this verse to a certain Jotipāla, who Cousins has suggested may be identical to an Indian Mahāvihāran monk mentioned in the *Cūḷavaṃsa* as defeating in debate a Vetullavāda or Mahayana opponent called Dāṭhāpabhuti.[89] If this narrative does refer to Jotipāla the commentator, we can date the scholar to the reign of Aggabodhi I (571–604) and thus to the early seventh century. This would place Jotipāla's *floruit* at the heart of an era of Pallava influence on the island, in which forms of Tantric and Mahayana doctrine were widespread.[90] It is perhaps not surprising, then, that a Mahāvihāran apologist like Jotipāla might make some concessions when debating opponents who adhered to definitions of scripture less literal than those of his own tradition.[91]

Sumaṅgala shows he was very much aware of the challenge to orthodoxy posed by conceptual views of scripture for he quickly follows his mention of this standpoint by contrasting it with the opinions of 'others', in this case, the more traditional view expressed by the *Vibhaṅga* commentator that scriptural language was in essence the precise wording of a text.[92] There the *Vibhaṅga* commentator states that the 'natural expression' (*sabhāvanirutti*), that is, scriptural language, is recognized by its sounds (*sadda*) rather than its concepts

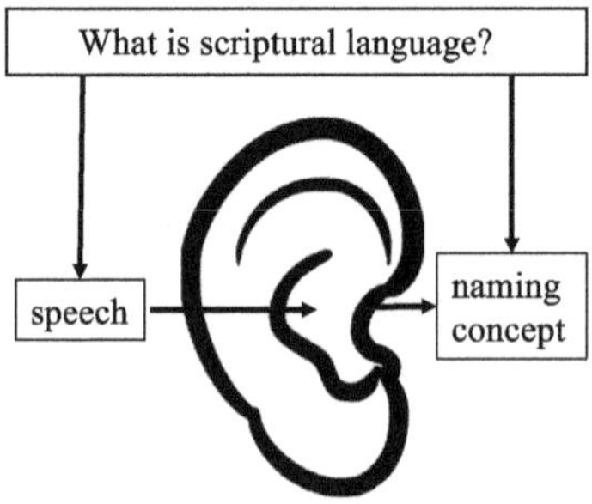

Figure 5.4 Scripture as either speech or concept

(*paññatti*) and furnishes this distinction with an example. The Pali word *phasso* (a masculine noun meaning 'sense-contact'), he states, can be considered scripture but incorrect grammatical forms such as **phassā* (*f.*) and **phassam* (*n.*) are not, despite the fact they may convey the same idea. The commentary refers to the ability to distinguish scriptural language as the *niruttipaṭisambhidā* or 'analysis of scripture'.[93] These views conform with the general approach of the other early commentaries, traditionally ascribed to Buddhaghosa, that treat scriptural meaning (*attha*) as rich and expansive but never as detached from or as more important than scripture's phrasing (*vyañjana*).[94]

Sumaṅgala, however, remains markedly silent about whether he agreed with the *Vibhaṅga* commentator here, probably because, as we have discussed, he actually accepted a largely conceptual understanding of language. And yet, in an exegetical move that is potentially conciliatory to those who defined scripture principally as sound, he quotes in agreement a discussion in Ānanda's subcommentary on this *Vibhaṅga* passage concerning when in the cognitive process the 'analysis of scripture' takes place. There, Ānanda states that, while the analysis of the 'natural expression' occurs as soon as the sounds of the language are heard, it is not impossible that this analysis continues at a secondary, conceptual stage of cognition.[95] There is potentially room in Ānanda's comments here, however intentional, for both views of scripture to be seen as compatible without overtly impinging on commentarial orthodoxy and it is no coincidence, I think, that Sumaṅgala draws our attention to this passage.[96]

There is evidence that the two competing views on scriptural language as concept or speech found their way outside of elite philosophical circles too. We find, for instance, the debate referenced in Sāriputta's Vinaya subcommentary where it seems the glossaries (*gaṇṭhipada*) available to him on the Vinaya and Abhidhamma contained conflicting views about the matter. Commenting on the opening to the Vinaya commentary, where the commentator defines the Dhamma specifically as the texts listed in the Tipiṭaka, Sāriputta raises the question of what exactly is meant by the word 'Dhamma'. He initially appears to follow the Vinaya commentator by defining the Dhamma specifically as *pāḷi*, that is, as a canonical text.

He then, however, raises the issue of what is meant by such a 'text' and offers two different interpretations. The first opinion, supposedly taken from a Sinhala Abhidhamma glossary, argues instead that a canonical text is in actuality a conceptual entity.[97] The second opinion, which he states derives from a Vinaya glossary, follows the traditional view in claiming that a canonical text is defined primarily by its sounds, that is, its exact wording. Of the two views, Sāriputta explains the former at length whereas he only cursorily defends the latter by quoting Dhammapāla's *Dīgha Nikāya* subcommentary.[98] His principal argument for the first position is that if the expression 'canonical text' refers primarily to the words of the text rather than the concepts conveyed by them, then there would be no difference between the Dhamma and the teaching (*desanā*) of the Dhamma. According to this reasoning, then, the Dhamma is a nominal entity and scriptural language itself is its verbal articulation.[99]

Reading between the lines, the silence of Sumaṅgala and Sāriputta – their reluctance to explicitly take the early commentators' side against those like Jotipāla – is revealing in that previously heterodox views of scripture as a concept were now presented as plausible, if not preferable. In exegetical fidelity to the handbook authors, both scholars expound a view of scriptural language that takes into account that scripture could be identified as a conceptual entity; an object of the mind rather than something heard. This was not to the exclusion of the traditional standpoint, of course. There were clear dangers in defining scripture as something *solely* conceptual, for the Mahāvihāra's identity and authority was based on the very idea that its Pali scriptures were spoken by the Buddha. Sumaṅgala seems to agree that while scripture can be analytically separated as a conceptual entity and potentially reformulated, these concepts must ultimately derive at some point from Pali sounds.

It is tempting to view this accommodation as part of the subtle loosening of the traditional link between the phrasing and meaning of scripture among the scholar-monks of the era, as discussed at the beginning of the chapter. Such a shift in emphasis perhaps makes sense when we consider the changes in the monastic curriculum, where condensations of the canon's meaning, with little exegetical connection to the wording of scripture, had begun to be viewed as commentaries too. Only a few elite monks had much sustained contact with the actual text of the Pali canon and most increasingly encountered conceptual abstractions: summaries, anthologies and grammars. Summaries could repackage this 'essential meaning' (*sārattha*) with a new wording and anthologies too could detach commentarial passages from their root text and still treat them as part of the meaning of scripture as an analytical domain. And yet these new formulations needed an authoritative connection with the Pali canon as a text, even if this was an increasingly rhetorical gesture that masked the reality of scholarly practice.

5.5. Summary

There is a great deal of overlap between the intellectual orientations of the reform-era grammarians and commentators. Both share a similar care and attention for the formal handling of scriptural meaning. We find, in general, increasingly systematic forms of exegesis, in particular, in the handbook commentarial tradition, based on an innovative application of commentarial models that, we can hypothesize, had first circulated in the Sanskrit tradition. The new formalism that characterized the exegetical culture of the era likely reflected the reform-era desire, as expressed by the grammarians, to stem the perceived religious decline of the period. It is also clear, at the same time, that these new models of writing responded to the practical needs of the late medieval school (*pariveṇa*) system, with older exegetical procedures deployed in greater frequency and specificity for pedagogical purposes. This new scholastic formalism was accompanied too by new ways of thinking about scripture. Scholar-monks, for instance, began to regard handbooks as 'commentaries', though ones that explain only the meaning and not the wording of scripture. This accompanied a reappraisal too of once heterodox views of scripture as something conceptual that could be analytically separated from scriptural wording.

Notes

1. It is possible to argue for the existence of 'scholasticism' in the sense of a systematic and rational exegetical method in earlier Pali literature. On the use of the term in this more general sense, see Cabezón, ed. 1998, 1–18; also, Ronkin, 2005, 7–9. Here, however, I wish to draw a more explicit comparison with the so-called European 'twelfth-century renaissance' where the scholastic method was intimately tied to the development in northern Europe, in particular, of new centres of learning in the form of schools or universities. See Southern, 1970.
2. Bond, 1982; Endo, 2013; Heim, 2018.
3. See, for instance, *Dīghanikāyaṭīkā* of Dhammapāla I, $19_{,22}$: attho kathīyati etāyā ti aṭṭhakathā; *Vinayatthamañjūsā* of Buddhanāga, 124: vaṇṇīyati attho kathīyati etāyā ti vaṇṇanā, aṭṭhakathā, taṃ vaṇṇanaṃ; *Moggallānapañcikāṭīkā* of Saṅgharakkhita, $3_{,15-17}$: anvattha byapadesena saṃvaṇṇīyati vivaritvā vitthāretvā kathīyati attho etāyā ti saṃvaṇṇanā; *Saddanīti* of Aggavaṃsa II, $326_{,5-6}$: ettha ṭīkā ti ṭikīyati jānīyati saṃvaṇṇanāya attho etāyā ti ṭīkā.
4. This is a general trend rather than a rule, for there are some commentaries, such as Sāriputta's *ṭīkā* on his *Vinayasaṅgaha*, that rearrange material from the canonical *ṭīkā*s. Others, such as the *Mūlasikkhāṭīkā*, while reflecting the reform-era concern for simplicity and concision, do not employ the full range of exegetical methods that we find systematically applied in some of the other handbook commentaries of the age.
5. Frauwallner, 1995, 11.
6. Von Hinüber, 1996, §343; Wijeratne and Gethin, trans. 2007, xvi–xvii. Sumaṅgala may also be identified with the initiator of the *Vinayavinicchayaṭīkā* and *Khuddasikkhābhinavaṭīkā*, though he is referred to in the latter work as a 'constant forest dweller'. See Gunawardana, 1979, 156; Kieffer-Pülz, 2017b, 36. Mayūrapāda also mentions in his *Pūjāvaliya* a famous relative, Sumaṅgala, who shared his Gaṇavāsi and Pāṇḍya descent. Similarly, there is a reference to a Sumaṅgala in Medhaṅkara's *Payogasiddhi* who was head of a monastery at Jambudoṇi (Daṁbadeṇiya). See Kieffer-Pülz, 2018, 195, n. 15.
7. Von Hinüber, 1996, §343; §346.
8. See, for instance, Skilling, 2010, 10–15.
9. *Sumaṅgalavilāsinī* of Buddhaghosa I, $1_{,15-18}$.
10. *Samantapāsādikā* I, $2_{,27}$–$3_{,12}$.
11. *Sāratthadīpanī* of Sāriputta I, $21_{,19-22}$: na hi bhagavatā abyākataṃ nāma tantipadaṃ atthi, sabbesaṃ yeva attho kathito. tasmā sammāsambuddhen'eva tiṇṇaṃ piṭakānaṃ atthavaṇṇanākkamo pi bhāsito ti daṭṭhabbaṃ. tattha tattha bhagavatā pavattitā pakiṇṇakadesanā yeva hi aṭṭhakathā.
12. *Nettipakaraṇaṭīkā* of Dhammapāla, 56: yadi pi tattha tattha pavattā bhagavato pakiṇṇakadesanā aṭṭhakathā, sā pana dhammasaṅgāhakehi tepiṭakaṃ buddhavacanaṃ saṅgāyitvā tassa atthasaṃvaṇṇanānurūpena vācanām aggaṃ āropitattā ācariyavādo nāma.

13. Dhammapāla explicitly refers to the *Abhidhammāvatāra* as an independent work (*pakaraṇa*) rather than a commentary. *Visuddhimaggamahāṭīkā* of Dhammapāla I, $2_{,21-6}$, cited in Von Hinüber, 1996, §340.
14. The *Saddhammasaṅgaha*, for instance, includes handbooks, exegetical manuals and grammars under the category of *pakaraṇa*. See *Saddhammasaṅgaha* of Dhammakitti, 62–4.
15. *Abhidhammāvatāravikāsinī* of Sumaṅgala I, $157_{,17-19}$: atthavasena pakārena kathento pi saddavasena saṅkhipitvā kathessāmī ti dassento āha "samāsenā" ti.
16. Similarly, in Sāriputta's *Abhidharmārthasaṅgrahasannaya* and Sumaṅgala's *vibhāvinī*, for instance, it is made clear that Anuruddha, author of the *Abhidhammatthasaṅgaha*, was thought to have explained the meaning of the Abhidhamma texts, 'having gathered that meaning in one place' (i.e. 'in one book'). See *Abhidharmārthasaṅgrahasannaya* of Sāriputta, $1_{,16-21}$ = *Abhidhammatthavibhāvinī* of Sumaṅgala, $54_{,7-11}$, trans. Wijeratne and Gethin, 2007, 2. The term *attha* here is difficult to translate since, on the one hand, *attha* refers specifically to the meaning of the Abhidhamma canonical texts and, on the other, it may also refer to commentaries in so far as they establish the *attha* of the canon.
17. *Abhidhammāvatāravikāsinī* of Sumaṅgala I, $157_{,11-15}$.
18. See Buddhadatta, ed. 1980, xiv. I have searched for the citation given by Buddhadatta in the *Pūjāvaliya* but, due to the work's large size, it is difficult to confirm his reading without reference to a chapter or page number. On the use of the term *aṭṭhakathā* to refer to handbooks in the early modern Burmese tradition, see Kieffer-Pülz, 2020, § 2.
19. See, for instance, the *Sāratthadīpanī* of Sāriputta, the *Sāratthamañjūsā* of Sāriputta, the *Sārasaṅgaha* of Siddhattha, the *Vinayasāratthasandīpanī* of Vācissara, the *Sāratthasālinī* of Vācissara (?), the *Sāratthasamuccaya*, and the *Sāratthavilāsinī* of Saṅgharakkhita. The uniformity of these titles has already been noted by Kieffer-Pülz, 2018, 191, n. 10 and Agostini, 2015, 2, n. 2.
20. *Sāratthadīpanī* of Sāriputta I, $2_{,3-16}$:
    vinayaṭṭhakathāyāhaṃ līnasāratthadīpaniṃ
    karissāmi suviññeyyaṃ paripuṇṇam anākulaṃ.
    porāṇehi kataṃ yaṃ tu līnatthassa pakāsanaṃ
    na taṃ sabbattha bhikkhūnaṃ atthaṃ sādheti sabbaso.
    duviññeyyasabhāvāya sīhaḷāya niruttiyā
    gaṇṭhipadesv anekesu likhitaṃ kiñci katthaci.
    māgadhikāya bhāsāya ārabhitvāpi kenaci
    bhāsantarehi sammissaṃ likhitaṃ kiñcideva ca.
    asāraganthabhāro 'pi tatth' eva bahu dissati
    ākulañ ca kataṃ yattha suviññeyyam pi atthato.
    tato aparipuṇṇena tādisen' ettha sabbaso
    katham atthaṃ vijānanti nānādesanivāsino.
    bhāsantaraṃ tato hitvā sāram ādāya sabbaso
    anākulaṃ karissāmi paripuṇṇavinicchayan ti.
    My translation differs slightly from Petra Kieffer-Pülz's recent rendering. See Kieffer-Pülz, 2013, 62–3, n. 131.
21. Kieffer-Pülz, 2013, 62–4. See also Bollée, 1969, 824–35; Dimitrov, 2016, 479.
22. Petra Kieffer-Pülz has plausibly suggested that Sāriputta here is rather referring to Sanskrit forms of language used in the *Vajirabuddhiṭīkā* (*gri* for *giri*, for instance). See Kieffer-Pülz, 2013, 130–1. As Sāriputta speaks of the 'unessential books' (*asāragantha*) as an obstacle in this connection, I am inclined, therefore, to hypothesize that he may also have in mind instances in the *Vajirabuddhiṭīkā* where the author cites Sanskrit works (albeit in Pali translation). See Dimitrov, 2016, 467–512. There was perhaps a convention that Sanskrit works should not be cited in Pali compositions. It is noteworthy, in this regard, that Sumaṅgala, when rendering Sāriputta's *sannaya* on the *Abhidhammatthasaṅgaha* into Pali, omits and never translates the work's Sanskrit citations.
23. Coḷiya Kassapa, for instance, plays on the double meaning of *laghu/lahu* ('light') by stating that his concise commentary is best suited for those of 'light' or 'lowly' behaviour (*lahuvutti*). See the incipit of the *Vimativinodanī* of Kassapa.
24. Adapted from Kieffer-Pülz, 2018, 194.
25. See the colophon of the *Vinayatthamañjūsā* of Buddhanāga, $407_{,13}$–$409_{,23}$.
26. *Abhidhammatthavibhāvinī* of Sumaṅgala, $212_{,18-25}$, trans. Wijeratne and Gethin, 2007, 267.
27. For details see chapter three.
28. There is some evidence that late Southeast Asian commentaries on the canon also began to employ this more systematic form of exegesis. See, for instance, Von Hinüber, 1997.

29. See, for instance, Kieffer-Pülz, 2013, 87, n. 192; See also Nance, 2012, 98–122; Skilling, 2000, 318.
30. Petra Kieffer-Pülz has compiled mentions of such *mātikā* in Pali works. See Kieffer-Pülz, 2013, 86–95. I have represented below those from the pre-reform era and I have added to this collection also a second *mātikā* cited in the *Dīghanikāyaṭīkā* of Dhammapāla I, $245_{,9}$–$246_{,15}$. These lists can be summarized in the following table:

	Vajirabuddhiṭīkā	Nettipakaraṇa-aṭṭhakathā 1	Nettipakaraṇa-aṭṭhakathā 2	Nettipakaraṇa-aṭṭhakathā 3	Dīghanikāya-ṭīkā 1	Dīghanikāya-ṭīkā 2
1	upogghāṭa	samuṭṭhāna	payojana	upogghāṭa	samuṭṭhāna	samuṭṭhāna
2	pada	adhippāya	piṇḍattha	X	pada	payojana
3	padattha	padattha	padattha	padaviggaha	padavibhāga	bhājana
4	padaviggaha	vidhi/anuvāda	anusandhi	padattha	padattha	piṇḍattha
5	codanā	virodha	codanā	cālanā	anuyoga	X
6	pratyavajja	anusandhi	parihāra	paccupaṭṭhāna	parihāra	X

31. This is evident, for instance, in Dhammapāla's subcommentary on the *Brahmajāla Sutta* of the *Dīgha Nikāya*. In an excursus at the end of his commentary he states that now he will present an 'explanation of the meaning of the text according to the method of the exegetical treatises (*pakaraṇanayena*)'. It is there that he introduces another list of exegetical principles and briefly discusses the Sutta on the basis of this list, though his main interest in this appendix is to demonstrate the many other exegetical techniques described in the *Nettipakaraṇa*. Dhammapāla treats the points in this list, however, as referring to what a commentary on a Sutta should contain as a whole and not necessarily how it should comment on each and every passage. He understands *samuṭṭhāna* 'context', for instance, as the context of the Sutta as a whole and, likewise, he takes *piṇḍattha* 'concise meaning' as referring to a summary of the Sutta too. See *Dīghanikāyaṭīkā* of Dhammapāla I, $245_{,9}$–$267_{,29}$, trans. Bodhi, 2007, 215–42. This corresponds with how these commentarial principles were implemented in certain works in the Mahayana Buddhist commentarial tradition. See, for instance, Nance, 2012, 98–122; Schoening, 1991, esp. 49–57.
32. The Burmese edition of the commentary, for instance, includes at the beginning of Vimalabuddhi's discussion of Kaccāyana's second rule the following schema, which is almost identical to the one found in the *Vajirabuddhiṭīkā* and the *Suttaniddesa* of Chapaṭa. Its awkward placement, however, suggests that the verse is not original to the *Mukhamattadīpanī*. See *Mukhamattadīpanī* of Vimalabuddhi B^e 7 (= *Suttaniddesa* of Chapaṭa, $3_{,33-4}$):
    sambandho ca padañ c'eva padattho padaviggaho,
    codanā parihāro ca chabbidhā suttavaṇṇanā.
    For other texts citing this verse, see Kieffer-Pülz, 2013, 91.
33. There has been some recent work on Sanskrit philosophical commentaries, however. See Ganeri, 2010; Eltschinger, 2018.
34. Vimalabuddhi's application of the principle of 'word analysis' (*padaviggaha/padavibhāga*) is innovative in that he uses it to refer to any form of grammatical analysis, including semantic analysis, and not only as the parsing of compounds, as it is often taken to mean.
35. *Mukhamattadīpanī* of Vimalabuddhi, $19_{,28}$–$20_{,5}$: **sarā sare lopaṃ:** kim attham idam uccate. anantaresu pubbasarassa lopatthaṃ. **sarā** ti ekaṃ padaṃ, **sare** ti ekaṃ, **lopan** ti ekaṃ, tipadam idaṃ suttaṃ. sarā kho sare pare lopaṃ pappontī ti attho. ettha ca **sarā** ti kārino nidasseti. **sare** ti nimittaṃ. **lopan** ti kāriyaṃ. sarantī ti **sarā**. lutti **lopo**. sarānaṃ paṭhamaṃ nidditthattā paṭhamaṃ tesaṃ sandhividhānaṃ vattabban ti ihedaṃ vuttaṃ. ettha ca saresū ti avatvā **sare** ti vacanaṃ ekekasmiṃ yevā ti ñāpanatthaṃ. yadi evaṃ saro ti avatvā kasmā **sarā** ti vuttaṃ ti. ekadviticatunnam pi lopo hotī ti ñāpanatthaṃ. "tena sakhāto gass' e vā" (*Kaccāyana* 113) ti ettha a ca ā ca i ca ī ca e cā ti viggahaṃ katvā "nāmānaṃ samāso yuttattho" (*Kaccāyana* 318) ti adhikicca "nāmānaṃ samuccayo dvando" (*Kaccāyana* 331) ti dvandasamāsaṃ katvā "vuttaṭṭhānam appayogo" ti casaddam appayogaṃ katvā a ā i ī e ti evaṃ ṭhite ekāre pare sesasarānaṃ lopo hotī ti daṭṭhabbaṃ. Translation amended from Gornall and Gunasena, 2018, 14–15.
36. On the types of Sinhala *sannaya*s and their style, see Bechert, 2005, 26–9; Blackburn, 2001, 68–9; 107–38.

37. See *Rūpasiddhisannaya*. Also, Kieffer-Pülz, 2013, 91. This is in contrast to earlier Sinhala commentaries, such as the *Siyabaslakarasannaya*, which very often only consist of a word-by-word translation of each passage commented upon, sometimes followed by a brief paragraph explaining the passage's underlying idea or *bhāva*. See *Siyabaslakarasannaya* of Ruvanmī. For a translated example of its analysis, see Dimitrov, 2016, 105–6. The Sinhala *sannaya* tradition also influenced the development of the Burmese *nissaya*. See Pruitt, 1994.
38. See Auroux, 1994.
39. Wijeratne and Gethin, trans. 2007, 367.
40. *Abhidhammatthasaṅgaha* of Anuruddha 2.8: karuṇā-muditā-appamaññāyo nāmā ti sabbathāpi paññindriyena saddhiṃ pañcavīsat' ime cetasikā sobhanā ti veditabbā. The translation is slightly adapted from Wijeratne and Gethin, 2007, 65.
41. *Abhidharmārthasaṅgrahasannaya* of Sāriputta, $48_{,31}$–$49_{,7}$: **karuṇāmuditā pana** duḥkhita sattvayangē duḥkhāpagamaya kaṭäṭi **karuṇāya** sukhita sattvayangē sukhayehī pramuditava pavatnā **muditāya** yana mē dedenā vanāhi; **appamaññā nāmā ti**, apramāṇa sattvayan viṣayakoṭa pavatnāheyin aprāmāṇya nam veti.
42. *Abhidhammatthavibhāvinī* of Sumaṅgala, $86_{,11\text{-}26}$ (= *Abhidharmārthasaṅgrahasannaya* of Sāriputta $49_{,8\text{-}22}$): **karoti** paradukkhe sati sādhūnaṃ hadayakhedaṃ janeti, **kirati** vā vikkhipati paradukkhaṃ, kiṇāti vā taṃ hiṃsati, **kiriyāti** (*corr.* kiriyati) vā dukkhitesu pasārīyatī ti **karuṇā**. sā paradukkhāpanayana**kāmatā**lakkhaṇā; tāya hi paradukkhaṃ apanīyatu vā, mā vā tadākāren' eva sā pavattati. modanti etāyā ti **muditā**. sā parasampatti-anumodana-lakkhaṇā. appamāṇasattārammaṇattā appamāṇā, tā eva **appamaññā**. nanu ca "catasso appamaññā" (*Abhidhammatthasaṅgaha* 9.9) ti vakkhati. kasmā pan' ettha dve yeva vuttā? ti. adosa-tatramajjhattatāhi mettupekkhānaṃ gahitattā. adoso yeva hi sattesu hitajjhāsayavasappavatto **mettā** nāma, tatramajjhattatā yeva tesu paṭighānunayavūpasamappavattā **upekkhā** nāma. ten' āhu porāṇā: "avyāpādena mettā hi tatramajjhattatāya ca, upekkhā gahitā yasmā tasmā na gahitā ubho" ti. Translation adapted from Wijeratne and Gethin, 2007, 65.
43. Here borrowing from Deleuze and Guattari, 1994, 15–34.
44. *Dīghanikāyaṭīkā* of Dhammapāla I, $43_{,17}$.
45. See *Abhidhammatthasaṅgaha* of Anuruddha, 2.6.
46. For instance, *Abhidhammāvatāravikāsinī* of Sumaṅgala II on vv. 74–80. This is also not uncommon in the canonical *ṭīkā* literature, with both Dhammapāla and Sāriputta sometimes referring to hidden (*antolīna*) objections that 'Buddhaghosa' was responding to. To give but one example from each work, see *Dīghanikāyaṭīkā* of Dhammapāla I, $269_{,22\text{-}4}$; *Sāratthadīpanī* of Sāriputta I, $204_{,23}$.
47. Patel, 2014, 89.
48. On Sāriputta's conciliatory approach, see Kieffer-Pülz, 2005.
49. I presented some of the material that has been used to write this section at a talk at the Oxford Centre of Buddhist Studies in 2012. I had the pleasure there of discussing these issues with Lance Cousins, who kindly sent me a number of references and pointers that greatly enriched my understanding of the topic. The presentation of the debate here owes much to his wisdom and kindness. There are few secondary sources on the topic. See Warder, 1971.
50. Useful summaries of Abhidhamma thought and the content of the Abhidhammapiṭaka can be found in Crosby, 2014, 175–93; Gethin, 1998, 202–23; Nyanatiloka, 2008.
51. See, in particular, *Puggalapaññattiaṭṭhakathā*, 171–5. See also Priestley, 1999, 139–42.
52. Designations can also be a combination of both such as 'a designation of what is not real by means of what is real' (*vijjamānena-avijjamāna-paññatti*), as in the word *chaḷabhiñña* 'one with the six knowledges'. Also, in this regard, Karunadasa, 2010, 57–8.
53. *Abhidhammāvatāra*, $83_{,3\text{-}4}$.
54. *Abhidhammāvatāra*, $83_{,16}$: ahan ti hi rūpādayo dhamme upādāya paṭicca kāraṇaṃ katvā yathā te rūpādayo dhammā uppāda-vaya-vanto na evaṃvidhā. See the translation below. Sumaṅgala (*Abhidhammāvatāravikāsinī*, $201_{,1\text{-}6}$) comments here as follows: ahan ti rūpādivinimuttaṃ ahaṃkārabuddhivisayabhūtaṃ attano khandhasamūhasantānam upādāya paññattaṃ, tadaññānaññabhāvena anibbacanīyaṃ upādāpaññattiṃ vadati. tenāha **ahan ti hī** ti ādi. "ahan ti ... pe ... katvā" ti upādāpaññattiyā uppattiṃ dassetvā **yathā** ti ādinā taṃ pakāseti. 'The [concept] "I" is conceptualized (*paññatta*), having as its cause (*upādāya*) the continuity of one's own mass of aggregates (*khandha*), which become an object of the self-conscious intellect, independent of form, etc. (i.e. dhammas). He (Buddhadatta) states that the dependent concept (*upādāpaññatti*) cannot be explained as either being different from that [mass of aggregates] nor as non-different from that. For this reason, [he] begins **ahan ti hi**. Having pointed to the arising of the dependent concept, [by stating] **ahan ti ... pe ... katvā**, he explains this with [the statement] beginning **yathā**.'

55. Later in his commentary Sumaṅgala explicitly treats *paññatti*s as neither conditioned nor unconditioned and speaks of *saṅkhata*, *asaṅkhata* and *paññatti* dhammas, though the latter, of course, are essenceless (*asabhāva*). See *Abhidhammāvatāravikāsinī* of Sumaṅgala on v. 1395. Y. Karunadasa notes this too, though he is less attentive to the historical development of this categorization of *paññatti*s. See Karunadasa, 2010, 50–1. Sāriputta in his *Abhidharmārthasaṅgrahasannaya* states that *paññatti*s, like nirvana, are free from time (*kālavinirmukta*). See *Abhidharmārthasaṅgrahasannaya*, $209_{,18}$ (= *Abhidhammatthavibhāvinī* of Sumaṅgala, $193_{,14}$).
56. *Dhammasaṅgaṇi*, §§1306–1308 (B^{e}, §§1312–1314). See also, Karunadasa, 2010, 48.
57. *Dhammasaṅgaṇi*, §1308: katame dhammā paññatti? yā tesaṃ tesaṃ dhammānaṃ saṅkhā samaññā paññatti vohāro nāmaṃ nāmakammaṃ nāmadheyyaṃ nirutti vyañjanaṃ abhilāpo, ime dhammā paññatti. sabbe va dhammā paññattipathā.
58. This seems at least to be the view of the subcommentators on this passage. See below.
59. *Atthasālinī*, $390_{,14-19}$: saṅkhāyatī ti **saṅkhā**. saṅkathīyatī ti attho. kin ti saṅkathīyati? ahan ti maman ti paro ti parassā ti satto ti gāvo ti poso ti puggalo ti naro ti mānavo ti tisso ti datto ti mañco pīthaṃ (*corr.* pīṭhaṃ) bhisī bimbohanan ti vihāro pariveṇaṃ dvāraṃ vātapānaṃ ti evaṃ anekehi ākārehi saṅkathīyatī ti.
60. *Dhammasaṅgaṇimūlaṭīkā* of Ānanda, $177_{,13-16}$: **ahan ti** iti-saddaparena ahaṃ-saddena hetubhūtena yo attho viññāyati, so saṃkathīyati, udīrīyatīti attho. aññathā hi vuccamānassa vacanena pakāsiyamānassa padatthassa saṅkhādibhāve sabbesaṃ kusalādidhammānaṃ adhivacanāditā siyā ti. '**ahan ti:** as the word *iti* follows [the word *ahaṃ*], the sense is "the meaning which is understood with the word *ahaṃ* as its cause, that is spoken, [i.e.] it is uttered". For, otherwise, if the word-meaning which is being expressed, [i.e.] being designated by an expression, has the status of *saṅkhā*, etc., then all dhammas, wholesome, etc., would have the status of being *adhivacana* "designation", etc.'
61. This has also influenced contemporary interpretations of this *Dhammasaṅgaṇi* passage. See, for instance, Karunadasa, 2010, 48–9; Collins, 1998, 184.
62. *Abhidhammāvatāra* of Buddhadatta, $83_{,8-18}$: tattha saṅkhāyatī ti **saṅkhā** kathīyatī ti attho; kin ti kathīyati? ahan ti mamā ti paro ti parassā ti mañco ti pīṭhan ti anekehi ākārehi kathīyatī ti **saṅkhā**; samaññāyatī ti **samaññā**; paññāpīyatī ti **paññatti**; voharīyatī ti **vohāro**. kin ti voharīyati? ahan ti mamā ti paro ti parassā ti mañco ti pīṭhan ti. evaṃ tāva paññāpetabbato paññattī ti vuttā. ahan ti hi rūpādayo dhamme upādāya paṭicca kāraṇaṃ katvā yathā te rūpādayo dhammā uppāda-vaya-vanto na evaṃvidhā. kevalaṃ lokasaṅketena siddhā yā ahaṃ ahan ti kathīyati paññāpīyati ca, esā paññattī ti attho. idāni paññāpanato paññattiṃ pakāsetuṃ nāmaṃ nāmakamman ti ādim āha; tattha "nāman" ti taṃ taṃ dhammaṃ "esa itthan nāmo" ti paññāpeti, tasmā taṃ paññattī ti pavuccati; nāmakamman ti ādīni tassā eva vevacanāni. ayaṃ paññāpanato paññatti nāma.
63. This is Anuruddha's expression. See *Abhidhammatthasaṅgaha* $43_{,27}$, trans. Wijeratne and Gethin, 2007, 320.
64. *Abhidhammāvatāra* of Buddhadatta, $84_{,6-9}$: duvidhā pi pan' esā sotadvāra-javanānantaraṃ gahita-pubba-saṅketen' eva manodvāra-javana-viññāṇena viññāyati, sā 'yaṃ (B^{e}, yāya) gahita-pubba-saṅketena manodvāra-javana-viññāṇena paññāpīyati.
65. Anuruddha refers to the same *Dhammasaṅgaṇi* passage in introducing *atthapaññatti*s and *nāmapaññatti*s. See, in particular, *Paramatthavinicchaya* of Anuruddha, vv. 1073–80. But also, *Abhidhammatthasaṅgaha* of Anuruddha, $43_{,32}$.
66. *Abhidhammatthasaṅgaha* of Anuruddha, $43_{,18}$–$44_{,14}$; *Paramatthavinicchaya* of Anuruddha, vv. 1064–1142. The expression *nāmapaññatti* was first employed rather ambiguously in the *Dhammasaṅgaṇi* commentary to refer collectively to the list of linguistic terms the work introduces as designators of *dhammas*. *Atthasālinī*, $391_{,21-5}$, discussed in Ronkin, 2005, 161. See also *Puggalapaññattiaṭṭhakathā*, 171_{19}–$173_{,6}$.
67. *Abhidhammatthasaṅgaha* of Anuruddha, $44_{,9-12}$:
vacīghosānusārena sotaviññāṇavīthiyā
pavattānantaruppannamanodvārassa gocarā.
atthā yassānusārena viññāyanti tato paraṃ
sāyaṃ paññatti viññeyyā lokasaṅketanimmitā.
Translation slightly altered from Wijeratne and Gethin, 2007, 323.
68. *Dhammasaṅgaṇimūlaṭīkā* of Ānanda, $177_{,13}$–$181_{,19}$; *Dhammasaṅgaṇianuṭīkā* of Dhammapāla, $189_{,24}$–$197_{,31}$. It is noteworthy that the *Saccasaṅkhepa*, traditionally ascribed to Dhammapāla, essentially summarizes and supports Ānanda's arguments here too. See *Saccasaṅkhepa*, vv. 372–83. I was lucky to have Lance Cousins's rough translation of the *Dhammasaṅgaṇimūlaṭīkā* passage here to hand in order to refine my own translation. Lance was interested in this passage due to his work on the *Saccasaṅkhepa*. My understanding of the passage in the context of the debate on *paññatti* and as

a critique of views like those expressed in the *Abhidhammāvatāra* is my own. I plan in the near future to publish full translations of Ānanda's arguments along with Dhammapāla's subcommentary. For the purpose of this chapter, however, I will cite the sections relating to the individual arguments and only translate key points.

69. *Dhammasaṅgaṇimūlaṭīkā* of Ānanda, 178$_{,9-14}$: ettha pana saṅkhā samaññā paññatti vohāro ti catūhi padehi paññāpitabbato paññatti vuttā, itarehi paññāpanato. tattha ca purimā upādāpaññatti uppādavayakiccarahitā lokasaṅketasiddhā pacchimā nāmapaññatti yāya purimā paññatti rūpādayo ca sotadvāraviññāṇasantānānantaram uppannena gahitapubbasaṅketena manodvāraviññāṇasantānena gahitāya paññāpīyantī ti ācariyā vadanti.
70. *Dhammasaṅgaṇimūlaṭīkā* of Ānanda, 181$_{,18-19}$: ayaṃ saṅkhatāsaṅkhatavinimuttassa atthitāpaṭisedhaṃ sabbathā anuvattantānaṃ vinicchayo.
71. *Dhammasaṅgaṇimūlaṭīkā* of Ānanda, 180$_{,6}$–181$_{,19}$. See, esp. 180$_{,12-21}$: yasmā pana yesu rūpādīsu cakkhādīsu ca tathā tathā pavattamānesu "satto itthī ratho ghaṭo" ti ādikā vicittasaññā uppajjati, saññānulomāni ca adhivacanāni, tehi rūpacakkhādīhi añño sattarathādisaññāvalambito vacanattho vijjamāno na hoti. tasmā sattarathādi-abhilāpā "avijjamānapaññattī" ti vuccanti, na ca te "musā" ti vuccanti lokasamaññāvasena pavattattā. tato eva te abhilāpā "sammutisaccan" ti vuccanti. so ca vacanattho sayaṃ avijjamāno pi vijjamānassa vacanass' eva vasena paññattivohāraṃ labhati, "sammutisaccan" ti ca vuccati yathāgahitasaññāvasena pavattavacanatthabhāvato.
'Since, however, various perceptions, such as being, woman, cart, and pot, arise when form etc. (i.e. objects of senses) and eye etc. (i.e. the sense organs) are occurring this way and that (*tathā tathā*), and designations (*adhivacana*) conform with these perceptions, there is no real object of speech (i.e. a conceptual *paññatti*) other than form and eye etc. attached to the perception of being and cart etc. Therefore, the utterances of "being" and "cart" etc. are spoken of as "designations of what is unreal", though they are not spoken of as "false" since they occur as an ordinary category. Therefore, these utterances (*abhilāpa*) are referred to as "conventional truth". And that object of speech even though it itself is unreal obtains the label "*paññatti*" only by dint of real speech and it is referred to as "conventional truth" as its status (*bhāva*) as the object of speech occurs because of the perception (*saññā*) as grasped.'
72. His first three arguments are as follows:
(1) It contradicts what is said in the *Dhammasaṅgaṇi* commentary.
Dhammasaṅgaṇimūlaṭīkā of Ānanda, 178$_{,15-22}$: etasmiṃ pana imissā pāḷiyā aṭṭhakathāya ca atthe sati yaṃ vuttaṃ mātikāyaṃ "vacanamattam eva adhikāraṃ katvā pavattā adhivacanā nāma … sahetukaṃ katvā vuccamānā abhilāpā nirutti nāma … pakārena ñāpanato paññatti nāmā" ti (*Atthasālinī*, 51), tena virodho siyā. na hi uppādavayakiccarahitassa vacanamattaṃ adhikāraṃ katvā pavatti atthi uppādādisahitass' eva pavattisabbhāvato (*conj.* °sabhāvato?); na ca vacanavacanatthavimuttassa nāmassa niddhāretvā sahetukaṃ katvā vuccamānatā atthi; nāpi aniddhāritasabhāvassa padatthassa tena tena pakārena ñāpanaṃ atthī ti.
'If this here, however, is the meaning of this canonical text and commentary then there would be a contradiction with what is said with respect to the *mātikā*, [namely, that] "*adhivacana* is so-called as it occurs taking only speech as a support; *nirutti* is so-called as it is an utterance being spoken for a reason; *paññatti* is so-called since it is making known by a means." This is because (1) there cannot be the occurrence of what lacks the function of arising and ceasing having taken speech as a support, since only that accompanied by arising, etc. can by nature occur; (2) a name separate from speech and the meaning of speech cannot be expressed with specificity, with a cause; (3) nor can a meaning element (*padattha*) of unspecified nature (*sabhāva*) be made known by this or that means.'
(2) The two-fold division of dependent and naming concepts, as described, is not found in any other commentary.
Dhammasaṅgaṇimūlaṭīkā of Ānanda, 178$_{,23}$–179$_{,7}$, esp. 179$_{,4-6}$: avijjamānapaññattivacanena paññāpitabbā upādāpaññatti, tassā paññāpanabhūtā nāmapaññatti ca vuttā, itarehi nāmapaññatti yeva yathā vuttā ti ce? na, asiddhattā.
'What if by the expression *avijjamānapaññatti* one refers to both the dependent concept which is to be designated and the naming concept which designates it, just as by the others (i.e. the other combinations of designating *vijjamāna* and *avijjamāna paññatti*s) one refers only to the naming concept? No, for it is not established.' Ānanda argues here that the *upādā-* and *nāmapaññatti* distinction, as described, cannot be inferred from the *Puggalapaññattiaṭṭhakathā* categorization of the various combinations of *vijjamāna* and *avijjamānapaññatti*s.
(3) If the unreal things words denote have the status of 'unreal concepts' then one might think that signified dhammas too have the status of 'real concepts', contradicting the *Dhammasaṅgaṇi* statement that dhammas themselves have a 'way of designation' (*paññattipatha*).

Dhammasaṅgaṇimūlaṭīkā of Ānanda, $179_{,7}$–$179_{,26}$, esp. $179_{,11\text{–}14}$: yathā ca paññāpitabbato avijjamānānaṃ sattādīnaṃ avijjamānapaññattibhāvo, evaṃ rūpādīnaṃ vijjamānānaṃ paññāpetabbato vijjamānapaññattibhāvo āpajjati. tato "sabbe dhammā paññattī" ti paññattipathehi avisiṭṭho paññattidhammaniddeso vattabbo siyā.

'And since, as [something] to be designated, unreal beings etc. have the status of *paññatti*s of what is unreal, then there is the unwanted consequence that real forms (*rūpa*) etc., as [something] to be designated, would have the status of *paññatti*s of what is real. Then, one would have to specify that dhammas *are paññatti*s, [stating,] "all dhammas are *paññattī*", without qualifying them as "having ways of *paññatti*" (as in *Dhammasaṅgaṇi*, §§1306–8).'

73. *Dhammasaṅgaṇimūlaṭīkā* of Ānanda, $179_{,26}$–$180_{,1}$, esp. $179_{,26\text{–}9}$: yadi hi tesaṃ vinā paññattiyā atthapaññāpane asamatthatā siyā, paññattipaññāpane ca asamatthatā ti tassā aññā paññatti vattabbā siyā, tassā tassā ti anavatthānaṃ. tato atthavijānanam eva na siyā.

'For if it were impossible for a [naming] *paññatti* to designate the meaning without them (i.e. understandings of a convention), then it would also be impossible to designate the [naming] *paññatti*. Thus, one would have to speak of another [naming] *paññatti* for that (i.e. to designate that naming *paññatti*), and for that, and that. There would be infinite regress and, thus, no signification of meaning at all.'

74. *Dhammasaṅgaṇimūlaṭīkā* of Ānanda, $180_{,1\text{–}5}$: "buddhassa bhagavato vohāro lokiye sote paṭihaññati" (*Kathāvatthu* 2.10), "abhijānāsi no tvaṃ ānanda ito pubbe evarūpaṃ nāmadheyyaṃ sutaṃ yadidaṃ javanasabho" (*Dīgha Nikāya* II, 18.9) ti, "nāmañ ca sāveti koṇḍañño ahaṃ bhagavā" (*Saṃyutta Nikāya* I, 8.9) ti ādīhi ca paññattiyā vacanabhāvo siddho. tasmā pāḷiyā aṭṭhakathāya ca aviruddho attho vicāretvā gahetabbo.

'Through [statements], such as, "the discourse of the enlightened Bhagavan impinges on the ordinary ear", "Are you not aware, Ānanda, that before [now] there was such a one known by the name of 'Javanasabha'?", and "He announced his name: I am Koṇḍañña, Bhagavan", it is established that *paññatti* is by nature speech. Therefore, upon examination, a meaning that does not contradict the canonical text and its commentary should be accepted.'

That the Pali commentaries lack any detailed discussion on the ontological nature of concepts has been noted, however. Nyanaponika Thera, for instance, criticized the Venerable U Ñāṇa, translator of Ledi Sayadaw's *Vipassanā Dīpanī*, for 'ascribing the teaching on the "eternal nature" of concepts and space to Buddhist philosophy in general' and remarks that 'this teaching is obviously of late origin, being found neither in the Abhidhamma Piṭaka nor in the old Abhidhamma commentaries'. See Ledi Sayādaw, 2007, 38.

75. *Abhidhammāvatāravikāsinī* of Sumaṅgala II, $200_{,14\text{–}17}$.

76. *Abhidhammāvatāravikāsinī* of Sumaṅgala II, $200_{,8\text{–}13}$: tattha "paññāpetabbato" ti iminā paññāpīyati pakārena ñāpiyatī ti paññattī ti evaṃ kammasādhanavasena atthapaññattibhūtā upādāpaññatti vuttā. "paññāpanato" ti iminā paññāpeti pakārena ñāpetī ti paññattī ti evaṃ kattusādhanavasena tassā abhidhāyakabhūtā nāmapaññattī ti veditabbaṃ.

77. *Abhidhammāvatāravikāsinī* of Sumaṅgala II, $203_{,13\text{–}19}$ (≈ *Abhidharmārthasaṅgrahasannaya* of Sāriputta, $214_{,20\text{–}6}$; *Abhidhammatthavibhāvinī* of Sumaṅgala, $195_{,12\text{–}17}$): katarajavanavīthiyaṃ panāyaṃ viññāyatī ti? ghaṭo ti ādisaddaṃ suṇantassa ekamekaṃ saddaṃ ārabbha paccuppannātītārammaṇavasena dve dve javanavārā honti. tato saddasamudāyam ārabbha eko, tato nāmapaññattim ārabbha eko ti evaṃ saddasamudāyārammaṇāya javanavīthiyā anantaraṃ nāmapaññatti pākaṭā hoti. tato paraṃ atthāvabodho ti ācariyā.

78. *Abhidhammatthavibhāvinī* of Sumaṅgala, $195_{,8\text{–}9}$: manodvāragahitā akkharāvalībhūtā paññatti viññeyyā. But see the slightly different *Abhidharmārthasaṅgrahasannaya* of Sāriputta, $214_{,15\text{–}17}$: viññeyyā manodvārika vijñānayen gannālada akṣarāvali saṃkhyāta nāmaprajñaptiya yi datayuttī yi.

79. The emphasis is my own. Note that here the opponent evokes the Buddha's statement that the Dhamma and Vinaya share the singular taste (*ekarasa*) of liberation. See, for instance, *Vinaya* II, $239_{,33\text{–}4}$. In speaking specifically of the *teaching* (*desanā*) having no singular taste, the opponent is making a distinction between the ideal Dhamma and its verbal articulation.

80. I would have expected *dukkhāpi sukhā vedanā* here. This is a tentative translation, though I am confident Dhammapāla is raising the issue of textual variation.

81. *Dhammasaṅgaṇianuṭīkā* of Dhammapāla, $197_{,24\text{–}31}$:

vohāro lokiyasote paṭihaññatī ti ādisu sotabbassa saddassa vasena tabbisayabhūtā vohārādayo paṭihananasotabbatāpariyāyena vuttā ti daṭṭhabbā. saddo yeva vā tattha vohārādisahacāritāya tathā vutto. na hi sakkā sabbattha ekarasā desanā pavattī ti vattuṃ. tathā hi katthaci sukhā dukkhā, sukhā pi vedanā dukkhā ti vuccanti, dukkhā sukhā dukkhā pi sukhā ti. evaṃ yathāvuttā duvidhāpi paññatti adhivacanādipāṭhassa atthabhāvena aṭṭhakathāyaṃ vuttā yevā ti. ayaṃ saṅkhatāsaṅkhatavinimuttaṃ ñeyyavisesaṃ icchantānaṃ vasena vinicchayo.

82. *Abhidhammāvatāravikāsinī* of Sumaṅgala II on v. 1189, 301–2, (≈*Sammohavinodanī* 387,$_{4-9}$). *Abhidhammāvatāra* of Buddhadatta, v. 1189:
tasmiṃ atthe ca dhamme ca yā sabhāvanirutti tu,
niruttī ti ca niddiṭṭhā niruttikusalena sā.
'The natural expression (*sabhāvanirutti*), however, with respect to both *attha* and *dhamma*
is also referred to as the "*nirutti*" by those skilled in *nirutti*.'
I agree with Brian Levman, here, that *nirutti* in Pali literature seems to refer specifically to the Pali lexicon, that is, to words rather than 'language' in general. Levman, 2008–9.
83. *Abhidhammāvatāravikāsinī* of Sumaṅgala II, 301,$_{9-15}$: **sabhāvaniruttī** ti aviparītanirutti, aviparītaniruttī ti tassa tassa atthassa bodhane sabbakālaṃ paṭiniyatasambandho abyabhicāravohāro māgadhabhāsā ti vuttaṃ hoti. sā hi sabbakālaṃ paṭiniyatasambandho, itarā bhāsā pana kālantarena parivattanti (≈ *Sammohavinodanī*, 387,$_{4-17}$). atthato pan' esā nāmapaññattī ti ācariyā. yathāhu: "nirutti māgadhā bhāsā, atthato nāmasammutī" ti.
84. See chapter three, §1.
85. It is possible that *atthato* in the passage means more literally 'as to the meaning'. I interpret the term *attha* more figuratively here, however, as being used to mean 'in fact' or 'in reality' since the *nāmapaññatti*, while conceptual, is not technically the referent or meaning of a word.
86. Cousins, 2011, 17–21.
87. Dhammapāla uses an almost identical expression to represent his and Ānanda's views. See *Vibhaṅga-anuṭīkā* of Dhammapāla, 192,$_{17-18}$: viññattivikārasahito saddo paññattī ti attano adhippāyo.
88. In the Theravada Abhidhamma the term *vijñapti* (P. *viññatti*) is difficult to translate. It refers here, it seems, to a mode of the earth element born from the mind that helps produce speech when one wants to say something. Y. Karunadasa states that the 'so-called *ākāra-vikāra* of the earth-element (= *vācīviññatti*) strikes against the vocal apparatus (*upādiṇṇaka, akkharuppattiṭṭhāna*) and produces (vocal) sound through which the thought is communicated.' Karunadasa, 1967, 76.
89. *Cūḷavaṃsa* 42.35–8 cited in Cousins, 2011, 2–3.
90. See chapter one.
91. See Skilling, 2010. A similar debate on the nature of scriptural language took place between the Sautrāntikas and the Vaibhāṣikas. See, for instance, Jaini, 2001. Jaini perceives some similarities in this regard between the *nāmapaññatti*, as developed in Abhidhamma handbooks, and the Vaibhāṣika's *nāmakāya*, a linguistic dhamma separate from verbal sound.
92. *Abhidhammāvatāravikāsinī* of Sumaṅgala II on v. 1189, 301–2 (≈ *Sammohavinodanī* 387).
93. *Sammohavinodanī*, 387, 4–17.
94. Heim, 2018, 73–85, esp. 84.
95. *Abhidhammāvatāravikāsinī* of Sumaṅgala II on v. 1189, 301,$_{25}$–302,$_{19}$ (= *Vibhaṅgamūlaṭīkā* of Ānanda, 191,$_{26}$–192,$_{13}$). See in particular, 302,$_{13-15}$ (= *Vibhaṅgamūlaṭīkā* 192,$_{8-11}$): taṃ sabhāvaniruttiṃ saddaṃ ārammaṇaṃ katvā paccavekkhantassā ti ca paccuppannasaddārammaṇaṃ paccavekkhaṇaṃ pavattayantassā ti na na sakkā vattuṃ. 'For it is not impossible to say with respect to the statement, "one who investigates having taken the sound of the natural expression as cognitive object", that [it means]: "one who keeps investigating the cognitive object of present sound".'
96. I disagree with Lance Cousins's interpretation here that in this passage Ānanda 'avoids the two alternatives' and 'speaks instead of a *paññatti* which is not speech'. See Cousins, 2013, 7. According to my reading, both Ānanda and Dhammapāla follow the *Vibhaṅga* commentator in advocating that the principal analysis, the *niruttipaṭisambhidā*, occurs as soon as Pali sounds are heard, though they concede that further analysis occurs after speech has been cognized.
97. *Sāratthadīpanī* of Sāriputta I, 77,$_{2-8}$. On the *gaṇṭhipada*s quoted by Sāriputta, see also Kieffer-Pülz, 2013, 22–39, esp. 27.
98. *Sāratthadīpanī* of Sāriputta I, 77,$_{20-7}$ = *Dīghanikāyaṭīkā* of Dhammapāla I, 37,$_{21}$–38,$_{21}$.
99. *Sāratthadīpanī* of Sāriputta I, 77,$_{8-19}$. Later commentators, such as Coḷiya Kassapa, see both views as compatible too. See *Vimativinodanī* of Kassapa I, 21, and, for a lengthier, erudite summary of this whole debate, see *Dīghanikāya-abhinavaṭīkā* of Ñāṇābhivaṃsa I, 102–8.

6
Eschatological Encyclopedism: Siddhattha's Anthology

The techniques of organization found in the pedagogical commentaries of the reform era are complemented by those of the new handbooks composed during the period. Many of these handbooks differ from the earlier condensations of Buddhist doctrine and practice in that they can be defined more precisely as anthologies, that is, they cut, rearrange and weave together passages mostly from the commentaries in order to create new formulations of Buddhist thought more suited to the monastic community's changed circumstances. The creation of anthologies involved also the development of new philological practices of compilation, including, for instance, the creation of contents lists, detailed referencing and forms of bibliography. This need for textual control not only related to the educational function of these works but also, this chapter argues, to the desire for concise, comprehensive and efficient charters for Buddhist practice in an age of foreseen civilizational collapse.

In one sense, an intellectual tendency towards condensation and encyclopedism has been ever-present in Buddhist thought, even in the earliest Pali literature. The Buddha of the Suttas, for instance, often favoured explaining his doctrine using numerical lists, such as the four noble truths or noble eight-fold path.[1] These mnemonic lists were then systematized and consolidated in the conceptual matrices (*mātikā*) of the Abhidhamma.[2] In the *Khuddaka Nikāya* of the Suttapiṭaka we also find early anthologies of teachings, such as the *Khuddakapāṭha* ('Short recitation'), in which different discourses of the Pali canon were collected and rearranged.[3] The first evidence of the handbook as a distinct genre, however, can be traced to the fourth or fifth century. Buddhaghosa composed the *Visuddhimagga* ('Path of purification'), which, to some extent, summarizes the ideas contained in his commentaries on the Suttapiṭaka.[4] After Buddhaghosa we then find Buddhadatta's two primers for the Vinaya and two more for the Abhidhamma.[5] We also know of a few handbooks composed in the second half of the first millennium, such as Dhammasiri's fifth- or sixth-century *Khuddasikkhā* ('Minor rules') and the post-fifth-century (?) *Saccasaṅkhepa* ('Summary of truth').[6]

The reform era witnessed increased interest in the study and composition of handbooks. Scholar-monks wrote new Pali and Sinhala commentaries for older works, as discussed in the previous chapter, and translated early handbooks into Sinhala too. The most striking formal innovation during the period, however, was the creation of anthologies of Buddhist doctrine and practice.[7] One new anthology in particular stands out for its unique scope. The *Sārasaṅgaha* ('Compendium of the essence'), composed in the late thirteenth century by a monk known as Siddhattha,[8] was the first work in Pali history that attempted to collate in a single text information from the three baskets of the canon and its commentaries that Siddhattha deemed essential (*sāra*) for happiness and well-being.[9] Siddhattha's work, then, provides us with a unique insight into the ways in which monastic elites were using their Pali textual tradition in practice and how new techniques of compilation enabled them to innovate in representing the religious outlook of their canon and its commentaries.[10]

The 'essence' of Buddhism for Siddhattha, in this regard, focuses almost exclusively on what Melford Spiro called 'kammatic' Buddhism, that is, the accrual of merit and better rebirth, not necessarily to the exclusion of nirvana as a soteriological goal, but certainly as part of an awareness of the ever-tightening karmic limits on human effort.[11] Siddhattha's soteriology calls into question a common sociological assumption in Buddhist history that such a shift in emphasis towards kammatic practices primarily developed to accommodate the laity as part of the emergence of Buddhism as a cultural religion of the masses.[12] The *Sārasaṅgaha* shows us, however, that the shift in orientation towards karma and rebirth may not have been solely a result of popular diffusion but was simultaneously a form of Buddhist life cultivated at the very heart of elite intellectual culture. The increased emphasis on kammatic practices that we see, at least in the *Sārasaṅgaha*, was rather likely a response to the social and political chaos of the era; a conscious decision by elites to involve themselves more intensely with the karmic conditions that shaped their lives.

6.1. Embattled Encyclopedists

It is difficult to define the term *saṅgaha* (lit. 'gathering together') since it can refer to a variety of different types of compendia. Early handbooks, such as the aforementioned treatises of Buddhadatta and those of Anuruddha, discussed in the previous chapter, summarize the meaning (*attha*) of either the Abhidhamma or Vinaya in a new composition. Most of the handbooks of the reform era differ, however, in that four of them, namely, Sāriputta's *Vinayasaṅgaha* ('Compendium of the Discipline'), Ānanda's *Upāsakajanālaṅkāra* ('Ornament of lay followers'), Siddhattha's *Sārasaṅgaha*, and the *Bhesajjamañjūsā* ('Casket of medicine'), can be thought of as anthologies, since they compile material largely excised from the canon and its commentarial tradition or, in the case of the *Bhesajjamañjūsā*, other Sanskrit medical works.[13] These anthologies are more encyclopedic in nature in that, rather than summarizing a single basket of the canon, they attempt to consolidate and organize a diverse array of canonical and commentarial material that the tradition had produced over more than a thousand years.[14] Ānanda acknowledges and celebrates the broad scope of his source material in his opening, stating that 'craftsmen make the best crown with gems coming from several mines'.[15] Siddhattha similarly boasts in his colophon of memorizing 100,000 books, though frames this goal in terms of his desire to protect his scriptural tradition.[16]

This interest in encyclopedism in reform-era Sri Lanka mirrors to some degree contemporary developments in Sanskrit literature throughout South Asia. The early second millennium, for instance, witnessed the first digests of Hindu Dharma (*nibandha*), Jain manuals of lay conduct (*śrāvakācāra*) and also the earliest anthology of Sanskrit court poetry.[17] Sri Lanka played an important but little recognized role in this development and monks on the island wrote the earliest known Sanskrit grammatical handbook as well as the first Sanskrit digest of astronomy and astrology.[18] Sheldon Pollock has speculated that the production of digests of Hindu Dharma, in particular, may be connected with the Turkic invasions of North India, noting that 'totalizing conceptualizations of society became possible only by juxtaposition with alternative lifeworlds', and that, 'they became necessary only at the moment when the total form of the society was for the first time believed, by the privileged theorists of society, to be threatened'.[19]

Setting aside possible objections to the specifics of his historical analysis, Pollock's general observation concerning the connection between encyclopedism and perceived threats to the social order may be useful for thinking about the creative influence of the reform era's chaotic political environment, described in part one of this book.[20] Many of the authors of these reform-era handbooks were responding to social and political changes that often had directly impacted their lives. We learn from the colophon to the *Upāsakajanālaṅkāra*, for instance, that Ānanda composed his work in exile in Pāṇḍya country in South India.[21] Remembering the events that had caused him to flee to South India, he writes that:

> When the whole island of Laṅkā was destabilized (*samākula*) by the fire of the Damiḷas, in order to protect themselves for the future growth of the teaching, the elders came and resided there. They were like banners [to the island of] Tambapaṇṇi, always abiding in the pasture land of the true Doctrine, preserving the tradition.[22]

It is likely that Ānanda here was referring to the rule of the anti-Buddhist Kāliṅga king Māgha (1215–36), who having invaded Sri Lanka with an army of South Indian mercenaries remained a destructive force in Buddhist politics until his death in 1255.[23] These political events radically altered Ānanda's social environment and in the opening of his work he states that he composed the treatise for those he describes as 'people who recently became pious' (*abhinava-sādhujana*), likely pointing to the fact that his benefactors in Pāṇḍya country had only latterly begun to favour his Buddhist tradition. He explains too that the expanded scope of his work was suitable for these newcomers (*abhinavāvatāri*) who were not satisfied with an older work on lay conduct, the *Paṭipattisaṅgaha* ('Compendium of conduct').[24] Ānanda is explicit then that his encyclopedic concerns were inspired by existential threats to his religious community and the perceived need to protect and transmit his religious heritage in a new social environment.

Our author Siddhattha, unlike Ānanda, never directly addresses his specific social circumstances, though we know that the upheaval Ānanda experienced persisted late into the thirteenth century. The colophon to the *Sārasaṅgaha* states that Siddhattha was the governor (*pati*) of the Dakkhiṇārāma monastery, a temple possibly located in Poḷonnaruva, and that he was the last pupil of his teacher, Buddhappiya.[25] We can tentatively identify this Buddhappiya with the thirteenth-century scholar-monk who composed the *Pajjamadhu* ('Nectar of verse'), an ornate, devotional poem to the Buddha. We know that other pupils of Buddhappiya, such as Vedeha, author of the *Rasavāhinī* ('Stream of aesthetic moods'), likely wrote during the reign of Parākramabāhu II (1236–70) and it is reasonable to think that Siddhattha was also active towards the end of his rule, if not shortly after.[26]

The relatively long reign of Parākramabāhu II and its eulogistic portrayal in the *Cūḷavaṃsa* ('Little history') masks the fact that his beleaguered rule was marred by continuous wars with foreign invaders, in particular Māgha, who we discussed above, the ascendant Pāṇḍya kings, Sundara Pāṇḍya (*a.* 1251) and Vīra Pāṇḍya (*a.* 1253/4), who record military victories in Sri Lanka between 1258–63, and the Javanese king Candrabhānu, who invaded twice in 1247 and 1261. Such was Parākramabāhu II's frailty that his forces were only able to enter Poḷonnaruva in 1262, twenty-six years after his coronation, as a result of a fragile peace brokered by Vīra Pāṇḍya, who, having killed

Candrabhānu alongside Parākramabāhu's forces, reinstated Candrabhānu's son to maintain a fragmented political landscape on the island advantageous to his South Indian kingdom.[27]

Ensconced for much of his reign on the rocky outcrop of Daṁbadeṇiya situated 150 kilometres southwest of Poḷonnaruva, Parākramabāhu II's struggle to protect and preserve his power in a small fortress mirrors somewhat the battle of Siddhattha, our reform-era archivist, who was intent on protecting the essence of his religion from destruction and decline.[28] These events, we can speculate, may have fuelled Siddhattha's karmic and eschatological interests. The first twelve chapters of his work, for instance, broadly focus on buddhas, in particular, future buddhas, the Dhamma and Saṅgha as objects of devotion and sources of merit, with a particular interest in their ritual veneration. After three short chapters dealing with morality, meditation and nirvana, perhaps consciously echoing the arrangement of Buddhaghosa's *Visuddhimagga* ('Path of purification'),[29] Siddhattha attends solely to issues of karma and rebirth. He describes in chapters sixteen to twenty-four different types of karma and their consequences and continues in chapters twenty-five to thirty-four to categorize the various living beings in the universe and the different types of rebirth possible. He concludes his work with six detailed chapters describing the life-cycle and physical attributes of the universe.[30]

G.P. Malalasekera wrote with some bemusement about the work's focus that, it is 'a curious medley of matter of diverse interest, jumbled together anyhow, with no attempt at arrangement.'[31] We do not, however, need to assume, like Malalasekera, that the work had been 'tampered with by later editors' to account for its karmic and eschatological interests. Siddhattha's focus can make sense if we view it as a hopeful response to his political circumstances, one that saw in the chaos of his era signs and portents of a new buddha age in the distant future.[32] As Steven Collins once noted, 'just as one can be sure that knowledge of the truth will fade so one can (now, in the present) be reassured that someday – even if theoretically very far distant – there will be Buddhas to rediscover it'.[33] It is relevant in this respect that in his colophon Siddhattha explicitly declares that he desired to become a bodhisattva himself, that is, a buddha-to-be, and, in comparing his own path with the previous lives of Gotama Buddha, dedicates the merit accrued in writing the work to his fulfilment of the ten perfections of a bodhisattva:

> … with this merit, in birth after birth until enlightenment,
> having fulfilled all perfections – that is, by giving like Sasarāja,
> being moral like Saṅkhapāla, in renouncing like Hatthipāla,
> being wise like Sānaka, having energy like king Janaka,
> by being patient like Khantivāda, truthful like Sutasoma,

determined like Mūgapakkha, by being kind like Ekarāja,
and having equanimity like Lomahaṃsa –
may I obtain the ultimate, perfect enlightenment
and teach the immaculate four truths to all living beings.[34]

Siddhattha is but one of a number of scholar-monks in the reform era who primarily aspired to buddhahood or at least better rebirths instead of nirvana.[35] This shift in attention away from nirvana to the attainment of a remote and distant buddhahood involved, perhaps paradoxically, an intensified engagement with the world, since it was the main task of a bodhisattva to accumulate vast merit capable of producing a birth in which buddhahood is possible.[36] We can possibly view the spread of the bodhisattva ideal among elites during the reform era as a lingering residue of the esoteric Buddhist practices cultivated, in particular, when the Abhayagiri was at the height of its powers before the tenth century.[37] Yet there is only so far that such external contact can be used as a total explanation for cultural change. For whether or not the bodhisattva path as imagined by the Mahāvihāra developed, even in part, due to attraction or rivalry with the previous era's Mahayana and Tantric practices, it is clear from reform-era writings that the pursuit of buddhahood was a genuine response to the chaos of the reform period and that Mahāvihāran monks created a conceptual framework for this path from within their own Pali tradition.

6.2. Authority, Control and the Art of the Anthology

We have already seen in the preceding chapters how the intertwined exigencies of staving off religious decline and establishing monastic unification had brought about a new systematicity in the way the Saṅgha handled its scriptural tradition. The anthologists, in this regard, shared the same desire for systematicity, concision and comprehensiveness as the reform-era commentators, indicated in particular by the word *sāra* ('essence') found in the title of Siddhattha's *Sārasaṅgaha*, or '*Sārattha*'-*saṅgaha* ('essential meaning') as attested by later tradition;[38] a word which, as discussed in chapter five, denotes both semantic totality and also compact utility.[39]

Like the commentators, the anthologists employed new philological approaches to recover and control this essence. One such technique that became pervasive in reform-era works was the introduction of a contents list at the beginning of each handbook, often referred to as a *mātikā* ('matrix'), providing the chapter divisions of the work. Prior to the reform era, the only handbook to include such a list was Dhammasiri's fifth- or sixth-century *Khuddasikkhā*.[40] There is no other evidence, as far as I am aware, of the use of a contents list in works contemporary with Dhammasiri, even in Sanskrit, and this possibly represents the first use of such a metatextual device in South Asian intellectual history. The list re-emerges in Sāriputta's *Vinayasaṅgaha* and can be found in the other anthologies of the era, including the *Sārasaṅgaha*, the *Upāsakajanālaṅkāra*, the *Bhesajjamañjūsā* and the *Daivajñakāmadhenu* ('Wish-fulfilling cow of divine insight'). The device also emerges outside of the Sri Lankan tradition in contemporary twelfth-century works, such as the *Kṛtyakalpataru* ('Wish-fulfilling tree of rites'), a manual of *Dharmaśāstra* or Hindu law, though it is referred to there as the 'introduction' (*pratijñā*).[41]

The term *mātikā* has a long history in Buddhist thought. It refers most commonly to the lists of phenomena that were derived from the Suttas and systematized in the Abhidhamma.[42] These lists of entities, sometimes referred to also as *uddesa* ('topics'), begin certain Abhidhamma texts, such as the *Vibhaṅga* ('Analysis'), and are then explained at length in the so-called *niddesa* ('explication') section. Even in certain Suttas, such as the *Bhaddekaratta Sutta* ('One fortunate attachment'), the Buddha explicitly separates his discourse into an initial summary (*uddesa*) followed by an extended explanation (*vibhaṅga*).[43] Commenting on this Sutta, Buddhaghosa defines *uddesa* simply as *mātikā*.[44] Writing sometime after the seventh century, Dhammapāla adds here that, 'He (Buddhaghosa) uses [the word] *mātikā* as it (i.e. the 'summary') is like a mother (*mātā*) since it is engaged in producing words of explication (*niddesapada*).'[45]

The exegetical character of the early *mātikā* continues in the commentarial tradition in the form of exegetical schemas (also called *mātikā*) used to guide commentarial analysis, as discussed in the previous chapter.[46] There is a clear conceptual continuity, then, throughout the tradition's history in the productive and exegetical function of these lists.[47] In the reform-era handbooks, however, we begin to see a subtle shift in the perceived role played by these schemas. Sāriputta, for instance, when defining the term *mātikā* used to introduce the contents list of his Vinaya handbook, differs from previous tradition by explicitly stating that this schema serves as a 'finding device' in that it enables those searching for a particular disciplinary judgement to find it easily and thus remove their doubts (*kaṅkhā*).[48] It is perhaps for this reason that the contents lists of the anthologies were more elaborate than the exegetical schemas of the commentaries. See, for instance, the contents list of Siddhattha's *Sārasaṅgaha*:

> This here is the contents list (*mātikā*):
> (1) The resolve of buddhas, etc.; (2) the marvellous deeds of the teacher; (3) the five disappearances; (4) defining a Wheel-Turning monarch;

> (5) characterizing the shrines of buddhas and Wheel-Turning monarchs; (6) the benefits of sweeping [a shrine]; (7) the marvel of the Dhamma; (8), the marvel of the Saṅgha; (9) defining sleep; (10) explaining dreams; (11) exchanging things belonging to the Buddha and Dhamma; (12) types of refuge; (13) types of morals; (14) meditation; (15) nirvana (*anālaya*); (16) disrespecting the [three] jewels; (17) defining the types of karma; (18) karma with immediate [consequences]; (19) defining false views; (20) the karma of finding fault with the noble; (21) the danger of deceit; (22) types of envy; (23) characterising the three-fold fire; (24) meritorious karma, such as, giving; (25) specifying the nutriments of living things; (26) types of reproductive structure of living things; (27) exchanging male and female genders; (28) types of women; (29) types of eunuch (*paṇḍaka*); (30) types of dragons; (31) types of snakes; (32) types of ghost; (33) types of demigod; (34) types of god; (35) the evolution of the earth; (36) earthquakes; (37) explaining rain and wind, etc.; (38) miscellaneous discussions; (39) extraordinary powers; (40) the form of the world.[49]

These contents lists usually give the book's chapters in order and are often composed in verse, presumably to facilitate memorization. Handbooks, like the *Sārasaṅgaha*, clearly demarcate the beginning and end of each chapter by citing the name of the topic as given in the contents list. Echoing older textual models, Siddhattha presents each chapter, at least at the outset, as an exegesis on the wording of the topic given in the contents. This all helps bind the work's content to its organizational structure and allows the reader to browse topics of interest more easily.

Another complementary innovation that we find in the anthologies of the reform era is that authors provide detailed information about the works used as source material. Unlike older commentaries and handbooks, for instance, there is an increasing tendency in works such as the *Sārasaṅgaha* and, to a lesser extent, the *Upāsakajanālaṅkāra*, to cite with great specificity the authoritative source for a particular passage or quotation.[50] While Siddhattha usually provides the name of his source immediately after citing a particular text, on occasion he also innovatively chooses to provide a list of the sources he has used at the very end of a longer passage or chapter in the form of a bibliography. This enables him to seamlessly weave his disparate source material together without interruption. We can speculate that this strategy also allowed him to mask the fact that some passages in his work cannot be traced to any of the texts that he cites as sources.[51] The occasional preference for endnotes rather than in-text citations is most pronounced in his final discussion of cosmology (*lokaṭṭhiti*) where the entire chapter is appended with a long list of authoritative sources, the beginning of which is as follows:

> In this chapter, then: (1) the mode of destroying and establishing an eon (*kappa*) due to three causes is taken from the *Aggañña Sutta* ('What is primary') in the *Dīgha Nikāya* and the *Visuddhimagga*; (2) how the seat of awakening (*bodhimaṇḍa*) is established is mentioned in the commentary on the *Mahāpadāna Sutta* ('Great lineage') in the *Dīgha Nikāya*; (3) the two-fold division of an established eon as either 'empty' or 'not empty' is mentioned in the commentary on the history of Padumuttara Buddha in the *Buddhavaṃsa* ('History of the buddhas'); (4) the analysis (*vibhāga*) of the size and motion of the moon and sun is mentioned in the commentary on the *Aggañña Sutta*, etc.; (5) the seizing [of the sun] by Rāhu (i.e. an eclipse), furthermore, is mentioned in the commentary on the *Devaputtasaṃyutta* in the *Saṃyutta Nikāya* …[52]

Chiara Neri in a recent pioneering study has pointed to a couple of passages in the *Sārasaṅgaha* where Siddhattha explains the purpose of such detailed referencing.[53] Early on in his work he specifically asks the question, 'What is the purpose in saying "this here is stated in such and such a source (*ṭhāna*)"?'[54] Siddhattha's answer indicates that he was concerned primarily with the legitimacy and credibility of his sources, in particular the authoritative status of his commentarial material, which by far represents the main source of information for his handbook.

He first paraphrases a discussion found in Sāriputta's Vinaya subcommentary, already discussed in our previous chapter, where commentaries are referred to as the 'miscellaneous teachings' (*pakiṇṇakadesanā*) of the Buddha himself since 'only the perfectly enlightened one uttered the method (*kkama*) of commenting on the meaning of the three baskets'. He continues, 'only the miscellaneous teachings that were initiated by the Buddha here and there are called a commentary (*aṭṭhakathā*). More generally, however, in some cases they are called a commentary (*aṭṭhakathā*) and in others a subcommentary (*ṭīkā*).' Siddhattha, then, differs from Sāriputta by including here even the subcommentaries as 'teachings initiated by the Buddha' and it is noteworthy that he also cites doctrinal handbooks in his anthology, further indicating that these works were now treated as commentaries.[55] Siddhattha viewed his sources as part of a tradition established by the Buddha and our anthologist concludes that, 'therefore when a source is specified the wise understand this well'.[56]

These references, according to Siddhattha, were not only provided to lend authority to his work but served a practical purpose in that they could act as a guide for students who wished to study a topic in more detail. He writes at the end of his thirty-eighth chapter, to quote Chiara Neri's translation, that 'it is necessary to refer back [to the quoted texts] continually so as to understand the true essence (*sāra*) [of these teachings] and furthermore to understand the essence [of the teachings] not explained here'.[57] To this end, the references in the *Sārasaṅgaha* act as a further matrix that orientates and organizes the reader's systematic investigation of the Pali textual tradition as a whole. The effect of this 'binding back' into his sprawling textual heritage is that, through the lens of the anthology, the canon and its commentaries appear organized and coherent and can be studied as such.[58] By shifting the framework in which the Pali textual tradition is analysed, Siddhattha, with the aim of conserving the tradition of the Mahāvihāra, is able to innovate in the way he represents the essence of his tradition and can provide a creative reading of this material to accommodate the interests of his contemporary monastic community.

6.3. Buddhology, Eschatology and Immanence

We can better appreciate the creativity inherent in the practice of compilation by exploring in more detail the emphasis the *Sārasaṅgaha* places on Buddhology, eschatology and karma, characterized, in particular, by the cultivation of merit and the pursuit of better rebirths. This reformulation of what was thought to be essential in the Buddha's teachings represented a marked shift from the earliest tradition. Siddhattha, for instance, spends a good forty-three pages in the Pali Text Society edition discussing the 'form of the world' and only one-and-a-half on the topic of nirvana. Rather than viewing these topics as a 'curious medley' with little connection to one another, it is possible by exploring how Siddhattha knits together in his anthology diverse topics, such as the portents of dreams and the cleaning of shrines, to discern how they form part of a coherent religious orientation.

The work's fundamental concern with the bodhisattva path is apparent at the outset where it begins with a chapter dedicated to the formal 'undertaking' (*abhinīhāra*) of buddhahood, that is, the resolution one makes to become a buddha when entering the bodhisattva path.[59] Excised almost exclusively from the opening or *nidāna* to the commentary on the *Khaggavisāṇa Sutta* ('Rhinoceros horn'), Siddhattha includes detailed descriptions of the length of time needed to achieve buddhahood, the eight prerequisites needed to make such an undertaking, as well as details on when and how a buddha arises in the world. He includes, for instance, information that buddhahood takes a minimum of 'four incalculables and one hundred thousand eons' to achieve and that to make a formal aspiration to buddhahood one must be a human, a male, a renunciate, have the capacity to achieve Arahantship, possess excellent qualities, have performed exceptional deeds of self-sacrifice, harbour the strong desire to achieve the goal and, importantly, make one's formal aspiration only after having personally seen a buddha.

This commentarial introduction originally served to contextualize the commentator's subsequent discussions on the nature of a *paccekabuddha* ('solitary buddha'), so-called because these buddhas do not teach others and live, supposedly like rhinoceroses, as solitary ascetics. Siddhattha, however, skilfully excises key passages from the commentary and uses them as a source to teach the doctrinal technicalities and prerequisites of making an aspiration to pursue buddhahood.[60]

We can detect a concern in Siddhattha's work also for information on how one can gain certainty that buddhahood will be obtained. It is in this light that we can understand the two chapters in the first quarter of his work concerning sleep (*niddā*) and dreams (*supina*).[61] He shows an interest in explanations of how we dream as well as the types of dream one can have, in particular prognosticatory dreams (*pubbanimittabhūta*).[62] These dreams are further classified by the level of truth (*sacca*) that one can derive from such visions. The omens from prognosticatory dreams, for instance, are regarded by the commentarial tradition as entirely true (*ekantasacca*).[63] Siddhattha's main concern in his chapter are the five great dreams (*mahāsupina*) that a bodhisattva sees in his last birth before enlightenment. G.P. Malalasekera summarizes them as follows:

> (i) that the world is his couch with the Himalaya as his pillow, his left hand resting on the eastern sea, his right on the western and his feet on the southern; (ii) that a blade of *tiriyā* (*kusa*) grass, growing from his navel touches the clouds; (iii) that white worms with black heads creep up from his feet, covering his knees; (iv) that four birds of varied hues from the four quarters of the world fall at his feet and become white; and (v) that he walks to and fro on a heap of dung, by which he remains unsullied.[64]

His concern for prognosticatory signs extends to cosmological portents and their relationship with the fate of his Buddhist tradition (*sāsana*). This is most evident in the prominent place Siddhattha assigns in his work to the so-called 'five disappearances' (*pañca-antaradhāna*), discussed in chapter three, that are said to characterize the inevitable decline and destruction of Buddhism, namely the gradual disappearance of realization, practice, scripture, monastic signs and relics.[65] Siddhattha's discussion of this topic is based largely on Buddhaghosa's prophecy in his *Aṅguttara Nikāya* commentary concerning the decline of the Buddhist tradition over the course of 5,000 years after the Buddha's death.[66] This decline, Buddhaghosa writes, is ultimately brought about by the disappearance of scriptural knowledge due to kings whose immorality (*adhammika*) causes the rain gods to create a drought.[67] This results in famine and the ultimate loss of religious patronage due to the impoverishment of society.

Siddhattha further cites in the chapter a number of other commentarial accounts of religious decline, focusing in particular on the diminishing scope of religious attainments possible in each age. In the most pessimistic but widely cited of these accounts, the commentator on the Vinaya states that the first 1,000 years after the Buddha's death will mark the end of the attainment of the so-called 'analytical insights' (*paṭisambhidā*) and that after the second 1,000 years monks will lose the possibility of 'dry insight' (*sukkhavipassana*) and, seemingly, of enlightenment itself.[68] The remaining 3,000 years witness the disappearance, in turn, of becoming a 'non returner' who is spontaneously reborn in the realm of form, a 'once returner' who has one life left, and finally a 'stream enterer' who has entered onto the path of enlightenment.

There is a connection in Buddhist eschatology between the decline of the Dhamma, the destruction of the cosmos as a whole and the appearance of buddhas. Siddhattha writes at length about cosmic decline and he dedicates the final and longest chapter in the work to a detailed description of the cosmos, its creation, maintenance and eventual destruction. There, he quotes Buddhaghosa's *Visuddhimagga* and describes the three ways the universe can be destroyed, either by fire, water or wind. With respect to fire, for instance, he describes the future appearance of seven suns that will eventually destroy the universe in an apocalyptic inferno, 'leaving no ash like a flame burning ghee and oil'.[69]

The Buddha's relationship to this universe is characterized as a threefold 'Buddha field' (*buddhakhetta*), divided into his 'field of birth' (*jātikhetta*), 'field of influence' (*āṇākhetta*) and 'field of scope' (*visayakhetta*). His 'field of birth' extends to the 10,000 world-systems (*cakkavāḷa*) that shook upon his entrance into his mother's womb. His 'field of influence', defined as the scope of the power of certain protective Suttas (*paritta*), further extends to 100,000 myriad world-systems.[70] Finally, his 'field of scope', that is, the scope of his omniscience, is boundless and has no spatial limit. It is the end of the Buddha's 'field of influence', Buddhaghosa writes, that brings about the destruction of the 10,000 world systems that constitute his 'field of birth' and the world as we know it.[71] The root cause of this destruction is said to be the accumulation of the so-called 'three fires', namely, greed (*rāga*), hatred (*dosa*) and delusion (*moha*).[72]

Implicit in the stages of religious decline set out in the 'five disappearances' is a steady transition from religious transcendence to immanence.[73] After the possibility of transcendent enlightenment and other realizations (*adhigama*) has been lost along with doctrine (*pariyatti*) and correct practice (*paṭipatti*), we are left with only the outward, worldly signs (*liṅga*) of the religious tradition – those who look like monks, for instance, despite being morally corrupt – and, finally, also the Buddha's relics (*dhātu*).[74] It is perhaps owing to his eschatological interests, then, that Siddhattha places such emphasis on relic worship. In a detailed description of the types of relics and the benefits of worshipping them in chapter five, Siddhattha cites the Buddha's statement in the *Mahāparinibbāna Sutta* ('Great passing') that, 'Whoever, Ānanda, wanders visiting shrines and dies with a serene (*pasanna*) mind will, after the break-up of the body at death, be reborn in a good destiny, a heavenly world.'[75] Siddhattha then immediately quotes Buddhaghosa's explanation:

> Here, **wanders visiting shrines** means those who, so far, wander (*āhiṇḍati*), i.e. roam (*vicarati*), here and there sweeping a shrine's courtyard, washing its seats and watering the Bodhi tree. These need no explanation. [The Buddha] reveals that those possessed of a serene heart, even if they die having set out with the intention, 'we will worship the shrine at such and such a monastery', will in fact immediately reappear in heaven.[76]

He explains here a stipulation that was originally about making pilgrimages to shrines in terms that instead emphasize their maintenance. Of the ritual acts mentioned, the sweeping of a shrine in particular appears to have captured the monastic imagination in the reform era. Siddhattha devotes an entire chapter to the topic including a passage in the Vinaya dedicated to the five benefits of sweeping and its commentarial explanation.[77] The passage states, 'there are five benefits in sweeping: one pleases (*pasīdati*) one's own mind, one pleases the mind of another, deities become delighted, one accumulates merit that leads to what is pleasing (*pasādika*), and, after the break-up of the body, that is, after death, one is reborn in a good destiny, a heavenly world'.[78]

We can see from the Buddha's statement in the *Mahāparinibbāna Sutta* and from this Vinaya passage that even in the very earliest tradition the religious importance of shrines and their associated ritual acts lay in their role as emotional stimulants, in particular their ability to bring about pleasing feelings. The words used here are the verb *pasīdati* (*pa* + *sad*, Sk. *pra* + *sad*), its nominal derivative *pasāda* or its past participle *pasanna*. It literally means to be 'bright' or 'pleased' but it is also used in the sense of gaining peace, clarity and confidence. Summarizing well the wide semantic range of the word, Edith Ludowyk-Gyömröi wrote that it refers to 'a mental attitude which unites deep feeling, intellectual appreciation and satisfaction, clarification of thought and attraction toward the teacher'.[79]

Throughout his work but in particular when discussing the 'marvels' (*acchariya*) of the Buddha, Dhamma and Saṅgha in his opening chapters, Siddhattha emphasizes the role of these devotional objects in inspiring among Buddhist devotees this feeling of 'serene joy', as Kevin Trainor succinctly renders the term.[80] These are not passive aesthetic objects, rather they are described as agents inculcating *pasāda* among devotees: the Buddha is a 'conveyer' (*āvaha*) of this emotion, the Dhamma actively 'pleases' (*pasīdati*) and monks are 'stimulators' (*saṃvaddhaka*) of *pasāda*.[81] Even in the earliest tradition this emotion is highlighted as an important karmic condition for bringing about a heavenly rebirth and even buddhahood itself. The enacting of wholesome karma through relic worship was traditionally always tied to the arising of the emotion, for, as Jonathan Walters states, 'such mental pleasure constitutes the operative element of meritorious karma, good actions being efficacious to the extent that they are performed with delight …'.[82] A soteriology centred on devotion, then, was primarily focused on finding ways to cultivate in oneself and others this serene joy since, throughout the tradition's history, it was this emotion that was a primary means of karmic transformation.

This fact is underlined by a charming story from Buddhaghosa's *Majjhima Nikāya* commentary that Siddhattha relates at the end of his chapter on the marvel of the Saṅgha, where an owl comes to worship the Buddha, bowing its head and folding its wings together in reverence. The Buddha smiles and declares that 'having cultivated serene joy (*pasādetvā*) in his heart with respect to me and the unsurpassed monastic community, he will not go to a bad rebirth for 100,000 eons. Having left the realm of the gods, impelled by a virtuous beginning (*mūla*), he will become an omniscient buddha named Somanassa.'[83] The prominence given to such stories reflects Siddhattha's soteriological interest in the transformative capacity of serene joy as one of the most potent means by which he could escape the chaos of his social and political circumstances and ensure a heavenly rebirth or perhaps even buddhahood in the distant future.

6.4. The Cult of the Book and Monastic Property

The widespread eschatological concerns and increasing popularity of the bodhisattva path among high status intellectuals must have rebalanced the social order by shifting the collective aim of a good number of monastic elites towards rebirth-orientated practices, in particular the cultivation of favourable emotions using the island's aesthetically-charged relics and other pleasing traces of Gotama Buddha's dispensation.[84] The danger, however, of shifting religious hierarchies around the immanent power of the Buddha, as embodied in his shrines in particular, is that it made the monastic elite more vulnerable to competition from other religious groups since it could allow the concentration of elite monastic power to weaken through the loss of control and possible proliferation of relics.[85] Such a concern is evident in Siddhattha's handling of one of the reform era's most striking developments in ritual practice, namely the acceptance of scriptural texts as Buddha relics.

Prior to tenth century, relic worship had been particularly prominent in the royally-favoured Abhayagiri fraternity, as a result, perhaps, of the court's interest in their apotropaic power.[86] After the unification of 1165 there is evidence that certain ritual practices found originally in the Abhayagiri appear to have continued within the Mahāvihāra, the most prominent of which was the practice of depositing scriptural texts in shrines and worshipping them as relics of the Buddha. Gregory Schopen famously referred to this long-standing practice among Mahayana and Tantric Buddhists as the 'cult of the book'.[87] From at least the second century, as Daniel Boucher has described, we find Sanskrit inscriptions of short *sūtra*s describing the Buddhist doctrine of dependent co-arising (*pratītyasamutpāda*, P. *paṭiccasamuppāda*) etched on reliquaries (*stūpa*) in India and Central Asia.[88] We also find, from around the sixth century until the twelfth, variations on the following Sanskrit verse summarizing the doctrine of dependent co-arising deposited as a relic itself often etched on clay tablets inside reliquaries:

> ye dharmā hetuprabhavā hetuṃ teṣāṃ tathāgato hy avadat
> teṣāṃ ca yo nirodha evaṃvādī mahāśramaṇaḥ.[89]
>
> The Buddha spoke of the cause of those dhammas that arise from a cause and the cessation of them. The great renunciate has taught this much.

The worship of scripture as a relic of the Buddha was based in part on the ancient identification of the Buddha with his teachings as reflected in scriptural statements found also in the Pali canon, such as, 'One who sees the Dhamma, Vakkali, sees me; one who sees me, sees the Dhamma.'[90] As the central doctrine of Buddhist thought, dependent co-arising was regarded by the earliest tradition as the epitome of the Buddha's teachings. Developing on the perceived identity between the Buddha and his doctrine, early Mahayana *sūtra*s explicitly equate the doctrine of dependent co-arising with the Buddha himself. In the *Śālistamba Sūtra* ('Rice stalk') the bodhisattva Maitreya addresses Śāriputra as follows: 'He, monks, who sees dependent co-arising sees the Dharma; he who sees the Dharma sees the Buddha.'[91] It is not difficult to see, then, how scripture began to be treated as a relic equivalent to the

Buddha's body. The middle of the first millennium further witnessed a parallel development where these textual formulas became increasingly cryptic and were deposited as relics in the form of *dhāraṇī*s, that is, 'coded systems of the Buddha's speech' often consisting of ritualized symbols sometimes in the form of mantras. These mantras served in Tantric soteriology to expedite religious attainments and also as apotropaic spells for karmic protection.[92]

The Pali tradition in Sri Lanka by contrast remained for much of its history remarkably ambivalent about such ritual practices.[93] This is not to say that the 'cult of the book' was not found in Sri Lanka. In fact there is some evidence that the ritual use of Sanskrit texts, incised as inscriptions or deposited as relics, was not uncommon on the island.[94] While we can conventionally speak of these as evidence of Mahayana or Tantric Buddhism in Sri Lanka, the boundaries between Buddhist traditions are much harder to differentiate in practice. We have already discussed in chapter one that the Abhayagiri fraternity, in particular, embraced Tantric Buddhist practices, including the enshrining of protective *dhāraṇī*s. One *dhāraṇī* dating to around the ninth century is especially interesting since it was inscribed on six tablets at the Abhayagiri monastery in Anurādhapura.[95] It records a discourse between the bodhisattva Vajrapāṇi and the Buddha in which the Buddha proclaims that if someone were to deposit the sūtra within a reliquary or *stūpa* then 'that *stūpa* would become a *stūpa* of the relics of the "essence" of *vajra* of all *Tathāgata*s'.[96]

There are some rare examples too of ritual deposits of Pali canonical formulas in Sri Lanka at sites associated with the Abhayagiri in particular. A gold foil Pali eulogy, giving the *iti pi so* formula, for instance, was discovered underneath a pillar of a relic shrine (*vaṭadāge*) at Mädirigiriya, which, according to Jeffrey Sundberg, may have been affiliated with the Abhayagiri fraternity. The first account of the etching dates it to the construction of the shrine in the reign of Aggabodhi VI (733–72). Sundberg, however, has recently speculated that it may date to one of the later renovations of the shrine and represent an attempt on the part of Abhayagiri monks to 'accommodate' or 'revalorize' Pali religious symbolism.[97] Sundberg has also plausibly suggested that the revival of the Mahāvihāra after Sena II (853–87) led the fraternity to adopt some of the ritual practices of their competitors and it is possible that the use of the Pali canon as a ritual deposit, first among Abhayagiri monks, was incorporated by Mahāvihāran monks into their own ritual repertoire during the tenth century.[98] It appears, for instance, that Kassapa V (914–23), an ardent supporter of the Mahāvihāra, enshrined the Abhidhamma text, the *Dhammasaṅgaṇi* ('Enumeration of dhammas'), within a temple in Anurādhapura, and that this relic became an important ritual object for his successors, in particular, Mahinda IV (954–72).[99]

By the reform era the treatment of scripture as a relic had become formally incorporated within the Pali matrix. Writing in his voluminous commentary on the Vinaya, for instance, Sāriputta states that there are three types of shrine to the Buddha (*buddhacetiya*), namely a shrine to items he used (*paribhogacetiya*), a shrine to his corporeal relics (*dhātucetiya*) and finally a shrine to his teachings (*dhammacetiya*). He defines the latter in terms familiar from Mahayana practice as 'a shrine built having deposited therein a book inscribed with dependent co-arising, etc.'[100] Siddhattha in his *Sārasaṅgaha* incorporates this passage in his discussion in chapter five of the shrines of Sages and Wheel-Turning kings. He also further dedicates an entire chapter to a particularly creative discussion on the legal status of offerings made to such a Dhamma shrine and their interchangeability with offerings made to the Buddha's corporeal relics:[101]

> **The exchange of things belonging to the Buddha and Dhamma:** This here is an explanation. Is it permissible to make an offering to the Buddha with the property of the Dhamma or an offering to the Dhamma with the property of the Buddha or not? They say that it is permissible since there is the statement (*vacana*), 'This, Vāseṭṭha, is a designation of the Tathāgata, namely, the body of Dhamma (*dhammakāya*)' (*Dīgha Nikāya* III, $84,_{23-4}$), and also, 'one who sees the Dhamma, Vakkali, sees me' (*Saṃyutta Nikāya* III, $120,_{28-31}$).
>
> Some, however, say that it is not permissible since, if this were the case, due to the statement 'a monk who would care for me, should care for the ill' (*Vinaya* I, $302,_{19-20}$), there would be the unwanted consequence that one would be allowed to make medicine also for an ill [person] using the property of the Buddha (on account of a perceived equivalence between the two).
>
> This is baseless since, in the statement 'a monk who would care for me, should care for the ill', not a single similarity (*ekasadisatā*) is mentioned between himself (Buddha) and the ill, nor is an equal benefit (*samaphalatā*) mentioned for the one who cares for them. For this here is the meaning: One who would care for me by delivering advice (*ovāda*) and instruction (*anusāsanī*), should care for the ill. By delivering my advice, the ill are to be cared for. In terms of any similarity between caring for the Buddha and for the ill, however, we do not accept such a sense here.
>
> Because of the statement, 'the doctrine and discipline, Ānanda, that I taught and declared to you will be your teacher after my passing' (*Dīgha Nikāya* II, $154,_{6-8}$); and because it was said, 'at present, furthermore, it is I alone who admonishes and instructs you. After I have completely

> passed away these 84,000 buddhas will admonish and instruct you'; and because, when praising a learned monk, it was also said, 'You should not call him a "hearer", Cunda, this one is called "awakened"' (*Sumaṅgalavilāsinī* III, $912,_{11-12}$); and because the Buddha has the status of teacher of the Dhamma, only the first reasoning should be praised (i.e. it is permissible to exchange the property of the Buddha and Dhamma). This is mentioned in the subcommentary (*ṭīkā*) on the Vinaya.[102]

In this fascinating discussion taken from Sāriputta's *Sāratthadīpanī* ('Illuminator of essential meaning') we can see that reform-era scholar-monks were less concerned with the doctrinal implications of the cult of the book than with the social and economic consequences of this ritual practice. Sāriputta, for instance, cites a number of key passages where the ontological and functional equivalence between the Buddha and his Dhamma is made explicit.

His imagined opponent argues against this not on any philosophical basis but simply because of what he perceives to be the possible economic consequences of this doctrine. Sāriputta's adversary argues that if the Buddha and Dhamma are treated as identical on account of passages comparing them, then – since there is also a canonical passage that seems to compare caring for the Buddha with caring for the ill – one unwanted consequence of this logic would be that the Buddha's property may be used to care for the ill as well. While Sāriputta does not disagree with his opponent's fear about the distribution of the Buddha's wealth, he views the comparison between the Buddha and the ill as different from passages comparing the Buddha and Dhamma. It is possible, therefore, to transfer property between shrines to the Buddha and Dhamma, though this logic should not extend to the comparison between the Buddha and the ill, and thus the Buddha's wealth cannot be used for the commonweal. This passage is buried deep within Sāriputta's Vinaya commentary and could easily be missed. Its relative importance, however, for reform-era practice is reflected in the fact that Siddhattha highlighted it and placed it as a chapter at the beginning of his anthology.

Siddhattha at the end of the chapter departs from Sāriputta's Vinaya subcommentary and, for good measure, reminds his reader also about the legal rules concerning the exchangeability of the property of relic shrines and that of the monastic community as a whole. He quotes Buddhaghosa's Vinaya commentary, for instance, as stating:

> It is permissible to have the property of a relic shrine maintained with the property of either a relic shrine or the Saṅgha. It is not permissible to have the Saṅgha's property maintained with the property of a relic shrine. The property of the Saṅgha, however, which is deposited together with

> the property of a relic shrine, can only be maintained when the property of the relic shrine is maintained.[103]

Buddhaghosa here states quite clearly that the property of a shrine cannot be transferred to the Saṅgha whereas the Saṅgha's property can be invested in a shrine. We can infer from this that the elite monks who managed such shrines must have long formed a fiscally and in part legally independent faction within the Saṅgha. There was an economic incentive in the post-reform era then to maintain control of such shrines, not only because of their ritual power in facilitating karmic transformation, but because these sites represented a common market for the Buddha's transferable property and the pinnacle of wealth within the Saṅgha's own courtly hierarchy. We can speculate further that Dhamma shrines, while a useful karmic technology, represented an economic challenge to monastic elites since they had the potential to radically distribute the Buddha's power and wealth on the island through proliferation. By incorporating Dhamma shrines within the Pali matrix and by legislating for the transferability of wealth between Dhamma shrines and Buddha shrines, the monastic leadership, in principle, was able to maintain control of the Buddha's immanent power on the island within their protectionist relic market.

6.5. Summary

The *Sārasaṅgaha* in many ways sits at the nexus of the main strands of thought that governed reform-era monastic life. As one of the new anthologies composed during the reform era, the *Sārasaṅgaha* displays a number of innovative philological techniques to extract and organize the semantic essence of the Pali scriptural tradition, using contents lists, citations and bibliographies to curate the substance of the canon into something that could stand for scripture in its totality as well as in its compact utility. Siddhattha's decision to present a totalizing depiction of his scriptural tradition in an anthology stems perhaps from the threat posed by the social and political turmoil of the age and his desire to intervene in these circumstances by pursuing buddhahood. This required a new charter for monastic action based on an engagement with karmic rituals that could bring vast amounts of merit, centred primarily on cultivating the transformative emotion of serene joy. To some extent, then, the task of a bodhisattva was to seek out stimulation, in particular from the inspiring traces of the Buddha, Dhamma and Saṅgha. This shift in soteriological emphasis among elites, however, while encouraged by the eschatologically orientated reforms, also needed to be formalized in Pali theory due to its concurrent potential to undermine the reformed Saṅgha's authority and economic hierarchy. Relics and other such sacred stimulants are treated in Siddhattha's manual not only as objects of religious transformation but also as potentially destabilizing entities that had to be controlled and legislated for within the monastic disciplinary code.

Notes

1. Dessein, 2013.
2. Gethin, 1992. Concerning Vinaya *mātṛkā*s, see Clarke, 2004.
3. Von Hinüber, 1996, §§86–7.
4. Von Hinüber, 1996, §245.
5. Von Hinüber, 1996, §325; §340.
6. See Kieffer-Pülz, 2013, 194–7; 2015, 435. On the authorship of the *Saccasaṅkhepa*, see Von Hinüber, 1996, §351; Cousins, 2013; Kieffer-Pülz, 2018, 190, n. 4. Other handbooks from this era include Mahāsāmi's (?) *Mūlasikkhā* and possibly also the Abhidhamma works of Anuruddha.
7. See Heim, 2004, 21–8.
8. Malalasekera, 1994, 228–9; Sasaki, ed. 1992, vii–xiii; Neri, 2015, 337–9.
9. *Sārasaṅgaha* of Siddhattha, $1_{,5}$. Reading *sāta*° instead of *sata*° in the compound *satasukhāvahaṃ*. On *sātasukha*, see *Aṅguttara Nikāya* I, $81_{,27}$.
10. I am influenced here by Blackburn, 1999a; Collins, 1990; Heim, 2004, 1–31; McDaniel, 2008, 191–204; Parkes, 1991.
11. Spiro, 1982.
12. As well as Spiro, 1982, esp. 69–70, see Ames, 1963; Deegalle, 1997; 2006; Keyes, 1995, 86; Reynolds and Hallisey, 1989, esp. 19. This is not to deny that a form of Buddhist public did start to emerge during this period or that this was linked to the development of vernacular preaching texts, but simply to question whether this process was the sole cause for the kammatic focus of much of the literature composed during the reform era and its aftermath. On the connection between eschatological notions of decline and popular religion in Japan, see Strathern, 2019, 96.
13. One exception is Vācissara's *Sīmālaṅkārasaṅgaha*. Another anthology is the *Suttasaṅgaha*, though attempts to date the work are highly speculative. See Chaudhuri and Guha, eds. 1957, xii–xiii.
14. I use the term 'encyclopedism' advisedly to denote the compilation of material from a wide range of disciplines, often collected in relation to a single topic. On the history of the term in early modern Europe, see Blair, 2013. See also, Blair, 2010, 168–72.
15. *Upāsakajanālaṅkāra* of Ānanda, 123, v. 4, trans. Agostini, 2015, 2.
16. *Sārasaṅgaha* of Siddhattha, $344_{,20–5}$.
17. For an overview, see Cox, 2017, 19–22, esp. 19, n. 35; Heim, 2004, 1–31.
18. On the *Rūpāvatāra* of Dharmakīrti, see Cardona, 1976, 285. On the *Daivajñakāmadhenu* of Anavamadarśin, see Pingree, 1981, 115.
19. Pollock, 1993a, 105–6, also discussed in Heim, 2004, 8.
20. For possible objections, see Brick, 2015, 14–15, also discussed in De Simini, 2016, 428–34.
21. Vācissara, author of the *Sīmālaṅkārasaṅgaha*, may also have fled to South India during the invasion of Māgha, if the author is identical with a Vācissara mentioned in *Cūḷavaṃsa* 81.17–22. See Kieffer-Pülz, 1999b; 2020.
22. *Upāsakajanālaṅkāra* of Ānanda, $358_{,15–22}$, trans. Agostini, 2015, 337–8. I have added the text in parentheses.
23. Liyanagamage, 2001a; Kieffer-Pülz, 2015a.
24. Agostini, 2015, xi–xii. The *Paṭipattisaṅgaha*, for instance, is more closely aligned with the structure of the *Visuddhimagga*. See Young, 2011, 33.
25. *Sārasaṅgaha* of Siddhattha, $344_{,16–17}$. On the monastery's possible location, see Sasaki, ed. 1992, viii.
26. It is more likely that Siddhattha is referring here to the thirteenth-century Buddhappiya, author of the *Pajjamadhu*, rather than the eleventh or early twelfth-century author of the *Rūpasiddhi*. The *Sārasaṅgaha* must date after the 1165 reform since it cites Sumaṅgala. See *Sārasaṅgaha* of Siddhattha, $105_{,15–18}$ = *Abhidhammatthavibhāvinī* of Sumaṅgala, $201_{,19–20}$, cited in Von Hinüber, 1996, §385.
27. Here following Liyanagamage, 1968, 133–59.

28. I am inspired here by Whitney Cox's recent comparison of the monumental character of Bhoja's *Śṛṅgāraprakāśa* and the same king's expansive irrigation works at Bhojpur. See Cox, 2012, 61–3.
29. On the influence of the *Visuddhimagga* on the *Sārasaṅgaha*'s discussion of meditation, see Neri, 2015, 339–42.
30. Other scholars have identified patterns in the work's arrangement of topics. Citing N. Nobuaki's work, which I have not been able to access, Chiara Neri quotes Nobuaki as identifying 'five macro subjects in the chapters of the Ss: Buddha, *Dhamma* and *Saṅgha*; spiritual exercises; problems linked to *kamma* in the *saṃsaric* [sic.] life; the various types of sentient beings; issues concerning the natural world.' See Nobuaki, 1998, 2, cited in Neri, 2015, 338.
31. Malalasekera, 1994, 230.
32. The category 'millennialism' has been used in this context as a catch-all description for both the devotional, karmic soteriology of the bodhisattva path and its attendant eschatological concerns. For an overview of studies relating to Theravada Buddhism and millennialism, see Collins, 1998, 395–413. If, as Collins argues, we take millennialism in a Theravada context as 'an overall category for Buddhist ideas of future felicity associated with Metteyya and other future Buddhas' (413), then I think the term only covers a part of the mentality of scholars such as Siddhattha. While our author certainly hoped to be consecrated as a bodhisattva in the presence of Metteyya, he is aware that this will only occur in the unfathomable future and much of his concern as a bodhisattva is drawn rather to karmic practices in the here and now.
33. Collins, 1998, 394.
34. *Sārasaṅgaha* of Siddhattha, $344_{,6-13}$:
    … tena puññena ābodhā jātijātiyaṃ
    sasarājā va dānena saṅkhapālo va sīlavā
    hatthipālo va nekkhamme sānako viya paññavā
    viriyavā janakarājā va khantivādo va khantiyā
    saccavā sutasomo va adhiṭṭhāne mūgapakkha va
    mettāya ekarājā va lomahaṃso v'upekkhavā
    pūretvā pāramī sabbā patvā sambodhim uttamaṃ
    bodheyyaṃ sabbasattānaṃ catusaccaṃ sunimmalaṃ.
35. Here is an admittedly tentative list of authors, who either directly state that they aspired to buddhahood or who hint at it. In this regard, see also Dimitrov, 2016, 226; 230; 375; 548.

Text	Author	Date	Aspiration
Amatarasadhārā	Upatissa	900–1000	Buddhahood
Vaṃsatthappakāsinī	Upatissa?	900–1000	Buddhahood
Mahābodhivaṃsa	Upatissa	900–1000	Liberate all beings
Jinālaṅkāra	Buddharakkhita	1157	Buddhahood
Abhidhammatthavibhāvinī	Sumaṅgala	1165–1232	To see Metteyya
Pajjamadhu	Buddhappiya	1200–1300	Rebirth for others
Sārasaṅgaha	Siddhattha	1250–1300	Buddhahood
Sumaṅgalappasādanī	Saṅgharakkhita	after 1232	Rebirth for others
Hatthavanagallavihāravaṃsa	Anon.	1236–66	Buddhahood
Payogasiddhi B[e]	Medhaṅkara	1272–84	To see Metteyya
Jinacarita	Medhaṅkara	1236–70	Buddhahood
Sambandhacintāsannaya	Gotama	after 1232	Buddhahood
Pūjāvaliya	Mayūrapāda	1266	Buddhahood
Pāramīsataka	Dhammakitti	1300–50	Buddhahood
Saddharmālaṅkāraya	Dhammakitti II	1350–1400	Buddhahood
Jinabodhāvalī	Dhammakitti II	1350–1400	Buddhahood

36. On the Bodhisattva ideal in Theravada Buddhism, see, in particular, Samuels, 1997.

37. See R.A.L.H. Gunawardana, 1966, also cited in Holt, 1991, 66. More generally, Jeffrey Sundberg has argued that after the reign of Sena II the Mahāvihāra incorporated a number of 'Esoteric Buddhist practices' within their Pali-based religious framework, perhaps in order to compete with the apotropaic expertise of the Abhayagiri. See, in particular, Sundberg, 2018, 214.
38. *Gandhavaṃsa*, 72,$_{3-4}$.
39. The *Abhidhammāvatāra*, for instance, is described as 'portable wealth' (*hatthasāra*). See *Abhidhammāvatāra* of Buddhadatta, 1,$_{16}$.
40. *Khuddasikkhā* of Dhammasiri, 88,$_{3-19}$.
41. See, for instance, *Kṛtyakalpataru* of Lakṣmīdhara I, 4,$_{5}$.
42. See Gethin, 1992. On the development of the Abhidhamma, see Anālayo, 2014.
43. See the whole of the *Vibhaṅgavagga* of the *Majjhima Nikāya* III.131–42, in particular the *Bhaddekaratta Sutta* (131). I have followed Bhikkhu Ñāṇamoli and Bhikkhu Bodhi's translation of these terms. See Ñāṇamoli and Bodhi, trans. 1995, 1039–41.
44. *Papañcasūdanī* of Buddhaghosa V, 1,$_{11}$.
45. *Majjhimanikāyaṭīkā* of Dhammapāla III, 366,$_{8-9}$: yasmā pana niddesapadānaṃ jananiṭṭhāne ṭhitattā mātā viyā ti mātikā ti vuccati.
46. See chapter five. The productive sense of *mātikā* as a 'point of origin' can be found throughout Pali commentarial literature. Maria Heim has shown, for instance, that the *Kathāvatthu* was regarded as canonical on the basis that it was thought to be an expansion of a *mātikā* laid down by the Buddha. See Heim, 2018, 42. I differentiate these uses from those of the reform era, however, as our 'contents lists' served the additional purpose of allowing students to systematically browse a work of interest.
47. See for instance, *Sāratthadīpanī* of Sāriputta I, 25,$_{10-11}$; *Mohavicchedanī* of Kassapa, 2,$_{10-13}$; *Vimativinodanī* of Kassapa I, 9. See also, Gethin, 1992, 161.
48. *Vinayasaṅgahapurāṇaṭīkā* of Sāriputta, 2,$_{12-16}$: idāni sukhagahaṇatthaṃ vattabbavinicchayaṃ sakalam pi saṅgahetvā mātikaṃ ṭhapento "tatrāyaṃ mātikā" ti ādim āha, vijjamānesu hi mātikāpadesu ye yaṃ yaṃ vinicchayaṃ kātum icchanti, te mātikāpadānasārena (*corr.* °anusārena) taṃtad eva gahetvā olokentā attano kaṅkhaṃ vinodenti. I borrow this expression 'finding devices' from Blair, 2010, 117–72.
49. *Sārasaṅgaha* of Siddhattha, 1,$_{6-23}$.
tatrāyaṃ mātikā
buddhādi-m-abhinīhāro kiriyaṃ satthu-m-abbhutaṃ
pañca antaradhānāni cakkavattī-vibhāvanaṃ.
saṃbuddhacakkavattīnaṃ cetiyānaṃ nidassanaṃ
sammajjanānisaṃsañ ca dhammasaṅghānam abbhutaṃ.
niddāvibhāvanañ c'eva supinassa ca dīpanaṃ
buddhadhammānam āyatto (*corr.* āyatta°) vatthūnaṃ parivattanaṃ.
pabhedo saraṇasīlānaṃ kammaṭṭhānam anālayaṃ
agāravo ca ratanānaṃ kammabhedavibhāvanaṃ.
ānantariyakammaṃ ca micchādiṭṭhivibhāvanaṃ
ariyūpavādakammañ ca kohaññadīnavam pi ca.
maccherānaṃ pabhedo ca tividhagginidassanaṃ
dānādipuññakammañ ca sattāhāravivecanaṃ.
yonippabhedo sattānaṃ pumitthiparivattanaṃ
ṭhīnaṃ paṇḍakanāgānaṃ supannānañ ca bhedanaṃ.
petāsurānaṃ devānaṃ bhedā paṭhavivaḍḍhanaṃ
mahīkampaṃ tathā vuṭṭhivātādīnaṃ pakāsanaṃ
pakiṇṇakakathā iddhi lokasaṇṭhānam eva cā ti.
50. Similarly, see Kieffer-Pülz, 2015b, 438–9.
51. On the 'hidden texts' cited in the *Sārasaṅgaha*, see Neri, 2015, 342–4. Also, Blair, 2010, 134.
52. *Sārasaṅgaha* of Siddhattha, 343,$_{13-22}$:
ettha pana tīhi kāraṇehi kappassa vināsasaṇṭhahanākāro dīghanikāye aggaññasutte ca visuddhimagge ca āgato. bodhimaṇḍassa saṇṭhahanākāro dīghanikāye mahāpadānasutta-vaṇṇanāya vutto. saṇṭhitassa kappassa suññāsuññavasena duvidhādibhedo buddhavaṃse padumuttarabuddhavaṃsa-vaṇṇanāyaṃ vutto. candimasuriyānaṃ parimāṇagamanādivibhāge (*corr.* °vibhāgo) aggaññasutta-vaṇṇanādisu vutto. rāhuggahaṇaṃ pana saṃyuttanikāye devaputtasaṃyutta-vaṇṇanāya vuttaṃ.
53. Neri, 2015, 342; 347.
54. My translation differs from Neri, 2015, 347.
55. For a list of the *Sārasaṅgaha*'s sources, see Neri, 2015, 349–82.
56. *Sārasaṅgaha* of Siddhattha, 26,$_{31-8}$:

kim ettha-m-idam asukaṭhāne vuttan ti kathane payojanan ti ce. sammāsambuddhen' eva hi tiṇṇaṃ pi piṭakānam atthavaṇṇanākkamo bhāsito. tattha tattha bhagavatā pavattitā pakiṇṇakadesanā yeva hi aṭṭhakathā nāma. yebhuyyena pana aññattha aṭṭhakathā, aññattha ṭīkā nāma. tasmā ṭhānaniyame kate medhāvino idaṃ suṭṭhu gaṇhantī ti. idam ettha ṭhānaniyame prayojanan ti.

57. *Sārasaṅgaha*, 278,$_{21-3}$, cited and translated in Neri, 2015, 342.
58. I borrow the idea of a commentary 'binding' a root text back within a wider textual tradition from Hallisey, 2017.
59. *Sārasaṅgaha* of Siddhattha, 2–6, trans. Neumann, 1891.
60. *Paramatthajotikā* II of Dhammapāla I, 46,$_{15}$–52,$_{9}$, trans. Bodhi, 2017, 401–7.
61. *Sārasaṅgaha* of Siddhattha, 76–82.
62. *Sārasaṅgaha* of Siddhattha, 78,$_{23-5}$. On sleepiness and sleep, see Gethin, 2017.
63. *Sārasaṅgaha* of Siddhattha, 79,$_{13-14}$.
64. Malalasekera, 1938, 326; *Sārasaṅgaha* of Siddhattha, 80,$_{41}$–82,$_{25}$.
65. *Sārasaṅgaha* of Siddhattha, 27–37. See chapter four.
66. *Manorathapūraṇī* of Buddhaghosa I, 87,$_{1}$–93,$_{26}$. See also Clark, 2018; Endo, 2013, 121–42.
67. *Manorathapūraṇī* of Buddhaghosa I, 88,$_{3-14}$.
68. *Sārasaṅgaha* of Siddhattha, 36,$_{40}$–37,$_{3}$, citing *Samantapāsādikā* VI, 1291,$_{18-23}$.
69. *Sārasaṅgaha* of Siddhattha, 306,$_{4-8}$, citing *Visuddhimagga* of Buddhaghosa, 351,$_{23-6}$. See also, *Aṅguttara Nikāya* IV, 7.62, *Sattasuriya Sutta*.
70. On *paritta*, see most recently Shulman, 2019.
71. *Sārasaṅgaha* of Siddhattha, 302,$_{12}$–303,$_{14}$.
72. *Sārasaṅgaha* of Siddhattha, 314,$_{1-16}$. That a new buddha arises only after the cosmos has been destroyed is made clear in the *Anāgatavaṃsa Desanā*. See Meddegama, trans. 1993, 26.
73. On the analytical distinction between 'immanentism' and 'transcendentalism', see Strathern, 2019, 27–106.
74. *Sārasaṅgaha* of Siddhattha, 28,$_{14}$–32,$_{20}$.
75. *Sārasaṅgaha* of Siddhattha, 40,$_{21-4}$, citing *Dīgha Nikāya* II, 141,$_{9-11}$: ye hi keci Ānanda cetiyacārikam āhiṇḍantā pasannacittā kālaṃ karissanti, sabbe te kāyassa bhedā param maraṇā sugatiṃ saggaṃ lokam uppajjissanti. See also Schopen, 1997, 115–18.
76. *Sārasaṅgaha* of Siddhattha, 40,$_{24-30}$, citing *Sumaṅgalavilāsinī* of Buddhaghosa II, 582,$_{20-5}$: tattha **cetiyacārikam āhiṇḍantā** ti ye tāva tattha tattha cetiyaṅgaṇaṃ samajjantā āsanāni dhovantā bodhimhi udakaṃ āsiñcantā āhiṇḍanti vicaranti. tesu vattabbam eva n'atthi. "asuka-vihāre cetiyaṃ vandissāmā" ti nikkhamitvā pasannacittā antarā kālaṃ karontā pi anantarā yeva sagge patiṭṭhahissanti yevā ti dassetī ti.
77. *Sārasaṅgaha* of Siddhattha, 42–4.
78. *Sārasaṅgaha* of Siddhattha, 42,$_{4-8}$: pañcānisaṃsā sammajjaniyā; sakacittaṃ pasīdati, paracittaṃ pasīdati, devatā attamanā honti, pasādikasaṃvattanikaṃ puññam upacināti, kāyassa bhedā param maraṇā sugatiṃ saggaṃ lokam uppajjatī ti.
79. Ludowyk-Gyömröi, 1943, 82, also cited in Trainor, 1997, 167.
80. Trainor, 1997, 167.
81. Sārasaṅgaha of Siddhattha, 26,$_{17-29}$; 55,$_{27-31}$; 62,$_{30}$. Andy Rotman has noted that this experience is involuntary for there is a presumption within Buddhist texts 'that Buddhist cognitive and causal realities are natural laws, not religious creations.' See Rotman, 2003, 561.
82. Walters, 2014, 144. *Sārasaṅgaha* of Siddhattha, 73,$_{23-41}$, citing *Papañcasūdanī* of Buddhaghosa II, 16,$_{17}$–17,$_{9}$.
83. *Sārasaṅgaha* of Siddhattha, 73,$_{38-41}$, citing *Papañcasūdanī* of Buddhaghosa II, 17,$_{1-4}$.
    mayi cittaṃ pasādetvā bhikkhusaṅghe anuttare
    kappāni satasahassāni duggatiṃ so na gacchati.
    devalokā cavitvāna kusalamūlena vodito
    bhavissati anantañāṇo somanasso ti vissuto.
84. See chapter seven.
85. See Strathern, 2019, 148–50.
86. Sundberg, 2018, 214.
87. Schopen, 1975.
88. Boucher, 1991.
89. This verse is also found in the Pali canon. See *Vinaya* I, 40,$_{28-9}$.
90. *Saṃyutta Nikāya* III, 120,$_{28-31}$.
91. Boucher, 1991, 2, citing Poussin, 1913, 70.
92. Davidson, 2009, 141.

93. This is not the case for the Theravada world in general. See, most recently, Skilling, 2008.
94. Mudiyanse, 1967; Von Hinüber, 1983. Daniel Drewes, however, has questioned whether the gold plates of the *Pañcaviṃśatisāhasrikā Prajñāpāramitā* found deposited in an earthenware pot at the Jetavanārāma in Anurādhapura were buried for ritual purposes. See Drewes, 2007, 132.
95. Mudiyanse, 1967, 99–105.
96. Schopen, 1982, 104. Schopen identified the inscription on these stones with the *Ārya-sarva-tathāgatādhiṣṭhāna-hṛdaya-guhya-dhātu-karaṇḍa-mudra-nāma-dhāraṇī Sūtra*. Chandawimala has further identified stones VI and VII with the *Sarvatathāgatatattvasaṃgraha*, an influential esoteric Buddhist work that had a wide circulation in Sri Lanka and an important place in esoteric Buddhist practice on the island. Chandawimala, 2016, 165–90. See also Powell, 2018, 5–26; Sundberg, 2017, 294–9; 2018, 182, n. 222.
97. Sundberg, 2017, 253–5.
98. Sundberg, 2018, 348, n. 451. There is evidence that the scholar-monks of the era viewed the ritual veneration of Sanskrit texts as a threat. The *Cūḷavaṃsa* (41.37–40), for instance, refers to a certain *dhammadhātu* ('Dhamma relic') brought by a merchant to Sri Lanka during the reign of Silākāla (518–31), who mistakenly took it to be the 'true doctrine of the Buddha'.
99. The *Saddharmālaṅkāraya* also refers to the depositing of the *Dhammasaṅgaṇi* within a Dhamma shrine. See Gunawardana, 1979, 230–1; *Epigraphia Zeylanica* III, 133.
100. *Sārasaṅgaha* of Siddhattha, $40_{,10-19}$, citing *Sāratthadīpanī* of Sāriputta I, $172_{,2-8}$. See also Skilling, 1997, 102, n. 35.
101. *Sārasaṅgaha* of Siddhattha, 83.
102. *Sārasaṅgaha* of Siddhattha, $83_{,3-29}$, citing *Sāratthadīpanī* of Sāriputta II, $166_{,20}$–$7_{,10}$: buddhadhammānām āyattavatthūnaṃ parivattanan ti etthāyaṃ vibhāvanā. dhammasantakena buddhapūjaṃ kātuṃ buddhasantakena vā dhammapūjaṃ kātuṃ vaṭṭati na vaṭṭatī ti. "tathāgatassa vā kho etaṃ vāseṭṭha adhivacanaṃ dhammakāyo" (*Dīgha Nikāya* III, $84_{,23-4}$) iti pi ca "yo kho vakkali dhammaṃ passati so maṃ passatī" (*Saṃyutta Nikāya* III, $120_{,28-31}$) ti vacanato vaṭṭatī ti vadanti. keci pana evaṃ sante "yo bhikkhu mam upaṭṭhaheyya so gilānam upaṭṭhaheyyā" (*Vinaya* I, $302_{,19-20}$) ti vacanato buddhasantakena gilānassāpi bhesajjaṃ kātuṃ yuttan ti āpajjeyya tasmā na vaṭṭatī ti vadanti, tam akāraṇaṃ. na hi "yo bhikkhave mam upaṭṭhaheyya so gilānam upaṭṭhaheyyā" ti iminā attano ca gilānassa ca ekasadisatā tad-upaṭṭhānassa vā samaphalatā vuttā. ayaṃ h'ettha attho: yo mam ovādānusāsanīkaraṇena upaṭṭhaheyya so gilānam upaṭṭhaheyya. mama ovādakārakena gilāno upaṭṭhātabbo ti. bhagavato ca gilānassa ca upaṭṭhānam ekasadisan ti evaṃ pan'ettha attho no gehetabbo (*Sāratthadīpanī*, na gahetabbo). "yo vo ānanda mayā dhammo ca vinayo ca desito paññatto so vo mamaccayena satthā" (*Dīgha Nikāya* II, $154_{,6-8}$) ti vacanato "ahañ ca pan'idāni eko va tumhe ovadāmi anusāsāmi, mayi parinibbute imāni caturāsīti buddhasahassāni tumhe ovadissanti anusāsissantī" ti vuttattā ca bahussutaṃ bhikkhuṃ pasaṃsantena ca "na so tumhākaṃ sāvako nāma buddho nāma eso, cundā" (*Sumaṅgalavilāsinī* III, $912_{,11-12}$) ti vuttattā ca dhammagarukattā ca tathāgatassa pubbanayo eva pasatthataro ti vinayaṭīkāya vuttaṃ.
103. *Sārasaṅgaha* of Siddhattha, $83_{,29-35}$, citing *Samantapāsādikā* of Buddhaghosa II, $358_{,16-21}$: cetiyassa vā saṅghassa vā santakena cetiyassa santakaṃ rakkhāpetuṃ vaṭṭati. cetiyassa santakena saṅghasantakaṃ rakkhāpetuṃ na vaṭṭati. yaṃ pana cetiyassa santakena saddhiṃ saṅghasantakaṃ ṭhapitaṃ hoti, taṃ cetiyasantake rakkhite rakkhāpitam (*Samantapāsādikā*, rakkhāpite rakkhitam) eva hotī ti cīvarakkhandhakavaṇṇanāya vuttaṃ.

Part III
Emotion

7
Sense and Sensibility: Saṅgharakkhita's Poetics

In seeking to improve their circumstances through the performance of virtuous karma and the accrual of merit, elite reform-era monks sought out religious stimulation and were focused in particular on cultivating an experience of karmically transformative emotions. In the third part of this book we will explore how this shift may have contributed to a revalorization of aesthetically pleasing literature as a means of such stimulation both on an individual level and also within the Saṅgha as a whole. This, to a large degree, meant finally embracing traditional theories of aesthetics as developed in the Sanskrit tradition, for it was Sanskrit that had long provided the paradigmatic framework for literary expression, in particular in the royal courts of Southern Asia. The two textual traditions of court and monastery, however, were not seamlessly compatible and we can see in the new literary and devotional works of the reform era a conscious reconceptualization of literary eloquence as a virtue suited to monastic goals as well as royal amusement. This issue was confronted directly during the reform era most notably by Saṅgharakkhita, who wrote after the 1165 reforms and who presided over Vijayabāhu III's reform council, c. 1232–6.

Saṅgharakkhita was one of the most prolific authors of the Pali reform period, composing at least seven works in Pali, six of which concerned grammar (*vyākaraṇa*) and poetics (*alaṅkāra*).[1] Of the works relating to poetry, he composed the *Subodhālaṅkāra* ('Lucid poetics') its *mahāsāmiṭīkā* ('Grandmaster commentary') and the *Vuttodaya* ('Exposition of metres'), a treatise on metrics. The title of his commentary on the *Subodhālaṅkāra* refers to the fact that he composed the work after having risen within the monastic community to the position of *mahāsāmi* or 'grandmaster'.[2] He appears to have composed the *Subodhālaṅkāra* itself before he became grandmaster, most probably between 1186 and 1232, a period characterized by almost constant war.[3] The *Cūḷavaṃsa* records that Vijayabāhu III (1232–6) appointed Saṅgharakkhita to the role and entrusted him with the education of his eldest son, the future Parākramabāhu II (1236–70), with the tooth and alms bowl relics of the Buddha, with the Saṅgha and with all the subjects living in Laṅkā.[4] The allusions in this passage to Saṅgharakkhita's sovereignty may not have been entirely rhetorical since he was well-connected with the increasingly powerful nobility outside of the weakened royal court and dwelt in monasteries that had been donated by powerful warlords.[5] There is also a fourteenth-century Burmese tradition, according to G.P. Malalasekera, that Saṅgharakkhita was descended from nobility and that he was a distant relative of king Dāṭhopatissa I (639–50).[6]

The composition of the *Subodhālaṅkāra* represented a profound shift in Pali literary culture for a number of reasons. It engaged openly, for instance, with the cosmopolitan world of Sanskrit pandits, it formally sanctioned sensual, devotional poetry to the Buddha as a religious practice and it set itself the aim of disseminating this knowledge throughout the Saṅgha. Those unfamiliar with reform-era Buddhism in Sri Lanka may be struck by the seemingly paradoxical celebration of passionate devotion to an ascetic who spent much of his life teaching the value of dispassion. If we were to take into account only the early Buddhist tradition, one would have to admit that there was a certain ambivalence, if not antipathy, towards ornate literature or *kāvya* in Buddhist monastic life.

While the Pali canon contains some of South Asia's oldest examples of poetic expression, the Buddha on a number of occasions makes his dislike for this literary form known. He states in the *Brahmajāla Sutta* ('Supreme net') that poetry is 'bestial knowledge' (*tiracchānavijjā*) and that being a poet is an immoral occupation.[7] In the same discourse he criticizes ascetics for continuing to engage in a number of activities associated with court culture, including listening to literary recitals (*akkhyāna*), and categorizes talk of kings, armies and heroes as 'bestial conversation' (*tiracchānakathā*).[8] Elsewhere, the Buddha criticizes those trained in the rhetorical arts rather than philosophical enquiry who are unable to question his discourses and who instead are content, he states, to listen to 'mere poetry composed by poets'.[9] Writing in the fourth century, Buddhaghosa, when discussing what counts as a 'literary recital', 'bestial conversation' or 'senseless babble' (*samphapalāpa*) specifically targets Brahmanical court culture and refers a number of times to the two Sanskrit epics, the *Mahābhārata* and *Rāmāyaṇa*.[10]

Textual sources, of course, cannot tell us the whole story about early Buddhist attitudes to poetry. Still, it is the case that in the Pali tradition no independent works of ornate poetry, with the possible exception of the *Mahāvaṃsa* ('Great history'), were composed in the language for much of the first millennium.[11] It is perhaps not surprising then that monks who engage in such worldly activity are often perceived as deviating from some Buddhist ideal type, famously characterized by Max Weber as otherworldly, mystic and sense-denying in nature.[12] In his translation of the *Subhāṣitaratnakośa* ('Treasury of well-turned verse'), a compendium of Sanskrit court poetry compiled by a Buddhist monk, Vidyākara, in twelfth-century Bengal, Daniel H.H. Ingalls remarked that Buddhist monks 'could succeed in the court tradition only by forgetting that they were Buddhists'.[13] More recently, with respect to the same text, Sheldon Pollock has asked in understandable puzzlement, 'What do we make of the fact that a collection of this-worldly poetry, three-quarters of it dealing with the physical love of men and women, was prepared at an institution for Buddhist renunciates?'[14]

As the first treatise on Pali poetics, the *Subodhālaṅkāra* offers a unique insight into a shift in attitude during the reform era among the Saṅgha's hierarchy towards the composition of ornate poetry based on Sanskrit models. Representing the only surviving explicitly Buddhist work on the subject, the *Subodhālaṅkāra* also potentially sheds light too on how monks in the wider region may have thought about poetry, sensuality and their monastic vocation. This chapter then investigates the way in which Saṅgharakkhita abstracts theories of poetic eloquence from the Sanskrit tradition and how he uses these theories to reframe Buddhist devotion. The most radical contribution Saṅgharakkhita makes to Buddhist thought, in this regard, is the central place he gives to morality and civility in the composition and appreciation of poetry. In fusing eloquence and morality, Saṅgharakkhita not only manages to assimilate the intellectual cultures of the monastery and royal court but also provides a moral framework for all monks within the Saṅgha to compose and enjoy devotional literature. This was necessary since, in the decades before, as we will explore in the next two chapters, scholar-monks had begun to compose ornate, literary works as a means of inculcating in themselves and others karmically transformative devotional feelings.[15]

7.1. Reframing Devotion

Saṅgharakkhita had two main objectives when writing the *Subodhālaṅkāra*. He wanted to formally define the full literary potential of the Pali language, which to a large extent meant showing that Pali possessed the same literariness as Sanskrit (though he treats literary eloquence as an ideal type not restricted to any one particular language). Saṅgharakkhita also intended to demonstrate to the wider Saṅgha the compatibility between this literary ideal and Buddhist norms by using the Sanskritic model to write devotional poetry to the Buddha.

While he adopts and adapts the latest ideas in Sanskrit literary theory from places as far away as Kashmir, the devotional content of his work reflects more local literary developments. Prior to the composition of the *Subodhālaṅkāra*, for instance, we find in the tenth century the first treatise on Sinhala poetics, the *Siyabaslakara*, focused similarly on Buddhist devotional poetry and inspired by Daṇḍin's *Kāvyādarśa* ('Mirror of literature') as well as a number of twelfth-century devotional works, such as the *Amāvatura* ('Flood of nectar') and *Jinālaṅkāra* ('Ornament of the conqueror').[16] This focus on devotion, as discussed in the previous chapter, reflected a wider feeling in the reform era that it was increasingly difficult to achieve any religious attainment without the help of a massive accumulation of merit.[17] The primary source of this merit was devotion to the Buddha, as represented by his relics, the Dhamma and Saṅgha. New forms of literature, it seems, had begun to play a key role in facilitating this devotion and Saṅgharakkhita's *Subodhālaṅkāra* is in many respects the culminating reflection on this artistic shift, setting out formally a theoretical model for the composition and appreciation of Pali devotional poetry. After each poetic figure, Saṅgharakkhita wastes no opportunity to furnish his work with an illustration in praise of the Buddha. Take, for instance, the following verse used to illustrate the poetic merit of delicate sounds (*sukhumālatā*):

> romañcapiñcharacanā sādhuvādāhitaddhanī
> laḷanti 'me munimeghummadā sādhusikhāvalā.[18]

> These peacock-like devotees,
> fanning the feathers of their wings
> and crying in appreciation,
> frolic in frenzied madness
> at [the sight of] the cloudlike sage.

Saṅgharakkhita uses the light, pitter-pattering alliteration of the verse here to evoke the image of rain and cleverly exploits the Sanskritic trope of excited peacocks awaiting the rains as a metaphor for the enthralment felt by Buddhist devotees at the sight of their master. The metaphor skilfully encompasses all objects in the comparandum. The Buddha is a raincloud, the devotees are peacocks, the devotees' utterances of approbation are the peacocks' cries and their feather fans (a sign of royalty) are their wings. Why the peacocks celebrate the rains, furthermore, is not made explicit and is left open to suggestion. A skilled reader, however, knows that peacocks rejoice at the sight of the rain clouds as the rains mark the beginning of their mating season. The unstated extension of the metaphor is that Buddhist devotees celebrate the coming of the Buddha as he signals their impending liberation.

The devotional focus of the *Subodhālaṅkāra*, however, did not overwhelm the courtly tenor of its Sanskrit framework. Saṅgharakkhita follows the authors of treatises on Sanskrit poetics and likens poetry to a woman's body, and compares the arrangement of chapters in his work to the successive stages of beautifying her appearance.[19] His *Subodhālaṅkāra* consists of five chapters, namely: (1) poetic faults (*dosa*); (2) their removal (*dosaparihāra*); (3) poetic merits (*guṇa*); (4) ornaments (*alaṅkāra*), that is, figures of sense; and (5) aesthetic moods and feelings (*rasabhāva*).[20] The *Subodhālaṅkāra* begins with poetic faults and their removal on the basis that, 'like a good wife' (*vadhū*), a faultless poem is implicitly virtuous.[21] Saṅgharakkhita then turns to poetic merits in chapter three, which he defines as a poem's phonetic configuration (*saddālaṅkāra*).[22] His chapter on poetic ornaments proper describes figures of sense (*atthālaṅkāra*), metaphors, similes and suchlike. He writes that these figures are dealt with after the merits as it is through ornamentation that a virtuous (*saguṇa*) lover becomes exceptionally attractive.[23] Finally, aesthetic moods and feelings (*rasabhāva*) are treated last, he says, since they are occasioned by ornamentation.[24] Yet these moods and feelings, he notes, cannot be attributed to any particular formal feature of a poem, just as a woman's beauty cannot be attributed to any one attribute.[25]

Daṇḍin's *Kāvyādarśa*, arguably the most influential work on Sanskrit poetics in South Asian history, was the principal source of inspiration for the literary ideal that Saṅgharakkhita formally wanted to introduce into the Saṅgha.[26] Saṅgharakkhita cites Daṇḍin as a source for his chapter on ornaments of sense and it is there that the *Kāvyādarśa*'s influence is most pronounced.[27] The small amount of historical information about Daṇḍin suggests that the author was active around 680–720 in Kāñcī in South India during the reign of the Pallava king, Narasiṃhavarman II Rājasiṃha (690/1–728/9).[28] Heramba Chatterjee has surveyed the thirty-seven ornaments of sense in Saṅgharakkhita's work and has shown that nearly all are adopted from Daṇḍin's *Kāvyādarśa*.[29] As well as following Daṇḍin's definitions of poetic figures, Saṅgharakkhita often adopts the examples he gives for each of these figures too. This occasionally means he takes one of Daṇḍin's amorous illustrations and with some minor changes, such as a well-placed vocative 'O Buddha', turns it into a poem of devotion and piety. Take, for example, his minor amendment to Daṇḍin's illustration of a simile through negation (*paṭisedhopamā*), that is, a simile where a comparison between two objects is refuted in order to heighten the intended point of comparison.[30] Daṇḍin in his example likens a lover's face to the moon, whereas Saṅgharakkhita changes the subject of the comparison to the Buddha's face.

na jātu śaktir indos te mukhena pratigarjitum
kalaṅkino jaḍasyeti pratiṣedhopamaiva sā. (*Kāvyādarśa* 2.34)

'The frigid, mottled moon does not have the power to ever rival your face.' This is a simile through negation (*pratiṣedhopamā*).

asamattho mukhen' indu **Jina** te paṭigajjituṃ
jaḷo kalaṅkī ti ayaṃ paṭisedhopamā siyā. (*Subodhālaṅkāra* 193)

'The frigid, mottled moon, **O conqueror,** is incapable of rivalling your face.' This is a simile through negation (*paṭisedhopamā*).

The burgeoning interest in Daṇḍin's *Kāvyādarśa* in Sri Lanka from the tenth century onwards was highly influenced by the works of Ratnamati or Ratnaśrījñāna, as he is otherwise known. We have already noted the great influence this scholar's Sanskrit commentary on the *Cāndravyākaraṇa* ('Grammar of Candragomin') had on the development of Moggallāna's new system of Pali grammar.[31] Writing under the name Ratnaśrījñāna, his Sanskrit commentary on the *Kāvyādarśa* too appears to have played an important role in the development of literary theory in Sri Lanka. Dragomir Dimitrov has argued that this commentary was an important source for a tenth-century (?) Sinhala commentary, the *Kāvyādarśasannaya*, too.[32] He has shown, furthermore, that whenever Saṅgharakkhita relies upon Daṇḍin's *Kāvyādarśa* in composing the *Subodhālaṅkāra*, he also follows Ratnamati's commentary on the *Kāvyādarśa* when writing his autocommentary.[33]

Alongside Daṇḍin's *Kāvyādarśa*, there is a pronounced strand of influence on the *Subodhālaṅkāra* from the Kashmiri tradition of poetics. It is unclear how this Kashmiri literature arrived in Sri Lanka though we can speculate, following Whitney Cox, that increased trade between Kashmir and South India during the period may have led to this drift South.[34] The order of chapters in the *Subodhālaṅkāra* deviates markedly from the *Kāvyādarśa* and better resembles the chapter divisions of the *Kāvyālaṅkāra* ('Ornament of poetry') of Vāmana, a minister in the court of the Kashmiri king Jayāpīḍa (779–813).[35] Saṅgharakkhita's opening two chapters on faults and their removal have an affinity, at least in terms of their subdivisions, with Vāmana's *Kāvyālaṅkāra* too. Like Vāmana, he divides his analysis of faults into the faults of words, the faults of sentences and the faults of the meaning of sentences.[36] He also mirrors the more expansive treatment of faults in the *Kāvyālaṅkāra* and discusses twenty-three faults in comparison to the reduced ten discussed by Daṇḍin.[37]

In general, Saṅgharakkhita places his faults in the same categories as Vāmana and adopts some of his innovations such as the introduction of the generalized fault of *grāmya* or 'coarse language'.[38] Despite defining poetic merits as primarily phonetic embellishments (*saddālaṅkāra*), Saṅgharakkhita occasionally borrows Vāmana's division of poetic merits into both merits of sense (Sk. *arthaguṇa*) and merits of sound (Sk. *śabdaguṇa*). He relies on Vāmana in his discussions on both the phonetic and semantic aspects of the poetic merits known as *oja* ('strength'), *sukhumālatā* ('tenderness') and *atthavyatta* ('the explicit').[39] Saṅgharakkhita adopts, for instance, Vāmana's idea that the merit of 'tenderness' refers to either the use of light, delicate sounds or of tender sentiments and uses an example given in the *Kāvyālaṅkāra* to illustrate the latter, namely, that instead of stating directly that someone has 'died' (*mata*) one should instead say that only their 'fame remains' (*kittisesa*).[40]

In his final chapter, Saṅgharakkhita borrows from another ninth-century Kashmiri work, Ānandavardhana's *Dhvanyāloka* ('Light on suggestion'), and introduces a standard framework of aesthetic moods and feelings (*ras-abhāva*).[41] Like the *Dhvanyāloka*, the *Subodhālaṅkāra* posits nine possible aesthetic moods culminating in *santarasa* (Sk. *śāntarasa*) or the mood of quiescence. According to the *Rājataraṅgiṇī* ('River of kings'), Ānandavardhana was a poet in the court of the Kashmiri king Avantivarman (855–83).[42] He revolutionized the study of Sanskrit poetry by developing a theory of aesthetics centred on the idea that aesthetic moods or *rasa* were brought about ultimately by the suggestive capacity (*dhvani*) of the artistic object as a whole and not solely due to formal combinations of poetic merits and figurations, as had been previously thought.[43] As we will see below, Saṅgharakkhita directly praises literary suggestion over formalist figuration when commenting on the second verse of his *Subodhālaṅkāra* and quotes Ānandavardhana's famous pronouncement in his *Dhvanyāloka* that literary suggestion, 'is a distinct element in the language of great poets, which appears separately from the well-known parts (of a poem), like beauty in women'.[44]

The point here is that, just as the beauty of a woman cannot be attributed to a particular body part or ornament, the suggested meaning of a literary work, which is, for Ānandavardhana, the determining factor in the enjoyment of a reader or listener, cannot be explained through a purely formalist analysis of a poem's parts and figures. We can speculate, in this regard, that just as theories of deep-level semantics in contemporary Sanskrit grammatical literature facilitated the grammatization of languages other than Sanskrit in Sri Lanka, as discussed in chapter three, the discussions on suggestion among the Kashmiri poeticians of the age provided the conceptual resources necessary to think about aesthetic beauty separately from the formal features of any one particular language or literature.[45]

7.2. The Pure Reader

The intellectual challenge of fusing Buddhist devotional sentiment with Sanskrit literary models was relatively simple when compared with the political task of appealing to a Saṅgha that was conflicted about the need for such a work of Pali poetics. We learn from the *Subodhālaṅkāra*, for instance, that access to Sanskrit education and Sanskrit poetry was very uneven within the Saṅgha and that some monks viewed an engagement with these worldly works as morally problematic. It becomes clear that the multilingual nature of late medieval scholastic culture had created new hierarchies based on one's level of literacy in Sinhala, Pali and Sanskrit and that these emergent forms of social stratification had become the site of political agitation and contest. Saṅgharakkhita maintains the mollifying tone of his predecessors, such as Sāriputta and Sumaṅgala, and attempts to reconcile the competing views of his various constituencies. In doing so he presents the study of literary theory as a moral practice while simultaneously criticizing Sanskrit and its literature for being polluting and impure. He argues at the beginning of his work that the *Subodhālaṅkāra* was designed to bring the morally transformative power of Sanskrit literary theory into monastic education without exposing young monks to content that some scholars perceived to be dangerous.[46]

Saṅgharakkhita establishes at the beginning of his treatise, for instance, that he has composed his work for monks who he refers to as 'pure Magadhans', that is, those who only know Pali or Māgadha, and writes in his second verse that, 'even though there are good, old works on poetics (*alaṅkāra*), such as Rāmasamma (Sk. Rāmaśarman), the pure Magadhans do not use them'.[47] Saṅgharakkhita explains in his commentary on this verse what he means by the term 'pure Magadhan' and also discusses why poetics had been neglected by the monastic community in the past:

> **The pure Magadhans** (*suddhamāgadhikā*): Māgadha [means] either the people of Magadha or the words that are understood there. Magadhans (*māgadhikā*) are those who are from Magadha or who learn (lit. are tied to) Māgadha [words]. Pure Magadhans, (i.e.) novices (*yatipota*), are those Magadhans who are pure (*suddha*), that is, they are completely pure or unmixed since they are unfamiliar with the impurity of Sanskrit literature, etc. (*sakkaṭādibhāsita*). They (i.e., the pure Magadhans) do not use the aforementioned treatises on poetics (*alaṅkāra*), which differentiate ornaments (i.e. poetic figures), nor can they tell the difference [between literary] styles (*pasādhana*). This is because, furthermore, one becomes a pure Magadhan by specifically studying and memorizing different books (i.e. Pali texts), whereas [works on poetics], such as

Rāmasamma, are in languages such as Sanskrit. This is the meaning of the word 'pure Magadhan' here.

A subtle, implied sense also obtains in this verse, according to the usual, well-known use [of these words]. The pure Magadhans, [for instance], due to being completely pure in themselves, previously did not use [figures of speech], [thinking] that 'these figures of speech, even though beautiful, have now become stale, what use are stale things for pure beings like us?' For [Ānandavardhana] has said: 'Further, what is implicitly understood is a particular object in the speech of great poets, which, like the beauty of women, is distinct from the well-known parts [of speech]' (*Dhvanyāloka* 1.4).[48]

In this rather dense discussion, Saṅgharakkhita draws out a number of the overlapping meanings of the term. To be a Magadhan, then, one can either be from Magadha or simply be a speaker of the Pali language. A 'pure' (*suddha*) Magadhan, however, is one who has not been polluted by 'what is spoken in Sanskrit, etc.' (*sakkaṭādibhāsita*). We should likely infer from the open-ended 'etc.' that Saṅgharakkhita also includes here the literary Prakrits and other languages of classical India. The word *kālusiya* ('impurity') refers both to Sanskrit literature's perceived immorality and also to its difficulty, literally, its turbidity. It is likely Saṅgharakkhita further intended to make an ethical connection here too between Pali's status as a pure language, underived from Sanskrit, and the moral purity of its users.

Even though Saṅgharakkhita speaks in this verse of Sanskrit poetics as 'good' (*santa*), he reveals in his commentary that, at the same time, Sanskrit figures of speech, while beautiful, were not good enough for the pure Magadhans since they were perceived to be stale or mouldy (*malaggahita*). It is here that Saṅgharakkhita quotes the aforementioned verse in Ānandavardhana's *Dhvanyāloka* concerning literary suggestion. In using a metaphor of decay, Saṅgharakkhita acknowledges the beauty of formalistic ornamentation, while attacking the stale and perhaps immoral application of the ornaments as developed in the tradition of Sanskrit court poetry. We can speculate, furthermore, that by quoting the *Dhvanyāloka* here he indicates that the old schematic formalism of the *alaṅkāra* tradition had been supplanted to an extent with Kashmiri theories of suggestion (*dhvani*) that subordinated formal figuration and which were viewed as new and sophisticated. It seems possible, in this respect, that these new theories allowed monks to reconsider the nature of good poetry separate from the morally suspect, ornamental formalism of earlier Sanskrit poetics.

In what at first may seem like a contradiction in terms, Saṅgharakkhita continues in his commentary to praise those who have mastered these formal aspects of poetry, namely literary merits and faults, as virtuous people (*sappurisa*) and those who have not as nothing more than beasts (*pasu*). He manages to reconcile his praise for experts in Sanskrit literary theory with his previous praise for those who know no Sanskrit at all, by speaking of the knowledge of poetic merits and faults less in terms of its importance in creating beautiful poetry and more as a marker of one's wisdom, civility and morality. In doing so, he develops upon ideas presented in the opening to the *Kāvyādarśa* and reinterprets them in light of Ratnamati's commentary.

Daṇḍin writes at the beginning of the *Kāvyādarśa*, for instance, that language (*śabda*) is a light that stops the world being conquered by darkness.[49] He then lends a social and moral inflection to this connection between language and the world and, by employing a witty pun on the word *go*, which means both 'cow' and 'language', argues that anyone who uses language ineloquently reveals their bovine nature (*gotva*).[50] Ratnamati overlooks the jocular nature of this verse, however, and takes it rather literally. He states that well-composed literature is constitutive of the four wholesome goals of life (Sk. *caturvarga*), which are classified traditionally as *artha* ('material wealth'), *kāma* ('physical pleasure'), *dharma* ('duty') and *mokṣa* ('liberation'), and that, since good literature reproduces social values, literary erudition – the composition and appreciation of *kāvya* – reveals in many ways one's own moral and social condition. He extends Daṇḍin's metaphor and writes, for instance, that those who know the *śāstra*s, that is, any prescriptive science, including literary science, are to be treated like gods whereas those who do not are nothing more than beasts (*paśu*).[51]

Saṅgharakkhita reproduces this social and moral understanding of literary erudition in his introduction and similarly speaks of those who study the discipline of poetics as 'virtuous people' (*sappurisa*) and those who do not as 'beast-like people' (*purisapasu*).[52] He writes, echoing Ratnamati (and partly Daṇḍin himself), that 'only those who know *śāstra* can discriminate between different merits and faults. Those who do not know *śāstra* – the beast-like men (*purisapasu*) – cannot.'[53] He places the science of poetry (*alaṅkārasattha*) alongside Buddhist scripture (*tipiṭaka*), philosophy (*takka*) and grammar (*vyākaraṇa*) as a source of wisdom (*paññā*) and speaks of the opportunity to learn poetics from a teacher as the result of the accumulation of merit.[54] Saṅgharakkhita presents the relationship between teacher and pupil in the study of poetics as not only marked by differing levels of wisdom but also by levels of civility too. He reiterates that the wisdom gained through education in literary theory distinguishes those who are virtuous from those who are bestial and quotes in support the following canonical verse from the *Sevitabba Sutta* ('Who is to be associated with'), which originally concerns the need to associate with those accomplished in morality, meditative concentration and wisdom:

> A man who associates with a lower descends,
> and one who associates with an equal never fails.
> The wise one who attends upon a superior rises,
> therefore, revere one who is superior to yourself![55]

Alongside the 'pure Magadhans' who only know Pali and the 'virtuous people' who have mastered literary theory, Saṅgharakkhita mentions a third constituency in his work, namely, those who were disinterested in poetry and whose sole focus was the attainment of nirvana. In his final chapter on aesthetic moods and feelings, beginning with the erotic (*siṅgāra*, Sk. *śṛṅgāra*), Saṅgharakkhita provides only definitions of these aesthetic moods and feelings and does not include example verses for he admits in his commentary that this worldly topic is 'not studied by those of high faith whose minds are gladly focused on analyzing the tradition of the pure, true Dhamma, which is the sole *rasa*, the *rasa* of liberation, and the only cause for escaping the suffering of *saṃsāra* entirely'.[56] The earliest Sinhala commentary on the *Subodhālaṅkāra* was less wary of the criticism of those who it describes as 'greedy' (*luddha*) for nirvana and rectifies Saṅgharakkhita's indecisive treatment of the topic by composing example verses for all of the aesthetic feelings using the narrative of the *Vidhurapaṇḍita Jātaka* ('Birth story of wise Vidhura').[57] The tension between those engaging with the world and those wanting to escape it reemerges decades later in the Daṁbadeṇiya edict, which advises that 'despicable arts such as poetry and drama should neither be studied nor taught to others'.[58] It is possible that Saṅgharakkhita's willingness to engage in worldly matters reflected the fact, as he seems to declare in two of his works, that he pursued the bodhisattva path. He writes, for instance, in the colophon to his *Khuddasikkhābhinavaṭīkā* ('New commentary on the Minor rules'), to quote Petra Kieffer-Pülz's translation, 'May I, by the merit acquired from working for the benefit of others become one who works for the benefit of others in successive births.'[59] Whether he pursued buddhahood or not, he certainly presents his study of impure Sanskrit literature as an act of charity that was solely for the benefit of the pure Magadhans.

7.3. Propriety as the Secret of Poetry

Saṅgharakkhita's depiction of those who study poetic figuration as essentially moral beings in opposition to the bestial inerudite anticipates the main innovation of his work, namely the centrality with which he places the poetic virtue of 'propriety' (*ocitya*) in literary practice. Writing at the beginning of his final chapter on aesthetic moods and feelings Saṅgharakkhita states, for instance, that, '[this chapter] has been composed by a poet possessed of creative eloquence (*paṭibhāna*), who relies on worldly discourse (*lokavohāra*), and who feels the exhilaration of utter propriety'.[60] Clearly having his nirvana-orientated opponents in mind when writing this verse, Saṅgharakkhita provocatively declares that as a poet his engagement with the world is necessarily moral. He writes in his commentary that:

> What is known as 'propriety' is the greatest secret among poets and only the one who knows what is acceptable (*ucita*) also in worldly discourse (*lokavohāra*) is to be praised. Only by relying on completely suitable worldly discourse can a poem, composed according to what is said below (i.e. in the chapter on moods and feelings), produce the taste of an aesthetic mood (*rasa*) for sentient beings. It is permissible, therefore, to compose a literary work (*bandhana*) only when it shines and reveals the exhilarating state of propriety.[61]

Saṅgharakkhita here brings out the connection between morality and the aesthetic experience. He argues that in order to produce an aesthetic experience for another one must know about worldly norms and conventions, with the implication that to transgress what is tasteful in worldly society would be to be render one's poem ineffective.

In referring to propriety as 'the greatest secret among poets' Saṅgharakkhita paraphrases Ānandavardhana's famous pronouncement in his *Dhvanyāloka* that 'a composition containing well-known propriety is the utmost secret of *rasa*'.[62] While the *Dhvanyāloka* first articulated the idea that propriety (*aucitya*) was an important part of affective poetry, it was developed upon more fully by other later Kashmiri literary theorists. Kṣemendra, a mid-eleventh-century polymath, in particular, wrote a treatise on the topic called the *Aucityavicāracarcā* ('Discourse on deliberating propriety') and defined *aucitya* as a kind of correspondence or alignment (*sadṛśa*) between a text and what it signifies.[63]

Kṣemendra uses similes in each verse of his work to connect poetic propriety with worldly propriety. He writes that 'the excellence, the lovely metre, and the goodness of a poem become prominent (lit. shine) if the verb is proper, just as the virtues, the behaviour, and the nobility of a person shine, if his deeds are good'.[64] This connection is not simply figurative since he understands the conventions of poetry as on a continuum with the social norms and proper behaviours of Brahmanical, monarchical society. This is most apparent when Kṣemendra discusses propriety in the topics and themes of poetry. He writes with respect to the need for a poem to depict 'appropriate' (*ucita*) families or lineages, for instance, that 'the propriety surrounding a family lends special excellence to the charm of the poetry, just as the propriety of the lineage of a person is generally dear to those who have a heart to feel'.[65] As an example he quotes a verse from Kālidāsa's *Raghuvaṃśa* ('Dynasty of Raghu'), in which prince Raghu is installed on the throne by his father, king Dilīpa, who then retires with his queen to the forest:

> Then, he (Dilīpa), whose heart had turned away from the sensual sphere, gave the white parasol, a symbol of kingship, to his young son (Raghu), according to the traditional rites. Together with his queen, he took refuge under the shady tree of an ascetic grove. For this is the familial custom of Ikṣvāku kings who have reached old age.[66]

Kṣemendra was one of the first authors to emphasize the role of propriety, that is, the poem's connection with the world outside the text, as the determining factor in its aesthetic success. If the poetic text does not properly relate to the social conventions of its audience then it will fail to convey an aesthetic mood.[67] Referring to this intellectual shift as the development of Sanskrit's 'social aesthetic', Sheldon Pollock writes that:

> Kṣemendra's importance for us, if not his novelty, lies in his unequivocal affirmation of the constitutive relationship of propriety and aesthetic sentiment: *Aucitya* now has become explicitly the life-force (*jīvita*) of *rasa* itself: how laughable and disruptive of the heroic mood, Kṣemendra says, is martial violence directed toward a suppliant, or, in the case of the piteous mood, compassion towards an enemy.[68]

We can account for the centrality of propriety in the *Subodhālaṅkāra* by hypothesizing that Saṅgharakkhita was likely a close reader of Kṣemendra's work. In explicitly pointing out the connection, between aesthetic feelings, propriety and what he calls 'worldly discourse' (*lokavohāra*), which could just as easily be translated as 'social discourse', Saṅgharakkhita goes even further than Kṣemendra in emphasizing the centrality of the social and moral construction of good poetry. The development of this new social aesthetic revalorized literary eloquence and allowed poetry to take on a new significance in the Sri Lankan monastic sphere, as a necessarily moral practice rather than as valueless sensuality.

Saṅgharakkhita not only discusses propriety in the context of his final chapter on aesthetic moods and feelings but references the value of propriety throughout his work. He explains, for instance, why he refers to the Buddha as 'lord of sages' (*muninda*) in his opening verse in which he implores the goddess of speech, who is said to reside in the *muninda*'s lotus-like mouth, to gladden his mind.[69] Saṅgharakkhita writes that the word *muninda* is the most tasteful name for the Buddha in this verse since it signifies the fact that in knowing both worlds – this life and the world beyond – the Buddha is the ultimate ruler (*paramissariya*) of both the sages (*muni*) and those people (*puggala*) (we can assume kings) who wield supreme power on earth. For this reason, he states, this word, *muninda*, is exceptionally pleasing and as such it also sustains the propriety of the other words in the verse.[70]

The Sinhala commentary here ties Saṅgharakkhita's discussion to another one of his innovations, namely his introduction of a new poetic fault, the 'lack of propriety' (*ocityahīna*) and quotes a verse from this section stating, 'that which is called "propriety" (*ocitya*) in the world should be learned out of respect. For the greatest poets, who are good people, are a source of instruction in [propriety].'[71] The late 'new commentary' on the *Subodhālaṅkāra*, possibly composed in Burma in the fifteenth century, remarks on this topic that while Saṅgharakkhita wanted to write a brief work, he explains propriety at length due to his fondness for it.[72]

Whereas Kashmiri theorists such as Kṣemendra framed propriety almost exclusively in terms of the social norms of the Brahmanical court, Saṅgharakkhita uses Buddhist ideals as the norm by which the propriety of poetry should be judged. In his discussion of the fault that he calls 'a lack of propriety' (*ocityahīna*), he presents the following example, for instance, based on the *Vessantara Jātaka* ('Birth story of Vessantara') narrative:[73]

> If asked, how could I not give up even my life?
> Even so, my heart trembles to give up my son.[74]

With respect to this verse, Saṅgharakkhita argues that the impropriety (*anucita*) here lies in Vessantara's expression of trepidation in giving away his son. This he argues transgresses the merit of loftiness (*udāra*) that was initially conveyed by the first half of the verse: 'If asked, how could I not give up even my life?'[75] The merit of loftiness (*udāra*), first described in Daṇḍin's *Kāvyādarśa* but also adopted in the *Subodhālaṅkāra*, refers to any quality in a verse that is uplifting (*ukkaṃsavanta*). Daṇḍin illustrates this merit with a verse describing the uplifting nature of a king's royal demeanour, though for Saṅgharakkhita it is of course the Buddha who evokes such feelings of elation.[76] When discussing the removal of the fault of propriety, Saṅgharakkhita provides the following verse as an example:

> He set up a victory festival right in front of Māra's army,
> and did not consider it to be worth even a blade of grass.
> May the conqueror give us victory![77]

The Buddha, then, is the ideal and most fitting subject of artistic expression according to Saṅgharakkhita's conception of propriety. Yet Pali poetry composed in a *kāvya* mode, even when in devotion to the Buddha, cannot escape the heroic tropes of court society, and the assimilation of the values of court poetry within a Buddhist frame still requires some accommodation. In this verse, for instance, the praiseworthy heroism of a king in battle is appropriated figuratively to describe the Buddha's spiritual conquest and his bravado in the face of his foe. Saṅgharakkhita, then, found a way to reconcile the roles and ideals of both poet and priest. Inspired by the latest literary theory from Kashmir, represented, in particular, by Kṣemendra, Saṅgharakkhita was able to build a bridge between the aesthetic sensibilities of court poetry and Buddhist devotion. He focused on the idea of propriety as the governing principle of poetry and established his devotional writings as primarily a moral practice.

7.4. The Buddha as a Literary Figure

By reframing the composition and appreciation of poetry as a religious practice, Saṅgharakkhita is careful not to present aesthetic experiences as liberating or otherworldly. In restricting aesthetic experience to the realm of worldly discourse, Saṅgharakkhita's thought runs counter to the general intellectual trajectory of Sanskrit poetics in India. There is a noticeable claim in the works of tenth- and eleventh-century Kashmiri scholars, such as Kuntaka and Abhinavagupta, that aesthetic experience, at least in part, is a transcendental (*alaukika*) one rather than simply a mundane experience (*laukika*).[78] This appeal to the extraordinary nature of aesthetic sentiment develops in later poetical theory from Northeast India in particular, where we find claims in the work of the fifteenth-century scholar Bhānudatta, for instance, that devotional experience is by nature a transcendent phenomenon.[79]

In the midst of the emerging trend for theistic devotional poetry or *bhakti* poetry in the region it is not surprising to find scholars advocating aesthetic experience as a means of salvation.[80] Saṅgharakkhita, on the other hand, maintains a strict distinction between mundane (*lokiya*) poetry and the transcendent nature of the Buddha and nirvana. Rather than shying away from the paradox inherent in writing devotional poetry to a being who in essence transcends the world, Saṅgharakkhita is keen throughout the *Subodhālaṅkāra* to draw attention, often playfully, to the problem in his work.[81] He writes in one particularly ironic verse that:

> One should pay homage to the Tathāgata who is beyond all similes,
> for him who has obtained the highest world no likeness (*upamā*) can be used.[82]

Saṅgharakkhita reflects on the tension between the worldly and otherworldly in Pali *kāvya*, in particular when discussing a poetic fault fittingly known as 'contradiction' (*virodhi*). Following Daṇḍin, Saṅgharakkhita speaks of contradictions in the description of places (*desa*), time (*kāla*), art (*kalā*), the world (*loka*), logic (*ñāya*) and tradition (*āgama*) as possible faults that a poet should be aware of.[83] The point is that a poet may fall into contradiction if he transgresses the conventions governing what he is depicting. For instance, if a poet writes, as Daṇḍin imagines, that 'day lotuses bloom at night', this would be classed as a fault since it contradicts conventions regarding time.[84] Daṇḍin adds, however, that a poet may occasionally through his own literary skill turn such a contradiction into a poetic merit and provides a number of examples where contradiction adds to the eloquence of a verse.[85] One verse in particular, illustrating how a logical contradiction can in fact be a poetic merit, stands out among Daṇḍin's courtly examples for its devotional and religious content:

> Although you are knowable, you are unknowable;
> Although you bear fruit, you possess no fruit;
> Although you are one, you are many;
> Homage to you, the universal form.[86]

Ratnamati, when commenting on this verse, writes tersely that there is no fault of contradiction here since 'such is the nature (*vidha*) of the ultimate Brahman.'[87] Inspired by this accommodation of Hindu devotional poetry, Saṅgharakkhita proceeds to demonstrate in a series of devotional verses corresponding to each of these faults that none of the types of contradiction obtains when the Buddha is the subject of a poem, since the Buddha, his miracles and even the merit he accrued as a bodhisattva are all incomprehensible (*acintanīya*) and immeasurable (*aparimāṇa*).[88] The implication is that, like Brahman, descriptions of the Buddha and bodhisattva do not contradict worldly discourse but rather transcend the very possibility of contradiction. Saṅgharakkhita composes an equivalent verse in praise of the Buddha using Daṇḍin's as a model:

> Although you have abandoned birth, you bring about (good) rebirth;
> Homage to you, best among sages, whose essential virtues are unknowable.[89]

Saṅgharakkhita here addresses the apparent contradiction in the fact that the Buddha, though he has escaped cyclic existence, is able to bring about a good rebirth for his devotees. He does not choose to engage fully with this difficult issue, however, perhaps because for him it was an obvious statement of fact, and instead simply echoes Ratnamati's explanation in stating that there is no contradiction since 'such is the nature of the best of sages'.[90] Saṅgharakkhita is concerned more with moulding Buddhist devotion on to the armature of Sanskrit poetics than with metaphysical issues. That said, we can detect an implicit aesthetic pragmatism in his writing. It seems that, for Saṅgharakkhita, so long as devotional poetry to the Buddha inspires the audience then it is good poetry, regardless of possible contradictions.

His discussion of the fault of 'contradiction in art' (*kalānirodha*) is interesting in this regard. In his example of how such faulty depictions of art can actually be a poetic merit, Saṅgharakkhita composes a verse recalling the celestial minstrel, Pañcasikha, who in the *Sakkapañha Sutta* ('Question of Sakka') serenades the Buddha with a song extolling the qualities of the Buddha, the Dhamma, the Buddha's enlightened disciples and, finally, of love itself:[91]

> What people would not be pleased by the discordant notes of the lute of Pañcasikha, whose mind is submerged in the qualities of the Buddha?[92]

Saṅgharakkhita writes in his commentary on this verse that there is no mistake in depicting the faulty performance of the arts, in this case the incorrect playing of a lute, since the clumsy performance is due to the fact that the performer, Pañcasikha, is immersed in meditation on the immeasurable (*aparimāṇa*) qualities of the Buddha.[93] We can infer that because the performance was inspired by meditation on the Buddha, any error that is produced is, in some respects, negligible since the audience is enraptured by the artist, who acts as a medium between the transcendent Buddha and the world.

Saṅgharakkhita is careful to note the subtle distinction between the Buddha's status as transcendent muse and his worldly representation in poetry in his commentary. He describes Pañcasikha, for instance, as immersed in the immeasurable qualities of the Buddha, that is, in his transcendent virtues, though takes care to note that the listening audience only has a sense of the Buddha's worldly (*lokiya*) qualities.[94] While he never spells it out explicitly, we obtain a glimpse in this verse as to how Saṅgharakkhita imagined devotional poetry to function, where the transcendent Buddha acts as a muse for the artist who creates in a worldly form an experience of pleasure for an audience, who cannot grasp the nature of the Buddha in actuality. The idea of the transcendent, not transcendence itself, becomes a worldly object of pleasure for devotees and a means of karmic transformation and better rebirth.

The old Sinhala commentary to the *Subodhālaṅkāra* provides another perspective on the matter when interpreting one of the Buddha's birth stories or *jātaka*s in terms of the aesthetic feelings it depicts. Whereas Saṅgharakkhita was hesitant to illustrate such moods and feelings in his own explication of his final chapter, the Sinhala commentary composes Pali examples based on the narrative of the *Vidhurapaṇḍita Jātaka* for each of the foundational aesthetic feelings (*ṭhayībhāva*), which are said to bring about the experience of aesthetic moods (*rasa*). In interpreting the *Vidhurapaṇḍita* narrative in terms of the aesthetic feelings it conveys, the commentary not only shows that traditional Pali literature can evoke the same range of aesthetic sentiments as Sanskrit *kāvya* but, in attributing these emotions to the characters involved in the birth story, in particular to the Bodhisattva himself, it presents some of these emotions as virtuous mental states on the bodhisattva path. In illustrating the aesthetic feeling of *sama* or 'calming', for instance, the commentary describes how the demon (*yakkha*), Puṇṇaka, at the behest of the dragon (*nāga*) king whose daughter he wished to marry, attempted to kill the Bodhisattva, who had been born as Vidhura, the wise, royal advisor of the Kurus:

> Even though lions and elephants charged [Vidhura],
> a serpent wrapped round [his body],
> and the demon [Puṇṇaka], like an elephant in rut,
> shook the mountain as if it were a bunch of bamboo,
> experiencing a sweet feeling, Vidhura did not shake in the slightest,
> as if having gone to a state of peace.[95]

Relying further on complex Sanskrit aesthetic theory, the Sinhala commentary on this verse explains that, while factors such as the charging of lions should inspire terror, Vidhura's experience of calm emerges here due to other factors, namely friendship (*mettā*), compassion (*dayā*) and joy (*moda*). This is made explicit in the verse when Vidhura is described as attaining a state peace on account of joyful feelings. The commentary further adds that these determining feelings are accompanied in the verse by other, more transitory feelings (*vyabhicāribhāva*), namely steadfastness (*dhiti*), intelligence (*mati*) and mindfulness (*sati*), and other physical effects (*anubhāva*), such as not shaking.[96] This bundle of emotion and action created by the verse produces the overall foundational feeling of calm, which for the audience transforms into the aesthetic mood known as *santa* or 'quiescence'.

When placed within the framework of a birth story of the Buddha, in this case his previous life as the pandit Vidhura, the aesthetic feelings associated with artistic representation are transformed into Buddhist virtues and the audience identifies with our hero Vidhura and emulates somewhat his virtuous mental state. While the line between reality and representation becomes blurred in the aesthetic experience of worldly emotions, the commentary still draws a sharp line between such experiences and the transcendence of nirvana. It is careful to highlight in the verse, for instance, that such a feeling of peace is only *like* the attainment of nirvana and is not liberation in and of itself.[97]

7.5. Summary

Writing in the middle of the thirteenth century, Saṅgharakkhita's *Subodhālaṅkāra* was the first attempt by the Saṅgha's hierarchy to propagate knowledge of literary theory to the whole monastic community. Previously, elite scholar-monks had incorporated Sanskrit literary models in their Pali works by means of a direct engagement with Sanskrit poetry and treatises on poetics. In creating the *Subodhālaṅkāra*, Saṅgharakkhita was able to successfully abstract an ideal literary model from Sanskrit treatises on poetics and use it as the framework for a specifically Pali poetics based on Buddhist norms and values. This act of formally sanctioning the study of poetics, a subject defined by its sensuality and worldliness, was not without controversy. The image of the late medieval Saṅgha that emerges from the *Subodhālaṅkāra* is one that is deeply conflicted about the value of studying poetics as part of a monastic vocation. Saṅgharakkhita skilfully negotiates the different views within the monastic community by praising literary theory as an intrinsically moral system while denigrating Sanskrit literature itself as impure. It is his re-centring of Pali poetics around notions of morality, civility and propriety that represents his most innovative contribution to Buddhist intellectual culture. In placing a knowledge of worldly propriety as the essence of composing and appreciating good poetry, Saṅgharakkhita manages to present Pali poetics to his sceptical audience as not only an acceptable object of study but one that is essential for the cultivation of morality and for one's self-presentation as a moral individual. He is careful, however, not to overexaggerate the liberating capacity of poetry and emphasizes that, while devotional poetry is wholesome and inspiring, it can never directly free a practitioner, nor can it capture the true nature of either the Buddha or nirvana. Rather, it produces virtuous emotions that can bring about better rebirths, even though, as Saṅgharakkhita notes, the Buddha himself has abandoned birth altogether.

Notes

1. On Saṅgharakkhita and his works, see Kieffer-Pülz, 2017b.
2. Kieffer-Pülz, 2017b, 31–4. Note, however, that Saṅgharakkhita did not replace Sāriputta as grandmaster but rather Moggallāna.
3. Kieffer-Pülz, 2017b, 49.

4. *Cūḷavaṃsa* 81.76–8. The Saṅgha, like the royal court, had its own system of appointing the grandmaster and, thus, like its own role in the coronation of kings, royal oversight in the selection of the grandmaster could have been largely ceremonial in nature. See chapter three.
5. See Kieffer-Pülz, 2017b, 49, referring to Saṅgharakkhita's *Khuddasikkhābhinavaṭīkā* and the *Moggallānapañcikāṭīkā*.
6. Malalasekera, 1994, 198, citing the *Candasāratthaṭīkā*, a commentary on Saṅgharakkhita's *Sambandhacintā*.
7. *Dīgha Nikāya* I, $11_{,10\text{–}12}$; $69_{,5\text{–}7}$. See Collins, 2003, 670.
8. *Dīgha Nikāya* I, $7_{,27}$–$8_{,6}$. This passage and its commentary remained significant for reform-era intellectuals. The Sinhala *Karmavibhāgaya* (twelfth century?), for instance, takes these topics and qualifies that if literature depicts the impermanence of kings, heroes and armies then such literature is in fact conducive to nirvana and heavenly rebirth. See *Karmavibhāgaya*, $79_{,9}$–$83_{,11}$.
9. *Aṅguttara Nikāya* I, $72_{,20}$–$73_{,23}$, trans. Bodhi, 2012, 163–4. Bodhi translates the terms *paṭipucchāvinīta* ('trained in philosophical enquiry') and '*ukkācitavinīta*' ('trained in rhetoric') as 'trained in interrogation' and 'trained in vain talk', respectively. See also Bodhi, trans. 2012, 1630, n. 284. This passage is also cited in Collins, 2003, 670, n. 50.
10. *Sumaṅgalavilāsinī* of Buddhaghosa I, $76_{,12}$; $84_{,15}$; $89_{,26}$. See also Guruge, 1993–4, 134. This attitude to the two Sanskrit epics continues in late medieval Sri Lanka. See, for instance, the thirteenth-century Sinhala commentary on the *Maṅgala Sutta*, translated in Hallisey, 2007, 299. On the more favourable reception given to the *Rāmāyaṇa* after the fourteenth century, see Henry, 2017, 145–81.
11. Collins, 2003, 649–50. On what Collins refers to as the '*problem* of literature in Pali', see chapter three. For a recent, literary reading of the *Mahāvaṃsa*, see Scheible, 2016.
12. Załęski, 2010. Since the 1960s, however, a number of excellent anthropological studies have challenged the very idea of such an ideal type, in particular one based on the Pali canon, and instead point to ethnographic evidence for the Saṅgha's intimate engagement with society and politics. For a recent overview see Schober, 2011, 1–14.
13. Ingalls, trans. 1965, 59.
14. Pollock, 2003, 114.
15. Many of my insights in this chapter are indebted to questions first posed by Charles Hallisey. See Hallisey, 2003, esp. 702–3.
16. See, for instance, Hallisey, 1988; 2003, 703–7; Dhammapala, 2003. On the *Jinālaṅkāra*, see chapter nine.
17. With respect to this period, Hallisey (1988, 17–18) perceptively writes that 'during a period of roughly three centuries beginning around 1200 C.E., Theravadin intellectuals in Sri Lanka became increasingly concerned with the significance of a juxtaposition of self-effort and human limitations … When the medieval thinkers reflected on what amounts to the effective dependence of human beings on the career of the Buddha, they also asked what human responses might be appropriate when an individual recognized this antecedent grace.'
18. *Subodhālaṅkāra* of Saṅgharakkhita, v. 138.
19. See, for instance, *Subodhālaṅkāra* of Saṅgharakkhita, v. 14; *Kāvyādarśa* of Daṇḍin, v. 1.7.
20. On the more logical structure of the *Subodhālaṅkāra* compared with the *Kāvyādarśa*, see Wright, 2002.
21. *Subodhālaṅkāra* of Saṅgharakkhita, v. 16. Compare this with the *Kāvyālaṅkāra* of Vāmana, where 'faults are in essence the opposite of merits' (2.1.1: guṇaviparyayātmāno doṣāḥ) and, similarly, they are to be understood by implication (2.1.2: arthatas tadavagamaḥ).
22. *Subodhālaṅkāra* of Saṅgharakkhita, v. 116. I am not aware of a similar definition in other works on Sanskrit poetics, though this requires further investigation.
23. *Subodhālaṅkāra* of Saṅgharakkhita, v. 164.
24. *Subodhālaṅkāramahāsāmiṭīkā* of Saṅgharakkhita on v. 338, $272_{,5}$.
25. See below on Saṅgharakkhita's adoption of Ānandavardhana's theory of suggestion (*dhvani*).
26. See, for instance, Wright, 2002.
27. *Subodhālaṅkāramahāsāmiṭīkā* of Saṅgharakkhita on v. 337, $270_{,9}$. The second verse of the *Subodhālaṅkāra* also refers to a theorist called Rāmaśarman (P. Rāmasamma) who, as Yigal Bronner has shown, was a predecessor of both Bhāmaha and Daṇḍin. See Bronner, 2012.
28. Bronner, 2012, 76.
29. Chatterjee, 1960.
30. I borrow here Yigal Bronner's translation of this term (personal communication).
31. See chapter three.

32. Dimitrov, 2016, 125–54. Dimitrov rather attributes the authorship of the *Kāvyādarśasannaya* and also the *Siyabaslakarasannaya* to Ratnamati/Ratnaśrījñāna. His arguments concerning the *Kāvyādarśasannaya*, in particular, are quite speculative. See Gornall, 2017, 476–7.
33. Dimitrov, 2016, 99–101.
34. Cox, 2011.
35. The chapter divisions of Vāmana's *Kāvyālaṅkāra* are as follows: (1) 'the body' (*śarīra*), that is, the components of poetry; (2) defects (*doṣa*); (3) merits (*guṇa*); and (4) figures of speech (*alaṅkāra*). Vāmana is also mentioned in verse two of the *Siyabaslakara*. See Hallisey, 2003, 695, n. 25. On the date of Vāmana, see McCrea, 2008, 50, citing *Rājataraṅgiṇī*, v. 4.497.
36. The divisions of faults in Vāmana's *Kāvyālaṅkāra* are: (1) the faults of words and the meanings of words; (2) the faults of sentences; and (3) the faults of the meanings of sentences.
37. Yet where there is agreement with the *Kāvyādarśa*, such as on the fault of tautology (*ekārtha*), Saṅgharakkhita still prefers to adopt the wording of Daṇḍin's definitions. See *Subodhālaṅkāra* of Saṅgharakkhita, v. 40 = *Kāvyādarśa* of Daṇḍin, v. 3.135.
38. See *Subodhālaṅkāra* of Saṅgharakkhita, v. 45 and *Kāvyālaṅkāra* of Vāmana, 2.1.7. Another general fault developed by Vāmana that Saṅgharakkhita borrows is the fault of meaninglessness (*anatthaka*). See *Subodhālaṅkāra* of Saṅgharakkhita, v. 39 and *Kāvyālaṅkāra* of Vāmana, 2.1.9.
39. In Saṅgharakkhita's definition of *oja* (Sk. *ojas*), for instance, he adopts two aspects of Vāmana's description of *ojas*, namely, *samāsa* (brevity) and *vyāsa* (diffuseness). Compare *Subodhālaṅkāra* of Saṅgharakkhita, v. 123 with *Kāvyālaṅkāravṛtti* of Vāmana, 3.2.2, $32_{,10}$. On *sukhumālatā*, see *Subodhālaṅkāra* of Saṅgharakkhita, v. 135 and *Kāvyālaṅkāra* of Vāmana, 3.2.12. For *atthavyatta*, see *Subodhālaṅkāra* of Saṅgharakkhita, v. 147 and *Kāvyālaṅkāra* of Vāmana, 3.2.14.
40. Compare *Subodhālaṅkāra* of Saṅgharakkhita, v. 139 and *Kāvyālaṅkāravṛtti* of Vāmana on 3.2.12, $35_{,14}$: *yathā mṛtaṃ yaśaḥśeṣa ity āhuḥ*.
41. It is quite possible that there is also an influence from Udbhaṭa on this chapter, though this needs to be explored. See Bronner, 2016.
42. McCrea, 2008, 99, citing *Rājataraṅgiṇī*, 5.34. It is worth noting here that Senarat Paranavitana invented and published in the *Journal of the American Oriental Society* a fictitious 'Sanskrit inscription' that purportedly recorded a debate on the authorship of the *Dhvanikārikā*s which ascribed them to a Buddhist monk, Dharmadāsa. See Paranavitana, 1974. The veracity of the inscription was taken seriously, for instance, by Daniel H.H. Ingalls in his translation of the *Dhvanyāloka* and its *Locana*. See Ingalls *et al.*, trans. 1990, 27, n. 12.
43. McCrea, 2008, 99–164. Also, 2016.
44. *Subodhālaṅkāramahāsāmiṭīkā* of Saṅgharakkhita on v. 2, $7_{,23\text{–}26}$ = *Dhvanyāloka* of Ānandavardhana, 1.4, translated in McCrea, 2008, 105.
45. On the connection between *alaṅkāraśāstra* and *vyākaraṇa* as 'grammars', see Bronner, 2007b.
46. We find a similar concern in Saṅgharakkhita's *Moggallānapañcikāṭīkā* concerning Moggallāna's use of a grammatical example that appears to reflect Jain philosophy. He argues in this case, however, that an exposure to the doctrines of other religious communities is beneficial since it allows a practitioner to see the flaws in these doctrines and to develop stronger faith in the Buddha. See *Moggallānapañcikāṭīkā* of Saṅgharakkhita, $85_{,1\text{–}16}$, discussed and translated in Gornall, 2013, 58.
47. *Subodhālaṅkāra* of Saṅgharakkhita, v. 2:
rāmasammādyalaṅkārā santi santo purātanā
tathā pi tu vaḷañjenti suddhamāgadhikā na te.
48. *Subodhālaṅkāramahāsāmiṭīkā* of Saṅgharakkhita on v. 2, $7_{,12\text{–}27}$: **suddhamāgadhikā** ti magadhesu bhavā, tattha viditā vā māgadhā saddā. te etesaṃ santi, tesu vā niyuttā ti māgadhikā. suddhā ca sakkaṭādibhāsitakālusiyābhāvena visuddhā, asammissā vā aparicitattā te māgadhikā cā ti suddhamāgadhikā, yatipotā. te yathāvutte alaṅkāre ābharaṇavisese na vaḷañjenti, pasādhanavisese nānubhavanti, ganthavisese pana uggahaṇadhāraṇādivisesena attano suddhamāgadhikattā, rāmasammādīnañ ca sakkaṭādibhāvato ti ayam ettha saddattho. bhāvatthaleso p' ettha paripūrati, tathāvidhapatītiyogato. suddhamāgadhikā attano parisuddhabhāvena pubbe sobhanā pi te alaṅkārā idāni malaggahitabhāvappattā, kiṃ tehi malaggahitehi amhādisānaṃ suddhasattānan ti na vaḷañjentī ti.
"patīyamānaṃ pana kiñci vatthu atth' eva vāṇīsu mahākavīnaṃ,
yaṃ taṃ pasiddhāvayavātirittaṃ ābhāti lāvaṇyam iva 'ṅganāsū" (*Dhvanyāloka* 1.4) ti hi vuttaṃ. On the derivation of *māgadhikā*, see also *Moggallānavyākaraṇa* of Moggallāna, 4.20; 4.26.
49. *Kāvyādarśa* of Daṇḍin, vv. 1.3–4.
50. *Kāvyādarśa* of Daṇḍin, v. 1.6.
51. *Ratnaśrīṭīkā* of Ratnaśrījñāna, $5_{,26}$–$6_{,9}$.

52. For a useful discussion of the *satpuruṣa* as a category of reader in medieval Sri Lankan literature, see Berkwitz, 2004, 258–70.
53. *Subodhālaṅkāramahāsāmiṭīkā* on v. 5, 11,$_{19-20}$: tasmā guṇadosavibhāgavicāraṇaṃ nāma tabbidūnaṃ yeva, nāsatthaññūnaṃ purisapasūnaṃ. He further writes that these beast-like people do not have the authority or entitlement (*adhikāra*) to discriminate between these literary merits and faults. See *Subodhālaṅkāramahāsāmiṭīkā* of Saṅgharakkhita on v. 5, 12,$_{24-5}$ ≈ *Kāvyādarśa* of Daṇḍin, v. 8.
54. *Subodhālaṅkāramahāsāmiṭīkā* of Saṅgharakkhita on v. 5, 12,$_{6-9}$.
55. *Subodhālaṅkāramahāsāmiṭīkā* of Saṅgharakkhita on v. 5, 12,$_{19-22}$ = *Aṅguttara Nikāya* I, 126,$_{1-4}$:
nihīyati puriso nihīnasevī
na ca hāyetha kadāci tulyasevī,
seṭṭham upanamam udeti dhīro
tasmā 'ttano uttaritaraṃ bhajethā ti.
56. *Subodhālaṅkāramahāsāmiṭīkā* of Saṅgharakkhita on v. 338, 272,$_{5-7}$: ... sakala-saṃsāra-dukkha-nissaraṇekanimitta-vimuttirasekarasa-visuddha-saddhammāgama-viggāha-sampīṇanoṇata-matīnaṃ parama-saddhālūnam anadhigatatthe pi ....
57. *Subodhālaṅkārapurāṇasannaya*, 177,$_{24}$ = *Subodhālaṅkāra-abhinavaṭīkā* on 338, 272,$_{24}$. This was also noted by Padmanabh S. Jaini in relation to the *sannaya*'s Pali translation, the *abhinavaṭīkā*. See Jaini, ed. 2000, xviii.
58. Ratnapāla, 1971, 150. See also, Gornall and Henry, 2017, 86. In this article I wrongly refer to Saṅgharakkhita as the hierarch during the 1266 reform when in fact it was Medhaṅkara.
59. Kieffer-Pülz, 2017b, 38, translating verse five of the colophon of the *Khuddasikkhābhinavaṭīkā* of Saṅgharakkhita, 440. A similar verse is found in the *Vuttodaya* colophon (v. 134). See Kieffer-Pülz, 2017b, 48.
60. *Subodhālaṅkāra* of Saṅgharakkhita, v. 338:
paṭibhānavatā lokavohāram anusārinā
kat' ocityasamulhāsavedinā kavinā paraṃ.
61. *Subodhālaṅkāramahāsāmiṭīkā* of Saṅgharakkhita on v. 338, 272,$_{13-17}$: yato ocityaṃ nāma kavīnaṃ paramaṃ rahassaṃ lokavohāre pi ucitaññu yeva pasaṃsīyate, samucitalokavohārānusāren' eva ca vakkhamānāukkamena viracitā racanā sacetanānaṃ rasassādāya sampajjate, tasmā ocitye samulla-sattaṃ (*corr.* samullāsattaṃ) dittaṃ phuṭam eva bandhanaṃ kātuṃ vaṭṭati.
62. *Dhvanyālokavṛtti* of Ānandavardhana on vv. 3.10–14, 145,$_{17-18}$:
anaucityād ṛte nānyad rasabhaṅgasya kāraṇam
prasiddhaucityabandhas tu rasasyopaniṣat parā.
63. *Aucityavicāracarcā* of Kṣemendra, v.7ab: ucitaḥ prāhur ācāryāḥ sadṛśaṃ kila yasya yat. See Pollock, 2001b, 213.
64. *Aucityavicāracarcā* of Kṣemendra, v. 19, ed. and trans. Sūryakānta, 1954, 142.
65. *Aucityavicāracarcā* of Kṣemendra, v. 28, ed. and trans. Sūryakānta, 1954, 157.
66. *Raghuvaṃśa* of Kālidāsa, v. 3.70, cited in *Aucityavicāracarcā* of Kṣemendra, 49,$_{4-7}$:
atha sa viṣayavyāvṛttātmā yathāvidhi sūnave
nṛpatikakudaṃ dattvā yūne sitātapavāraṇam
munivanatarucchāyāṃ devyā tayā saha śiśriye
galitavayasām ikṣvākūṇāṃ idaṃ hi kulavratam.
In translating this verse, I consulted the translation by Sūryakānta, 1954, 157.
67. Verse twelve of the *Aucityavicāracarcā* mentions explicitly the 'approbation of the wise' as a determining feature of propriety, for instance.
68. Pollock, 2001b, 213.
69. *Subodhālaṅkāra* of Saṅgharakkhita, v. 1 ≈ *Kāvyādarśa* of Daṇḍin, v. 1.1. His appeal here for divine inspiration imitates the *Kāvyādarśa*, which begins similarly by imploring the Hindu goddess Sārasvatī to inspire its author. Whereas Daṇḍin describes Sārasvatī as dwelling in the mouth of the god Brahma, 'like a she-goose in a lotus garden', Saṅgharakkhita conjures an explicitly Buddhist image and reimagines the goddess of speech as 'born in the womb of the Buddha's lotus-like mouth'.
70. *Subodhālaṅkāramahāsāmiṭīkā* of Saṅgharakkhita on v. 1, 2,$_{27}$–3,$_{6}$.
71. *Subodhālaṅkārapurāṇasannaya* on v. 1, 4,$_{1-2}$ = *Subodhālaṅkāra-abhinavaṭīkā* on v. 1, 6,$_{24-5}$, citing *Subodhālaṅkāra* of Saṅgharakkhita, v. 103:
ocityaṃ nāma viññeyyaṃ loke vikhyātam ādarā
tatthopadesappabhavā sujanā kavipuṅgavā.
72. *Subodhālaṅkāra-abhinavaṭīkā* on v. 106, 114,$_{16-19}$. This passage is not found in the older Sinhala *sannaya* (on v. 106, 66) on which the *abhinavaṭīkā* is based. See Jaini, ed. 2000, xiv; xviii.

73. Charles Hallisey was the first to note the potential significance of the introduction of this fault. See Hallisey, 2003, 703.
74. *Subodhālaṅkāra* of Saṅgharakkhita, v. 62:
yācito 'haṃ kathaṃ nāma na dajjāmy api jīvitaṃ
tathā pi puttadānena vedhate hadayaṃ mama.
75. *Subodhālaṅkāramahāsāmiṭīkā* on v. 62, 80,$_{21-3}$.
76. *Kāvyādarśa* of Daṇḍin, vv. 1.76–77; *Subodhālaṅkāra* of Saṅgharakkhita, vv. 142–3.
77. *Subodhālaṅkāra* of Saṅgharakkhita, v. 106:
yo mārasenam āsannam āsannavijayussavo,
tiṇāya pi na maññittha so vo detu jayaṃ jino.
78. Cuneo, 2013; Kulkarni, 1986; McCrea, 2008, 392–6; Shulman, 2012, 93.
79. See, for instance, Pollock, trans. 2009, 251.
80. See, for instance, Haberman, 2001, 30–9.
81. A similar aesthetic exploitation of the perceived incongruity between poetic speech and the divine can be found in much Hindu devotional poetry too. See, for instance, Bronner, 2007a, 119–23.
82. *Subodhālaṅkāra* of Saṅgharakkhita, v. 52:
name taṃ sirasā sabbopamātītaṃ tathāgataṃ
yassa lokaggataṃ pattassopamā na hi yujjati.
83. *Subodhālaṅkāra* of Saṅgharakkhita, v. 34; *Kāvyādarśa* of Daṇḍin, vv. 3.162–85.
84. *Kāvyādarśa* of Daṇḍin, v. 3.167.
85. *Kāvyādarśa* of Daṇḍin, v. 3.179.
86. *Kāvyādarśa* of Daṇḍin, v. 3.184:
prameyo 'py aprameyo 'si saphalo 'py asi niṣphalaḥ
ekas tvam apy aneko 'si namas te viśvamūrtaye.
87. *Ratnaśrīṭīkā* of Ratnaśrījñāna, 275,$_{22-3}$: itīdṛśaṃ na nyāyaviruddham evaṃvidhatvād brahmaṇaḥ paramasyeti.
88. *Subodhālaṅkāra* of Saṅgharakkhita, vv. 75–80.
89. *Subodhālaṅkāra* of Saṅgharakkhita, v. 79:
pariccattabhavo pi tvam upanītabhavo asi
acintyaguṇasārāya namo te munipuṅgava.
90. *Subodhālaṅkāramahāsāmiṭīkā* of Saṅgharakkhita, 97,$_{6-7}$: īdisaṃ na nyāyaviruddham evaṃvidhattā munipuṅgavassa.
91. *Dīgha Nikāya* II, 265,$_{16}$–267,$_{13}$.
92. *Subodhālaṅkāra* of Saṅgharakkhita, v. 77:
nimuggamanaso buddhaguṇe pañcasikhassa pi
tantissaravirodho so na sampīṇeti kaṃ janaṃ.
93. *Subodhālaṅkāramahāsāmiṭīkā* of Saṅgharakkhita, 95,$_{19-26}$.
94. *Subodhālaṅkāramahāsāmiṭīkā* of Saṅgharakkhita, 95,$_{24}$.
95. *Subodhālaṅkārapurāṇasannaya*, 186,$_{28-32}$ (= *Subodhālaṅkāra-abhinavaṭīkā*, 304,$_{16-19}$):
entesu kesarikarīsv api veṭhayante nāge nagaṃ madagaje viya veḷugumbaṃ
yakkhe vicālayati no cali īsakam pi santiṃ gato va vidhuro madhurāpi bhāvā.
96. *Subodhālaṅkārapurāṇasannaya*, 187,$_{10-18}$ = *Subodhālaṅkāra-abhinavaṭīkā*, 304,$_{29}$–305,$_{6}$.
97. *Subodhālaṅkārapurāṇasannaya*, 187,$_{5-8}$ = *Subodhālaṅkāra-abhinavaṭīkā*, 304,$_{24-7}$.

8
The Politics of Relics: Dhammakitti's History

Saṅgharakkhita's poetics, fusing eloquence and morality, turned ornate literature from an object of spiritual danger into a potent source of stimulation for seekers of devotional sentiments. Saṅgharakkhita did not forge the connection between ornate literature and devotional practice himself, however. Rather, it had emerged in historiographical works composed in the decades prior to the composition of his treatise. These experimental texts reveal more clearly the role this new form of *kāvya* was thought to play in monastic life and underscore the fact that elite monks had begun to use the Buddha's relics, reliquaries and ornamental Pali literature alike as tools in the search for serene joy (*pasāda*). There is, of course, a long-standing tradition that speech can inspire such devotional feeling. The *Mahāvaṃsa* ('Great history') sets out explicitly that one of its aims was to inculcate serene joy in its audience. Reform-era histories differed, however, in that a new poetic form modelled on Sanskrit *kāvya* was now used as an affective soteriological tool and, due to its historical associations with political power, also as *the* appropriate medium for aesthetically instantiating new relationships with the Buddha that were at once devotional and political.

The term *vaṃsa* when used as a genre of literature is most often translated either as 'chronicle' or 'history'. The original meaning of the word though was 'bamboo'; the successive segments of clumping bamboo stems provided an apt metaphor for the multiple lineages of buddhas and kings described in these texts.[1] The *vaṃsa*s most often begin by recounting certain episodes in the lives of Buddha Gotama (the buddha of our current age) – or even of previous buddhas – and go on to narrate the fate of the *sāsana*, that is, the Buddhist tradition,[2] during the reigns of successive monarchs, one after the other. The linearity of historical description in these texts serves both to cast the Buddhist tradition in Sri Lanka as the sole continuation of the *sāsana* established by the Buddha and to underscore its steady, uninterrupted march through the fleetingly fragile structures of temporal power.[3]

The earliest example of a Pali *vaṃsa* is the *Buddhavaṃsa* ('History of the buddhas'), which was written in India possibly around the second century BCE.[4] The text is an account of the succession of previous buddhas beginning with Buddha Dīpaṅkara '100,000 eons and four incalculable eons ago' and ending with Buddha Gotama, his life, death and the distribution of his relics.[5] This work was followed centuries later by two *vaṃsa*s composed in Sri Lanka that continued the account from where the *Buddhavaṃsa* left off. The earlier *Dīpavaṃsa* ('History of the island'), most likely composed in the fourth century, again narrates the life of the Buddha, his visits to Sri Lanka, the establishment of Buddhism there, and its subsequent history in the reigns of kings up until Mahāsena (274–301).[6] The later *Mahāvaṃsa*, likely composed in the fifth century, is a more coherent work and is essentially a systematic revision of the *Dīpavaṃsa* narrative.[7]

The motivation to compose these early histories was not to provide a chronicle of past events for posterity or to detail the genealogies of royal dynasties to serve the political ends of the royal court.[8] First and foremost these histories can be understood as documenting 'successions of the Buddha's presence', as Jonathan Walters fittingly puts it, that is, they describe the interconnections of karma that influence the fate of the Buddhist tradition, age after age, king after king. As Walters says, 'more important than who a king's mother was, in the eyes of the authors of the Pāli Vaṃsas, is the question of his *kamma*: what merit, and what demerit, did he accrue as king? How will this affect where he is going? Did he assist, or injure, the instituted Discipline on the island?'[9] Kings and their polities are at once subject to previous karma stretching back to the incalculable past and agents of karma that will produce effects for future generations. This desire to provide causal, ethical explanations for history is always underpinned by a deep soteriological concern for the health and state of the *sāsana*.

By the tenth century scholar-monks began to compose histories influenced by new, Sanskritic ideas of literary beauty, including, for instance, a continuation of the *Mahāvaṃsa*, known as the *Cūḷavaṃsa* ('Little history'), and a number of new histories that narrate the fate of the different relics of the Buddha. While parts of older histories may have, on occasion, addressed royal audiences,[10] the later *vaṃsa*s sometimes explicitly address elites and often focus on deeds of royal heroism in the protection and preservation of the Buddha's relics. These *vaṃsa*s adopt conventions of Sanskrit narrative literature in a seemingly conscious move away from the previous *vaṃsa* style and consist for the most part of a self-contained, episodic story of how a particular Buddha relic travelled from India and became enshrined in a certain location in Sri Lanka.[11] Their literary quality meant that early Orientalists, such as Wilhelm Geiger (1882–1945), whose approach to the *vaṃsa*s focused on separating historical facts from 'fables, legends and tales of marvels', viewed them as particularly 'artificial and sometimes even abstruse' when compared with the 'sober and reliable form' of the *Mahāvaṃsa*.[12]

Focusing on Dhammakitti's *Dāṭhāvaṃsa* ('History of the tooth'), a history of the Buddha's tooth composed for the court of Queen Līlāvatī (1211–12), we will explore how such ornamental poetry supported the centrality of relic worship in reform-era practice and how these texts became agents themselves in enhancing the affective power of the relics they described. The aesthetic of these poems was not only devotional but also simultaneously political, since monks employed this courtly form of writing to assert the Buddha's spiritual and temporal sovereignty over the island. In thinking about the political function of relic histories we will move beyond previous approaches that treated these poems solely as forms of state ideology and as tools of royal legitimation.[13] This is not to deny, as others have, the existence of group ideologies or of legitimation as a possible outcome of premodern politics but rather to highlight, from a *monastic* perspective, how the relic *vaṃsa*s served the autonomous political interests of monastic elites during the reform era and how monks viewed relics, not as tools of court power, but as potent agents in emotionally instantiating the king and the court's status as devotional vassals to the Buddha and the Saṅgha.[14] In exploring the Saṅgha's political agency this chapter thus emphasizes the historical contingency, rather than natural 'symbiosis', inherent in the emergence of Saṅgha-state co-operation;[15] co-operation that was not *met* as a result of social needs but rather *made* as a result of the political endeavours of the scholar-monks of the era.[16]

8.1. The Political Aesthetic and Sociokarmic Figuration

The *Dāṭhāvaṃsa* is a Pali poem in five chapters composed by the royal preceptor (*rājaguru*) Dhammakitti at the request of the warlord Parakkama, who was army commander during the reign of Queen Līlāvatī and protector of her young Pāṇḍya successor, prince Madhurinda. In his opening verses, Dhammakitti states that his Pali poem is in fact a rendering of an older Sinhala history of the tooth relic and that he composed it for those who live on the other island (*dīpantaravāsi*).[17] The Sinhala commentary on this verse clarifies that the author meant that the history was composed both for those in Sri Lanka and India.[18] The work is composed in a Sanskrit literary mode, a 'political aesthetic' that Sheldon Pollock has shown was intimately tied to court culture and expressions of political power.[19] It opens with a eulogy or *praśasti* praising the court and in both form and content presupposes an elite audience.

Since Dhammakitti praises the royal court and adopts a literary form associated with celebrating sovereignty, we could feasibly interpret the poem as a work of court poetry. This genre, however, is often too mechanically applied to premodern South Asian *kāvya* and obscures the complex political relationships underpinning literary production. We cannot say, for instance, that Dhammakitti was a dependent member of the royal household like the poets in the lettered courts of late medieval Europe, nor did he necessarily intend to sustain the royal court as a social group.[20] The tendency to frame literary works such as the *Dāṭhāvaṃsa* as reflective of a single interpretative community or dominant class – what we can call 'court culture' – could easily lead us to overlook the complicated political situation of the poem, which represents in actuality a monastic intervention in a trialogue between local powerholders, namely monastic elites, a warlord, and the royal court, that was intended at least in part to declare the lordship of the Buddha over the island and to turn the newly arrived Pāṇḍya prince into a Buddhist devotee and tributary supplicant. The opening eulogy of the history hints at some of the complexities in the work's production:

> An ornament in the lineage of the inhabitants of Kāḷaka, the compassionate warlord Parakkama – who strives for the advancement of the conqueror's religion and who longs for what is good for the people – appointed into royal dominion over the whole land of Laṅkā Queen Līlāvatī, who was born of the pure, resplendent, and stainless Paṇḍu lineage, who is highly devoted to the religion of the king of sages, pleasant in speech, like a parent, a mother, to the people who follow the path of guidance at all times, loving queen to King Parākramabāhu, possessed of discriminating intelligence, and one who gives what is needed. He (Parakkama) appointed as her heir-apparent a scion of the lineage of Paṇḍu kings named Madhurinda – who pleases his honourable ministers, is kind-hearted, faithful, and well-learned in religious matters and worldly arts – and dispelled the disgrace known as 'Tisīhaḷa',[21] which was kingless for so long, and always made the well-disciplined Saṅgha pleased with good robes and other requisites.[22]

The timeless motifs of power, fame and valour contained in these opening verses project a sense of stability that contrasts with the reality of the historical context, which we know was characterized by chaos and violence. The eulogy is particularly unusual since it primarily glorifies the warlord Parakkama and only praises Queen Līlāvatī and Prince Madhurinda as his dependents, both of whom were of Pāṇḍya descent. During this era, the so-called 'period of sixteen kings'[23], rulers of both the Kāliṅga and Pāṇḍya lineages fought over the throne of Laṅkā and were supported by various local warlords who acted as kingmakers.[24]

Writing in 1211, Dhammakitti had just witnessed the young Kāliṅga prince Dharmāśoka (1208–9) put to death possibly by his own father Anīkaṅga (1209) of the Eastern Gaṅgas, who in turn was killed by a warlord Vikkanta-Camūnaka to make way for Līlāvatī's second reign (1209–10).[25] Her first reign (1197–1200) had similarly come about due to the murder of Coḍagaṅga (1196–7) at the hands of a Pāṇḍya-supporting warlord named Kitti. At the end of her third and final reign in around 1212, both Līlāvatī and the young Madhurinda were deposed by another Pāṇḍya prince also called 'Parākrama' (1212–15) who landed in Sri Lanka with an army from South India. His fleeting reign, in turn, was put to a violent end by Māgha of Kaliṅga who invaded in 1215 and ruled until 1236.[26] In the midst of this pan-South Asian internecine war on the island, we have two local actors, namely, a warlord, Parakkama, and a monk, Dhammakitti, who both have interests in cultivating one of these monarchs into a favourable ally for their respective causes. For Dhammakitti, in particular, this critically involved maintaining a monarch who was favourable to the monastic community and who, most importantly, would respect its sovereignty and land rights.

Dhammakitti's choice to compose his work in Pali was an attempt to bring the history of the Buddha's tooth to a foreign audience. At the same time his claim to be a translator rather than an author lends his work a certain authority in the local *vaṃsa* tradition while also reinstating the authority of his Sinhala sources in transregional Buddhist history more generally. In the plot of the *Dāṭhāvaṃsa* itself we can read an attempt to frame the Indian genealogies of both the Pāṇḍya and Kāliṅga lineages within the karmic history of Buddhism in order to encourage a sense of communality with and favourability towards the Buddhist tradition. The *Dāṭhāvaṃsa* begins by relating the Buddha's previous life as an ascetic Sumedha who in the presence of the previous Buddha Dīpaṅkara made the aspiration to become a buddha himself. We are then given a brief account of the life of the Buddha Gotama, his princely upbringing, his renunciation and enlightenment.

When describing the Buddha's cremation and the distribution of his relics the *Dāṭhāvaṃsa* states that the monk Khema who had been apportioned the left canine tooth took the relic to Brahmadatta, king of Kaliṅga, in Dantapura ('Tooth city'). Khema introduced Brahmadatta to the Buddha's teachings and the king established a temple to house the relic. The subsequent kings of Kaliṅga continued to worship the relic until a certain ruler Guhasīva ascended the throne. Guhasīva was less discriminating in his patronage of religious sects and began to adhere to wrong views (*diṭṭhi*).[27] The Kāliṅga king, however, eventually relinquished his false views and banished non-Buddhist ascetics (*nigaṇṭha*) from his kingdom, having witnessed the Buddhist festivals of the city-dwellers and having listened to his minister's advice about the benefits of worshipping the relic.

The non-Buddhist ascetics went to Pāṭaliputta and appealed to king Paṇḍu, lord of Jambudīpa, as 'a worshipper of the gods such as Śiva and Brahma' to reprimand king Guhasīva.[28] King Paṇḍu sent a suzerain, king Cittayāna, to bring Guhasīva and the tooth relic to Pāṭaliputta. Paṇḍu then had the non-Buddhist ascetics at his court throw the tooth relic into a fire and pound it with a hammer, though each time the relic performed a miracle and remained undamaged. A noble of Paṇḍu's court, Subhadda, who had become pleased with the relic's power, then eloquently sang the praises of the Buddha and touched the hearts of the assembly. Responding to Subhadda's worship, the relic performed a miracle and 'lit up all the directions like the star Venus'.[29] Paṇḍu's ministers appealed to the king to favour the Buddha 'in order to reach heaven and nirvana', at which point the king, full of joy, worshipped the relic, paraded it around the city, and built a gem-studded temple for it.

King Paṇḍu then ruled virtuously, defeated his enemy Khīradhāra in battle, gave to the poor and lived with self-control into old age. Before passing away and attaining his heavenly goal he entrusted the throne to his son and returned the tooth relic to king Guhasīva. Guhasīva then married his daughter, Hemamālā, to prince Danta, the son of the king of Ujjenī. Soon after, relatives of king Khīradhāra attempted to invade Kaliṅga and seize the tooth relic, forcing Guhasīva to give prince Danta and his daughter the tooth relic so that they could take it to the Buddhist king Mahāsena in Sri Lanka to ensure its safety. Finding Mahāsena had passed away, the two were greeted instead by his successor, king Kittisirimegha, also known as Sirimeghavaṇṇa (301–28), who, in devotion, offered the island of Sri Lanka to the relic. At Kittisirimegha's request, the relic miraculously travelled in a golden chariot in a celebratory procession through the streets of Anurādhapura and, after circumambulating the city, settled beyond its northern gate at the Abhayagiri monastery, bathing the city in light:

> sā dantadhātu sasikhaṇḍasamānavaṇṇā
> raṃsīhi kundanavacandanapaṇḍarehi
> pāsādagopurasiluccayapādapādiṃ
> niddhotarūpiyamayaṃ va akā khaṇena.[30]
>
> The tooth relic, coloured like a crescent moon,
> with rays white like jasmine and fresh sandalwood,

made the palace, the city gates, hills, and trees
appear for a moment as if made of pure silver.

Dhammakitti in his narrative modifies traditional accounts connecting the tooth relic with the Kāliṅgas, as found in the *Mahāparinibbāna Sutta* ('Great passing'), for instance, and introduces for the first time the figure of king Paṇḍu, who it seems we are to identify as an ancestor of the Pāṇḍya royal family. There was a popular South Indian tradition of tracing the Pāṇḍya dynasty to North Indian predecessors and it is noteworthy that Dhammakitti speaks of the 'Paṇḍu lineage' (*paṇḍuvaṃsa*) when referring to Līlāvatī and Madhurinda's Pāṇḍya ancestry.[31] King Paṇḍu, perhaps like Madhurinda, was not a Buddhist but a Hindu and it is only by witnessing the miracles performed by the relic that he turns his favour towards Buddhism. It seems likely that Dhammakitti intended the Pāṇḍyas in the Laṅkan court, in particular the heir apparent prince Madhurinda, to identify with their heroic Buddhist ancestor.

Kings in the narrative also do not act independently but are heavily influenced by their ministers and there may well be other correspondences between ministerial figures in the poem and those surrounding prince Madhurinda. It is the army commander (*senāpati*), for instance, who propitiates the relic on behalf of king Paṇḍu and entreats it to travel to the royal palace and have the king favour the triple gem. The army commander's role as a powerful facilitator of the king's conversion here clearly mirrors the possible role played by the warlord Parakkama who was the patron of the *Dāṭhāvaṃsa* and protector of prince Madhurinda. More generally, we can speculate too that the co-operation that results between king Paṇḍu, the Kāliṅga Guhasīva, and the Laṅkan monarch Kittisirimegha reflects Dhammakitti's desire for unity among the royal court's factions centred on a common concern for the well-being of the monastic community and the Buddhist tradition in general.

It seems likely, then, that one of Dhammakitti's aims in narrating the ancient history of the tooth in his *Dāṭhāvaṃsa* was to provide a framework for contemporary political action.[32] It would be overly simplistic, however, to view this representation of the past simply as a pragmatic instrumentalization of myth. Rather, Dhammakitti was perhaps seeking karmic explanations for the events unfolding before his eyes. This karma was not just personal but rather what Jonathan Walters calls 'sociokarma', in which the social relations that bind communities are thought to transmigrate and karmically continue in successive lives.[33] We can speculate that Dhammakitti intended his audience to identify as heirs of this sociokarma, either by identifying as their ancestor reborn or as a recipient of karmic 'overflow', that is to say, they viewed themselves as indirectly benefiting from the good karma of their ancestors. Through this sociokarmic figuration Dhammakitti skilfully intertwines the consanguineous descent of the royal houses he depicts with their karmic ties to the Buddhist tradition and, in doing so, redefines kinship in karmic terms, allowing him to localize these foreign rulers. This karmic model, of course, did not 'overwhelm political exigency' and Dhammakitti's vision was adapted, reinterpreted and selectively ignored at various points in the course of its reception in Laṅkan political life.[34] This point is starkly reinforced by the fact that within months of its completion both royal Pāṇḍyas, Madhurinda and Līlāvatī, were likely killed before Dhammakitti's vision of Buddhist Pāṇḍya kingship could be realized.

8.2. Serene Joy and the Poetics of Relics

The drama of the central chapters of the *Dāṭhāvaṃsa* centres on the shifting religious identities of the two kings, Guhasīva and Paṇḍu, and the role of the tooth relic's miracles, ornamented reliquaries, public festivals and royal ministers' speeches in reshaping their sensibilities in favour of Buddhism. Descriptions in the history of the religious power of each of these spectacles combine traditional ideas about the emotional charge of religious wonders with courtly attitudes about the moral value of ornamentation and beautification.[35] We can detect in the *Dāṭhāvaṃsa*, for instance, subtle shifts in emphasis, first within its descriptions of the power of these objects in terms of their ornamental configuration, and second in the inclusion of a broader array of sensual objects that are not directly religious as stimulators of serene joy (*pasāda*) in the conversion of kings and their courtiers, including ornate speeches, courtly behaviour and well-governed kingdoms.[36]

The short conversion narrative of the non-Buddhist king Cittayāna, who was sent by king Paṇḍu to bring both Guhasīva and the tooth relic to Pāṭaliputta, illustrates well how kings in the *Dāṭhāvaṃsa* are brought to a state of serene joy through a complex construction of diverse events and objects. Over the course of twenty-five verses (2.99–124), Cittayāna experiences a number of pleasing events that gather in intensity until finally he witnesses the tooth relic of the Buddha produce a spectacular miracle and renounces his false views. These events, however, are not all specifically Buddhist and the first descriptions of Cittayāna's change of heart occur as a result of Guhasīva's courtly decorum and the good governance of the city of Dantapura. We are told that upon his arrival king Guhasīva pleased (*tosesi*) his guest with gifts of elephants and that Cittayāna became well-disposed (*sumana*) when surveying the capital city which was 'decorated with walls, gates, towers, palaces and garlands' and was 'well furnished with alms-houses'.[37]

Incidentally, a fourteenth-century Sinhala rendering of the *Dāṭhāvaṃsa*, the *Daḷadāpūjāvaliya* ('Garland of offerings to the tooth'), places greater emphasis on the spectacle of Dantapura and expands in opulent detail on the wonderful construction of the city.[38] The descriptions of diplomatic decorum in the *Dāṭhāvaṃsa* conform to tropes of royal virtue derived from Indian court culture and the inclusion of ornate descriptions of cities, for instance, likewise follows the prescriptions of Sanskrit poetical treatises.[39] At the same time, however, our author Dhammakitti situates these courtly emotions as part of a cumulative aesthetic experience that ultimately will lead to Cittayāna's conversion.

The subsequent objects that bring Cittayāna to an experience of serene joy are more recognizably Buddhist. At their first meeting Guhasīva delivers a short sermon praising the Buddha and his path to enlightenment that produces in Cittayāna a state of serene joy (*pasannatā*) accompanied by a flood of joyful tears (*ānandassu*°). There is a clear connection here between Cittayāna's sensitivity to courtly beauty, garlands, palaces, etc., and his emotional receptiveness to the poetic praise of the Buddha. At this point Cittayāna has yet to renounce his non-Buddhist views and it is only through a series of visual sights, namely an ornate relic temple, a glittering reliquary and finally a miracle 'pleasing to the eye' performed by the tooth relic itself, that brings Cittayāna and his entire army to such a state of pleasure (*haṭṭha*) that they renounce their false views. We can perhaps also read into Dhammakitti's descriptions of these spectacles elements of a courtly aesthetic, in particular, in the construction of the tooth relic temple, which is described as having been built with sandalwood, jewels and gems and decorated with coral images and other paintings.[40]

It is useful to compare the conversion narrative of Cittayāna with that of king Paṇḍu. Our author, Dhammakitti, relates the indecorous courtly behaviour of Paṇḍu and his advisors with their lack of emotional receptiveness to the religious spectacles that they witness. Paṇḍu is described as arrogant and bad-tempered and surrounded by a court of deceitful advisors. He becomes filled with rage, for instance, when observing the celebratory procession that accompanies Guhasīva and the relic to Pāṭaliputta and continues to remain emotionally unmoved and full of suspicion when viewing the many miracles performed by the relic in his court. Conversely, Paṇḍu's virtuous royal conduct after his conversion only further serves to underscore the connection between Buddhist and courtly sensibilities.[41] It is only after a number of royal courtiers are moved to petition Paṇḍu to change his mind that finally the king becomes overjoyed (*pahaṭṭha*) with his 'doubts dispelled' (*vitiṇṇakaṅkha*).[42]

It is a longstanding trope of Pali *vaṃsa*s that inspiring speech has transformative, pleasing effects in the same way as other visual marvels. The *Mahāvaṃsa*, for instance, claims both in its opening verses and at the end of each chapter that the history was composed to arouse the 'serene joy (*pasāda*) and powerful emotion (*saṃvega*) of the good people'.[43] Eloquent speech in the *Dāṭhāvaṃsa* similarly instils in kings feelings of joy and happiness in identical ways to religious spectacles. The speech that finally brings Paṇḍu to a joyful state is as follows:

> What advantage is having wisdom, king, if, upon seeing such extraordinary power of the chief of sages (i.e. Buddha), one does not experience even a little serene joy? It is the nature of good people [to experience] serene joy, king, with respect to qualities that should inspire serene joy. All the buds of white waterlilies blossom automatically at moonrise. Do not then, king, abandon the path to heaven on account of the speech of the ill-minded. What unconfused person in search of a good path would walk holding on to the blind? Even powerful kings such as Kappiṇa, Bimbisāra and Suddhodana came to the Dhamma king (i.e. Buddha) for refuge and attentively drank the immortal Dhamma. Even [Indra] the thousand-eyed king of the gods (lit. 'the thirty'[44]) whose life was spent came to the king of sages, who had destroyed birth, listened carefully to the pure Dhamma and, having realized the Dhamma, obtained also [a longer] life. You too, supreme king of men, for the sake of obtaining heaven and nirvana quickly make your mind serenely joyful with respect to the destroyer of the five Māras[45], preeminent god of gods[46], the best Dhamma king.[47]

This speech introduces historical models of ideal devotion in the form of the ancient kings Kappiṇa, Bimbisāra and Suddhodana, and also the king of the gods, Indra, who sought long lives and immortality. After narrating these past events, the speech sharply turns to the present with a direct imperative (make your mind serenely joyful!) instructing the king to act similarly.

Dhammakitti in the narrative here presents the past as a model for royal behaviour and seems to have viewed his own history as similarly politically instructive.[48] Here, the model emphasizes as a rhetorical strategy the karmic rewards of Dhammic action, notably extended life and immortality. In structure, the passage resembles to some extent the so-called 'acts of truth' (*sacca-kiriyā*) common in early Buddhist literature, defined by Eugene Burlingame as a 'formal declaration of fact, accompanied by a command or resolution or prayer that the purpose of the agent shall be accomplished'.[49] Even in the *Dāṭhāvaṃsa* we have three explicit instances of the ritual performance of 'acts of truth' in which the previous deeds of the Buddha are narrated in order to move the tooth relic to perform a miracle.[50] While similar, the speeches of ministers – variously described in the poem as *subhāsita* 'eloquent expositions' (2.86) or *vaṇṇanā* 'praises' (2.108), for instance – differ from these 'acts of truth', however, in that they are not just effective in terms of the truth they convey but are also affective due to their ornate, formal composition and rhetorical power.

The first two verses of the speech help us understand something of the 'mechanism' of *pasāda* in the *Dāṭhāvaṃsa*, that is to say they explain explicitly why some do and do not experience serene joy when witnessing religious spectacles.[51] First, it is noteworthy that there is little emphasis here on the agency or power of the Buddha in bringing about serene joy in the audience witnessing his wonders.[52] Rather, Dhammakitti chooses to stress instead the morality and wisdom of the spectator as the determining factor in the experience of this joy. He treats as a natural indicator of one's moral condition the ability to experience serene joy with respect to an object that should produce this emotion. He reinforces the morally normative nature of this experience by likening it to the natural world where forest water lilies blossom automatically in the moonlight. There is a similarity here between the moral basis of the aesthetic appreciation of Buddhist miracles and Saṅgharakkhita's ideas about the importance of propriety in one's emotional response to poetry.[53] In both cases morality is the foundation of a transformative emotional experience that, as Dhammakitti reminds us, can take us to heaven or even lead to nirvana. The similarity in the dynamics of religious and artistic experience underscores the continuity in Dhammakitti's poem between Buddhist religious sensibilities and the normative behavioural and emotional repertoire of courtly society.

8.3. Assembling an Affective Community

Dhammakitti presents religious wonders, relics, reliquaries and ornate speech, including his own poem, as potent tools in the cultivation of serene joy.[54] By placing emphasis on the audience's role in the affective success of Buddhist spectacles, Dhammakitti provides a framework to imagine the parameters of a Buddhist community, defined by what Émile Durkheim would call a 'collective effervescence', a shared emotional response towards some material object that creates social solidarity. Yet in speaking of the social, ritual function of the religious spectacle, whether relics, festivals or poetry, I do not mean to suggest, following Durkheim, that such rituals are a 'social necessity', that is, a manifestation of the needs of an *a priori* social whole.[55] Rather, we can see in the *Dāṭhāvaṃsa* how relic worship functions as a focal point for the creative reorganization of a particular monastic conception of society. At any one time, kings, ministers and ascetics move in and out of the Buddhist community depending on whether they participate in the solidarity engendered by shared serene joy.[56]

We can see such a dynamic process at work in the *Dāṭhāvaṃsa* in the way the poem frames the struggle to win the favour of kings within a conflict between Buddhists and non-Buddhists. As mentioned, these non-Buddhists in the *Dāṭhāvaṃsa* are referred to as *nigaṇṭha*s, a word that in earlier Pali literature especially referred to Jain ascetics. In Dhammakitti's history, however, the term is employed in a more capacious manner to denote all theists. Dhammakitti is rather insensitive to the various sectarian distinctions among his adversaries and largely lumps all gods together in what we might understand as an early delineation of Hindu identity, albeit in opposition to Buddhist ritual practice.[57] He initially describes king Paṇḍu, for instance, as a worshipper of gods, 'such as Śiva and Brahma', and yet when Paṇḍu is inspecting the relic his advisors claim that the tooth is a bone from Rāma, an incarnation of Viṣṇu, and the king initially worships it as such.[58] The sly *nigaṇṭhas* function both as a foil for their moral Buddhist counterparts but also as a means for Dhammakitti to stress the exclusivity of Buddhist sensibilities. The experience of serene joy and the rewards of relic worship, such as a heavenly rebirth, are not available for those who hold sympathies for non-Buddhist sects.[59]

The sharp contours of Buddhist identity that emerge in the *Dāṭhāvaṃsa* take on a spatial dimension too and are explicitly linked with political territory. Upon experiencing serene joy in relation to the three jewels, for instance, Guhasīva has the *nigaṇṭhas* banished from his kingdom.[60] Similarly, in contrast to the hostile religious competition of northern India, Dhammakitti depicts the island of Sri Lanka or Sīhaḷa in the reign of Kittisirimegha as a Buddhist utopia filled with monks, relics and a devoted populace. While never a lived reality, we can hypothesize that the idea of an exclusively Buddhist kingdom in the *Dāṭhāvaṃsa* was an articulation of Dhammakitti's desire to overcome the antagonistic religious rivalries of the thirteenth century. The choice of Kittisirimegha's reign is suggestive too in that the monarch ensured the survival and eventual triumph of the Mahāvihāra by restoring its properties and plunder taken during the reign of his father, Mahāsena, whose support for competing fraternities had almost eradicated the Mahāvihāra entirely. Writing half a century after these rival monastic fraternities were reunified in 1165, Dhammakitti perhaps chose to strike a conciliatory note in situating the arrival of the tooth relic at the Abhayagiri during the reign of such a harmonizing figure, rather than the historically divisive Mahāsena.[61]

The contestation with Hindu ascetics in the narrative simultaneously underscores the fragility and malleability of a Buddhist community bound by a common emotional response to the Buddha's relics. In the court of Paṇḍu, for instance, the king's Hindu advisors employ a number of strategies to exploit the 'ambiguity of miracles' and undermine both the affective success of witnessing the tooth relic and its exclusively Buddhist significance.[62] They first inform Paṇḍu that Guhasīva despises the gods and worships the 'bone of a corpse' (*chavaṭṭhi*).[63] Confronted with the relic's miracles, however, the Hindu ascetics first claim that the bone is a relic of one of Viṣṇu's incarnations and, when the relic fails to respond to their worship of it as such, they then claim that its miracles derive from the magical powers (*vijjābala*) of the Buddhist monks and not the relic itself.[64]

On the one hand, the Hindu ascetics seek to subordinate Buddhist relic worship against the transcendental position of their own gods by first framing the veneration of the tooth as a form of animism and later by explaining the relic's miracles as a product of the monk's immanent magical power. The other more disruptive strategy employed by the ascetics is the attempt to incorporate the tooth within their own theistic framework by claiming that it is a bone from an avatar of Viṣṇu. Phyllis Granoff has perceptively noted with respect to this episode that it is only among audiences of 'non-believers' that the miracles of relics are treated and contested as evidence of the Buddha's power and continued presence.[65] By having the relic perform such 'evidential miracles' to disprove the suppositions of the Hindu ascetics about its natural, divine or magical origin, Dhammakitti seeks to remove the ambiguity of the relic's miracles and in particular to prohibit, at least within his own aesthetic community, the assimilation of the relic within another religious assemblage.[66]

The dramatic threat posed by the Vaiṣṇava appropriation of the Buddha's relics in the narrative can be possibly connected with contemporary historical events in northeast India, in particular in Kaliṅga, which we can infer Dhammakitti's courtly audience would be aware of. Less than 100 years prior to the composition of the *Dāṭhāvaṃsa*, the Eastern Gaṅgas, beginning with Coḍagaṅga, turned away from Śaivism to Vaiṣṇavism, incorporating in particular the local cult of Jagannātha, a deity that had longstanding associations with the Buddha.[67] From the tenth century, the Orissan Vaiṣṇava tradition equated Jagannātha with the ninth avatar of Viṣṇu, who prior to this period was identified with the Buddha.[68] We can possibly read Dhammakitti's conscious allusions to Hindu appropriation in the ancient past as a contemporary response to the threat of the 'theistic inclusivism' of Vaiṣṇavism, a trait that is readily apparent in the religious sensibilities of the Eastern Gaṅgas, who were likely an important force in the Kāliṅga-Pāṇḍya contest over the Sri Lankan throne.[69]

While the construction of a Buddhist community in the *Dāṭhāvaṃsa* centres on the king and the royal court, a Buddhist public sphere also plays an important, stabilizing role in the narrative by highlighting the constancy of the

Buddhist tradition in the midst of shifting royal sensibilities.[70] In describing the kingdoms of both Guhasīva and Kittisirimegha, Dhammakitti introduces the idea of a Buddhist populace, principally, to act as a religious spectacle that can inspire joy in much the same way as a reliquary. As such, for the most part, the public in the *Dāṭhāvaṃsa* are a faceless entity that are only encountered indirectly during festivities and other displays of religious and political power. Even the vernacular retellings of the history, while elaborating on the ornate processions and festivals described in the *Dāṭhāvaṃsa*, continue to centre on the perspective of the king and the court, where the flags, drums and chariots of a city's festivals remain a disembodied presence with no mention of the types of people and characters who may be contributing to these effects.[71]

There are occasions, however, where the public can be understood as an agent capable of petitioning the king and his court. In the episode of Guhasīva's conversion, for instance, the king gazes out of his palace window and witnesses the wonderful spectacle of his subjects participating in a Buddhist festival.[72] While the people here play a passive role in this scene, in the fourteenth-century *Daḷadāpūjāvaliya* the city-dwellers host an elaborate festival for the tooth relic '*having understood* that the king neglected to worship the tooth relic'.[73] In this vernacular account it is the people who are active participants in the attempt to convert the king and are not simply a passive object to be gazed upon.

Similarly, in the *Dāṭhāvaṃsa*'s depiction of the utopian kingdom of Kittisirimegha, the countryfolk, townsfolk and city-dwellers, gather together in the presence of the king and protest (*ugghosayiṃsu*) that they have not seen the relic, stating, 'the lord of Dhamma was born in the world (*loka*) for the benefit of all people (*loka*) and worked for the benefit of all humanity (*janatā*). His relics were distributed for the masses (*bahujana*) and we too desire to worship the [tooth] relic.'[74] A Buddhist monk advises the king to display the relic outside every spring so that the people (*jana*) may make merit, since, he argues, 'it is the nature of great men to act for the benefit of those dependent [on them] (*anujīvi*)'.[75]

In evoking the spectre of the public in the latter episode, in particular, Dhammakitti skilfully instils a sense of religious obligation in his royal audience by assimilating the role of monarch with a priestly responsibility for providing merit and by conflating the Buddha's universal mission with a king's duty to his people. Throughout the *Dāṭhāvaṃsa* Dhammakitti speaks of the benefits of tooth relic worship most often in terms of its power to provide a heavenly rebirth for his audience. Dhammakitti usually depicts any connection between relic worship and a king's ability to govern in terms of the perceived continuity between Buddhist and royal virtues, as mentioned above. In this late passage, however, we see for the first time Dhammakitti appeal to the Buddhist sensibilities of the masses as a potential reason for Sri Lanka's kings to favour the Buddhist tradition. In happily conflating the ritual agency of the public with their potential for collective political agency, Dhammakitti thus presents the Buddhist public as an arbiter on royal authority.[76]

8.4. Offering the Island to the Buddha

While co-operation between Saṅgha and state was by no means inevitable in late medieval Sri Lanka – as the relatively long reign of the anti-Buddhist king Māgha attests (1215–36) – it was often the case that, even in times of upheaval, kings conformed to Buddhist norms and respected the property rights of the Saṅgha. R.A.L.H. Gunawardana has described this tendency as a reflection of a natural, if occasionally antagonistic and disputatious, symbiosis between the institutions of court and monastery, based on their differing political and religious social functions.[77] In naturalizing their relationship, we can often overlook the inherent, political contingency of relations between court and monastery, the fluidity of social functions across these institutions, and the hierarchical relationship that often resulted from competition over shared social terrain.[78] Focusing on the concluding episode of the *Dāṭhāvaṃsa*, namely Kittisirimegha's offering of Sīhaḷa island to the tooth relic, and the earliest prescriptions for royal tooth relic worship contained in the *Daḷadāsirita* ('Acts of the tooth'), we will explore the monastic conception of Saṅgha-court relations and, in particular, how royal relic worship was thought of as a ritual instantiation of a monarch's subordinate position to monastic elites.

In the climactic scene where king Kittisirimegha, overwhelmed with joy, offers Sīhaḷa island to the tooth relic, the king confesses that no offering is suitable to the Buddha, 'even the entire earth with its abundant gems, wealth and pleasures'. He then laments that as his kingdom is 'very small' he does not possess enough wealth to worship the Buddha, 'the sole lord of the three worlds' (*tibhavekanātha*). Overcome with emotion he faints but on regaining consciousness he consoles himself that even a 'small seed' can produce many desired fruits and, 'with a face resembling the full moon due to a great amount of joy', promptly offers 'the whole Sīhaḷa island' to the tooth relic in order to attain the happiness of heaven and nirvana.[79] The scene is framed by a complex interplay between temporal and spiritual kingship. The Buddha is characterized, for instance, as 'lord of the three worlds', a figurative reference both to his escape from and, by implication, mastery of all of cyclic existence.

In response Kittisirimegha first assimilates into the role of subordinate king by depicting his offering solely in material terms, as if he was a suzerain relinquishing territory to his imperial overlord. Then taking on a priestly role, Kittisirimegha subsequently appeals to a spiritual teleology and reconciles that even a small offering to the Buddha, now referred to as the sovereign of the Dhamma (*dhammissara*), may bring about the rewards of a heavenly rebirth through the merit generated. We can see here in the offering of the kingdom to the tooth relic that, at least in the monastic imagination, the Buddha takes the form of both the king's political and religious overlord and the monarch likewise assimilates into a political vassal and a priestly devotee.[80] From a monastic perspective, then, there is no symbiosis of function between the two and the king is simply a pale imitation of the Buddha in what Ronald Inden referred to as a 'hierarchy of lordship'.[81]

The personages adopted by the king and the Buddha in such passages, furthermore, should not be understood as entirely symbolic either, especially when taken in the context of the material realities of the period. The shrine of the tooth relic in late medieval Sri Lanka, for instance, had become one of the largest landholding temples on the island and kings after the Anurādhapura period would make regular land grants to the temple as part of their rituals in association with the tooth relic.[82] We learn from the eleventh-century Vēlaikkāra inscription that the Saṅgha employed, at least on this occasion, a mercenary company to guard the tooth relic temple and rewarded the custodians with some land owned by the temple, in this case between 36 and 54 acres, that is, around the size of Grand Central Station in New York.[83] The Buddha then was quite literally not only lord of the Dhamma but also a landlord.

This is not to say that all offerings of kingdoms to the Buddha and Saṅgha should be understood literally. Certainly in earlier periods we find similar instances of the king giving his kingdom to the Buddha's relics.[84] The first such example is found in the *Vinayanidāna*, where Aśoka 'honours the Bodhi tree with sovereignty over all Jambudīpa'.[85] In some of these instances, however, the symbolic nature of the gift is made explicit either through the return of the gift or through its substitution for wealth. According to the *Cūḷavaṃsa*, Moggallāna I (491–508) offered the Saṅgha his royal parasol, a symbol of his rule, but this was promptly returned to him by the monastic community.[86] Similarly, Aggabodhi VIII (804–815) had his mother offer his own body to the Saṅgha but this was later exchanged for his equivalent value in gold.[87] In the *Dāṭhāvaṃsa*, though, Kittisirimegha's offering of the physical island is not qualified by any substitution, metaphorical interpretation or abstract reference to 'sovereignty'. That the offering of the island to the Buddha should be taken quite literally, albeit with of pinch of poetic hyperbole, as referring to an ideal transfer of territory to monastic elites is hinted at in the *Daḷadāsirita*, an early fourteenth-century Sinhala retelling of the *Dāṭhāvaṃsa*, which, in rendering this passage, refers to the 'land' (*tala*) of the kingdom.[88]

The earliest detailed regulations for worshipping the tooth relic found in the *Daḷadāsirita*, first translated by A.M. Hocart and Senarat Paranavitana, further reveal how the monarchical role played by the Buddha during rituals was intended to translate into real monastic autonomy.[89] In describing the later tooth relic rituals of the Kandyan period, H.L. Seneviratne depicts these events essentially as instruments of state, an opportunity for the king to legitimize his rule and consolidate his power.[90] In the regulations given in the *Daḷadāsirita*, however, the Saṅgha plays the orchestrating role and the king, both spiritually and temporally, is subordinated to the Buddha who is represented by the tooth relic. The king, as A.M. Hocart once wrote, 'used to act as priest for a greater king than himself, the Buddha'.[91] According to the *Daḷadāsirita* each day kings must:

> leave all their retinue outside, cleanse themselves, enter the house with devotion and respect, take a broom and sweep the house, wash their hands, offer gold, flowers, etc., worship by meditating on the nine virtues of the Buddha, such as sainthood, make obeisance, and take upon themselves the five commandments.[92]

At the New Year and Kārtika festivals too it explicitly specifies that those who wish to make offerings to the king must first make offerings to the tooth relic temple. The ministers of the royal court are also ritually subordinated to their counterparts in the monastic community. In the description of the ritual procession of the tooth relic, the relic is accompanied first by the Saṅgha, protected by sacred threads and other rites, along with temple officials and ritual drummers, who are then followed, finally, by the musicians of the royal court and the king's ministers protected by the army.[93] The rituals depicted in the *Daḷadāsirita* further give prominence to lay Buddhist functionaries and other nobility with a longstanding connection to the Saṅgha. The Saṅgha's own 'acolytes' (*kapuvā*) guard the tooth relic temple, for instance, and the families of the Gaṇaväsi and Kiliṁ, the latter being of Kāliṅga ancestry, act as officiants, second only to the chief monk of the Uttaromūla monastery.[94] Note that the king provides no military support to the Saṅgha or tooth relic in the ritual and his army participates in the parade only to guard his own ministers.

The last temple regulations in the *Daḷadāsirita* do not concern ritual directly but rather establish rules for the handling of donations and the resolution of legal disputes, all of which reveal how the ritual superiority of the Buddha over the king was meant to translate into the Saṅgha's autonomy. We learn, for instance, that if a matter of dispute arose concerning the tooth relic temple, there would first be an attempted resolution between the head of the Uttaromūla monastery, chief custodian of the relic temple, and the ministers of the king. If no resolution could be found, the authority for the final decision is said to rest with the monastic community. Similarly, the work specifically states that 'not even a *kahāpaṇa* coin', that is, 'a cent', donated to the tooth relic temple, should be moved to the king's palace. Finally, the work claims legal autonomy from the royal court in declaring the temple a place of sanctuary, stating that 'anyone coming to the Tooth-relic house in fear of something should not be molested'.[95] The *Daḷadāsirita* ends its regulations by detailing arrangements for taxation. Gifts, it states, should be given by 'those holding grants of freeholds', 'oil and wicks from villages holding service lands' and from others regular dues should be paid.

By noting the translation of ritual to temporal sovereignty, I do not wish to argue for a form of ritual determinism, that is, we cannot say that belief in such rituals ensured that the personages adopted within the ritual sphere led to their translation outside of this arena. The tumultuous events of this century suggest that many monarchs may have ignored such prescriptions and may have had their own understanding of the rituals they participated in. Rather, what is certain is that monastic elites at least did not regard the temporal and spiritual personages adopted in ritual and narrative works such as the *Dāṭhāvaṃsa* as purely symbolic. There was a palpable desire on behalf of the leaders of the Saṅgha that the lordship of the Buddha as embodied, in particular, in the ritual and literary representation of the tooth relic should translate into real legal and fiscal autonomy for themselves.

8.5. Summary

Dhammakitti's *Dāṭhāvaṃsa* employed a number of strategies to cultivate in his audience devotional sentiments sympathetic to the Buddhist tradition. Dhammakitti instilled in his audience, for instance, feelings of identification with the historical figures depicted in the narrative by framing the events as a sociokarmic figuration. He stressed in his work the continuity between relics, courtly behaviour and literary speech as religious stimulants, creating a new, holistic social aesthetic, combining courtly and Buddhist values, conducive to the cultivation of serene joy. For Dhammakitti serene joy was an emotion not only of personal transformation but also of social unity and he viewed his religious community as primarily an aesthetic entity, that is, he describes it as a constantly shifting assemblage constructed primarily by shared devotional emotions. In constituting this affective community, the Buddha, as embodied in his relics, served, from the monastic perspective, as the temporal and spiritual overlord on the island, with the king and court serving as religious and political vassals. The metaphors and figurations of literature and ritual, in this regard, were not simply symbolic but were meant to translate into real social, material and economic changes for the monastic elites who wielded them.

Notes

1. Collins, 1998, 254.
2. On *sāsana*, see Carbine, 2012, 266.
3. Collins, 1998, 270; See also, Collins, 1990, 99–101.
4. Walters, 1997. Also, Von Hinüber, 1996, §§124–5.
5. See Steven Collins's translation of selected passages from the *Buddhavaṃsa* and his analysis of its depiction of time. Collins, 1998, 257–67; 577–92.
6. Von Hinüber, 1996, §183; Walters, 1999, 331–37, dates the work to the reign of Mahāsena's son and successor, Sirimeghavaṇṇa (301–28).
7. Von Hinüber, 1996, §185. Walters, 1999, 337, speculatively identifies the author of the *Mahāvaṃsa* with a certain Mahānāma, who was the teacher and maternal uncle of king Dhātusena (455–73).
8. Collins, 1998, 255.
9. Walters, 2000, 107.
10. Walters, 1999.
11. The author of the *Hatthavanagallavihāravaṃsa*, for instance, declares that in composing his work he relied upon stories (*kathā*) based on history (*itihānugata*). See *Hatthavanagallavihāravaṃsa*, $1_{,14}$; Godakumbura, ed. 1956, ix–xvii.
12. Geiger, 1930, 212–13. Even the *Mahāvaṃsa*, however, had been regarded as filled with 'intentional perversion'. See Turnour, 1838, 686–7, cited in Walters, 2000, 158–9.
13. See the recent summary of previous approaches to the *vaṃsa*s in Berkwitz, 2004, 55–6; Scheible, 2016, 117–54. On the tooth relic and royal legitimation, see, in particular, Seneviratne, 1978a; 1978b. For a critique of Seneviratne's Weberian approach and his neglect of monastic agency, see Appadurai, 1981.
14. Sheldon Pollock has provided a far-reaching critique of the often mechanical application of 'legitimation', 'ideology' and other sociological constructs in explaining the relationship between culture and power in premodern South Asia and my approach to Pali literature is influenced by his methodological focus on 'the subjective horizon' of historical actors or what he refers to in Sanskrit terminology as the *vyavahārika-sat* ('conventional truth'). See Pollock, 2006, 511–24. In his critique of legitimation and ideology, however, Pollock goes so far as to argue objectively that both were historical impossibilities in premodern South Asia. I rather agree with Alan Strathern, who has perceptively raised a number of problems with Pollock's analysis here. He argues, in particular, that, while legitimation may not be found in the intentions of historical actors, that is, in their 'subjective horizons', these processes can still be analysed as historical effects. See Strathern, 2019, 110–14.
15. Steven Collins argued, for instance, that 'this symbiosis was not a historically contingent alliance but an intrinsic feature of the civilizational work of articulating order'. See Collins, 1998, 32.
16. We can fruitfully read the *Dāṭhāvaṃsa*, here, in light of Whitney Cox's recent discussion of the political function of a Cōḻa-era temple chronicle, the *Cidambaramahātmya*, which he characterizes as a 'work that was intended to intervene within a set of material and symbolic relations among persons and institutions, and to present an argument for how this order should be maintained'. See Cox, 2016, 197.
17. *Dāṭhāvaṃsa* of Dhammakitti, 1.10.
18. *Dāṭhāvaṃsasannaya* on v. 1.10, $4_{,33-4}$: **dīpantaravāsinam api**, jambudvīpayehi ättavunṭada lakdiva ättavunṭada.
19. On the work's style, see Law, 2000, 579–81. On the close association between *kāvya* and the political culture of the royal court, see Pollock, 2006.
20. See Green, 1980. On court culture and the reproduction of 'interpretative communities', see Ali, 2006, 19.
21. *Tisīhaḷa* refers to a traditional three-fold political division of the island of Sri Lanka, namely, *rāja* (or *pihiṭi*, the northern portion of the island), *māyā* (the central highlands) and *rohaṇa* (*ruhuṇu*, the South). We can perhaps understand the dismissive use of the term here as reflecting the author's negative view of the political fragmentation that had emerged in the reform era.

22. *Dāṭhāvaṃsa* of Dhammakitti, 1.4–8:
vibhūsayaṃ kāḷakanāgaranvayaṃ parakkamo kāruṇiko camūpati
gavesamāno jinasāsanassa yo virūḷhim atthañ ca janassa patthayaṃ
sudhāmayūkhāmalapaṇḍuvaṃsajaṃ virūḷhasaddhaṃ munirājasāsane
piyaṃvadaṃ nītipathānuvattinaṃ sadā pajānaṃ janikaṃ va mātaraṃ
piyaṃ parakkantibhujassa rājino mahesim accunnatabuddhisampadaṃ
vidhāya līlāvatim icchitatthadaṃ asesalaṅkātalarajjalakkhiyaṃ
kumāram ārādhitasādhumantinaṃ mahādayaṃ paṇḍunarindavaṃsajaṃ
vidhāya saddhaṃ madhurindanāmakaṃ susikkhitaṃ pāvacane kalāsu ca
narindasuññaṃ suciran tisīhalaṃ iti ppatītaṃ ayasaṃ apānudi
ciram paṇītena ca cīvarādinā susaññate saṃyamino atappayi.
This translation has been amended from the one in Gornall and Henry, 2017, 89. In translating passages from the *Dāṭhāvaṃsa* I have also often consulted the translation of Mutu Coomāra Swāmy, 1874.
23. *Cūḷavaṃsa*, 80.
24. See chapter one for more details.
25. It is possible that Anīkaṅga had the support of the Cōḷas. See Pathmanathan, 2004, 31.
26. Liyanagamage, 1968, 42–75; De Silva, 1981, 63.
27. On the translation of *nigaṇṭha* in the sense of 'non-Buddhists' in the *Dāṭhāvaṃsa*, see Granoff, 1996, 82.
28. *Dāṭhāvaṃsa* of Dhammakitti, 2.93.
29. *Dāṭhāvaṃsa* of Dhammakitti, 3.53.
30. *Dāṭhāvaṃsa* of Dhammakitti, 5.63.
31. There is a late South Indian tradition, for instance, that Arjuna of the *Mahābhārata* married Citrāṅgadā, who is described in these works as the daughter of a Pāṇḍya king. See, for instance, Bishop Robert Caldwell, 1881, 12–13, who is likely referring to the *Villipāratam* of Villiputtar (c. 1400). William Taylor (Taylor, 1857, 488) describes a seventeenth-century Telugu work, the *Vijayavilāsam*, that similarly expounds on Arjuna's exploits in South India and marriage to the Pāṇḍya Citrāṅgadā. He also translated another late history connecting the Pāṇḍya dynasty with Arjuna, and thus the Pāṇḍavas, in an earlier work under the title 'An account of kings who reigned in the Cali-yuga and of those who ruled in Madhura'. See Taylor, 1835, 195–206. This connection between the Pāṇḍyas and the Pāṇḍava brothers is made far earlier in Jain literature. See Churn Law, 1949, 52.
32. On myth, history and politics, see Gunawardana, 1976; Pollock, 1993b and Cox, 2016, 34–42.
33. Walters, 2003. See also Appleton, 2014, 126–54; Crosby, 2008b; Strong, 1997.
34. See Cox, 2016, 38. The *Pūjāvaliya* of Mayūrapāda, 728,$_{18–29}$, provides an account of the tooth relic narrative, though omits any reference to the Paṇḍu episode altogether. The same is true for the fourteenth-century *Rājāvaliya*, 37,$_{7–28}$.
35. Pollock, 2001b; Ali, 2006, 175–82. See also, Gornall and Henry, 2017, 78–85. On the role of *pasāda* in early Buddhist literature, see Rotman, 2009, 65–150.
36. On 'conversion' as an analytical term in comparative history, see Strathern, 2007a.
37. *Dāṭhāvaṃsa* of Dhammakitti, 2.99–101.
38. *Daḷadāpūjāvaliya*, 17,$_{9–24}$.
39. *Kāvyādarśa* of Daṇḍin, 1.14–22. On Daṇḍin's definition of a *mahākāvya*, see Peterson, 2003, 8–13.
40. It is quite possible, of course, that this is simply part of a longstanding 'assimilation' between the Buddhist temple and the artistic traditions of the royal palace. See Schopen, 2006.
41. *Dāṭhāvaṃsa* of Dhammakitti, 4.1–5.
42. *Dāṭhāvaṃsa* of Dhammakitti, 3.76.
43. Trainor, 1997, 82, n. 54. See also Berkwitz, 2003; 2004, 231–86; Scheible, 2010–11; Trainor, 1989; 2003; Walters, 1997, 179–80.
44. Reading *tidasa* °for *tidisa*° in v. 3.74a.
45. On Māra and his five-fold nature, see Nyanatiloka, 1998, 184.
46. On *atideva* ('preeminent god'), see Norman, 1991.
47. *Dāṭhāvaṃsa* of Dhammakitti, 3.70–75:
disvāna yo īdisakam pi rāja iddhānubhāvaṃ munipuṅgavassa
pasādamattam pi kareyya no ce kimatthiyā tassa bhaveyya paññā.
pasādanīyesu guṇesu rāja pasādanaṃ sādhujanassa dhammo
pupphanti sabbe sayam eva cande samuggate komudakānanāni.
vācāya tesaṃ pana dummatīnaṃ mā saggamaggaṃ pajahittha rāja
andhe gahetvā vicareyya ko hi anvesamāno supathaṃ amūḷho.

narādhipā kappiṇabimbisārasuddhodanādī api tejavantā
tam̩ dhammarājam̩ saraṇam̩ upecca pivim̩su dhammāmatam̩ ādareṇa.
sahassanetto tidisādhipo pi khīṇāyuko khīṇabhavam̩ munindam̩
upecca dhammam̩ vimalam̩ nisamma alattha āyum̩ api diṭṭhadhammo.
tuvam pi tasmim̩ jitapañcamāre devātideve varadhammarāje
saggāpavaggādhigamāya khippam̩ cittam̩ pasādehi narādhirāja.

48. This is not to say that this was the purpose of the *Dāṭhāvam̩sa* in the entire history of its reception.
49. Burlingame, 1917, 429. See also Söhnen-Thieme, 1995. On *saccakiriyā* in Buddhist literature, specifically, see Fiordalis, 2008, 103–7.
50. *Dāṭhāvam̩sa* of Dhammakitti, 2.115 (*abhiyācana*); 3.53 (*sacca*); 3.81 (*ajjhesi*).
51. Here, borrowing the expression from Rotman, 2003, 557.
52. See Trainor, 1997, 164–5. Considerations about the Buddha's continuing power do arise with respect to secondary debates about the authenticity of the relics, as we see among the *nigaṇṭhas* in the court of Paṇḍu, for instance.
53. See chapter six.
54. Crosby, 2014, 61–4. On the *Mahāvam̩sa*, see similarly Scheible, 2016, 247–8.
55. Durkheim, 1964, 236–7.
56. In order to describe these dynamic relationships it is perhaps more useful to speak of a Buddhist 'assemblage' rather than 'society'. See DeLanda, 2006, 253.
57. On the emergence of a nascent Hindu identity between the twelfth and sixteenth centuries, see Nicholson, 2014.
58. *Dāṭhāvam̩sa* of Dhammakitti, 2.93; 3.19. See also in the *Daḷadāsirita* of Devrada Dampasaṅginā, $23_{,1}$, the use of the expression *brahma-viṣṇu-maheśvarādi* when referring to king Guhasīva's turn to theism. The author of the *Daḷadāsirita* demonstrates a greater knowledge of Vaiṣṇava theology, however, and explicitly refers to Rāma as one of the ten avatars of Viṣṇu. See *Daḷadāsirita* of Devrada Dampasaṅginā, $27_{,12–13}$.
59. Guhasīva, for instance, is never accused of converting exclusively to Hinduism, only of making offerings to the *nigaṇṭhas*. See *Dāṭhāvam̩sa* of Dhammakitti, 2.73.
60. *Dāṭhāvam̩sa* of Dhammakitti, 2.89.
61. On Mahāsena and the Mahāvihāra, see Walters 1999. I am grateful to Jonathan Walters for clarifying the historical significance of Kittisirimegha/Sirimeghavaṇṇa's reign. It is noteworthy too that, despite Mahāsena's evil reputation in older works, such as the *Dīpavam̩sa* and *Mahāvam̩sa*, in the *Dāṭhāvam̩sa* he is depicted as a pious Buddhist. As mentioned, Guhasīva initially instructs Prince Danta and Hemamālā to take the tooth relic to Mahāsena's kingdom, though when they arrive the monarch has passed away. It is possible the earlier source material Dhammakitti used to write his history of the tooth relic, which had historical associations with the Abhayagiri *nikāya*, originally situated the arrival of the relic in Mahāsena's reign, since he was likely viewed by the Abhayagiri fraternity as a just and benevolent monarch. Writing after the unification of the three *nikāyas*, however, in which the monks who identified with the Mahāvihāran lineage took prominent positions, it was perhaps necessary for Dhammakitti to tweak the narrative in order to promote reconciliation.
62. Granoff, 1996.
63. *Dāṭhāvam̩sa* of Dhammakitti, 2.94.
64. *Dāṭhāvam̩sa* of Dhammakitti, 3.19; 3.56. On *vijjā* (Sk. *vidyā*) in the sense of 'magical spell', see Fiordalis, 2008, 121.
65. Granoff, 1996, 81–2. See also Strong, 2007, 193.
66. I borrow the expression 'evidential miracles' from Verellen, 1992.
67. Mukherjee, 1940, 18–19; 1949, 291–2. On the development of the cult, see Kulke, 1981.
68. Mukherjee, 1939, 780.
69. Clooney, 2003. Evidence of such theistic inclusivism prior to the composition of the *Dāṭhāvam̩sa* is perhaps found in an inscription of Gajabāhu II (1132–53), a monarch known for his Hindu inclinations, dated to 1153, which records a land grant to a monastery, using the Vaiṣṇava terms *āḷvār* and *vallavaraiyan* for the Buddha. See Pathmanathan, 1995, 39–40.
70. On the 'public sphere' in premodern South Asia, see Novetzke, 2016 and Fisher, 2017. Both provide conceptions of the public sphere that usefully differ from Jürgen Habermas's characterization of the public sphere as an arena of secular rationality.
71. See, in particular, *Daḷadāpūjāvaliya* (on *Dāṭhāvam̩sa* 3.2), $18_{,8}$–$19_{,9}$.
72. *Dāṭhāvam̩sa* of Dhammakitti, 2.79–80.
73. *Daḷadāpūjāvaliya*, $16_{,3–4}$: … pūjāsatkārayehi raja upekṣakavū niyāva **dāna** nāgarika janayā divyapurayak men nuvara sarjjita koṭa … The *Daḷadāsirita* elaborates in greater detail on the faults of the

king but, like the *Dāṭhāvaṃsa*, presents the festival of the people as a coincidence rather than as an intentional form of political action. See *Daḷadāsirita* of Devrada Dampasaṅginā, 21.

74. *Dāṭhāvaṃsa* of Dhammakitti, 5.39–40.
75. *Dāṭhāvaṃsa* of Dhammakitti, 5.43.
76. Here we can see most clearly the importance, as Alan Strathern has argued, of distinguishing intention from effect when discussing legitimation. For while Dhammakitti's motivation here is to bolster monastic autonomy and status, one possible effect of his strategies, regardless of intention, is to legitimize any compliant and subordinate Buddhist court within his social model. See Strathern, 2019, 110–14.
77. Gunawardana, 1979, 343–4.
78. While Gunawardana does recognize the growing political autonomy of the monastic community, he never truly analytically separates political and religious functions from the institutions of the court and monastery. Gunawardana depicts competition or antagonism between the court and monastery in early medieval Sri Lanka as occurring almost *in spite* of their underlying, functional interdependence. The convergence of roles that we see in the reform era between court and monastery are difficult to analyse if function is seen as essentially contiguous with institution. Rather, if we separate the two analytically, then it is possible to view this convergence as a new institutional expression of the symbiosis of religious and political functions in the longue durée, albeit a symbiosis occurring within singular institutions rather than between institutions. The resulting relationship between such complex institutions, then, becomes primarily defined by political rivalry, a hierarchy of lordship, rather than symbiosis. The term 'antagonistic symbiosis' then cannot at least be used in the reform era to describe an institutional relationship and yet we can evoke its components so long as it is clear that symbiosis here can only refer to a relationship between functions and not one between institutions.
79. *Dāṭhāvaṃsa* of Dhammakitti, 5.14–21.
80. Hocart, 1970, 270.
81. See introduction.
82. Herath, 1994, 114–35.
83. Herath, 1994, 116; *Epigraphia Zeylanica* II, 242–55.
84. Rahula, 1956, 75.
85. *Samantapāsādikā* I, $93_{,27-8}$.
86. *Cūḷavaṃsa*, 39.31.
87. *Cūḷavaṃsa*, 49.63.
88. *Daḷadāsirita* of Devrada Dampasaṅginā, $42_{,11}$. The work was likely composed during the reign of Parākramabāhu IV (1302–26) by a lay minister in charge of 'ecclesiastical affairs'. See Herath, 1994, 10.
89. Hocart, 1996, 34–7.
90. Seneviratne, 1978b, 1–20. See also Holt, 1982, 23–8.
91. Hocart, 1970, 199.
92. Hocart, 1996, 35. The translations given are those of A.M. Hocart and S. Paranavitana. See *Daḷadāsirita* of Devrada Dampasaṅginā, 52–60.
93. Hocart, 1996, 36.
94. Hocart, 1996, 35–6.
95. Hocart, 1996, 37.

9
Devotional Power: Buddharakkhita's Buddha Biography

The turn towards devotion to the Buddha and his relics in the monastic literature of the reform era provided a means to counter perceived disorder, reassurance of better days to come and strengthened the monastic community's karmic relationships with each other and the laity in shared aesthetic experiences. There is a volatility, however, inherent in the immanence of devotional religion in that it has the potential to give rise to new, charismatic authorities in the religious landscape, fuelled by merit-making and claims of grand karmic inheritance. The rise of buddhahood as a prominent religious goal of elites, in particular, had the potential to unsettle the social hierarchies of the era. In this chapter, then, we will turn to a close reading of what was the reform era's first and arguably most ornate devotional poem, the *Jinālaṅkāra* ('Ornament of the conqueror'), so as to explore how a biographer of the Buddha carefully managed the aesthetic experiences of his audience in order to cultivate them into devotional subjects while subduing any destabilizing potential in their religious aspirations.[1]

Buddha biographies, such as the *Jinālaṅkāra* and *Jinacarita* ('Acts of the Buddha'), are unique in Pali literary history in terms of their devotional content and their highly ornate, literary style, marked in particular by the employment of poetic figures derived from Sanskrit literary theory.[2] While they represent a departure from previous tradition, at the same time, there is much continuity between these works and older Pali histories. Late medieval Buddha biographies, for instance, often commence in a similar fashion to earlier works by situating the Buddha's life on a cosmic scale and begin their accounts not with the birth of the Buddha but with his previous life as Sumedha in which he made the aspiration to buddhahood in the presence of the Buddha Dīpaṅkara. In narrating the Buddha's life and enlightenment prior to his death and distribution of his relics they further borrow from narratives found in post-Aśokan works such as the *Apadāna* ('Legends'), *Buddhavaṃsa*

('History of the buddhas'), *Cariyāpiṭaka* ('Basket of conduct') and the *Nidānakathā* ('Story of origins').[3]

Of these works, the *Nidānakathā* was the main source for the biographical framework adopted in the reform era, though it differs from later biographies both in terms of its intended audience and the message it conveys. The *Nidānakathā* is a prose work that serves as an introduction to the canonical *Jātaka*s or 'birth stories' of the previous lives of the Buddha.[4] The central drama of the *Nidānakathā* unfolds from a prediction by Brahmin soothsayers that the new-born prince would either become a universal sovereign (*cakkavatti*) or a buddha. To stop Siddhattha renouncing the world his father Suddhodana contrives to trap his son in a life of utter satisfaction free from its usual sufferings. The narrative depicts courtly life as ultimately a deceitful existence. Renunciation, by contrast, is presented as a necessity, not just for Siddhattha, but for all those who wish to follow him, as the Brahmin Koṇḍañña reminds us:

> Siddhattha the prince has taken the vows. Assuredly he will become a buddha. If your fathers were in health they would to-day leave their homes, and go forth: and now, if you should so desire, come, I will leave the world in imitation of him.[5]

The *Jinālaṅkāra* and *Jinacarita* differ in that they stress the long, karmic path to enlightenment or buddhahood instead of encouraging immediate renunciation.[6] The *Jinālaṅkāra*, for instance, emphasizes not the universal necessity of renunciation but the impossibly immense merit needed to give up the perfection of the royal court. There is a repeated refrain in the *Jinālaṅkāra* after describing each of the wonderful aspects of Siddhattha's courtly life: 'how did he, free from desires, walk away?'[7] Even the bees of the palace garden are so satisfied with their lives that they cry in astonishment, 'why did our lord abandon this?'[8] In the *Jinacarita* we find an explicit subordination of renunciation in favour of pursuing buddhahood when Gotama, in his previous life as Sumedha, remarks that:

> Today even, if I wished it, I could put an end to the endless fight, that is, existence, and, becoming a novice in the Saṅgha, enter the great city of nirvana! But what's the point of me extinguishing my defilements in another garb? Having, like this Buddha, become an incomparable buddha in the world, better for me complete extinction, when in the boat of Dhamma I have ferried humanity across the ocean of rebirths and brought them to the city of nirvana![9]

This path of merit-making and the pursuit of buddhahood among elites has most often been studied from the perspective of the royal court, with reference to what Emanuel Sarkisyanz called the 'bodhisattva ideal of kingship', that is, the belief expressed in the royal inscriptions of kings after the tenth century in both Sri Lanka and Burma that they were bodhisattvas, buddhas-to-be.[10] Scholars have generally interpreted such statements as part of the royal desire for 'unquestionable legitimacy', 'spiritual authority', and 'soteriological charisma'.[11] Echoing Max Weber, who argued that the bodhisattva ideal developed in the Buddhist tradition in response to the popular demand for a saviour,[12] Paul Mus even goes so far as to depict this shift in Sri Lanka as a 'messianic' response to 'Hindu' invasions that '*had* to be reconciled' with 'the most inflexible tenets of orthodoxy'.[13] In this chapter we will explore from the monastic perspective how scholar-monks rather promoted the bodhisattva path via the Buddha's life-story, in part, to control its charismatic potential within traditional devotional frameworks, to foster social support for monastic elites both within the Saṅgha and among the nobility and to establish a soteriological path compatible with their worldly engagements. This chapter argues, then, that at the stylus of Buddharakkhita the bodhisattva path emerges as a new form of virtuosity, rather than as source of charismatic authority, that, as a consequence, could support rather than disrupt elite monastic power in Sri Lanka's changing political landscape.[14]

9.1. The *Jinālaṅkāra* and Karmic Determinism

The *Jinālaṅkāra*'s colophon states that the work was written 1,700 years after the Buddha's passing, that is, in 1156 or 1157 CE, and that the author, Buddharakkhita, descended from a noble family (*sucivaṃsa*) in Rohaṇa and was the chief incumbent (*gaṇavācaka*) of his monastery.[15] The work's Pali commentary adds that Buddharakkhita had been initiated by the best scholars in Sri Lanka and the 'Tamba country' of the Cōḻas.[16] It is likely no coincidence that Buddharakkhita composed his poem at such an auspicious time and in the very same year that Parākramabāhu I (1157–86) was crowned ruler of Laṅkā in the capital of Poḷonnaruva.

Fresh in Buddharakkhita's mind when writing the *Jinālaṅkāra* must have been Parākramabāhu's spectacularly violent rise to power on the island. Buddharakkhita's native Rohaṇa in the South, in particular, had borne the brunt of the civil war that raged prior to Parākramabāhu's ascension to the throne. The young pretender had waged a bloody campaign in the region, hunting down Sugalā, mother of Mānābharaṇa, and recapturing the tooth and alms bowl relics hidden there. To win over the remaining resistance in Rohaṇa, the

Cūḷavaṃsa ('Little history') states that Parākramabāhu's army had hundreds of Mānābharaṇa's allies publicly impaled in villages and market towns. The history describes his brutality with an awe that usually accompanies religious miracles. The *vaṃsa* states, for instance, that 'they had many other foes hanged on the gallows and burnt and showed forth in every way the majesty – hard to subdue, scarcely to be surpassed, arousing astonishment – of the Ruler of men Parākramabāhu'. Following the conquest of the region, Parākramabāhu is said to have invited to Poḷonnaruva his army, the subdued dignitaries of Rohaṇa, as well as the monastic community of the region in order to 'cleanse their heads with the blossom dust of the foot-lotus of the illustrious King of kings enthroned (there) in splendour'.[17]

As a senior monk from the region, Buddharakkhita could well have made the long march from the ruins of his Rohaṇa homeland to the new king's capital and placed his head at Parākramabāhu's feet. When reading the unflinchingly eulogistic description of the king's rise in the *Cūḷavaṃsa* and also the praise openings of Parākramabāhu's royal inscriptions, one immediately gets the sense that the monarch saw himself as a karmically superior being, who was fulfilling his destiny in conquering the island. The *Cūḷavaṃsa* writes that the young prince, filled with a sense of his own cosmological importance, modelled himself as a bodhisattva, a buddha-to-be, as a king like Rāma in the *Rāmāyaṇa*, and as a hero like one of the five Pāṇḍava brothers of the *Mahābhārata*.[18] It is noteworthy, then, that a work like the *Jinālaṅkāra*, which was composed in the year of Parākramabāhu's coronation, presents a more nuanced vision of the bodhisattva path and of bodhisattvas, one that sanctifies lordship, to some degree, while subordinating elites by establishing devotional relationships with the historical Buddha.

While we can never know if Parākramabāhu was aware of Buddharakkhita's work, we can hypothesize with some confidence that the poem's immediate audience must have consisted of monastic and lay nobility. The poem does not cite its patron or contain an opening royal eulogy like the *Dāṭhāvaṃsa* but it frequently uses complex poetic figures that only the very few with a high level of education in Sanskrit, whether in the royal courts or elite monasteries, would be able to understand.[19] It is due to its prosaic difficulty, for instance, that the *Jinālaṅkāra* even became an object of satire in a fifteenth-century (?) Burmese biography of Buddhaghosa, where the poem is attributed incorrectly to Buddhadatta. The work describes a meeting between Buddhaghosa and Buddhadatta, in which Buddhadatta recites a verse from the *Jinālaṅkāra*. Upon listening to the ornate verse, Buddhaghosa responds dismissively that, even though the poem was 'beautifully composed', 'the ignorant will find it unintelligible' and 'those of noble birth will not understand it'.[20]

Buddharakkhita speaks in his work both of the pursuit of nirvana and of buddhahood, though it is the latter that he himself strived to attain. Echoing the consecration of Gotama's own path to buddhahood in the presence of former buddhas, in a series of aspirations (*patthanā*) at the end of the poem, Buddharakkhita imagines the future Buddha Maitreya prophesizing that 'he will become a buddha in the future'.[21] Written in the first person and in an inclusive tone these aspirations could equally apply to anyone who recites or listens to these verses.

Buddharakkhita opens his poem by stating that he will speak about the causes (*hetu*) necessary for buddhahood and the results (*phala*) obtained by the Buddha corresponding to these causes.[22] Here he advertises what is essentially unique about his method of biography in that he eschews the conventions of the older tradition, in which we find a linear narrative beginning with Gotama's aspiration to enlightenment under former buddhas, his arduous journey in fulfilling the perfections (*pāramī*) and finally his birth as Siddhattha, renunciation and enlightenment. The *Nidānakathā*, for instance, separates the events prior to his birth as Siddhattha in a long chapter referred to as the 'distant cause' (*dūrenidāna*). Buddharakkhita condenses this narrative and collapses its linear, cosmic timeline by interweaving occasional references to the events of Gotama's previous lives with the story of his renunciation and enlightenment in his final rebirth. This condensed form which weaves between Siddhattha's present condition and events in the cosmic past makes the connection between the cause, Gotama's karma, and the effect, his buddhahood, more tangible. One implication of this, however, is that, in literary terms, the courtly drama concerning whether Siddhattha will renounce is very much lost and, as a character, the prince becomes almost a karmic vessel without autonomy whose course is already set.

The emphasis in the biography on what we can call 'karmic determinism' is reflected in Buddharakkhita's decision to remove or modify the traditional episodes in which Brahmin soothsayers prophesize that the new-born prince would either become a universal sovereign (*cakkavatti*) or a buddha. King Suddhodana in the *Nidānakathā*, for instance, summons sixty-four Brahmins to interpret Queen Māyā's dream that a white elephant entered her side and all state that she is pregnant with a boy who will either become a universal sovereign or a buddha.[23] At the birth of the prince, an ascetic and royal advisor, Kāḷa Devala, provides a second prediction that the new-born would become a buddha.[24] At the prince's name-giving ceremony, seven Brahmins make a third prophecy and reiterate that the prince could either become a universal sovereign or a buddha, though another, the youngest Koṇḍañña, determines the new-born prince is destined for buddhahood.[25] In the *Jinālaṅkāra*, however, any dramatic ambiguity is removed. There is no mention of the first two prophecies concerning Queen Māyā's dream or Kāḷa Devala and the third prophecy at Siddhattha's name-giving ceremony is radically altered. There, all the Brahmins are in agreement and raise a single finger, declaring that 'he will become a buddha free from passion'.[26] There is a consensual uniformity in the *Jinālaṅkāra* between the predictions of the previous buddhas, who, in Gotama's former lives, determined that 'he will be a buddha in the future', and the prophecies made in his final life. There is no mention at all of the possible path of temporal lordship available to one born with the thirty-two marks of a great man.

Buddharakkhita perhaps pre-empts criticism of his deterministic depiction of the Bodhisattva's fate when narrating the episode of Gotama's initial aspiration to buddhahood in the presence of the Buddha Dīpaṅkara. There, our author clarifies that 'he [the Buddha] obtained this result, [i.e. buddhahood], only through the incomparable acts of giving, etc., that he performed himself. He did not obtain it without a cause, or due to previous buddhas, or because of agreement among many Brahmas, etc.'[27] Buddharakkhita wants to avoid any supposition that the Buddha gained enlightenment by chance or through divine predestination. It is the Bodhisattva's own karma, he emphasizes, that determines his eventual buddhahood.

Here, Buddharakkhita reiterates orthodox opinion regarding the predictions of former buddhas. 'Buddhas', writes the *Kathāvatthu*'s ('Topics of dispute') commentator,[28] 'through the power of their own insight, determine that "this being in the future will attain buddhahood" and speak of the Bodhisattva as assured [of buddhahood] by reason of the cumulative growth of merit'.[29] The commentator clarifies, however, that even though bodhisattvas can be conventionally referred to as 'assured of buddhahood', they only officially enter the 'path of assurance' (*niyāmaṃ okkamati*), that is, a guarantee of nirvana, when realizing the truth at the foot of the Bodhi tree.[30] By emphasizing the inevitability of the prince's enlightenment from birth, however, Buddharakkhita differs from the *Kathāvatthu* commentator in that, like the latter's opponents, he views the possibility of enlightenment as assured, at the very least, from the time that Siddhattha is born in Suddhodana's court.[31]

This subtle shift in emphasis has great repercussions for how Buddharakkhita depicts courtly life in the biography of the Buddha. Rather than simply a soteriological obstacle, Siddhattha's courtly upbringing is framed equally as a karmically necessary step towards buddhahood. At the beginning of a chapter entitled in James Gray's translation, 'verses illuminating the good fortune (*sampatti*) of being a householder (*agāriya*)', Buddharakkhita writes of the Bodhisattva's birth in the royal court that, 'over time, as his family prospered like a waxing moon, by accumulating merit, he grew up like the sun in the sky (*ambara*)'.[32] The point here is that the Bodhisattva's life as a royal householder was a necessary condition for the accumulation of further merit.[33]

Note, however, that the *Jinālaṅkāra*'s re-evaluation of the Bodhisattva's courtly life did not alter the basic nature of Buddhist soteriology. The Bodhisattva still detaches from his life of sensuality and comes to the conclusion that sovereignty is 'terrifying' (*sasārajja*).[34] We can read such statements as a critique of court culture but not one that is in any way subversive since, as we will discuss below, the *Jinālaṅkāra* does not present the Bodhisattva as a role model who should be emulated in the here and now. While the royal court is certainly an arena of sensuality that a bodhisattva must eventually renounce, the general tenor of Buddharakkhita's narrative focuses on the court as a model of material perfection, the fulfilment of lifetimes of good karma and the best possible birth before complete buddhahood.

This shift in emphasis is no better illustrated than in the eulogistic and idealized descriptions of Yasodharā, the Bodhisattva's wife, in the *Jinālaṅkāra* when compared with her depiction in the *Nidānakathā*. In the latter work, Yasodharā figures less prominently and is referred to only as 'mother of Rāhula', the Bodhisattva's son.[35] The *Jinālaṅkāra* by contrast spends many verses describing the virtues of Yasodharā as the perfect wife who only the Bodhisattva would have the strength to abandon.[36] It is possible that the nascent devotion to Yasodharā in the *Jinālaṅkāra* reflected a renewed interest in the *Apadāna* ('Legends'), in which we find an elaborate, eulogistic life-story of the queen.[37] This narrative, for instance, was rendered into Sinhala during the period.[38] In the *Pūjāvaliya* ('Garland of offerings') too Yasodharā is depicted in a devotional light. The author has Yasodharā defend her supposed previous misdemeanours in her relationship with the Bodhisattva, in particular in his previous life as king Kusa, on the basis that her wrongdoings helped 'to strengthen' the Bodhisattva's perfections (*pāramī*). She states then that, 'even wrongs done by me were in fact a source of benefit to you'.[39] There was a wider tendency during the period, then, found not only in *Jinālaṅkāra*, to present the Bodhisattva's family life as a model or, at least as karmically useful, rather than simply as a dangerous obstacle.

9.2. The Rhetoric of Distance

Buddharakkhita's emphasis on courtly life as an inevitable, meritorious condition on the path to buddhahood offers a new soteriological frame for those who held Buddhist sensibilities and who wielded temporal power, whether lay or monastic nobility. There is no contradiction, for instance, when Buddharakkhita aspires at the end of his poem to be both wealthy (v. 245) and a buddha (v. 250). This is not an Augustinian style self-delusion – Give me buddhahood, but not yet! – but rather a reflection of a twelfth-century view of the bodhisattva path as characterized by accumulating vast merit, often reflected in material prosperity, and of buddhahood as a worthy but utterly remote goal. In Buddharakkhita's own words, 'I will be a buddha *in future times*!'[40] Bernard Faure has written persuasively about a 'rhetoric of immediacy' in the Chan Buddhist tradition, that is, how the doctrine of immediate enlightenment functioned to construct a new religious elite in opposition to older gradualists.[41] Conversely, we can view the two aspects of Buddharakkhita's bodhisattva path, namely his accommodation of sensuality and material prosperity and his emphasis on the remoteness of buddhahood, as part of a 'rhetoric of distance' that on the one hand represents an expansion of Buddhist ideology into courtly society and on the other a desire to contain the aspirations of a community formed of those engaged with worldly power.

Buddharakkhita conveys the remoteness of buddhahood in the *Jinālaṅkāra* principally by emphasizing the inconceivable deeds necessary to fulfil the bodhisattva path. He emphasizes, for instance, that the Bodhisattva's impossible acts of gruesome self-sacrifice – whether cutting off his own head as a gift, cooking himself over a fire to feed others, plucking out his eyes, or spilling oceans of blood[42] – provide the exceptional karmic conditions for his renunciation. Our author constantly reminds his audience furthermore that these are karmic conditions that they sorely lack. In conversation with Māra, for instance, the Bodhisattva reminds us:

> Indeed, the good done by men in the innumerable world systems is not worth a sixteenth part of even one of my perfections. Once, as a hare, on seeing a mendicant coming, I fell into a fire and cooked myself so that I could offer my meat. Thus, I performed arduous deeds during endless ages; who other, indeed, possessed of intelligence, and not insane, could have acted thus?[43]

The implication here is not that the Bodhisattva's extreme acts of generosity should be imitated but that nobody else of sound mind could or should perform such an act.[44] By praising the inimitable nature of the Bodhisattva, Buddharakkhita elevates the Bodhisattva as an extraordinary object of devotion for his audience while also ensuring that the favourable Buddhist nobility did not renounce their power or develop charismatic authority by transgressing worldly norms in imitation of him.

Buddharakkhita further muddies the distinction between the transcendent status of the Buddha and his meritorious position in his last life as a buddha-to-be. He resituates a famous episode in the Pali canon, for instance, in which the enlightened Buddha declares that he is neither a god, spirit (*gandhabba*), demon (*yakkha*) or man, and instead places this speech in the mouth of the Bodhisattva in conversation with Māra prior to his final enlightenment.[45] In the canonical discourse, a Brahmin Doṇa encounters the Buddha's footprints when travelling along a path and notices that they contain wheels with thousands of spokes. He declares in astonishment that these footprints cannot belong to a human being and follows them until he finally encounters the Buddha sitting under a tree by the roadside. The Buddha then answers a series of questions about whether he is a god, spirit, demon or human, each time giving a negative reply.[46] He responds, instead, that he is awakened (*buddha*) and free from taints, like a lotus flower standing unsoiled above the water. In the *Jinālaṅkāra*, however, Buddharakkhita has the Bodhisattva proclaim before Māra that he is not 'a man, a demon, a god (*brahma*), or a minor deity (*devatā*)' since his body is created by infinite merit (*anantapuñña*).[47] Whereas here the Bodhisattva is regarded as beyond identification due to his unique karma, in the canonical discourse the Buddha transcends worldly designations precisely because he is free from karma.

Buddharakkhita further plays with the style of the poem itself in order to instil feelings of separation between his audience and the Bodhisattva. Buddharakkhita employs a variety of literary strategies, for instance, that encourage the reader to adopt the perspective of the astonished royal household rather than the prince who is renouncing courtly life.[48] Buddharakkhita often inserts rhetorical interjections to guide the reader's emotional experience of the unfolding events. In one particularly sonorous verse, designed to emulate the sounds and rhythm of courtly dance, a disembodied voice laments that the detached prince paid little attention to the beautiful dancing of his wife Yasodharā before abandoning the royal household:

> pāde pāde valayaviravā mekhalāvīṇānādā
> 'gītaṃ gītaṃ patiratikaraṃ gāyatī gāyatī sā
> hatthe hatthe valayacalitā sambhamaṃ sambhamantī
> disvādisvā iti ratikaraṃ yāti hāhā kim īhā.[49]

> With the jingling of anklets on each foot,
> and the lute-like tinkling of her girdle,
> she, Gāyatrī, sang a song not sung before
> to entice her lord,
> shaking the bangles on each hand,
> and whirling around in excitement.
> Though seeing her amorous advances,
> it is as if he does not see and leaves.
> Oh no, why the effort?[50]

It is not readily apparent who makes the interjection 'Oh no, why the effort?' ('*hā hā kim īhā*') in the final line. Could it be his wife, Yasodharā, who has gone to great lengths to entertain and offer herself to the prince? What about the poet and narrator himself who cannot fathom how the enlightened subject could reject such a spectacle? Or, quite possibly, the author is also pre-empting the response of his ideal audience, one educated and refined enough to understand something of the life on offer to the prince? Either way, the ambiguity of these interjections allows the reader to adopt these judgements as their own and to both commiserate with the Bodhisattva's wife and marvel in astonishment at his extraordinary detachment.

Buddharakkhita cleverly utilizes the poem's complex ornaments (*alaṅkāra*) or 'figures of speech' too in order to frustrate his audience and model the difficulty of the Buddha's renunciation. While the *Jinālaṅkāra* is arguably one of the most ornate Sanskritic poems composed in the reform era it is not uniformly so. Between stanzas forty-nine and one hundred and ten, as perceptively noted by Dragomir Dimitrov, there is a large concentration of *saddālaṅkāra*s or phonetic embellishments.[51] We can speculate that Buddharakkhita quite deliberately employs such complex verses here because the section (vv. 49–110) describes the Bodhisattva's incredible decision to renounce courtly life. The verses of this section get progressively more difficult ending with ones consisting of *yamaka*s, phonetically identical duplicates,[52] of only one consonant class, such as gutturals, palatals, etc., (*ekaṭhānika*, vv. 101–4) or of only one letter (*akkharuttarika*, vv. 105–8) and even one verse containing a riddle (*paheḷi*, v. 109). The poetic figures are among those that even Daṇḍin in his *Kāvyādarśa* describes as 'difficult' (*duṣkara*) to compose and that Saṅgharakkhita in the *Subodhālaṅkāra* omits entirely because they 'tire students' (*sissakheda*).[53] The difficulty of language mirrors the incomprehensibility of what Buddharakkhita refers to in the title of the opening chapter of this section as the Bodhisattva's 'astonishing (*vimhaya*) act of renunciation (*pāduddhāra*)'. By struggling to understand these verses the reader is given a taste of the effort required by the Bodhisattva to renounce the world and perhaps also a sense of the bemusement felt by the royal household in witnessing his departure.

It is likely that for many readers the section would prove difficult to comprehend and they would struggle to read beyond the Bodhisattva's life in the court. Buddharakkhita does provide some help though and in a few instances indicates the type of *yamaka* that is employed in a particular group of verses. The entire section itself is marked by a clever veneration to the Buddha that can be read identically both forwards and backwards, *namo tassa yato mahimato yassa tamo na* (Homage to him, the great one, he who has no darkness). One of the verses that is composed of only guttural sounds (*ka, kha, ga, gha, ṅa*) is as follows:

> ākaṅkhakkhākaṅkhaṅga kaṅkhāgaṅgāghāgahaka
> kaṅkhāgāhakakaṅkhāgha hā hā kaṅkhā kahaṃ kahaṃ.[54]
>
> O one whose senses [can obtain what they] desire, whose form removes doubt, who does not hold on to the suffering that is the river of doubt, who destroys the doubts of those who hold them – Oh, Oh! Where, o where can there be doubt?

The verse ends with an interjection by the narrator that is playfully ambiguous. One sense – and perhaps the dominant sense – of the rhetorical question is the total conviction of the narrator. No doubt about the Buddha remains. Yet the question could equally imply that the narrator has some doubt that he cannot quite comprehend himself, further underlining his distance from the subject of his poem who renounced the world. We can speculate too that there is likely a further meta-literary aspect to the verse, where the obvious repetition of the word 'doubt' in the puzzle stands out as a humorous comment on the linguistic difficulty of the verse itself.

We find in the *Jinālaṅkāra*, then, a soteriological path in which those wielding wealth and power are sanctified but subordinated as devotional subjects to the Buddha and, by implication, to monastic elites too. Those like Buddharakkhita were not the slightest bit interested in narrating the bodhisattva path to create messianic saviours either from their own fold or out of the nobility.[55] Some rulers of the era, such as Parākramabāhu I, who rose to power amid political and social conflagration, no doubt harboured and advertised a sense of their own cosmological importance – as buddhas-to-be or emanations of gods – but Buddharakkhita, at least, exhibits in his poem a desire to harness this will to power and contain it within models of virtuosity that maintain the social order, in particular the status of monastic elites. This model, Buddharakkhita's path, was focused primarily on the vast accumulation of merit through generosity to the Buddha and his poetic imagination, as we will now see, played an important role in instilling in the audience a sense of this devotional and political obligation.

9.3. The Literary Imagination and Meditative Visualization

As an ornate work of *kāvya*, the *Jinālaṅkāra* was not simply composed as a trojan horse to bring Buddhist ideology into courtly society, in the way, for instance, that Aśvaghoṣa states was the purpose of his *Saundarananda* ('Handsome Nanda'): 'This work, which contains liberation within it, is made for inner peace, not for pleasure, in the guise of a poem, so as to captivate hearers, who are concerned with other things.'[56] Rather, Buddharakkhita also understood his ornate poem as playing a role in the meditative contemplation of the Buddha. Buddharakkhita appeals to meditators in his third verse, for instance, and states that one who is devoted to the Buddha can obtain liberation through meditation (*bhāvanā*) and the contemplation of him (*buddhānussati*).[57]

Buddharakkhita again raises the practice of meditative contemplation at the end of his twenty-eighth chapter and states that the reader of the poem (*iha ... passatā*) must reflect (*cintanīya*) on the Buddha's awakening, which among other things he characterizes as a constant means of accumulating merit (*subha*).[58] He writes that the point of this spiritual exercise is that one who is wise – which he defines as one who is educated in philosophy (*takka*), grammar (*vyākaraṇa*) and the Buddha's teachings – having understood the poem completely, develops faith (*saddahate*) in the Buddha's enlightenment by perceiving its causes and results.[59]

The word *saddhā* 'faith' is difficult to translate in Buddhist literature due to the fact that in certain passages it seems to be a cognitive state, a reasoned belief, and in others it is quite clearly emotional or affective in nature similar to the state of *pasāda* 'serene joy' discussed in chapters six and eight.[60] Here Buddharakkhita presents the faith that arises in reading the *Jinālaṅkāra* as both cognitive and affective. It is an affective disposition that leads one to adore and venerate the Buddha but one that is developed through reasoning. This reasoning, it should be said, is not based on direct experience but a logical inference on the possibility of buddhahood through examining its causes and conditions. The reciprocal cognitive and affective aspects of faith are best illustrated in an episode from the *Mahāparinibbāna Sutta* ('Great passing') where Sāriputta proclaims with conviction, a 'lion's roar', that there is no one greater than the Buddha. The Buddha challenges Sāriputta about how he can say such a thing when he has no direct experience of the nature of a buddha, to which he responds that while he has not experienced buddhahood himself he has witnessed, in Kate Crosby's rendering, 'the logical consequences of the Dhamma' (*dhammanvaya*).[61]

In order to understand what these meditational instructions for reading the *Jinālaṅkāra* may have meant to Buddharakkhita's audience, it is helpful to turn to the work's commentary, the *Jinālaṅkāravaṇṇanā*. The colophon of the commentary claims that it was composed by Buddharakkhita himself. It states that this 'mass of texts' (*ganthapiṇḍa*), twenty-eight recitations (*bhāṇavāra*) long – a reference, according to Dragomir Dimitrov, to the cumulative length of the commentary and *Jinālaṅkāra* – was compiled (*sampiṇḍita*) by Buddharakkhita.[62] There is reason to doubt this attribution, however, since in at least one instance the commentary deviates subtly from the biographical account narrated in the main poem.[63] The commentary, furthermore, had a large influence on a Southeast Asian Buddha biography, the *Paṭhamasambodhi* ('First awakening'), and it quotes texts, such as the *Lokapaññatti* ('Description of the world'), which had a wide circulation in Southeast Asia but which are not cited in Sri Lanka until the early modern period.[64] The only evidence that the commentary was available in reform-era Sri Lanka is that it shares a quotation with Guruḷugomi's *Dharmapradīpikāva* ('Lamp on the Dhamma'), a work that also cites the *Jinālaṅkāra*.[65] Nevertheless, the commentary's colophon provides plausible information about Buddharakkhita's own life and, since it must date before the early sixteenth century, it remains a significant source for understanding how the *Jinālaṅkāra* was interpreted by its earliest monastic readers.[66]

The commentary explains that Buddharakkhita composed his poem principally for meditating nobles (*yogāvacarakulaputta*).[67] A *kulaputta* refers to a monk or layperson who is either a noble by birth (*jāti*) or one who has attained this status through his conduct (*ācāra*).[68] The commentary further refers to this meditating noble as a 'good worldling' (*kalyāṇaputhujjana*), a technical term employed in Pali commentaries to refer to a virtuous practitioner who has not yet attained stream entry (*sotapanna*), the lowest of the four religious attainments in the tradition.[69] While the commentator, like Buddharakkhita, speaks of both the pursuit of nirvana and buddhahood, he reads the *Jinālaṅkāra* primarily as a poem intended for bodhisattvas who aspired to the latter. The commentator on the *Jinālaṅkāra* fittingly employs a courtly analogy to explain the precise relationship between Buddharakkhita's ornate biography, which is likened to a casket of gems, the Buddha, and his meditating reader seeking buddhahood:

> It is just as a skilful treasurer would take the ornamental treasures of a Wheel-Turning (*cakkavatti*) king, deposit them in a jewelled chest and would instruct his most treasured counsellor (the king's heir) to 'guard this!' He (the counsellor) would take and guard it and, on the death of his father (the king), in becoming the Wheel-Turning king he would be adorned with that treasure and become lord of the world (*lokissara*). In the same way, the teacher Buddharakkhita, who is like the treasurer, has taken the treasure, that is, the virtuous ornaments of the blessed Buddha – lord of all worlds, boundless conqueror – has deposited them in a chest-like poem called the *Ornament of the conqueror* and has instructed the noble meditator who is like the most trusted counsellor. He (the noble meditator) receives it respectfully and humbly and protects it by engaging in meditation/imagining (*bhāvanā*). Practising as instructed he gradually achieves

> the Buddha domain and in becoming the boundless conqueror (i.e. a buddha) he is adorned with those virtuous ornaments.[70] Having made a single light for the entire world he shines and becomes lord of the world. [Buddharakkhita] thus describes the meditating noble [in verse three] as he is the principal recipient (*paṭiggāhaka*) of the *Ornament of the conqueror* that he will compose.[71]

The ornate biography, then, acts as a repository of the Buddha's qualities that can be used by a meditator when engaging in the practice of recollection (*anussati*). The analogy captures the multiple senses of the word *alaṅkāra* in the poem's title. The term refers both to the Buddha's virtues that are likened to treasures and also to the embellished nature of the poem ('the jewelled chest') decorated with ornaments or 'figures of speech'. The ornamental treasure chest, the *alaṅkāra*-filled poem, is a fitting vessel for the Buddha's qualities, both in terms of beauty and value, and is the most secure and difficult to access. As an idiom associated with royal power, it is the most suitable medium for conveying the Buddha's power, since, as Paul Mus observed, the model of the Wheel-Turning king traditionally provided the conceptual framework for imagining the Buddha's role as transcendent, universal overlord.[72]

Framed within the analogy of royal succession and inheritance, the commentary also points to the exclusivity and linearity of the succession of buddhas and to the fact that bodhisattvas, as heirs in waiting, cannot possess a buddha's qualities while he is still in power, that is, they do not decorate themselves in the Buddha's ornaments but guard them until the time they succeed the Buddha as the world's overlord. The analogy of royal inheritance thus touches upon a core aspect of Pali Buddhology that distinguishes the bodhisattva path of Theravada elites from other schools of Buddhism. Since Bodhisattvas, by definition, have not been taught by a buddha, the tradition classifies bodhisattvas as worldlings (*puthujjana*), and thus inferior to those on the noble path to enlightenment, up until they realize the Dhamma at the foot of the Bodhi tree.[73] Elsewhere, the commentary wryly states, for instance, that a such a worldling bodhisattva has a better chance of 'stabbing the back of a mosquito with a dagger' than directly comprehending the virtues of a buddha.[74]

We can speculate too that the ornamental imagery decorating the poem was thought to aid the process of contemplation, with an affinity perceived between meditative *bhāvanā* or 'becoming' and the poet's creative *bhāvanā* or 'imagination'. The *bhāvanā* of meditative rituals, as David Shulman states, is akin to the poet's *bhāvanā* 'insofar as we are dealing with vivid internal perceptions crystallized as mental images amenable to definition in words'.[75] It is within the sphere of the imagination, common to both the literary and ritual worlds, that we see most clearly the inapplicability in a Buddhist context of a distinction Sheldon Pollock makes in his analysis of Sanskrit court poetry between aesthetic power and material power.[76] The aesthetic cannot be separated from the quotidian here since both are encompassed by the moral laws of karma, in which one's emotions are an important causal condition for future material giving and the accrual of material rewards.[77] Within what Kevin Trainor fittingly describes as an 'aesthetically charged ritual environment'[78], the ornamental poem brings the reader into Buddhism's 'moral economy' and literature becomes a site of exchange, where one can convert moral action, including the cultivation of faith, into merit and in turn convert that merit into material and spiritual attainments. This merit, as Andy Rotman notes, is both 'the basis for future good deeds and attainments, and the purchasing power for current ones'.[79]

We find a compelling depiction of the interplay between the aesthetic and material worlds, for instance, in the penultimate chapter of the *Jinālaṅkāra*, entitled 'verses illuminating the rules for offerings (*pūjāvidhāna*)'.[80] Writing in the first person, Buddharakkhita describes the world system in which the Buddha was born as a devotional landscape, filled with valuable and beautiful objects, including, flowers, fruits, trees, birds, mountains, precious woods, gems, silver, gold, silks and fine cloths, and imagines himself, and by implication the reader, offering these items to the Buddha, as well as the Dhamma and Saṅgha, in devotion. This section serves as an opportunity for our poet to show his skill in naturalistic description (Sk. *svabhāvokti*) while simultaneously acting as an aesthetic, ritual environment in which Buddharakkhita and his readers can simulate undertaking great acts of giving to the Buddha.[81] He concludes that:

> I pay honour to his first inconceivable aspiration [to buddhahood] by means of all the existing objects in the world system.[82]

This exercise of imagining the world system and offering its treasures to the Buddha resembles, in many respects, the way the Bodhisattva, as described at the beginning of the *Apadāna,* imagines a Buddha field for himself in the form of a palace filled with buddhas, to whom he makes offerings in order to generate merit for his final birth.[83] The practice of creating the image of a buddha in one's mind and mediating with this image in order to generate merit has further parallels with South Indian Tantric and *bhakti* meditations contemporary with Buddharakkhita.[84] Unlike these practices of meditative imagination, however, there is never a sense in the *Jinālaṅkāra* or its commentary that a practitioner should identify with the Buddha. Both works stress the path of devotion, but this is one of long and arduous merit making and not immediate transformation. The meditator, the commentator states, only gradually gains a sense of the Buddha's virtues 'like a falling leaf' that becomes perfumed having brushed the back of a fragrant elephant.[85]

Buddharakkhita then ends his chapter by venerating in succession various important moments on the Bodhisattva's path to buddhahood, the Buddha's realizations, his teachings, the monasteries he founded, the Tipiṭaka that he preached, his relics and Buddha images.[86] In an apparent attempt to sanction the path of devotion towards the Buddha's relics, he creatively modifies the Buddha's famous injunction in the *Mahāparinibbāna Sutta* that, 'what I have taught and explained to you as doctrine and discipline will, at my passing, be your teacher'.[87] He rather quotes the Buddha as follows: 'The great Sage sanctioned that, "this doctrine and discipline that I have properly taught, as well as my bodily relics, are your teacher after my passing; the unconquerable throne and the splendid Bodhi tree are also your teacher after my passing".'[88] This expansion of religious authority to include material objects of devotion, such as relics and Buddha images, reinforces the fact that the Pali reform era was an age of emotion, where emotions as well as ideas were increasingly sources of authority, communal identity and religious transformation, especially for those who were taking their first lotus-like steps towards achieving buddhahood in the incalculable future.

9.4. The Buddha's Proprietary Rights

In presenting material generosity towards the Buddha as the natural outcome of developing faith in his enlightenment through reading his biography, the *Jinālaṅkāra* reflects a feature that became common to a number of other late medieval works of *kāvya* in Sri Lanka both in Pali and Sinhala. What Stephen Berkwitz notes with respect to the Sinhala rendering of the *Thūpavaṃsa* ('History of the relic shrine'), namely that it 'was composed and copied, as well as read and recited, in premodern Sri Lanka to instil emotions of serene joy and gratitude that compel acts of relic veneration', for instance, could equally apply to the *Jinālaṅkāra* and the *Dāṭhāvaṃsa* too.[89] Buddharakkhita in his work also hints at the social and political assumptions underpinning the poetic instantiation of relic worship. He frames his descriptions of the wealth contained in the universe and the imagined gifting of it to the Buddha in his final chapter not only as a spiritual obligation on the part of the reader but, uniquely, as the Buddha's proprietary right:

> I venerate him (the Buddha), who previously venerated those worthy of veneration (former buddhas), with the charming objects that exist in his birthing chamber, that is, the auspicious world system that belongs to him.[90]

In presenting the Buddha as one 'who previously venerated those worthy of veneration' the verse depicts the Buddha as a devotee of former buddhas and thus instils the reader with a familiar sense of obligation since this path of devotion should be followed by those who aspire to buddhahood.[91] The verse then uniquely turns to describe the world system in which the Buddha was born as his 'birthing chamber' (*jātovaraka*) and his property (*āyattaka*). The commentary elaborates on this statement using legal terminology from the Vinaya, stating, with respect to the contents of the universe, that, 'it belongs to him, [i.e.] it is his property (*santaka*). Even the living beings and material things that exist in that [world system]? [Yes,] all of it is only his property.'[92]

While references to the Buddha's ownership of property in texts from Sri Lanka are rare, as discussed in chapter five, we do find a discussion of the Buddha's property (*santaka*) in Sāriputta's Vinaya commentary, quoted also in Siddhattha's *Sārasaṅgaha* ('Compendium of the essence'), where the work sanctions the offering of property belonging to the Buddha as an offering to the Dhamma (*dhammapūjā*) and vice versa.[93] Here, however, Buddharakkhita goes even further and makes the extraordinary claim that the Buddha is in fact the legal owner of the entire universe.

There is an affinity here between this image of ownership and traditional ideas about the Buddha's relationship with his so-called 'Buddha field' (*buddhakhetta*). We have already noted, for instance, that in the first chapter of the *Apadāna*, the Bodhisattva becomes king of a heavenly realm that he creates in his mind, the 'Buddha field', in which he worships former buddhas, before being reborn in the Tāvatiṃsa heaven prior to his final birth as Siddhattha.[94] The concept of the Buddha field developed in later tradition to refer to the Buddha's sphere of power more generally, divided into 'the field of his birth' (*jātikhetta*), that is, the world system in which he is born, 'the field of influence' (*āṇākhetta*), the cosmological extent of the apotropaic efficacy of his teachings, and 'the field of scope' (*visayakhetta*), the infinite extent of his knowledge.[95]

In the Mahayana *sūtra*, the *Karuṇāpuṇḍarīka* ('Lotus of compassion'), we find an equivalent idea that the Buddha owns his 'field of birth' on the basis that it is his Dhamma, his moral law, that governs the world system in which he is born.[96] In depicting the Buddha as owner of all precious objects in the world, our author, Buddharakkhita, asserts the Buddha's proprietary rights over even the king; an important message when one considers that Buddharakkhita's fellow Rohaṇa monks had been ordered to Poḷonnaruva in order to prostrate before the 'king of kings' Parākramabāhu. The implication then, we can hypothesize, is that all devotees, including those in the highest social sphere, are obliged to make offerings to the Buddha both for future rewards and also in recognition that, in a certain sense, one's possessions are owned by the Buddha in that they were ultimately produced and acquired due to the Buddha's karmic laws. Clearly, this is not art for art's sake. It is ideological in that it naturalizes the tributary relationship between the monastic community and the nobility.

Ronald M. Davidson is one of the few scholars to recognize the political nature of the 'Buddha field' and he has argued that the word *kṣetra* ('field') 'should be understood in the sense of "domain" (rather than field) over which Buddha – as the pre-eminent *kṣatriya* and lord of that domain – presides with the dominion (*kṣatra*) of his Dharma'.[97] Even Davidson, however, ultimately regards the prevalence of such imperial metaphors in late medieval Indian Buddhism as 'only a weak imitation of the authentic imperial tradition'.[98] In the Sri Lankan context, at least, the very real temporal power wielded by the Saṅgha, as we have already discussed in previous chapters, makes it plausible that such feudal imagery reflected a form of genuine belief in the Buddha's, and, by implication, the Saṅgha's, rights over the island's wealth.

The Buddha's depiction here in the *Jinālaṅkāra* is another example of how scholar-monks in the reform era began to think about lordship, land and property in terms of what Ronald Inden referred to as an 'Indian imperial formation'.[99] Building on Inden's work, Daud Ali has recently explored conceptions of property in medieval India. He explains, following Inden, that the lordship of a creator deity, usually, Viṣṇu or Śiva, was thought to extend throughout the cosmos to all worldly agencies, which 'were in fact conceived of as the capacities of greater and lesser lordships anchored in the agency of the supreme lord'.[100] This cosmology formed the blueprint for the social organization of kingdoms, which were viewed similarly as a hierarchy of nested spheres of lordship encompassing one another, with the ruling monarch at its apex. This social order, Ali writes, 'enabled, ultimately, the extraction of surplus from the direct producer through a hierarchical chain of rights and privileges manifested through superior claims upon *places as the instantiation of moral value and social being*'.[101] Buddharakkhita appears to have conceived of his social structure similarly, with the Buddha, through his immense karma, acting as the all-encompassing moral sovereign of the world.

We have already seen in the *Dāṭhāvaṃsa* how the relationship between the king and Buddha was portrayed as a hierarchy of lordship rather than as a division of social functions. The grandmaster and his Saṅgha and the king and the royal court were two important links within a great chain of power that ultimately, from the Buddhist perspective, was anchored in the Buddha's Dharma. Even when Buddhist kings reigned Laṅkā, the site of ideological struggle, as presented in the Pali literature of the period, was not between the Saṅgha or royal court and agrarian producers, but between the royal court and monastic elites, competing for position at the apex of the social hierarchy with its attendant rights and privileges under the Buddha as cosmic overlord.

It is not necessary to assume, then, as both Sheldon Pollock and Steven Collins do in criticizing the idea that *kāvya* functioned ideologically, that ideology must be directed downwards towards an agrarian class, who may or may not have participated in the ideology of elites.[102] Nor was Pali *kāvya* the product of a homogeneous ruling class or 'civilization-bearing state-system', as Collins depicts, but rather an expression of particular monastic interests directed primarily, we can hypothesize, towards others who wielded political power.[103] The Theravada bodhisattva path in this regard served the nobility, both monks and the laity, in that it accommodated their lordship as karmically beneficial, while, at the same time, it established their devotional and political relationship with the Buddha (represented primarily by his relics administered by monastic elites) based on a confluence of spiritual and temporal rights and obligations.

9.5. Summary

As the first Pali poem composed by an aspirant to buddhahood, about the Buddha's final life, and for those interested in following this path, the *Jinālaṅkāra* provides a unique insight into the mentality of a bodhisattva at the cusp of the reform era recollecting the deeds of the Buddha of his current age. Contrary to previous views connecting the rise of the bodhisattva ideal with a supposed, popular desire for a Buddhist saviour, we have seen that the dominant tone in Buddharakkhita's work is rather one of devotional subordination. In the *Jinālaṅkāra*, Buddharakkhita depicts buddhahood as karmically determined and he accommodates materiality and sensuality as a sign of good karma and as an opportunity for creating more merit. The bodhisattva path sanctifies high status while at the same time it creates out of these figures subordinate, devotional subjects. Bodhisattvas are simply worldlings, the poem's commentator wrote, mere falling leaves that have the good fortune to brush against the back of the great elephant. Pali *kāvya*, in this regard, was not a non-ideological form of aesthetic politics as has been argued in the case of other 'court' literature. The aesthetic in Buddhist thought cannot be separated from the material since aesthetic pleasure was thought to manifest karmically in the form of material generosity and future material rewards. Pali *kāvya* was also more pointedly ideological than its Sanskrit counterpart in that it was used to extract wealth from its noble audience both through creating a sense of devotional obligation and, for the first time in Sri Lanka's history, instantiating the Buddha's proprietary rights over all things in the universe.

Notes

1. Berkwitz, 2004, 231–70. Also, Ladwig, 2014; Strathern, 2019, 148–50.
2. In this respect they are written in a literary style reminiscent of other Sanskrit biographies, such as Aśvaghoṣa's *Buddhacarita* and the ninth or tenth-century (?) *Padyacūḍāmaṇi*. See Hiltebeitel, 2006. Also, Franceschini, 2010; 2013.
3. Walters, 1997, 165. See also Reynolds, 1976; 1997, esp. 20, where Reynolds refers to histories of the Buddha's relics as the final part of the 'mythically constructed biography of the Buddha'.
4. Von Hinüber, 1996, §111. See also, Reynolds, 1997, 27–8.
5. *Jātakaṭṭhakathā* I, $56_{,29-32}$, trans. Rhys Davids, 1925, 162.
6. In this regard, these works share a certain similarity with Buddha biographies outside of the Theravada tradition, such as those found in the *Mahāvastu* and the *Lalitavistara*. On the *Mahāvastu*, in particular, see Tournier, 2017.
7. *Jinālaṅkāra* of Buddharakkhita, vv. 65d–69d: kathaṃ nu padam uddhari so nirāso. Trans. by James Gray (1894, 90). The expression *padam uddhari* literally means 'lifted the foot'.
8. *Jinālaṅkāra* of Buddharakkhita, v. 71d: jahitaṃ kim idaṃ patinā.
9. *Jinacarita* of Medhaṅkara, vv. 40–2:
   icchheyyañ ce 'ham ajj' eva hantvānantaraṇe bhave
   saṅghassa navako hutvā paṭiseyyaṃ puraṃ varaṃ.
   kiṃ aññātakavesena klesanibbāpanena me
   ayaṃ buddho va 'haṃ buddho hutvā loke anuttaro.
   janataṃ dhammanāvāya tāretvāna bhavaṇṇavā
   nibbānapuram ānetvā seyyaṃ me parinibbutaṃ.
   I have adapted this translation from Duroiselle, ed. and trans. 1906, 131. A similar passage occurs in the tenth-century *Mahābodhivaṃsa*, an important source for the *Jinacarita*, though it is notably absent from earlier works. See, in particular, Matsumura, 2010, 101–33. On textual parallels in the *Mahābodhivaṃsa* and *Jinacarita*, see Dimitrov, 2016, 515–52.
10. Sarkisyanz, 1965, 59–67.
11. See Holt, 1991, 57; Sarkisyanz, 1965, 59; Mus, 1965, xvii. See also Yabuuchi, 2007, 108–11. Steven Collins has rightly critiqued Mus and Sarkisyanz's interpretation that such inscriptions indicate that kings identified themselves with *the* future Buddha, Maitreya. Rather, as Collins notes, these kings were simply claiming to be *a* future buddha, not necessarily the next buddha. See Collins, 1998, 381.
12. Weber, 1958, 237; 249. See also Malalgoda, 1970, 426.
13. Mus, 1965, xviii. Emphasis in the original.
14. On the Weberian categories of virtuosity and charisma in a Theravada monastic context and their sometimes overlapping sense, in particular, when speaking of 'institutionalized charisma', see Silber, 1995.
15. *Jinālaṅkāra* of Buddharakkhita C^{e}, vv. 271–5 (*Jinālaṅkāravaṇṇanā*, $290_{,6-15}$). Dragomir Dimitrov has discussed in detail this unstable colophon, which is rightly included in Välipaṭanavila Dīpaṅkara and Baṭapolē Dhammapāla's edition but is missing in James Gray's edition of the poem. See Dimitrov, 2016, 272. On *gaṇa* and the related term *gaṇanāyaka*, see Ilangasinha, 1992, 75–7.
16. *Jinālaṅkāravaṇṇanā*, $290_{,16-17}$.
17. *Cūḷavaṃsa*, 75.185–204. These are Geiger and Rickmers' translations. See Geiger and Rickmers, 1998, 62–3. On Parākramabāhu I's Rohaṇa campaign, see Liyanagamage, 1968, 34–42.
18. *Cūḷavaṃsa*, 64.26–64.
19. See chapter six for a discussion of the social stratification of linguistic knowledge.
20. *Buddhaghosuppatti* of Mahāmaṅgala, $50_{,19-21}$.
21. *Jinālaṅkāra* of Buddharakkhita, vv. 242–50.
22. *Jinālaṅkāra* of Buddharakkhita, v. 2.
23. *Jātakaṭṭhakathā* I, $50_{,30}$–$51_{,3}$.
24. *Jātakaṭṭhakathā* I, $55_{,15-18}$. The ascetic is also referred to in the canonical biographical tradition as 'Asita'. See *Sutta Nipāta* 3.11.
25. *Jātakaṭṭhakathā* I, $56_{,8-15}$.
26. *Jinālaṅkāra* of Buddharakkhita, v. 44.
27. *Jinālaṅkāra* of Buddharakkhita, v. 14:
    nādhicca laddhaṃ na ca pubbabuddhā
    brahmādinaṃ sammutiyā bahūnaṃ
    sayaṃkaten' eva anopamena
    dānādinā laddham idaṃ vipākaṃ.

28. Von Hinüber, 1996, §312.
29. *Kathāvatthuaṭṭhakathā*, 143,$_{6-8}$. In translating this passage, I have consulted Bimala Churn Law's translation. See Law, 1940, 175.
30. *Kathāvatthuaṭṭhakathā*, 143,$_{18-20}$.
31. *Kathāvatthuaṭṭhakathā*, 143,$_{8-12}$. On this passage, see also McDermott, 1989. The issue is more ambiguous in canonical literature itself, see Anālayo, 2013, 178.
32. *Jinālaṅkāra* of Buddharakkhita, v. 46:
kālakkamena cando va vaḍḍhanto vaḍḍhite kule
puññodayen' udento so bhāṇumā viya ambare.
33. We find a much longer glorification of Siddhattha's family in chapter three of the *Lalitavistara*, for instance. See *Lalitavistara*, 11–21.
34. *Jinālaṅkāra* of Buddharakkhita, v. 60.
35. In this regard, see Bareau, 1982.
36. *Jinālaṅkāra* of Buddharakkhita, vv. 62, 77, 87–93.
37. *Apadāna* II, 584–90 (*Therīapadāna* 3.28). See Jonathan S. Walters' recent translation of the *Apadāna* (apadana.whitman.edu).
38. Obeyesekere, 2009, 1–35.
39. Cited and translated in Obeyesekere, 2009, 11–12.
40. *Jinālaṅkāra* of Buddharakkhita, v. 250, trans. by Gray, 1894, 112.
41. Faure, 1991, 32–52.
42. *Jinālaṅkāra* of Buddharakkhita, vv. 25, 31, 128.
43. *Jinālaṅkāra* of Buddharakkhita, vv. 127–9:
anantalokadhātumhi sattānaṃ hi kataṃ subhaṃ
mayhekapāramiyā pi kalaṃ n'agghati soḷasiṃ.
tiracchāno saso hutvā disvā yācakam āgataṃ
pacitvāna sakaṃ maṃsaṃ patito 'ggimhi dātave.
evaṃ anantakālesu kataṃ dukkarakārikaṃ
ko hi nāma kareyy' añño anummatto sacetano.
Trans. adapted from Gray, 1894, 98.
44. The inimitable nature of the Bodhisattva is stated more clearly in other Mahayana writings. See Ohnuma, 2000; 2007.
45. *Doṇa Sutta*, *Aṅguttara Nikāya* II, 37; *Jinālaṅkāra* of Buddharakkhita, vv. 130–1.
46. *Aṅguttara Nikāya* II, 38,$_{10-18}$: manusso no bhavaṃ bhavissatī ti, for instance. The interpretation of the verb *bhavissati* is problematic here. Buddhaghosa's commentary interprets it as a simple future and thus the Brahmin Doṇa is enquiring about the Buddha's future rebirth. See *Manorathapūraṇī* of Buddhaghosa III, 78,$_{21-3}$. It is more likely that, as the author of the *Samantapāsādikā* recognizes elsewhere, the future tense (*lṛt*) here is used in the sense of impossibility (*anavakḷpti*) or intolerance (*amarṣa*) as set out in Pāṇini's *Aṣṭādhyāyī* 3.3.146 *kiṃkilāstyartheṣu lṛt* ('The future tense is introduced after a verbal stem co-occurring with *kiṃ-kila* and expressions denoting the sense of the verbal stem *as-* "be"'). This is Katre's translation (*Aṣṭādhyāyī*, 313). See *Samantapāsādikā* I, 209,$_{27}$–210,$_{1}$, and the discussion of the related Sanskrit grammatical rules in Pind, 1989, 57–8.
47. *Jinālaṅkāra* of Buddharakkhita, vv. 130–1.
48. See, for instance, *Jinālaṅkāra* of Buddharakkhita, vv. 65–77.
49. *Jinālaṅkāra* of Buddharakkhita, v. 77.
50. The commentary on this verse in the *Jinālaṅkāravaṇṇanā* not unreasonably tries to read formal *yamakas* in lines one and three and, in doing so, states that the beginning of these lines prior to *sandhi* should read *pāde apāde* (lit. 'on the foot, not on the foot') and *hatthe ahatthe* (lit. 'on the hand, not on the hand'). The commentary, however, rather dubiously interprets the negation here as meaning that the limb is flung out (glossing *a-* as *apagata*). It interprets the verse, then, as depicting the jingling of bangles on two feet, with one placed on the floor and the other raised up, and, likewise, with one hand down and the other up. I am not completely satisfied with this explanation and thus provisionally translate the reduplication here as simply distributive ('on each hand', etc.). See *Jinālaṅkāravaṇṇanā*, 174,$_{20-2; 32-3}$.
51. Dimitrov, 2016, 262–4.
52. Bronner, 2010, 21.
53. *Kāvyādarśa* of Daṇḍin, vv. 3.78; 3.96; *Subodhālaṅkāra* of Saṅgharakkhita, v. 33.
54. *Jinālaṅkāra* of Buddharakkhita, v. 101.
55. Jonathan Walters, in this regard, has highlighted a claim made in the *Vaṃsatthappakāsinī* that, prior to attaining buddhahood as Gotama, the Bodhisattva in his previous lives had taken birth as various

paramount kings, including Mahāsammata. He interprets this, rather speculatively, as meaning that 'if the coming Buddha is to be found, like his predecessor Gotama Buddha, incarnate in the Śākya branch of the Okkāka dynasty, and if the only extant descendants of Okkāka rule Sri Lanka, then a Sri Lankan king who attains imperial status must also be the coming Buddha'. See Walters, 2000, 132. While it is, of course, possible that some kings may have identified themselves directly with Maitreya, this was not, I think, the Saṅgha's view of bodhisattva kings. Reform-era scholar-monks rather presented the bodhisattva path and buddhahood as an extremely distant goal to be followed by many and thus discourage and even preclude, at least from the monastic perspective, such a view.

56. *Saundarananda* of Aśvaghoṣa, v. 18.64ab, translated in McCrea, 2013, 121. Johannes Bronkhorst has described Aśvaghoṣa's *Buddhacarita* as a 'Trojan horse' intended to weaken Brahmanical court society from within. See Bronkhorst, 2011, 168.
57. *Jinālaṅkāra* of Buddharakkhita, v. 3.
58. *Jinālaṅkāra* of Buddharakkhita, v. 185. I follow the *sannaya* of the editors (C^{e}, v. 205) of the Sinhala edition here in taking *iha* 'here' in this verse as referring to the poem itself.
59. *Jinālaṅkāra* of Buddharakkhita, v. 186.
60. Gethin, 2001, 106–112; Rotman, 2009, 23–62.
61. *Dīgha Nikāya* II, 83$_{,8}$, trans. Crosby, 2014, 23–4.
62. *Jinālaṅkāravaṇṇanā*, 290$_{,16-27}$. For a discussion of this colophon, see Dimitrov, 2016, 266; also, Von Hinüber, 1996, §407.
63. As mentioned in verse forty-four in the *Jinālaṅkāra*, for instance, Buddharakkhita deviates from the *Nidānakathā* narrative and states that, upon seeing the new-born prince, Brahmin soothsayers declared that the prince would become a buddha. In the *Nidānakathā*, however, the seven Brahmin soothsayers disagree about whether the prince would become a world-conquering king (*cakkavatti*) or a buddha and only one Brahmin, Koṇḍañña, states with certainty that the new-born will certainly achieve buddhahood. The *Jinālaṅkāra* commentary, however, seems to try to reconcile the two versions. See *Jinālaṅkāravaṇṇanā*, 146$_{,8-16}$.
64. *Jinālaṅkāravaṇṇanā*, 50$_{,3}$. On the influence of the *Jinālaṅkāravaṇṇanā* in Southeast Asia, see Balbir, 2007, 336–46.
65. Rammandala, 1954, 53–5. Dragomir Dimitrov has noted too that, 'In Laṅkā the *Jinālaṅkāravaṇṇanā* seems to have been lost for several centuries, and presumably it has hardly been possible to procure copies of it on the island until the revival of the Sinhalese Sangha in the eighteenth and nineteenth centuries when many Pali texts have been (re)imported from Burma and Siam to Laṅkā.' See Dimitrov, 2016, 270.
66. The work is quoted in Ratanapañña's *Jinakālamālī*, composed around 1516–17, and also in a Pali translation of a Thai chronicle entitled the *Mūlasāsanā*. See Dimitrov, 2016, 264.
67. *Jinālaṅkāravaṇṇanā*, 12$_{,33-4}$. On the term *yogāvacara* in the early Pali tradition, see Silk, 1997. On its use in later Theravada writings, see Crosby, 2000; 2013, 154, n. 26.
68. See, for instance, *Sāratthappakāsinī* of Buddhaghosa II, 49$_{,13-14}$. This dual understanding of noble status persisted in the reform era. See Guruḷugomi on *kulaputta*: *Dharmapradīpikāva* of Guruḷugomi, 269$_{,6-15}$.
69. *Jinālaṅkāravaṇṇanā*, 13$_{,14}$.
70. A similar metaphor is used, but with the object of comparison reversed, in an inscription of the Pāla king Devapāla, which states that the king ascended the throne as a bodhisattva succeeds a buddha. See Davidson, 2002, 89, citing Kielhorn, 1892, 258.
71. *Jinālaṅkāravaṇṇanā* of Buddharakkhita, 12$_{,20-34}$: seyyathāpi nāma cheko bhaṇḍāgāriko cakkavattirañño alaṅkārabhaṇḍāni gahetvā ratanakaraṇḍake pakkhipitvā evaṃ "taṃ anurakkhāhī" ti parināyakaratanassa nīyyādeyya. so taṃ gahetvā anurakkhanto pitu accayena cakkavattirājā hutvā tenālaṅkārena alaṅkato lokissaro hoti. evam eva bhaṇḍāgārikasadiso buddharakkhitācariyo sabbalokissarassa anantajinassa buddhassa bhagavato guṇālaṅkārabhaṇḍāni gahetvā jinālaṅkārasaṃkhāte gandhakaraṇḍake pakkhipitvā parināyakaratanasadisassa yogāvacarakulaputtassa nīyyādeyya. yasmā ca so taṃ sakkaccaṃ sirasā paṭiggahetvā bhāvanānuyogavasena anurakkhanto yathānusiṭṭhaṃ paṭipajjanto anukkamena buddhabhūmiṃ patvā anantajino hutvā tena guṇālaṅkārena alaṅkato sakalalokaṃ ekobhāsaṃ katvā virocanto lokissaro hoti, tasmā sabbapaṭhamaṃ attanā vattabbassa jinālaṅkārassa paṭiggāhakaṃ yogāvacarakulaputtaṃ vaṇṇento āha: [v. 3].
72. Mus, 1928, 274.
73. Relatively little has been written about this important point of doctrine. Patrick Pranke has picked up on it in his recent paper on Buddhist saints in Burma. See Pranke, 2010–11, 457, n. 8, citing *Kathāvatthu* 4.8, 286–90. For a comprehensive overview of the Bodhisattva ideal in the different schools of Buddhism and the differing ideas about the Bodhisattva's status as a *pṛthagjana* (P. *puthujjana*), see Krishan, 1984, esp. 202.

74. *Jinālaṅkāravaṇṇanā*, 34,$_{11-12}$.
75. Shulman, 2012, 131.
76. Pollock, 2006, 14. With respect to the Sanskrit eulogy of royal inscriptions, in particular, Pollock writes that it 'was beyond the quotidian and the instrumental; it was directed above all toward articulating a form of political consciousness and culture, politics not as transaction of material power – the power of recording deeds, contracts, tax records, and the like – but as celebration of aesthetic power'.
77. For a similar criticism, see Ali, 2006, 16–17.
78. Trainor, 2003, 526.
79. Rotman, 2009, 9.
80. *Jinālaṅkāra* of Buddharakkhita, vv. 189–241.
81. *Kāvyādarśa* of Daṇḍin, v. 2.8; *Subodhālaṅkāra* of Saṅgharakkhita, v. 165.
82. *Jinālaṅkāra* of Buddharakkhita, v. 217:
pujemi paṭhamaṃ tassa paṇidhānaṃ acintiyaṃ
cakkavāḷamhi sabbehi vijjamānehi vatthuhi.
Trans. adapted from Gray, 1894, 108.
83. *Apadāna* I, 1–6. See also Bechert, 1992.
84. Shulman, 2012, 109–43.
85. The commentator also likens the bodhisattva meditator to one who uses a sesame seed to collect the ocean's water. See, for instance, *Jinālaṅkāravaṇṇanā*, 34,$_{7-8;\ 25-30}$.
86. *Jinālaṅkāra* of Buddharakkhita, vv. 218–41.
87. *Dīgha Nikāya* II, 154,$_{6-8}$. Trans. by Walshe, 1995, 270.
88. *Jinālaṅkāra* of Buddharakkhita, vv. 232–3:
svāyaṃ dhammo vinayo ca desito sādhukaṃ mayā
mamaccayena so satthā dhātu cāpi sarīrajā
apparājitapallaṅkaṃ (*corr.* aparājita°) bodhirukkhañ ca uttamaṃ
mamaccayena satthā ti anujāni mahāmuni.
Trans. adapted from Gray, 1894, 110.
89. Berkwitz, 2004, 281.
90. *Jinālaṅkāra* of Buddharakkhita, v. 189:
tasmā hi jātovarakamhi tassa āyattake maṅgalacakkavāḷe
bhūtehi vatthūhi manoramehi pūjemi taṃ pūjitapūjitaṃ pure.
Trans. adapted from Gray, 1894, 105.
91. *Jinālaṅkāravaṇṇanā*, 285,$_{13-18}$.
92. *Jinālaṅkāravaṇṇanā* of Buddharakkhita, 285,$_{8-11}$: tassa āyattakaṃ santakaṃ. tasmiṃ vijjamānaṃ yaṃ kiñci sattasaṅkhāragataṃ? taṃ sabbaṃ tass' eva santakaṃ hoti. On the Buddha as owner of property, see Schopen, 1990.
93. See chapter five. See also the *Caturārakkhadīpanī*, vv. 4.48–9.
94. Barua, 1946.
95. *Visuddhimagga* of Buddhaghosa, 349,$_{18-28}$. See also Rowell, 1934; Kloetzli, 1983, 56–7.
96. Rowell, 1934, 231.
97. Davidson, 2002, 133.
98. Davidson, 2002, 168.
99. Inden, 2000, 213–62.
100. Ali, 2008, 123.
101. Ali, 2008, 137. Emphasis in the original.
102. See, for instance, Collins, 2003, 682–3; Pollock, 2006, 511–24. For different reasons, Daud Ali states that Hindu cosmology was 'without ideology', on the basis that 'representations of society had a direct relationship to class hierarchies'; see Ali, 2008, 138. If I understand Daud Ali correctly, I think that in our context we can see that, while this may have been the case for those lower down the social hierarchy, the site of ideological struggle, that is the naturalization of social order, occurred between the royal court and the Saṅgha, rather than the royal court and agrarian producers. Therefore, representations did not necessarily reflect the social hierarchies of these elites, which were very much contested and unstable during the period in question.
103. Collins, 2003, 682–3.

10
Conclusion: Other Lives and Afterlives

Sri Lanka's reform era requires us to rethink a number of assumptions about the history of Buddhism, in particular about the agency of Buddhist scholar-monks in premodern politics and social life, about Pali literature as a dynamic and creative, rather than static and conservative, form of knowledge, and even about how we think of the island of Sri Lanka as a place deeply connected with, rather than isolated from, its neighbours in the wider region. This book has argued that the unprecedented cultural productivity of the reform era was not a by-product of political stability or of the munificent patronage of a single emperor, as has often been thought. Rather, it was rooted in chaos, the destruction of the old social order and the birth of a more fragmented political environment. The monastic community emerged from this era of war and strife with greater autonomy than it had possessed in the previous centuries. Through the dual reform processes of purification and unification the Mahāvihāra carefully crafted a new coherent identity. This coherence was sustained primarily within a matrix of Pali texts that provided a conceptual order within which monastic elites could think and act with a greater sense of control over their circumstances.

The process of reform was guided by textual production for a number of reasons. Most fundamentally, scholar-monks had traditionally believed in an ontological connection between the state of scriptural learning and the moral condition of their social and political environment. Faced with the unprecedented upheaval brought about by Cōḻa rule, the scholar-monks of the era sought in their philological practices explanations for the decline they perceived in their tradition. Religious decline, in this regard, was primarily interpreted as a philological problem and scholar-monks developed new textual forms as a means of countering the deterioration of their tradition and better protecting and propagating the doctrine and discipline within the Saṅgha. This project was accompanied by the expulsion of monks who did not suitably conform to the new orthodoxy and by the emergence of a more structured, courtly hierarchy among the remaining monks, which enabled them to act with greater autonomy in the midst of political uncertainty. This hierarchy was primarily educational in that a monk's level of training in Pali texts largely determined his social position in the monastic community. Not only, then, did Pali literature provide an organizational plane on which religious thought could be ordered but that same plane served as the performative means by which monastic social hierarchies could be established and consolidated.

On the face of it, there's something almost paradoxical in how scholar-monks experimented with Pali during the period. For, on the one hand, the aforementioned concern for social and textual order and the exigencies of reform meant that Pali grammars, commentaries and handbooks, in particular, were increasingly systematic in their construction. (The development of new textual forms, as we have seen, normally meant the adoption of models, often from Sanskrit, deemed more methodical than those that were used previously.) At the same time, the very ability of scholar monks to move beyond traditional philological forms was accompanied by more abstract and less formal notions of scriptural language and scriptural authority. The grammarians introduced philosophical ideas about universal semantics and the variability of phonetic representation; handbook commentators began to view their digests as authorities equal to commentaries, which in turn were now thought of as an analytical extension of the Dhamma's meaning, and also seemingly entertained previously heterodox ideas about scripture as a conceptual entity; and, finally, anthologists felt able to compile excerpts of largely commentarial material while supposedly protecting the 'essential meaning' of their scriptures.

The increasingly loose relationship in the reform era between Pali textual production and the formal canon is no better illustrated than in the proliferation of new literary works in Pali, in particular relic histories and Buddha biographies. While these works can be seen as a continuation of traditional historiography, they depart from pre-reform literature in both style and substance. They are particularly concerned with the traces of the Buddha's dispensation and their role in stimulating karmically transformative emotions, in particular serene joy. In many respects they are a literary expression of the immanent religious goals of the monastic elites of the period, as reflected, for instance, in the karmic focus of the new anthologies. While grammars, commentaries and handbooks, in this regard, served as new exegetical technologies, designed primarily to extract and protect the essence of scriptural tradition, reform-era Pali poetry was a complementary, karmic technology, one that utilized Sanskritic literary models and theories in order to better cultivate favourable emotions among an increasingly diverse audience of lay and monastic nobles. The soteriology of devotion, as developed in these works, reflected a reform-era concern with human limitations and a desire for control, though one that was more focused on shaping future circumstances than conservation.

A different tension between form and content also underpinned the development of ornate Pali poetry too. Traditionally scholar monks had, at least ideally, been wary of ornamentation, whether that meant wearing jewellery or enjoying the wordplays of a poem, since such decoration was viewed as an immoral distraction that may foster undesirable attachments. In the early works of the reform era, however, we have seen how the pressing karmic demands of this period of chaos led to a radical re-evaluation of emotionally charged ornamentalism. The era's foremost literary theorist, for instance, argued that the composition and appreciation of ornate poetry was inherently moral since literature's affective success was based on a knowledge of worldly morals and propriety; the relic historians also established an aesthetic continuity between relics, reliquaries, miracles and ornate, stylized poetry as stimulants of meritorious sentiments; and Buddha biographers too creatively adapted this traditional, courtly form of poetry and employed it to aesthetically instantiate the Buddha's religious and political sovereignty over the island.

10.1. The Post-Reform Sīhaḷa Saṅgha in Thirteenth-Century Pagan

The aim of this book has been to explore the intense production of monastic literature in reform-era Sri Lanka and to understand its importance in relation to the monastic community's changing social and political circumstances. In order to avoid a teleological reading of the period as a point of origin for later religious developments, I have consciously set aside much discussion of the *outcomes* of this era of change. And yet, having established the significance of the reform era on its own terms, it is worthwhile turning our attention to these outcomes if only to suggest some of the possible implications of the era for the history of Theravada Buddhism in Southern Asia and also for the literary culture in Sri Lanka in the centuries that followed.

It is well known that monastic centres that identified with Sīhaḷa monastic lineages, that is, post-reform Mahāvihāran lineages, were established from the twelfth century onwards in what is now Burma, Thailand and Laos.[1] This movement of monks is rightly regarded as an important moment in the development of Theravada Buddhism as an early modern, transregional religious formation. While it is no coincidence that this occurred during Sri Lanka's reform era, the question arises as to the exact causal relationship between the reforms on the island and the movement of monks abroad. The arrival of Sīhaḷa monastic lineages in Southeast Asia from the twelfth century is often depicted solely as a royal, political initiative, in which kings, eyeing the reforms in Sri Lanka, brought monks and texts to their kingdoms as part of their state-building enterprises.[2] This analysis is predicated, to a large extent, on the old view that Sri Lanka's reforms turned Buddhism into a kind of state religion. In light of the arguments made in this book, we can suggest that, rather than as a result of any imperial project, many of the monks who travelled to Southeast Asia may have actually done so as an indirect consequence of political fragmentation.

The kingdom of Pagan represents a useful case study in this regard since its history has been well documented by Michael Aung Thwin and Tilman Frasch.[3] Part of the problem in ascertaining how the Sīhaḷa lineage became established in Burma is the rather late source material describing these events. It is only in a fifteenth-century inscription, the *Kalyāṇī* inscription, for instance, that we find the first account of what went on. There, it is said that in 1170 the royal monastic preceptor Uttarajīva travelled to Sri Lanka in order to worship the island's relic shrines.[4] His pupil, Chapaṭa, returned ten years later (c. 1181) during the reign of king Narapatisithu (1174–1211) along with four other monks, Sīvali, Tāmalinda, Rāhula and Ānanda, thus introducing the Sīhaḷa ordination lineage to Pagan. It appears that these monks gained the favour of Narapatisithu and established monasteries in the city, though they soon splintered into rival monastic factions.[5] Michael Aung Thwin has framed the patronage they received as part of a process of royal monastic reform and has claimed that Narapatisithu himself intended to bring the Sīhaḷa order to Pagan, writing that, 'king Narapatisithu purified the Order by sending a few chosen monks to Ceylon to be reordained, then bringing them back to reform the Order in Burma'.[6]

The idea that Narapatisithu led reforms that brought the Sīhaḷa lineage to Pagan is often repeated and yet the sources on which these assertions are made do not explicitly state that such reforms ever took place.[7] We only learn, for instance, that Narapatisithu patronized the Sīhaḷa fraternity but there's no mention that he did so with the intention of reforming the Saṅgha in Pagan.[8] In the case of Uttarajīva, if the *Kalyāṇī* inscription is a reliable source, it seems rather that he went to Sri Lanka in search of relics and not as a result of any royal injunction instructing him to reform the monastic community in his homeland.[9]

This is not to say, of course, that religion did not play a role in the politics between the courts of Pagan and Laṅkā. King Anuruddha (1044–78) of Pagan, for instance, sent monks in aid of Vijayabāhu I (1055–1110), who the *Cūḷavaṃsa* ('Little history') rather dubiously states could no longer find fully ordained monks in Sri Lanka to carry out ordinations.[10] The same king supposedly invaded Thaton to obtain a copy of the Tipiṭaka and similarly sent 'four great warriors' to Sri Lanka to procure another as well.[11]

We do find mention of a possible royal monastic reform in Pagan after Narapatisithu's reign, however, in the fragmentary *Mahānāgakulasandesa* ('Message from Mahānāgakula'), a poem apparently composed in mid-thirteenth-century Sri Lanka. The work is an ornate *kāvya* containing a message sent to a monk in Pagan, Kassapa, from a certain Nāgasena who resided in the South of Sri Lanka.[12] Nāgasena writes that he was responding to a message originally sent by Kassapa through a minister Ñāṇa. The first editor of the poem, Lionel D. Barnett, identified the Pagan king 'Dhammarāja' mentioned in the poem with one of the three who ruled with this epithet between 1211 and 1256.[13] Epigraphic evidence from Pagan attests to the existence during this time too of a high status forest monk, Kassapa, and a minister, Ñāṇa.[14] The issue of reform, however, is only raised in the final verse of the poem; a verse that Barnett importantly deemed corrupt and a later addition.[15] In this verse Nāgasena asks Kassapa to encourage king Dhammarāja to reform the Saṅgha in Pagan like Parākramabāhu I (1157–86):

> saddhiṃ parakkamabhujena mahībhujena
> saṅgho visodhayi yathā jinasāsan' ettha
> tumhe pi tattha siri-dhammanarādhirājam
> ādāya sāsanavaraṃ suvisodhayātha.[16]
>
> As the Saṅgha purified the conqueror's religion here
> alongside Parakkamabhuja ('the strong armed'),
> ruler of the earth,
> so you too should purify it well there,
> seizing what is best in the religion
> with Siri-Dhammanara as king.

There are a few references to 'purifications' of the Saṅgha from this period in inscriptions from Burma too, though they provide little context for understanding the nature of these activities. Tilman Frasch, for instance, has pointed to a fifteenth-century inscription that claims a Cambodian monk, Subhūticanda, 'purified' (*visodhayi*) the *sāsana* in 1248.[17] Similarly, a 1259 inscription from Pagan, also states that a minister built a monastery for a certain Ānanda who had 'purified' the Buddha's religion.[18] While such references do attest to a continuing rhetoric of reform internal to monastic factions in Pagan, they do not explicitly point to reforms comparable to those that took place in Sri Lanka during the reform era.[19] This reform mentality, for instance, does not seem to have led to any greater unity or autonomy at least within the Sīhaḷa fraternity.

This is indicated by the fact that the Sīhaḷa lineages in thirteenth-century Pagan were greatly fractured and did not adopt centralized, monarchical hierarchies under a 'grandmaster' (*mahāsāmi*) as they had done during the reform era in their homeland.[20]

Inscriptional evidence in Burma contemporary with the arrival of Sīhaḷa monastic lineages in the thirteenth century suggests rather that the rise of this Sīhaḷa lineage in Pagan was far less centralized than is often appreciated. Tilman Frasch, for instance, has noted that the thirteenth century saw an increase in the number of inscriptions in Pagan mentioning monks who had 'arrived from Sri Lanka'.[21] Almost none of the monks can be identified with any of the senior prelates in Sri Lanka during the reform era and it is even unclear whether they were Sinhalese monks leaving Sri Lanka or Burmese monks returning home. One exceptional inscription, though, can speculatively be connected with concrete events and persons of the period. Incised at the Tāmanī-complex – a Sīhaḷa lineage monastery founded by Tāmalinda, one of Chapaṭa's companions who returned to Pagan in 1181 – the inscription refers to a certain 'Sīlavisuddhi, preceptor of king Sīri Dhammāsoka', who was staying at the monastery in 1228. Frasch has suggested that this Sinhalese (?) monk may well have been the preceptor of the young Kāliṅga prince Dharmāśoka, who nominally ruled Laṅkā for a few months in 1208/9 before being put to death.[22] Even in this case, however, it seems likely, as Frasch suggests, that Sīlavisuddhi travelled to Pagan due to political turmoil rather than some imperial mission.

The Pali literature produced by these early Sīhaḷa scholar-monks in Pagan also helps us better understand the knowledge flows underpinning the emergence of these groups. It seems that the monks who travelled to Burma brought with them a number of reform-era Pali works. We find, for instance, possibly mentioned in a 1236 inscription of a certain royal teacher, Sīri Mahādhamma, the *Dhātuvaṃsa* ('History of the relic') and Dhammakitti's *Dāṭhāvaṃsa* ('History of the tooth'). Similarly, the Kubyaukkyi pagoda in Myinkaba, built by king Kyanzittha's (1084–1112) son in around 1112/13, apparently contains murals that depict the reign of Vijayabāhu I, possibly as described in the *Cūḷavaṃsa*.[23] The Sīhaḷa-lineage monks in Pagan also composed new Pali works, though curiously those that survive are almost entirely grammatical works.[24] It may be that these are simply the extant remains of a more diverse literary culture or it is possible that monks focused on grammar, as they did in reform-era Sri Lanka, because it was perceived to be the foundation of religious and social order.[25] Nevertheless these earliest grammatical works contain a number of quotations from grammars composed in reform-era Sri Lanka and other Pali works too, attesting to the fact that the monks who travelled to Burma did so with the latest scholarship.[26]

In terms of the movement of texts from Burma to Sri Lanka, an eighteenth-century Burmese Pali history, the *Sāsanavaṃsa* ('History of the teaching'), states that when Uttarajīva travelled to Sri Lanka in 1170 he did so carrying a new Pali grammar composed in Pagan, Aggavaṃsa's *Saddanīti* ('Word guide'), and that the scholar-monks on the island marvelled at the scope of its erudition.[27] Setting aside the date of the *Saddanīti*, which is difficult to ascertain with any accuracy, the reform-era literature of Sri Lanka provides a rather different impression of cultural exchange between the regions.[28] The Pali and Sinhala literature composed prior to the fifteenth century, for instance, is remarkably silent about Burmese scholarship and I am not aware of a single Burmese work quoted in any text from Sri Lanka before Śrī Rāhula's Sinhala commentary on the *Moggallānapañcikā* ('Extensive commentary on Moggallāna's grammar') in 1458.[29] This apparent lack of intellectual exchange prior to the fifteenth century reminds us again to be cautious about projecting onto the twelfth and thirteenth centuries the more connected realities of a later historical period. In fact, before the fifteenth century, while there were knowledge flows from Sri Lanka to Burma, it seems that there was little in the way of intellectual exchange between the two regions, at least one recoverable from the available texts.

10.2. The 'Twilight Glow' Revisited, 1270–1527

If the long century beginning with the thirty-three-year reign of Parākramabāhu I was notable for its revitalized intellectual order sustained by new Pali works, the subsequent era prior to the beginning of European colonization reflects an almost opposite trend, where monastic interest in the composition of new Pali texts dwindled. G.P. Malalasekera is the only scholar, as far as I am aware, who has offered an explanation for this period of decline. He described this era, for instance, as the 'twilight glow' of Pali literature and attributed it to 'foreign influence', in particular, South Indian marriages with the Laṅkan monarchy and the increasing power of 'Tamil' polities in the north of the island, which, he argued, led to a widespread loss of patronage since 'the people were too much engrossed in the protection of their property and persons to have time for anything else'.[30]

The reduced interest in composing new Pali works in Sri Lanka, much like the posited 'death of Sanskrit' in India, was a highly complex affair involving a number of causes.[31] While a definitive account of the cultural changes of this period must wait, in this section we will explore alternative hypotheses that challenge the 'twilight glow' narrative. The main reason for doubting Malalasekera's account is that, while Pali literary production did notably diminish, the same cannot be said for Sinhala. In fact, the long century after the reform era has been rightly considered as something of a golden age for Sinhala literature.[32] For much of the reform era, poetic Sinhala remained on the whole a language of court culture. The royal courts of the twelfth and thirteenth centuries, for instance, produced three Sinhala *kāvya*s inspired by *jātaka*s, namely, the *Sasadāvata* ('Story of a hare'), *Muvadevdāvata* ('Story of king Makhadeva'), and the *Kavsiluminạ* ('Crown jewel of literature').[33]

These courtly works, modelled on Sanskrit literary forms and themes, reflect many of the features of 'cosmopolitan vernacularization', as defined by Sheldon Pollock, and accompanied a heightened awareness of Laṅkā's local political identity as a kingdom in the twelfth and thirteenth centuries.[34] At the same time, it is important to note that, contrary to Pollock's assertions, these works were not a product of the political unification of the island under Parākramabāhu I but rather they were likely composed during the chaotic aftermath of his rule, in particular, in the reigns of Līlāvatī (1197–1200; 1209–10; 1211–12) and Parākramabāhu II (1236–70), for instance. Their exclusively Buddhist content may suggest also that these works were not simply a celebration of royal sovereignty but were a product of the new, localized (and more religious) political discourse that had emerged during the reform era as part of the court's mimetic political dialogue with monastic powers.[35]

A related but rather different strand of vernacularization also continued to develop after the reform era, namely, the monastic use of Sinhala primarily for exegetical and pedagogical purposes; to comment on and sometimes translate Pali works, in particular, those that had been newly composed as part of the reform programme. Many of the Sinhala adaptations of this period expanded the intellectual scope of reform-era Pali works, spreading their doctrines to a wider audience of novice monks and the laity. It is in the latter half of the thirteenth century too that monks began to compose Sinhala preaching (*baṇa*) works, such as the *Butsaraṇa* ('Refuge of the Buddha') and *Pūjāvaliya* ('Garland of offerings'), which were only tangentially exegetical in purpose.[36] The author of the encyclopedic *Pūjāvaliya*, for instance, presents his work as an exposition of the Pali word *arahaṃ* ('worthy'), an epithet of the Buddha, though, in reality, the work is more a devotional anthology of Buddhist historical and didactic narratives than a commentary in the strict sense.[37]

It is possible to interpret the rise of such independent, Sinhala preaching works as in part a continuation of processes that had begun in the reform era. We have seen how during the reforms the strong traditional ties between the Dhamma and the precise wording of Pali texts was slowly loosening. This shift in emphasis accompanied the rise of newly authoritative Pali texts that would have previously fallen outside the strict parameters of what had been classed as a commentary. In the subsequent centuries the necessary connection even between the Dhamma and Pali language began to unravel and we see that scholar-monks start to justify the composition of preaching poems about the Dhamma in Sinhala on the basis that the vernacular too could be a means of enlightenment.[38] Writing in the fifteenth century at the beginning of his *Lōväḍa Saṅgarāva* ('Handbook for the world's welfare'), for instance, Vīdāgama Maitreya defended his use of poetic Sinhala or Eḷu to teach the Dhamma as follows:

> I thus venerate with devotion and respect the charming trainer of men (i.e. the Buddha), the Dhamma, and the Saṅgha and now declare in Eḷu the results of karma, especially for those who do not understand the Pali Dhamma (*peḷadam*).
>
> Formerly, sixty members of the Saṅgha, gladdened their minds and gained confidence when [listening] to an Eḷu poem that conformed (*sarikoṭa*) with the Dhamma and, reflecting on the many defects in the composition of the aggregates, they reached nirvana.
>
> Therefore, do not disparage that which is uttered in Eḷu. For if one listens to this charming Dhamma with respect and the pleasure of reverence, then you will surely obtain the glory of heaven and liberation.[39]

These verses also point to a second factor underpinning the development of independent preaching literature, namely, the need to extend the reach of the Dhamma to new audiences, in particular those who were unable to understand Pali. Whereas the development of vernacular court poetry, as Sheldon Pollock has argued, likely had little to do with any emerging popular or public audience, this second strand of monastic-led vernacularization was connected with the spread of Buddhism as a cultural religion.[40] Even in Mayūrapāda's *Pūjāvaliya*, composed in 1266, we find an early, programmatic description of this expanding audience. There, the author divides his imagined readership into eight groups and explains how each could benefit from appreciating expositions of the Dhamma written in Sinhala. The eight groups consist of kings, queens and women, deputy kings and ministers, Mahātheras, meditators, eloquent preachers, virtuous people, and 'the pious living in remote places'.[41]

It would be wrong, however, to treat court literature and preaching texts as completely distinct genres, since there was some overlap between the two in both style and audience.[42] In the fourteenth and fifteenth centuries, for instance, monks composed in poetic Sinhala a great number of 'messenger' (*sandeśa*) poems explicitly addressed to the monarchy, especially, the court of Parākramabāhu VI (1411–66), during a brief moment of political centralization. These poems were modelled on an older Sanskrit genre in which the plot centres on the delivery of a message and the journey undertaken by the messenger.[43] While originally a form of erotic, court literature, the genre as it developed in both Sri Lanka and South India in the fourteenth century became more devotional and religious. In almost every Sinhala messenger poem, as Justin Henry notes, 'the "message" to be delivered consists of a request to a Hindu deity to produce some benefit to a king or member of the royal family'.[44] Henry has skilfully shown, however, that alongside their theurgic, courtly role these poems also formed an arena for religious debate, with rival monastic factions – the forest dwelling monks and village or city dwelling monks – presenting to the court alternative articulations of Buddhist orthodoxy and religious pluralism.[45] We can speculate that these rival perspectives between factions within the Saṅgha on the island were perhaps best expressed in Sinhala, since the political univocality that had underpinned monastic scholarship in Pali was now lacking.

Alongside broad divisions between forest dwelling and village or city dwelling monks, for instance, the individual schools or *pariveṇa*s had also developed more autonomy and scholar-monks from these schools began to formally identify with a particular institution in their monastic title.[46] There has been some doubt too about whether the position of *mahāsāmi* or grandmaster continued in regular succession after the reform era. Some have argued that the position remained singular whereas others have noted that the plurality of 'grandmasters' mentioned during this period cannot be explained if regular succession had continued.[47] Monastic histories and inscriptions from Burma and Thailand further complicate the picture since we find accounts of monks from Sri Lanka, such as, 'Udumbara Mahāsāmi' and a certain 'Mahāsāmi Saṅgharāja', travelling to Southeast Asia in the fourteenth century. These monks clearly styled themselves as monastic hierarchs but cannot be identified with any of the known prelates in Sri Lanka from the period.[48] The agreement among scholar-monks in the reform era, then, had thus begun to break down and, both in terms of administration and monastic identity, the Saṅgha had once more fragmented, destined never again to achieve the same productive unity as it found in the twelfth and thirteenth centuries.

Notes

1. See Blackburn, 2015a; 2015b.
2. For instance, Keyes, 1995, 80–2; Collins, 2003, 680–4.
3. See Aung Thwin, 1985; Frasch, 1996.
4. *Kalyāṇī Inscriptions*, 50. See also *Epigraphia Birmanica* 3.2, no. XII. Later Pali and Burmese histories provide a similar account of these events. See *Sāsanavaṃsa*, 65; Pranke, 2004, 148–50; Maung Tin and Luce, 1923, 142–4.
5. Frasch, 1996, 292.

6. Aung Thwin, 1979, 673–4.
7. See Aung Thwin, 1985, 169–98; 1976, 215, citing the *Sāsanavaṃsa*, *Glass Palace Chronicle* and *Kalyāṇī* inscription. The idea of Narapatisithu's 'reforms', for instance, is repeated in Taylor, 1992, 164–8; also, Frasch, 1996, 288–305; 2001, 94. Similar doubts have been raised concerning the historical reality of the 'reforms' that Aung Thwin also claims took place during the reign of Narapatisithu's descendant Klacwā (1234–49). See Chan, 1988, 92–3.
8. This, of course, depends on how we define reform. Further work is needed to think more critically about the term as a category in the comparative history of Buddhist traditions. How can we differentiate reform from selective patronage, for instance?
9. Historians have tended to interpret Narapatisithu's reign rather anachronistically in light of the religious activities of king Dhammaceti (1460–91) who initiated the fifteenth-century *Kalyāṇī* inscription and who did send monks to Sri Lanka in order to purify the order in Burma in conscious imitation of the reforming activities Parākramabāhu I.
10. *Cūḷavaṃsa*, 60.4–7.
11. *Sāsanavaṃsa*, 63–4.
12. Von Hinüber, 1996, §441.
13. Barnett, 1905, 266. See also, Günther, 1942, 257–64.
14. Barnett, 1905, 266–7.
15. Barnett, 1905, 265. There's reason to doubt too whether Nāgasena would have solicited Kassapa's help in attempting to orchestrate a royal reform in Pagan based on Sīhaḷa orthodoxy since this Kassapa was perhaps a leading monk in the Burmese forest fraternity and was not of the Sīhaḷa lineage. See Frasch, 1996, 296–7.
16. *Mahānāgakulasandesa* of Nāgasena, v. 62. Herbert Günther ignores the strange accusative of the compound *Siri-Dhammanarādhirājam* and translates it as an instrumental ('mit dem König Siri-Dhammaraja') to mirror the syntax of the relative clause. See Günther, 1942, 281. The reading *suvisodhayātha* is also either a corrupt imperative plural (with elongated *ā*), as Günther translates it, or an ungrammatical imperative singular (sandhi with *atha*) that does not agree with the plural agent *tumhe*. On monastic agency in initiating 'royally sponsored ordination embassies' in Lān Nā, see Blackburn, 2015b, 324.
17. Frasch, 2017, 71; 2019, 143–4, citing *Inscriptions of Burma* III, plate 302.
18. Frasch, 1996, 294–5, citing *Inscriptions of Burma* III, plate 226.
19. Frasch does compare these references to the reforms that took place in twelfth- and thirteenth-century Sri Lanka, though defines 'reform' more capaciously as a joint recitation of texts and a renewal of ordination lineages. See Frasch, 2017, 148.
20. Frasch, 1996, 304–5.
21. Frasch, 2001, 92–6.
22. Frasch, 2001, 93–4. See also chapter seven.
23. Frasch, 1996, 327–8. See also Frasch, 1998, 86–7.
24. Frasch, 1996, 328–35. Gornall and Ruiz-Falqués, 2019, 426–31.
25. In this regard, see Ruiz-Falqués, 2017b. Frasch (1996, 328–35) also speculates that the focus on grammar was due to the fact that Burmese monks had to learn Pali as a second language. This is no doubt likely, though it does not adequately explain the composition of works on grammatical philosophy or other detailed, extensive commentaries.
26. Aleix Ruiz-Falqués is currently working on these thirteenth-century grammatical texts, such as, the *Sambandhacintāpurāṇaṭīkā* and *Mukhamattasāra*, and has found in them quotations of Moggallāna's grammatical works, for instance.
27. *Sāsanavaṃsa*, 74.
28. On the date of the *Saddanīti*, see Gornall and Ruiz-Falqués, 2019, 428.
29. The work apparently cites the *Saddanīti*. See Dharmārāma, ed. 1896, xix–xxi.
30. Malalasekera, 1994, 238–9.
31. See Pollock, 2001a. For some useful criticisms of the idea of such a 'death', see Hanneder, 2002.
32. See, for instance, Hallisey, 2003.
33. Godakumbura, 1955, 144–51.
34. See Pollock, 2006, 386–7.
35. See chapter one.
36. See Deegalle, 1997; 2006; Dhammapala, 2003; Godakumbura, 1955, 56–66; 73–6. The one early exception is Guruḷugomi's mid-twelfth-century *Amāvatura* ('Flood of nectar').
37. Godakumbura, 1955, 61.

38. This appears to run counter to the suggestion in the *Vibhaṅga* commentary that one can only obtain insight into scripture (*niruttipaṭisambhidā*) and, thus, seemingly enlightenment when it is in Pali and not when it is translated. See *Sammohavinodanī*, $388_{,13-16}$.
39. *Lōväḍa Saṅgarāva* of Vīdāgama Maitreya, vv. 4–6:
manaram naradam säridam saṅganaṭa
melesin bätiyen adarin nama koṭa
vesesin peḷadam nomadat danahaṭa
pavasam kaḷa kam pala dän heḷu koṭa.
dahamaṭa sarikoṭa eḷuven perakī
kaviyaṭa sita pahadā siṭa nisäkī
sihikoṭa kaṅda piḷiveḷa dos noyekī
nivanaṭa sapämiṇi saṅga säṭanamakī.
ebävin eḷuven kīvayi anadara
novamin bätiyen adarin namakara
satosin äsuvot medahaṃ manahara
säbavin siduveyi saga mok sirisara.
In translating these verses, I have consulted the translations in Ñāṇānanda, 2000 and *Lōväḍa Saṅgarāva* (ed. and trans. De Silva), 2007. See also Hallisey, 2003, 706–7.
40. See Pollock, 2006, 426.
41. See the analysis and translation of this passage in Deegalle, 1997, 189–91. See also Hallisey, 2003, 733. On social and political changes after the reform era, see Kulasuriya, 1976.
42. Śrī Rāhula in his *Kāvyaśekhāraya* (v. 260), for instance, speaks of his style as a combination of a 'poetic path' and a 'preaching path' (*kivilakara hā banamaga*). See Dhammapala, 2003, 200.
43. On these works, see Henry, 2017, 220–37. Henry notes, however, that the earliest poem of this type, the *Vuttamālāsandesasataka* ('Hundred-verse message in a garland of metres', c. 1340s), was actually composed in Pali.
44. Henry, 2017, 222.
45. Henry, 2017, 220–37.
46. Dhammavisuddhi, 1970, 86–131.
47. Dhammavisuddhi, 1970, 78–9, citing Jayatilaka, 1956, 137–8, and Buddhadatta, 1960, 142.
48. *Jinakālamālī* of Ratanapañña, 84. See also *Tamnān Mūlasāsanā Wat Pā Daeng*, translated in Premchit and Swearer, 1977; Cœdès, 1924, 99, cited in Sirisena, 1978, 93. On the possible identity of these individuals, see Griswold and Nagara, 1973.

References

I. Primary sources

Abhidhammatthasaṅgaha of Anuruddha:
Saddhātissa, Hammalawa, ed. *The Abhidhammatthasaṅgaha of Bhadantācariya Anuruddha and the Abhidhammatthavibhāvinī-ṭīkā of Bhadantācariya Sumaṅgala*. Oxford: Pali Text Society, 1989.

Abhidhammatthavibhāvinī of Sumaṅgala:
See *Abhidhammatthasaṅgaha* of Anuruddha.

Abhidhammāvatāra of Buddhadatta:
Buddhadatta, A.P., ed. *Buddhadatta's Manuals, Part 1: Abhidhammāvatāra and Rūpārūpavibhāga, Part 2: Vinayavinicchaya and Uttaravinicchaya*. 1915, 1928. Combined reprint, London: Pali Text Society, 1980.

Abhidhammāvatāra of Buddhadatta Bᵉ:
Chaṭṭhasaṅgāyana CD-ROM, Version 3.0. Igatpuri: Vipassana Research Institute, 1999.

Abhidhammāvatāravikāsinī of Sumaṅgala I:
Abhidhammāvatārapurāṇaṭīkā. Abhidhammāvatārabhinavaṭīkā. 2 vols. Rangoon: Buddhasāsana Samiti, 1961.

Abhidhammāvatāravikāsinī of Sumaṅgala II:
See *Abhidhammāvatāravikāsinī* of Sumaṅgala I.

Abhidhānappadīpikā of Moggallāna:
Subhūti, Waskaḍuwē, ed. and trans. *Abhidhānappadīpikā; or, dictionary of the Pali language. By Moggallāna Thero*. Colombo: W. Henry Herbert, Acting Government Printer, 1865.

Abhidharmārthasaṅgrahasannaya of Sāriputta:
Siri Pannamoli Tissa, ed. *Abhidharmārthasaṅgraha vistara sannaya*. Third edition, revised and edited. Ambalamgoḍa: Wijaya Printing Press, 1926.

Aṅguttara Nikāya I:
Morris, Richard, ed. *The Aṅguttara-Nikāya, Part 1: Ekanipāta, Dukanipāta, and Tikanipāta*. 1885. Second edition, revised by A.K. Warder, London: Pali Text Society, 1961.

Aṅguttara Nikāya IV:
Hardy, E., ed. *The Aṅguttara-Nikāya, Part 4: Sattaka-nipāta, aṭṭhaka-nipāta, and navaka-nipāta*. 1899. Reprint, London: Pali Text Society, 1958.

Apadāna I–II:
Lilley, Mary E., ed. *The Apadāna, Parts 1–2*. Oxford: Pali Text Society, 2000.

Aṣṭādhyāyī of Pāṇini:
Katre, Sumitra M., ed. and trans. *Aṣṭādhyāyī of Pāṇini in Roman Transliteration*. Austin: University of Texas Press, 1987.

***Atthasālinī*:**
Müller, Edward, ed. *The Atthasālinī: Buddhaghosa's Commentary on the Dhammasaṅgaṇi*. 1897. Revised edition, London: Pali Text Society, 1979.

***Aucityavicāracarcā* of Kṣemendra:**
Rāghavāchārya, Vidyāratna E.V.V. and D.G. Padhye, eds. *Minor Works of Kṣemendra*. Hyderabad: Sanskrit Academy Osmania University, 1961.

***Bālāvabodhana* of Kassapa:**
Sri Seelaskhandha, C.A., ed. *Balawa Bodhana, An Abridgement of Chandra's Grammar by the most venerable Sri Mahakasyapa Sangharaja Mahasthavira of Jētawana Mahāvihāra, Polonnaruwa*. Aluthgama: Saddharmaprakasa Press, 1924.

***Bālāvatāra* of Dhammakitti:**
Chaṭṭhasaṅgāyana CD-ROM, Version 3.0. Igatpuri: Vipassana Research Institute, 1999.

***Buddhaghosuppatti* of Mahāmaṅgala:**
Gray, James, ed. and trans. *Buddhaghosuppatti or The History Romance of the Rise and Career of Buddhaghosa*. London: Luzac, 1892.

***Buddhippasādanī* of Śrī Rāhula:**
Sri Dhirananda and Vachissara, eds. *Buddhippasadani. A commentary on Padasadhana, Grammar of the Pali Language. By Sangharaja Sri Rahula, Principal of the College Srisanghabodhi-Srivijayabahu Parivena, Totagamuwa*. Colombo: Vidyasagara Printing Works, 1908.

***Caturārakkhadīpanī*:**
Chaṭṭhasaṅgāyana CD-ROM, Version 3.0. Igatpuri: Vipassana Research Institute, 1999.

***Cūḷavaṃsa*:**
Geiger, Wilhelm, ed. *Cūlavaṃsa: Being the most recent part of the Mahāvaṃsa, Volumes, 1–2*. 1925, 1927. Combined reprint, London: Pali Text Society, 1980.

***Daḷadāpūjāvaliya*:**
Sugatapāla, T., ed. *Daḷadāpūjāvaliya*. Colombo: Vidyādarśa Press, 1929.

***Daḷadāsirita* of Devrada Dampasaṅginā:**
Rajasekhara, E.S., ed. *Daḷadā Sirita*. Colombo: Granthaprakasa Press, 1920.

***Dāṭhāvaṃsa* of Dhammakitti:**
Morris, Richard and T.W. Rhys Davids, eds. 'The Dāṭhāvaṃsa', *Journal of the Pali Text Society* (1884): 109–51.

***Dāṭhāvaṃsasannaya*:**
Āsabha Tissa, ed. *Dāṭhāvaṅso or The History of the Tooth Relic With its Sinhalese Paraphrase by Ācariya Dharmakīrti Mahā Terunnānsē of Pulastinagara A.B. 1762*. Kelaniya: Sastradhara Press, 1883.

***Dhammapadaṭṭhakathā* I:**
Norman, H.C., ed. *The Commentary on the Dhammapada, Volume 1, Part 1*. 1906. Reprint, London: Pali Text Society, 1970.

***Dhammasaṅgaṇi*:**
Müller, Edward, ed. *The Dhammasaṅgaṇi*. 1885. Reprint, London: Pali Text Society, 1978.

***Dhammasaṅgaṇi* B[e]:**
Chaṭṭhasaṅgāyana CD-ROM, Version 3.0. Igatpuri: Vipassana Research Institute, 1999.

***Dhammasaṅgaṇianuṭīkā* of Dhammapāla:**
See *Dhammasaṅgaṇimūlaṭīkā* of Ānanda.

***Dhammasaṅgaṇimūlaṭīkā* of Ānanda:**
Abhidhammapiṭake Dhammasaṅgaṇī-aṭṭhakathāya Atthavaṇṇanābhūtā Bhadantācariya-ānandattherena katā Dhammasaṅgaṇīmūlaṭīkā. Tapassānuvaṇṇanābhūtā Bhadantācariyadhammapālattherena katā Dhammasaṅgaṇī-anuṭīkā. Yangon: Ministry of Religious Affairs, 2008.

***Dharmapradīpikāva* of Guruḷugomi:**
Vimalavaṃsa, Baddēgama, ed. *Dharmapradīpikāva*. Colombo: M.D. Gunasena, 1967.

***Dhvanyāloka* of Ānandavardhana:**
Durgāprasāda, Mahāmahopādhyāya Paṇḍit and Wāsudev Laxmaṇ Śāstrī Paṇśīkar, eds. *The Dhvanyāloka of Ānandavardhanāchārya with the Commentary of Abhinavaguptāchārya* (Kāvyāmālā 25). Third edition. Bombay: Nirṇaya-Sāgar Press, 1928.

***Dhvanyālokavṛtti* of Ānandavardhana:**
See *Dhvanyāloka* of *Ā*nandavardhana.

***Dīgha Nikāya* I:**
Rhys Davids, T.W. and J. Estlin Carpenter, eds. *The Dīgha Nikāya, Volume 1*. 1890. Reprint, London: Pali Text Society, 1975.

***Dīgha Nikāya* II:**
Rhys Davids, T.W. and J. Estlin Carpenter, eds. *The Dīgha Nikāya, Volume 2*. 1903. Reprint, London: Pali Text Society, 1966.

***Dīghanikāya-abhinavaṭīkā* of Ñāṇābhivaṃsa I:**
Chaṭṭhasaṅgāyana CD-ROM, Version 3.0. Igatpuri: Vipassana Research Institute, 1999.

***Dīghanikāyaṭīkā* of Dhammapāla I:**
De Silva, Lily, ed. *Dīghanikāy-aṭṭhakathāṭīkā Līnatthavaṇṇanā, Volume 1*. London: Pali Text Society, 1970.

***Dīpavaṃsa*:**
Oldenberg, Hermann, ed. and trans. *The Dīpavaṃsa: An Ancient Buddhist Historical Record.* 1879. Reprint, London: Pali Text Society, 2000.

***Epigraphia Birmanica* 3.2:**
Duroiselle, Charles, ed. *Epigraphia Birmanica: Being Lithic and Other Inscriptions of Burma, Volume 3, Part 2: Mon Inscriptions: Section II, The Mediaeval Mon Records, No. XII The Inscriptions of the Kalyāṇīsīmā, Pegu*, edited by C.O. Blagden. Rangoon: Government Printer, 1928.

***Epigraphia Indica* 22:**
Chakravarti, N.P., ed. *Epigraphia Indica and Record of the Archaeological Survey of India, Volume 22, 1933–34*. Delhi: Manager of Publications, 1938.

***Epigraphia Zeylanica* I:**
Wickremasinghe, Don Martino De Zilva, ed. and trans. *Epigraphia Zeylanica: Being Lithic and Other Inscriptions of Ceylon, Volume 1*. London: Oxford University Press, 1912.

***Epigraphia Zeylanica* II:**
Wickremasinghe, Don Martino De Zilva, ed. and trans. *Epigraphia Zeylanica: Being Lithic and Other Inscriptions of Ceylon, Volume 2*. London: Oxford University Press, 1928.

***Epigraphia Zeylanica* III:**
Wickremasinghe, Don Martino De Zilva and H.W. Codrington, ed. and trans. *Epigraphia Zeylanica: Being Lithic and Other Inscriptions of Ceylon, Volume 3*. London: Oxford University Press, 1933.

***Epigraphia Zeylanica* IV:**
Codrington, H.W. and S. Paranavitana, ed. and trans. *Epigraphia Zeylanica: Being Lithic and Other Inscriptions of Ceylon, Volume 4*. London: Oxford University Press, 1934.

***Epigraphia Zeylanica* V.III:**
Paranavitana, S. and C.E. Godakumbura, ed. *Epigraphia Zeylanica: Being Lithic and Other Inscriptions of Ceylon, Volume 5, Part 3*. Colombo: The Archaeological Department, 1965.

***Gandhavaṃsa*:**
Minayeff, J.P., ed. 'Gandha-Vaṃsa', *Journal of the Pali Text Society* (1886): 54–80.

***Harivaṃsa*:**
Vaidya, Parashuram Lakshman, ed. *The Harivamsa: Being the Khila or Supplement to the Mahābhārata, Volume 1*. Poona: Bhandarkar Oriental Research Institute, 1969.

***Hatthavanagallavihāravaṃsa*:**
Godakumbura, C.E., ed. *Hatthavanagallavihāravaṃsa*. London: Pali Text Society, 1956.

***Inscriptions of Burma* 3:**
Inscriptions of Burma, Portfolio III: 630–662 B.E. (1268–1300 A.D.). London: Oxford University Press, 1939.

***Inscriptions of Ceylon* 5.1:**
Ranawella, Sirimal, ed. and trans. *Inscriptions of Ceylon, Volume 5, Part 1: Containing Pillar, Slab and Rock Inscriptions from 815 AD to 923 AD*. Colombo: Department of Archaeology, Sri Lanka, 2001.

***Inscriptions of Ceylon* 5.2:**
Ranawella, G.S., ed. and trans. *Inscriptions of Ceylon, Volume 5, Part 2: Containing Pillar Inscriptions and Slab Inscriptions from 924 AD to 1017 AD*. Colombo: Department of Archaeology, Sri Lanka, 2004.

***Inscriptions of Ceylon* 5.3:**
Ranawella, Sirimal, ed. and trans. *Inscriptions of Ceylon, Volume 5, Part 3: Containing Pillar, Slab and Rock Inscriptions from 9th Century to 10th Century AD*. Colombo: Department of Archaeology, Sri Lanka, 2005.

***Inscriptions of Ceylon* 6:**
Ranawella, G.S., ed. and trans. *Inscriptions of Ceylon, Volume 6: Containing Pillar Inscriptions, Slab Inscriptions and Rock Inscriptions of the Polonnaruva Period*. Colombo: Department of Archaeology, Sri Lanka, 2007.

***Jātakaṭṭhakathā* I:**
Faussbøll, V., ed. *The Jātaka Together with its Commentary: Being Tales of the Anterior Births of Gotama Buddha, Volume 1*. 1877. Reprint, London: Pali Text Society, 1962.

***Jinacarita* of Medhaṅkara:**
Duroiselle, Charles, ed. and trans. *Jinacarita or "The Career of the Conqueror". A Pali Poem Edited and Translated with Notes by Charles Duroiselle*. Rangoon: British Burma Press, 1906.

***Jinakālamālī* of Ratanapañña:**
Buddhadatta, A.P., ed. *Jinakālamālī*. London: Pali Text Society, 1962.

***Jinālaṅkāra* of Buddharakkhita:**
Gray, James, ed. and trans. *Jinālaṅkāra or "Embellishments of Buddha" by Buddharakkhita*. London: Luzac, 1894.

***Jinālaṅkāra* of Buddharakkhita Cᵉ:**
Dīpaṅkara, Välipaṭanvila and Baṭapolē Dhammapāla, eds. *The Jinālaṅkāra by Tripiṭaka Vāgīsvarācārya the Venerable Buddharakkhita Maha Thera*. Galle: Vidyaloka Press, 1900.

***Jinālaṅkāravaṇṇanā*:**
Dīpaṅkara, Välipaṭanvila and Baṭapolē Dhammapāla, eds. *Jinālaṅkāravaṇṇanā*. Aluthgama: Saddhammappakāsa Press, 1913.

***Kaccāyanavyākaraṇa* of Kaccāyana:**
Pind, Ole Holten, ed. *Kaccāyana*. Bristol: Pali Text Society, 2012.

***Kalyāṇī Inscriptions*:**
Taw Sein Ko, ed. and trans. *The Kalyānī Inscriptions, erected by King Dhammacetī at Pegu in 1476 A.D.: Text and Translation*. Rangoon: Government Press, 1892.

***Karmavibhāgaya*:**
Jinaratana, Isvällē and Saraṇapāla, Paluvälgālē, eds. *Karmavibhāgaya*. Colombo: Vidyārthaprakāśa Press, 1929.

Kāśikāvṛtti:
Shastri, Dwarikadas and Kalikaprasad Shukla, eds. *Nyāsa or Pañcikā Commentary of Ācārya Jinendrabuddhipāda and Padamañjarī of Haradatta Miśra on the Kāśikāvṛtti (Commentary on the Aṣṭādhyāyī of Pāṇini) of Vāmana-Jayāditya, Part 2: Chapter 2 and up to second section of Chapter 3.* Varanasi: Prachya Bharati Prakashan, 1965.

Kathāvatthu:
Taylor, Arnold C., ed. *Kathāvatthu, Volumes 1–2.* 1894, 1897. Combined reprint, London: Pali Text Society, 1979.

Kathāvatthuaṭṭhakathā:
Jayawickrama, N.A., ed. *Kathāvatthuppakaraṇa-aṭṭhakathā included in Pañcappakaraṇa-aṭṭhakathā named Paramatthadīpanī.* London: Pali Text Society, 1979.

Kavidappaṇanīti:
Chaṭṭhasaṅgāyana CD-ROM, Version 3.0. Igatpuri: Vipassana Research Institute, 1999.

***Kāvyādarśa* of Daṇḍin:**
Belvalkar, S.K., ed. and trans. *Kāvyādarśa of Daṇḍin: Sanskrit text and English translation.* Poona: Oriental Book-Supplying Agency, 1924.

***Kāvyālaṅkāra* of Vāmana:**
Durgāprasāda, Mahāmahopādhyāya Paṇḍit and Kāśināth Pāṇḍurang Parab, eds. *The Kāvyālankāra-Sūtras of Vāmana with his own Vṛtti.* Revised by Wāsudev Laxmaṇ Shāstrī Paṇśīkar. Third edition. Bombay: Nirṇaya-Sāgar Press, 1926.

***Kāvyālaṅkāravṛtti* of Vāmana:**
See *Kāvyālaṅkāra* of Vāmana.

***Khuddasikkhā* of Dhammasiri:**
Müller, Edward, ed. 'Khuddasikkhā and Mūlasikkhā', *Journal of the Pali Text Society* (1883): 86–132.

***Khuddasikkhābhinavaṭīkā* of Saṅgharakkhita:**
Chaṭṭhasaṅgāyana CD-ROM, Version 3.0. Igatpuri: Vipassana Research Institute, 1999.

***Kṛtyakalpataru* of Lakṣmīdhara I:**
Rangaswami Aiyangar, K.V., ed. *Kṛtyakalpataru of Bhaṭṭa Lakṣmīdhara, Volume 1, Brahmacārikāṇḍa.* Baroda: Oriental Institute, 1948.

Lalitavistara:
Vaidya, P.L. ed. *Lalita-vistara.* Darbhanga: Mithila Institute of Post-Graduate Studies and Research in Sanskrit Learning, 1958.

***Lōväḍa Saṅgarāva* of Vīdāgama Maitreya:**
de Silva, W.A., ed. and trans. *Lōväḍa Saṅgarāva: The Book of Public Welfare; Sinhala Text, English Transliteration and English Translation.* Colombo: Godage International, 2007.

***Mahābhāṣya* of Patañjali I:**
Kielhorn, F., ed. *The Vyākaraṇa-Mahābhāṣya of Patañjali, Volume 1.* Third edition revised and furnished with additional readings, references and select critical notes by MM. K.V. Abhyankar. Pune: Bhandarkar Oriental Research Institute, 1962.

***Mahābhāṣyadīpikā* of Bhartṛhari:**
Abhyankar, K.V. and Limaye V.P., eds. *Mahābhāṣyadīpikā of Bhartṛhari.* Pune: Bhandarkar Oriental Research Institute, 1970.

***Mahānāgakulasandesa* of Nāgasena:**
Günther, Herbert, ed. 'Der Mahānāgakula-sandeśa', *Wiener Zeitschrift für die Kunde des Morgenlandes* 49 (1942): 257–81.

***Mahāyānasūtrālaṅkārasvavṛtti* of Asaṅga:**
Bagchi, S., ed. *Mahāyāna-sūtrālaṅkāra of Asaṅga with its svavṛtti.* Darbhanga: Mithila Institute of Post-Graduate Studies and Research in Sanskrit Learning, 1970.

***Mahāvaṃsa* of Mahānāma:**
Geiger, Wilhelm, ed. *The Mahāvaṃsa*. London: Pali Text Society, 1908.

***Majjhima Nikāya* III:**
Chalmers, Robert, ed. *The Majjhima-Nikāya, Volume 3*. 1899. Reprint, London: Pali Text Society, 1977.

***Majjhimanikāyaṭīkā* of Dhammapāla III:**
Majjhimapaṇṇāsaṭṭhakathāya Atthavaṇṇanābhūtā Bhadantācariyadhammapālattherena katā Majjhimapaṇṇāsaṭīkā. Tathā — Uparipaṇṇāsaṭṭhakathāya Atthavaṇṇanābhūtā Uparipaṇṇāsaṭīkā. Yangon: Ministry of Religious Affairs, 2008.

***Manorathapūraṇī* of Buddhaghosa I:**
Walleser, Max, ed. *Manorathapūraṇī. Buddhaghosa's commentary on the Anguttara-nikāya after the manuscript of Edmund Hardy, Volume 1: Eka-nipāta-vaṇṇanā*. 1924. Second edition, revised. London: Pali Text Society, 1973.

***Manorathapūraṇī* of Buddhaghosa III:**
Kopp, Hermann, ed. *Manorathapūraṇī. Commentary on the Aṅguttara Nikāya, Volume 3: Catukka-pañcaka-chakka-nipāta-vaṇṇanā*. 1936. Reprint, London: Pali Text Society, 1966.

***Manorathapūraṇī* of Buddhaghosa B[e]:**
Chaṭṭhasaṅgāyana CD-ROM, Version 3.0. Igatpuri: Vipassana Research Institute, 1999.

***Moggallānapañcikā* of Moggallāna:**
See *Moggallānavyākaraṇa* of Moggallāna.

***Moggallānapañcikāpradīpaya* of Śrī Rāhula:**
Śrī Dharmārāma, ed. *Moggallāna Pañchikā Pradīpa: A Treatise on Moggallāna's System of Pali Grammar by Saṅgharāja Srī Rāhula Mahāsthavira*. Colombo: H.C. Cottle, Acting Government Printer, 1896.

***Moggallānapañcikāṭīkā* of Saṅgharakkhita:**
Moggallān pañcikā aphvaṅ. Sāratthavilāsinī maññ so Moggallān pañcikā ṭīkā. Rankun: Mrui jambū. mit chve piṭakat puṃ nhip tuik, 1413 (1955).

***Moggallānavutti* of Moggallāna:**
See *Moggallānavyākaraṇa* of Moggallāna.

***Moggallānavyākaraṇa* of Moggallāna:**
Srī Dharmānanda, ed. *Moggallāna Pañcikā with Sutta Vutti by the Venerable Moggallāna Mahā Sāmi*. Colombo: Satyasamuccaya Press, 1931.

***Mohavicchedanī* of Kassapa:**
Buddhadatta, A.P. and A.K. Warder, eds. *Mohavicchedanī Abhidhammamātikatthavaṇṇanā by Kassapatthera of Coḷa*. London: Pali Text Society, 1961.

***Mukhamattadīpanī* of Vimalabuddhi:**
Dhammaratana, Weliwiṭiyē, ed. *The Mukhamattadīpanī, with the Kaccāyana Vutti, and an appendix of useful information on nouns, verbs, &c.* Colombo: H.C. Cottle, Acting Government Printer, 1898.

***Mukhamattadīpanī* of Vimalabuddhi B[e]:**
Nyāsapāṭh. Yangon: Sudhammavatī Press, 1933.

***Nettipakaraṇa*:**
Hardy, E., ed. *The Netti-Pakaraṇa with extracts from Dhammapāla's commentary*. 1902. Reprint, London: Pali Text Society, 1961.

***Nettipakaraṇaṭīkā* of Dhammapāla:**
Chaṭṭhasaṅgāyana CD-ROM, Version 3.0. Igatpuri: Vipassana Research Institute, 1999.

***Nikāyasaṅgrahaya* of Devarakṣita Dharmakīrti:**
De Silva, Simon, A. Mendis Gunasekera, and W.F. Gunawardhana, eds. *Nikāya-Saṅgraha; or Sāsanāwatāraya: A history of Buddhism in India and Ceylon by Dewarakshita Dharmakīrti Saṅgharāja*. Colombo: H.C. Cottle, Acting Government Printer, 1907.

***Nyāsa* of Jinendrabuddhi:**
Chakravarti, Srish Chandra, ed. *The Kāśikā-vivaraṇa-pañjikā (The Nyāsa): A Commentary on Vāmana-Jayāditya's Kāśikā by Jinendra Buddhi, Volume 1: Adhyāyas 1–4*. Rajshahi, Bengal: The Varendra Research Society, 1916.

***Padasādhana* of Piyadassi:**
Dharmasena, Doḍandūvē, ed. *Padasādhanaya pūjācāryya Piyadassīmahāsthavira pādayanvahansē visin viracitayi. Dim̐bulāgala medhaṅkarābhidhāna mahāyati śreṣṭhayanvahansēgē śiṣyavū Ānandamahāsthavira pādayanvahansē visin liyanalada vyākhyānayen samupalakṣitayi*. Colombo: Lankābhinava Viśruta Press, 1905.

***Padasādhanasannaya* of Ānanda:**
See *Padasādhana* of Piyadassi.

***Papañcasūdanī* of Buddhaghosa II:**
Woods, J.H. and D. Kosambi, ed. *Papañcasūdanī Majjhimanikāyaṭṭhakathā of Buddhaghosācariya, Part 2: Suttas 11–50*. 1928. Reprint, London: Pali Text Society 1979.

***Papañcasūdanī* of Buddhaghosa V:**
Horner, I.B., ed. *Papañcasūdanī Majjhimanikāyaṭṭhakathā of Buddhaghosācariya, Part 4: Suttas 101–130, Part 5: Suttas 131–152*. 1937, 1938. Combined reprint, London: Pali Text Society, 1977.

***Paramatthajotikā* II of Dhammapāla I:**
Smith, Helmer, ed. *Sutta-Nipāta Commentary: Being Paramatthajotikā II, Volume 1: Uragavagga Cūḷavagga*. 1916. Reprint, London: Pali Text Society, 1966.

***Paramatthavinicchaya* of Anuruddha:**
Buddhadatta, A.P., ed. 'Paramatthavinicchaya by Anuruddha', *Journal of the Pali Text Society* 10 (1985): 155–226.

***Paribhāṣenduśekhara* of Nāgojī Bhaṭṭa:**
Abhyankar, K.V., ed. *Paribhāṣenduśekhara of Nāgojī Bhaṭṭa, Part 1*. New edition with the commentary *Tattvādarśa* of MM. Vasudev Shastri Abhyankar. Pune: Bhandarkar Oriental Research Institute, 1962.

***Payogasiddhi of Medhaṅkara*:**
Siri Ñāṇāloka Kōdāgoḍa, ed. *Payogasiddhi mugalan viyaraṇa äsiri koṭa Medhaṅkara vanaratana mahāsthavirayan vahansē visin viracitayi*. Colombo: Śrī Laṅkā Saṃskṛtika Maṇḍalaya, 1974.

***Peṭakopadesa*:**
Barua, Arabinda, ed. *The Peṭakopadesa*. 1949. Revised edition, London: Pali Text Society, 1982.

***Puggalapaññattiaṭṭhakathā*:**
Morris, Richard, ed. *Puggala-paññatti*. 1883. Georg Landsberg and Caroline Rhys Davids, eds. *Puggala-paññatti-atthakathā*. 1914. Combined reprint, London: Pali Text Society, 1972.

***Pūjāvaliya* of Mayūrapāda:**
Saddhatissa, Bentota, ed. *Pujawalie by the Venerable Buddhaputta Maha Thero, principal of the Maurapada Piriwena*. Panadura: Panadura Press, 1930.

***Raghuvaṃśa* of Kālidāsa:**
Kale, Moreshwar Ramachandra, ed. and trans. *The Raghuvamśa of Kālidāsa, with the Commentary (the Sanjīvinī) of Mallinātha. Cantos I–X*. Third revised edition. Bombay: Gopal Narayen, 1922.

***Rājataraṅgiṇī*:**
Bandhu, Vishva, ed. *Rājataraṅgiṇī of Kalhaṇa. Edited, critically, and annotated with text-comparative data from original manuscripts and other available materials, Part 1: Taraṅga-s 1–7*. Edited in collaboration with Bhīma Dev, K.S. Rāmaswāmi Sāstrī and S. Bhāskaran Nair. Hoshiapur: Vishveshvaranand Vedic Research Institute, 1963.

***Rājāvaliya*:**
Guṇasēkara, B., ed. *The Rājāvaliya: Or, A Historical Narrative of Siṇhalese Kings from Vijaya to Vimala Dharma Sūrya II*. Colombo: H.C. Cottle, Government Printer, 1911.

Rasavāhinī of Vedeha:
Saraṇatissa, ed. *Rasavāhinī. Patirājapariveṇajjhācariyavarena saddasatthāgamapāradassinā Vedehamahātherasāminā pubbaracanānirākulīkaraṇato sampāditā.* Second edition. Colombo: Vijjāsāgara Press, 1896.

Ratnaśrīṭīkā of Ratnaśrījñāna:
Thakur, Anantalal and Upendra Jha, eds. *Kāvyalakṣaṇa of Daṇḍin (also known as Kāvyādarśa) with commentary called Ratnaśrī of Ratnaśrījñāna.* Darbhanga: Mithila Institute of Post-Graduate Studies and Research in Sanskrit Learning, 1957.

Rūpasiddhi of Buddhappiya:
Dhammaratana, B.K., ed. *Maharupasiddhi by Ven. Choliya Buddhapriya Maha Thera, the Head of the Maha Vihara sect in Ceylon, with Sandehavighatani, a Sinhalese paraphrase by an ancient great scholar.* Weligama: Sathmina Press, 1936.

Rūpasiddhi of Buddhappiya B[e]:
Chaṭṭhasaṅgāyana CD-ROM, Version 3.0. Igatpuri: Vipassana Research Institute, 1999.

Rūpasiddhisannaya:
Dhammaratana, Baddegama Keertisri, ed. *Maha Rupa Siddhi Sanna or Paraphrase of Maha Rupa Siddhi by an Ancient Pandit.* Peliyagoda: Satyasamuccaya Press, 1926.

Saccasaṅkhepa:
Dharmārāma, P., ed. 'Sacca-Sankhepa, by Dhammapāla', *Journal of the Pali Text Society* (1917–19): 1–25.

Saddanīti of Aggavaṃsa II:
Smith, Helmer, ed. *Saddanīti: La Grammaire Palie d'Aggavaṃsa, Volume 2: Dhātumālā (Pariccheda 15–19).* Lund: C.W.K. Gleerup, 1929.

Saddhammasaṅgaha of Dhammakitti:
Saddhānanda, Nedimāle, ed. 'Saddhamma Samgaho', *Journal of the Pali Text Society* (1890): 21–90.

Samantapāsādikā I:
Takakusu, J. and M. Nagai, eds. *Samantapāsādikā: Buddhaghosa's commentary on the Vinaya Piṭaka, Volume 1.* 1924. Reprint, London: Pali Text Society, 1975.

Samantapāsādikā VI:
Takakusu, J. and Makoto Nagai, eds. *Samantapāsādikā: Buddhaghosa's commentary on the Vinaya Piṭaka, Volume 6.* 1947. Reprint, London: Pali Text Society, 1982.

Sambandhacintā of Saṅgharakkhita:
Sārānanda, Kalutara, ed. *The Sambandha-cintā by Venerable Sthavira Sri Sangha Rakshita, translated by Venerable Gotama Maha Sami.* Colombo: Lakrivikiraṇa Press, 1891.

Sambandhacintāsannaya of Gotama:
See *Sambandhacintā* of Saṅgharakkhita.

Sammohavinodanī:
Buddhadatta, A.P., ed. *Sammoha-vinodanī Abhidhamma-Piṭake Vibhaṅgaṭṭhakathā.* 1923. London: Pali Text Society, 1980.

Saṃyutta Nikāya III:
Feer, Leon, ed. *Saṃyutta-nikāya, Part 3: Khandha-vagga.* 1890. Reprint, London: Pali Text Society, 1975.

Sāratthadīpanī of Sāriputta I:
Samantapāsādikāya Vinayaṭṭhakathāya Atthavaṇṇanābhūtā Bhadantasāriputtattherena katā Sāratthadīpanīṭīkā (Paṭhamo bhāgo). Yangon: Ministry of Religious Affairs, 2008.

Sāratthadīpanī of Sāriputta II:
Samantapāsādikāya Vinayaṭṭhakathāya Atthavaṇṇanābhūtā Bhadantasāriputtattherena katā Sāratthadīpanīṭīkā (Dutiyo bhāgo). Yangon: Ministry of Religious Affairs, 2008.

Sāratthadīpanī of Sāriputta III:
Samantapāsādikāya Vinayaṭṭhakathāya Atthavaṇṇanābhūtā Bhadantasāriputtattherena katā Sāratthadīpanīṭīkā (Tatiyo bhāgo). Yangon: Ministry of Religious Affairs, 2008.

Sāratthappakāsinī of Buddhaghosa I:
Woodward, F.L., ed. *Sārattha-ppakāsinī: Buddhaghosa's commentary on the Saṃyutta-Nikāya, Volume 1: On Sagāthā-vagga.* 1929. Reprint, London: Pali Text Society, 1977.

Sāratthappakāsinī of Buddhaghosa II:
Woodward, F.L., ed. *Sārattha-ppakāsinī: Buddhaghosa's commentary on the Saṃyutta-Nikāya, Volume 2: On Nidāna-Vagga, Khandha-Vagga, Saḷāyatana-Vagga (First Part).* 1932. Reprint, London: Pali Text Society, 1977.

Sārasaṅgaha of Siddhattha:
Sasaki, Genjun H., ed. *Sārasaṅgaha.* Oxford: Pali Text Society, 1992.

Sāsanavaṃsa:
Bode, Mabel, ed. *Sāsanavaṃsa.* London: Pali Text Society, 1897.

Saundarananda of Aśvaghoṣa:
Johnston, E.H., ed. and trans. *The Saundarananda of Aśvaghoṣa.* 1928, 1932. Combined reprint, Delhi: Motilal Banarsidass, 1975.

Sidat Saṅgarāva of Vedeha:
Gair, James W. and W.S. Karunatillake. *The Sidat Saṅgarā: Text, Translation and Glossary* (American Oriental Series 95). New Haven, Connecticut: American Oriental Society, 2013.

Sinhala Inscriptions in the Colombo National Museum:
Ranawella, Sirimal, ed. and trans. *Sinhala Inscriptions in the Colombo National Museum.* Colombo: Department of National Museums, 2005.

Siyabaslakarasannaya of Ruvanmī:
Jayatilaka, Hendrick, ed. *Siyabas Lakara or Siṇhalese Rhetoric by king Silāmēghavarṇa. Paraphrased by Ratnamadhvāchārya Mahā Thēra.* Colombo: Lakrivikiraṇa Press, 1892.

South Indian Inscriptions IV:
Sastri, Rao Bahadur H. Krishna, ed. *South-Indian Inscriptions (Texts), Volume 4: Miscellaneous Inscriptions from the Tamil, Telugu and Kannada Countries and Ceylon (with eleven plates).* Madras: Government Press, 1923.

Subodhālaṅkāra of Saṅgharakkhita:
Jaini, Padmanabh S. ed., *Subodhālaṅkāra. Porāṇa-ṭīkā (Mahāsāmi-ṭīkā) by Saṅgharakkhita Mahāsāmi, Abhinava-ṭīkā (Nissaya) (anonymous).* Oxford: Pali Text Society, 2000.

Subodhālaṅkāra-abhinavaṭīkā:
See *Subodhālaṅkāra* of Saṅgharakkhita.

Subodhālaṅkāramahāsāmiṭīkā of Saṅgharakkhita:
See *Subodhālaṅkāra* of Saṅgharakkhita.

Subodhālaṅkārapurāṇasannaya:
Dharmasena, Doḍandūvē, ed. *Subodhālaṅkāraya. Mahā mahopādhyāya śrī saṅgharakṣita saṅgharāja svāmipādayan visin viracitayi. Purātanācāryyavarayaku visin liyanalada praśasta vyākhyātayakin yuktayi.* Colombo: Sevyaśrī Press, 1910.

Sumaṅgalavilāsinī of Buddhaghosa I:
Rhys Davids, T.W. and J. Estlin Carpenter, eds. *The Sumaṅgala-Vilāsinī, Buddhaghosa's Commentary on the Dīgha-Nikāya, Part 1.* 1886. Reprint, London. Pali Text Society, 1968.

Sumaṅgalavilāsinī of Buddhaghosa II:
Stede, W., ed. *The Sumaṅgala-vilāsinī, Buddhaghosa's Commentary on the Dīgha-Nikāya, Part 2: Suttas 8–20.* 1931. Reprint, London: Pali Text Society, 1971.

***Sumaṅgalavilāsinī* of Buddhaghosa III:**
Stede, W., ed. *The Sumaṅgala-vilāsinī, Buddhaghosa's Commentary on the Dīgha-Nikāya, Part 3: Suttas 21–24*. 1932. Reprint, London: Pali Text Society, 1971.

***Suttaniddesa* of Chapaṭa:**
Medhankara, Mabopiṭiyē, ed. *The Kachchayanasuttaniddesa. By the ven'ble neruttikachariya Cchappada maha thera.* Colombo: Vidyabhusana Press, 1915.

***Suttanipāta*:**
Andersen, Dines and Helmer Smith, eds. *Sutta-Nipāta*. 1913. Reprint, Oxford: Pali Text Society, 1948.

***Thūpavaṃsa* of Vācissara:**
Jayawickrama, N.A., ed. and trans. *The chronicle of the Thūpa and the Thūpavaṃsa*. London: Pali Text Society, 1971.

***Upāsakajanālaṅkāra* of Ānanda:**
Saddhatissa, H., ed. *Upāsakajanālaṅkāra: A critical edition and study*. London: Pali Text Society, 1965.

***Vajirabuddhiṭīkā*:**
Chaṭṭhasaṅgāyana CD-ROM, Version 3.0. Igatpuri: Vipassana Research Institute, 1999.

***Vākyapadīya* of Bhartṛhari:**
Subramania Iyer, K.A., ed. *Vākyapadīya of Bhartṛhari with the Commentaries, Vṛtti and Paddhati of Vṛṣabhadeva, Kāṇḍa 1*. Poona: Deccan College Postgraduate and Research Institute, 1966.

***Vibhaṅgamūlaṭīkā* of Ānanda:**
Abhidhammapiṭake Vibhaṅgaṭṭhakathāya Atthavaṇṇanābhūtā Bhadantācariya-ānandattherena katā Vibhaṅgamūlaṭīkā. Tapassānuvaṇṇanābhūtā Bhadantācariyadhammapālattherena katā Vibhaṅga-anuṭīkā. Yangon: Ministry of Religious Affairs, 2008.

***Vimativinodanī* of Kassapa:**
Chaṭṭhasaṅgāyana CD-ROM, Version 3.0. Igatpuri: Vipassana Research Institute, 1999.

***Vinaya* I:**
Oldenberg, Hermann, ed. *The Vinaya Piṭakaṃ: One of the Principal Buddhist Holy Scriptures in the Pāli Language, Volume 1: The Mahāvagga*. 1879. Reprint, Oxford: Pali Text Society, 1997.

***Vinaya* II:**
Oldenberg, Hermann, ed. *The Vinaya Piṭakaṃ: One of the Principal Buddhist Holy Scriptures in the Pāli Language, Volume 2: The Cullavagga*. 1880. Reprint, Oxford: Pali Text Society, 1995.

***Vinaya* IV:**
Oldenberg, Hermann, ed. *The Vinaya Piṭakaṃ: One of the Principal Buddhist Holy Scriptures in the Pāli Language, Volume 4: The Suttavibhāga, Second Part (End of the Mahāvibhaṅga; Bhikkhunīvibhaṅga)*. 1882. Reprint, Oxford: Pali Text Society, 1993.

***Vinayasaṅgaha* of Sāriputta:**
Chaṭṭhasaṅgāyana CD-ROM, Version 3.0. Igatpuri: Vipassana Research Institute, 1999.

***Vinayasaṅgahapurāṇaṭīkā* of Sāriputta:**
Pannasara, K. and P. Nanavimalatissa, ed. *Palimuttaka Vinaya Vinicchaya Sangahatika. Edited by Very Revd. Sariputra Sangharaja of Jetawanarama in Pollonnaruwa.* Matara: Sudarsana Press, 1908.

***Vinayatthamañjūsā* of Buddhanāga:**
Kaṅkhāvitaraṇīpurāṇaṭīkā. Kaṅkhāvitaraṇīabhinavaṭīkā. Rangoon: Buddhasāsana Samiti, 1961.

***Vinayavinicchaya* of Buddhadatta:**
See *Abhidhammāvatāra* of Buddhadatta.

***Visuddhimagga* of Buddhaghosa:**
Warren, Henry Clarke, ed. *Visuddhimagga of Buddhaghosācariya*. Revised by Dharmananda Kosambi (Harvard Oriental Series 41). Cambridge, Massachusetts: Harvard University Press, 1950.

***Visuddhimaggamahāṭīkā* of Dhammapāla I:**
Visuddhimaggassa Atthasaṃvaṇṇanābhūtā Bhadantācariyadhammapālattherena katā Paramatthamañjūsā nāma Visuddhimaggamahāṭīkā (Paṭhamo bhāgo). Yangon: Ministry of Religious Affairs, 2008.

***Vuttodaya* of Saṅgharakkhita:**
Ānandajoti, ed. and trans. *Vuttodaya: The Composition of Metre by Ven. Saṅgharakkhita.* 2016.

II. Secondary sources

Acri, Andrea. 'Introduction: Esoteric Buddhist Networks along the Maritime Silk Routes, 7th–13th Century AD', in *Esoteric Buddhism in Mediaeval Maritime Asia: Networks of Masters, Texts, Icons*, edited by Andrea Acri, 1–28. Singapore: ISEAS Publishing, 2016.

Agostini, Giulio, trans. *The Ornament of Lay Followers: Ānanda's Upāsakajanālaṅkāra.* Bristol: Pali Text Society, 2015.

Ali, Daud. 'Royal Eulogy as World History: Rethinking Copper-Plate Inscriptions in Cōḻa India', in *Querying the Medieval: Texts and the History of Practices in South Asia*, edited by Ronald Inden, Jonathan Walters and Daud Ali, 165–229. New York: Oxford University Press, 2000.

Ali, Daud. *Courtly Culture and Political Life in Early Medieval India.* Cambridge: Cambridge University Press, 2006.

Ali, Daud. 'Cosmos, Realm, and Property in Early Medieval South India', in *Tamil Geographies: Cultural Constructions of Space and Place in South India*, edited by Martha Ann Selby and Indira Viswanathan Peterson, 117–41. Albany: State University of New York Press, 2008.

Ames, Michael. 'Ideological and Social Change in Ceylon', *Human Organization* 22, no. 1 (1963): 45–53.

Anālayo, Bhikkhu. *The Genesis of the Bodhisattva Ideal* (Hamburg Buddhist Studies 1). Hamburg: Hamburg University Press, 2010.

Anālayo, Bhikkhu. 'The Evolution of the Bodhisattva Concept in Early Buddhist Canonical Literature', in *The Bodhisattva Ideal: Essays on the Emergence of Mahāyāna*, edited by Bhikkhu Ñāṇatusita, 165–208. Kandy: Buddhist Publication Society, 2013.

Anālayo, Bhikkhu. *The Dawn of the Abhidharma.* Hamburg: Hamburg University Press, 2014.

Appadurai, Arjun. 'Royal Rituals and Cultural Change', *Reviews in Anthropology* 8, no. 2 (1981): 121–38.

Apple, James B. 'Eschatology and World Order in Buddhist Formations', *Religious Studies and Theology* 29, no. 1 (2010): 109–22.

Appleton, Naomi. *Jātaka Stories in Theravāda Buddhism: Narrating the Bodhisatta Path.* Farnham: Ashgate Publishing, 2010.

Appleton, Naomi. *Narrating Karma and Rebirth: Buddhist and Jain Multi-Life Stories.* Cambridge: Cambridge University Press, 2014.

Archer, Margaret S. *Culture and Agency: The Place of Culture in Social Theory.* Cambridge: Cambridge University Press, 1988.

Ariyapala, M.B. *Society in Mediaeval Ceylon: The State of Society in Ceylon as Depicted in the Saddharma-ratnāvaliya and Other Literature of the Thirteenth Century.* Colombo: K.V.G. de Silva, 1956.

Aung Thwin, Michael Arthur. 'The Nature of State and Society in Pagan: An Institutional History of 12th and 13th Century Burma'. PhD thesis, University of Michigan, 1976.

Aung Thwin, Michael. 'The Role of *Sasana* Reform in Burmese History: Economic Dimensions of a Religious Purification', *Journal of Asian Studies* 38, no. 4 (1979): 671–88.

Aung Thwin, Michael. *Pagan: The Origins of Modern Burma.* Honolulu: University of Hawai'i Press, 1985.

Auroux, Sylvain. *La révolution technologique de la grammatisation: Introduction à l'histoire des sciences du langage.* Liège: Mardaga, 1994.

Aussant, Émilie. *Le nom propre en Inde: Considérations sur le mécanisme référentiel.* Lyon: ENS Éditions, 2009.

Balbir, Nalini. 'Three Pāli Works Revisited', *Journal of the Pali Text Society* 29 (2007): 331–64.

Bareau, André. *Les sectes bouddhiques du Petit Véhicule.* Saigon: École française d'Extrême-Orient, 1955.

Bareau, André. 'Un personnage bien mystérieux: L'épouse du Buddha', in *Indological and Buddhist Studies: Volume in Honour of Professor J.W. de Jong on His Sixtieth Birthday*, edited by L.A. Hercus, F.B.J. Kuiper, T. Rajapatirana and E.R. Skrzypczak, 31–59. Canberra: Faculty of Asian Studies, Australian National University, 1982.

Barnett, Lionel D. 'The Manavulu – Sandesaya', *Journal of the Royal Asiatic Society of Great Britain and Ireland* (April 1905): 265–83.

Barua, Dwijendralal. '"Buddhakhetta" in the Apadāna', in *B.C. Law Volume, Volume 2*, edited by D.R. Bhandarkar, K.A. Nilakanta Sastri, B.M. Barua, B.K. Ghosh and P.K. Gode, 183–90. Poona: Bhandarkar Oriental Research Institute, 1946.

Bechert, Heinz. 'Ways of Sasana Reform in Theravada Buddhism', in *Rhys Davids Memorial Volume*, edited by V. Ñāṇāloka, 145–57. Colombo: University of Ceylon, 1965.

Bechert, Heinz. *Buddhismus, Staat und Gesellschaft in den Ländern des Theravāda-Buddhismus, Volume 1: Grundlagen; Ceylon*. Frankfurt am Main: Alfred Metzner Verlag, 1966.

Bechert, Heinz. 'Theravāda Buddhist Sangha: Some General Observations on Historical and Political Factors in Its Development', *Journal of Asian Studies* 29, no. 4 (1970): 761–78.

Bechert, Heinz. 'Sangha, State, Society, "Nation": Persistence of Traditions in "Post-Traditional" Buddhist Societies', *Daedalus* 102, no. 1 (1973): 85–95.

Bechert, Heinz. 'Sāsana-Reform im Theravāda-Buddhismus', in *50 Jahre Buddhistisches Haus: Gegründet von Paul Dahlke 1924–1974*, edited by A. Sri Gnanawimala Maha Thera, Guido Auster and Ralf Leu, 19–34. Berlin-Frohnau: German Dharmaduta Society, 1974.

Bechert, Heinz. 'Sanskrit Literature in Sri Lanka as a Paradigm of Regional Sanskrit Literatures', in *Malalasekera Commemoration Volume*, edited by O.H. de A. Wijesekera, 23–35. Colombo: Malalasekera Commemoration Volume Editorial Committee, 1976.

Bechert, Heinz. 'Mahāyāna Literature in Sri Lanka: The Early Phase', in *Prajñāpāramitā and Related Systems: Studies in Honor of Edward Conze*, edited by Lewis Lancaster and Luis O. Gómez, 361–8. Berkeley: University of California Press, 1977.

Bechert, Heinz. 'Beginnings of Buddhist Historiography: *Mahāvaṃsa* and Political Thinking', in *Religion and Legitimation of Power in Sri Lanka*, edited by Bardwell L. Smith, 1–12. Chambersburg, PA: Anima Books, 1978a.

Bechert, Heinz. 'Remarks on Astrological Sanskrit Literature from Sri Lanka', in *Senarat Paranavitana Commemoration Volume*, edited by Leelananda Prematilleke, Karthigesu Indrapala and J.E. van Lohuizen-de Leeuw, 45–7. Leiden: Brill, 1978b.

Bechert, Heinz. 'Sanskrit-Grammatiken in singhalesischer Überlieferung', *Studien zur Indologie und Iranistik* 13/14 (1987): 5–16.

Bechert, Heinz. 'Buddha-Field and Transfer of Merit in a Theravāda Source', *Indo-Iranian Journal* 35, no. 2 (1992): 95–108.

Bechert, Heinz. 'The *Nikāya*s of Mediaeval Sri Lanka and the Unification of the *Sangha* by Parākramabāhu I', in *Studies on Buddhism in Honour of Professor A.K. Warder*, edited by N.K. Wagle and F. Watanabe, 11–21. Toronto: University of Toronto, Centre for South Asian Studies, 1993.

Bechert, Heinz. 'Remarks on Buddhist Sanskrit Literature in Sri Lanka from the 9th Century until the End of the Dambadeṇiya period', in *Sūryacandrāya: Essays in Honour of Akira Yuyama on the Occasion of His 65th Birthday*, edited by Paul Harrison and Gregory Schopen, 1–8. Swisttal-Odendorf: Indica et Tibetica, 1998.

Bechert, Heinz. *Eine regionale hochsprachliche Tradition in Südasien: Sanskrit-Literatur bei den Buddhistischen Singhalesen*. Vienna: Österreichischen Akademie der Wissenschaften, 2005.

Bell, H.C.P. 'Dimbulá-gala: Its Caves, Ruins, and Inscriptions', *Ceylon Antiquary and Literary Register* 3, no. 1 (1917): 1–12.

Berkemer, Georg. *Little Kingdoms in Kaliṅga: Ideologie, Legitimation und Politik regionaler Eliten*. Stuttgart: Franz Steiner Verlag, 1993.

Berkwitz, Stephen C. 'History and Gratitude in Theravāda Buddhism', *Journal of the American Academy of Religion* 71, no. 3 (2003): 579–604.

Berkwitz, Stephen C. *Buddhist History in the Vernacular: The Power of the Past in Late Medieval Sri Lanka*. Leiden: Brill, 2004.

Berkwitz, Stephen C. 'Reimagining Buddhist Kingship in a Sinhala *Praśasti*', *Journal of the American Oriental Society* 136, no. 2 (2016): 325–41.

Bhattacharyya, Dinesh Chandra. 'New Light on Vaidyaka Literature (from Niścalakara's *Ratnaprabhā*)', *Indian Historical Quarterly* 23, no. 1 (1947): 123–55.

Blackburn, Anne M. 'Looking for the *Vinaya*: Monastic Discipline in the Practical Canons of the Theravāda', *Journal of the International Association of Buddhist Studies* 22, no. 2 (1999a): 281–309.

Blackburn, Anne M. 'Magic in the Monastery: Textual Practice and Monastic Identity in Sri Lanka', *History of Religions* 38, no. 4 (1999b): 354–72.
Blackburn, Anne M. *Buddhist Learning and Textual Practice in Eighteenth-Century Lankan Monastic Culture*. Princeton: Princeton University Press, 2001.
Blackburn, Anne M. *Locations of Buddhism: Colonialism and Modernity in Sri Lanka*. Chicago: University of Chicago Press, 2010.
Blackburn, Anne M. 'Buddhist Connections in the Indian Ocean: Changes in Monastic Mobility, 1000–1500', *Journal of the Economic and Social History of the Orient* 58, no. 3 (2015): 237–66.
Blackburn, Anne M. 'Sīhaḷa Saṅgha and Laṅkā in Later Premodern Southeast Asia', in *Buddhist Dynamics in Premodern and Early Modern Southeast Asia*, edited by D. Christian Lammerts, 307–32. Singapore: ISEAS Publishing, 2015.
Blackburn, Anne M. 'Buddhist Technologies of Statecraft and Millennial Moments', *History and Theory* 56, no. 1 (2017): 71–9.
Blair, Ann M. *Too Much to Know: Managing Scholarly Information before the Modern Age*. New Haven: Yale University Press, 2010.
Blair, Ann. 'Revisiting Renaissance Encyclopaedism', in *Encyclopaedism from Antiquity to the Renaissance*, edited by Jason König and Greg Woolf, 379–97. Cambridge: Cambridge University Press, 2013.
Bloch, Marc. *Feudal Society, Volume 1: The Growth of Ties of Dependence*, translated by L.A. Manyon. London: Routledge and Kegan Paul, 1961.
Bodhi, Bhikkhu, trans. *The Discourse on the All-Embracing Net of Views: The Brahmajāla Sutta and Its Commentaries*. 2nd ed. Kandy: Buddhist Publication Society, 2007.
Bodhi, Bhikkhu, trans. *The Numerical Discourses of the Buddha: A Translation of the Aṅguttara Nikāya*. Somerville, MA: Wisdom Publications, 2012.
Bodhi, Bhikkhu, trans. *The Suttanipāta: An Ancient Collection of the Buddha's Discourses, Together with Its Commentaries: Paramatthajotikā II and Excerpts from the Niddesa*. Somerville, MA: Wisdom Publications, 2017.
Bollée, W.B. 'Die Stellung der Vinaya-ṭīkās in der Pāli-Literatur', *Zeitschrift der Deutschen Morgenländischen Gesellschaft, Suppl.* 1, no. 17 (1969): 824–35.
Bond, George D. *"The Word of the Buddha": The Tipiṭaka and Its Interpretation in Theravada Buddhism*. Colombo: M.D. Gunasena, 1982.
Boucher, Daniel. 'The *Pratītyasamutpādagāthā* and Its Role in the Medieval Cult of the Relics', *Journal of the International Association of Buddhist Studies* 14, no. 1 (1991): 1–27.
Bretfeld, Sven. 'The Later Spread of Buddhism in Tibet', in *The Spread of Buddhism*, edited by Ann Heirman and Stephan Peter Bumbacher, 341–77. Leiden: Brill, 2007.
Brick, David. *Brahmanical Theories of the Gift: A Critical Edition and Annotated Translation of the Dānakāṇḍa of the Kṛtyakalpataru* (Harvard Oriental Series 77). Cambridge, MA: Department of South Asian Studies, Harvard University, 2015.
Bronkhorst, Johannes. 'Sūtras', in *Brill's Encyclopedia of Hinduism, Volume 2: Sacred Texts, Ritual Traditions, Arts, Concepts*, edited by Knut A. Jacobsen, Helene Basu, Angelika Malinar and Vasudha Narayanan, 182–92. Leiden: Brill, 2010.
Bronkhorst, Johannes. *Buddhism in the Shadow of Brahmanism*. Leiden: Brill, 2011.
Bronner, Yigal. 'Singing to God, Educating the People: Appayya Dīkṣita and the Function of *Stotras*', *Journal of the American Oriental Society* 127, no. 2 (2007a): 113–30.
Bronner, Yigal. 'There is No Lotus, It is a Face: Poetics as Grammar in Daṇḍin's Investigation of the Simile', in *The Poetics of Grammar and the Metaphysics of Sound and Sign*, edited by S. La Porta and D. Shulman, 91–108. Leiden: Brill, 2007b.
Bronner, Yigal. *Extreme Poetry: The South Asian Movement of Simultaneous Narration*. New York: Columbia University Press, 2010.
Bronner, Yigal. 'A Question of Priority: Revisiting the Bhāmaha-Daṇḍin Debate', *Journal of Indian Philosophy* 40, no. 1 (2012): 67–118.
Bronner, Yigal. 'Understanding Udbhaṭa: The Invention of Kashmiri Poetics in the Jayāpīḍa Moment', in *Around Abhinavagupta: Aspects of the Intellectual History of Kashmir from the Ninth to the Eleventh Century*, edited by Eli Franco and Isabelle Ratié, 81–148. Berlin: LIT, 2016.
Buddhadatta, A.P. 'The Great Author of Summaries – Contemporary of Buddhaghosa', *University of Ceylon Review* 3, no. 1 (1945): 34–40.
Buddhadatta, A.P. *Pāli Sāhityaya*. 2 vols. Colombo: Maradāna Sāhitya Press, 1956–7.
Buddhadatta, A.P. *Theravādī Bauddhācāryayō*. Ambalamgoḍa: S.K. Candratilaka, 1960.

Buddhadatta, A.P., ed. *Buddhadatta's Manuals, Part 1: Abhidhammāvatāra and Rūpārūpavibhāga, Part 2: Vinayavinicchaya and Uttaravinicchaya*. London: Pali Text Society, 1980.
Burlingame, Eugene Watson. 'The Act of Truth (Saccakiriya): A Hindu Spell and Its Employment as a Psychic Motif in Hindu Fiction', *Journal of the Royal Asiatic Society* 49, no. 3 (1917): 429–67.
Cabezón, José Ignacio, ed. *Scholasticism: Cross-Cultural and Comparative Perspectives*. Albany: State University of New York Press, 1998.
Caldwell, Robert. *A Political and General History of the District of Tinnevelly, in the Presidency of Madras, from the Earliest Period to Its Cession to the English Government in AD 1*801. Madras: E. Keys, Government Press, 1881.
Carbine, Jason A. '*Sāsanasuddhi/Sīmāsammuti*: Comments on a Spatial Basis of the Buddha's Religion', in *How Theravāda is Theravāda? Exploring Buddhist Identities*, edited by Peter Skilling, Jason A. Carbine, Claudio Cicuzza and Santi Pakdeekham, 241–74. Chiang Mai: Silkworm Books, 2012.
Cardona, George. 'Studies in Indian Grammarians, I: The Method of Description Reflected in the Śivasūtras', *Transactions of the American Philosophical Society* 59, no. 1 (1969): 3–48.
Cardona, George. 'Pāṇini's *Kārakas*: Agency, Animation and Identity', *Journal of Indian Philosophy* 2, no. 3/4 (1974): 231–306.
Cardona, George. *Pāṇini: A Survey of Research*. The Hague: Mouton, 1976.
Carrithers, Michael B. '"Sie werden die Herren der Insel sein": Buddhismus in Sri Lanka', in *Der Buddhismus: Geschichte und Gegenwart*, edited by Heinz Bechert and Richard Gombrich, 140–68. Munich: C.H. Beck, 1984.
Chan, Aye. 'The Nature of Land and Labour Endowments to Sasana in Medieval Burmese History: Review of the Theory of "Merit-Path-to-Salvation"', *Southeast Asian Studies* 26, no. 1 (1988): 86–95.
Chandawimala, Rangama. *Heterodox Buddhism: The School of Abhayagiri*. Colombo: Rangama Chandawimala Thero, 2016.
Chatterjee, Heramba Nath. *Comparative Studies in Pāli and Sanskrit Alaṅkāras, Part 1*. Calcutta: Sanskrit Pustak Bhandar, 1960.
Chaudhuri, Ramaprasad and Devaprasad Guha, eds. *Suttasaṃgaha*. Calcutta: Asiatic Society, 1957.
Childers, Robert Cæsar. *A Dictionary of the Pali Language*. London: Trübner and Company, 1875.
Chimpa, Lama and Alaka Chattopadhyaya, trans. *Tāranātha's History of Buddhism in India*, edited by Debiprasad Chattopadhyaya. Delhi: Motilal Banarsidass, 1990.
Chin, Catherine M. *Grammar and Christianity in the Late Roman World*. Philadelphia: University of Pennsylvania Press, 2008.
Choompolpaisal, Phibul. 'Constrictive Constructs: Unravelling the Influence of Weber's Sociology on Theravada Studies since the 1960s', *Contemporary Buddhism* 9, no. 1 (2008): 7–51.
Clark, Chris. 'A Note on the Disappearance of the Dhamma According to the Manorathapūraṇī', *Journal of the Pali Text Society* 33 (2018): 101–14.
Clarke, Shayne. '*Vinaya Mātṛkā* – Mother of Monastic Codes, or Just Another Set of Lists? A Response to Frauwallner's Handling of the Mahāsāṃghika *Vinaya*', *Indo-Iranian Journal* 47, no. 2 (2004): 77–120.
Clooney, Francis X. 'Hindu Views of Religious Others: Implications for Christian Theology', *Theological Studies* 64, no. 2 (2003): 306–33.
Cœdès, G. *Recueil des inscriptions du Siam, Première partie: Inscriptions de Sukhodaya*. Bangkok: Bangkok Times Press, 1924.
Collins, Steven. 'On the Very Idea of the Pali Canon', *Journal of the Pali Text Society* 15 (1990): 89–126.
Collins, Steven. *Nirvana and Other Buddhist Felicities: Utopias of the Pali imaginaire*. Cambridge: Cambridge University Press, 1998.
Collins, Steven. 'What is Literature in Pali?', in *Literary Cultures in History: Reconstructions from South Asia*, edited by Sheldon Pollock, 649–88. Berkeley: University of California Press, 2003.
Coomāra Swāmy, Mutu, trans. *The Daṭhāvansa; or, The History of the Tooth-Relic of Gotama Buddha*. London: Trübner, 1874.
Copland, Ian, Ian Mabbett, Asim Roy, Kate Brittlebank and Adam Bowles. *A History of State and Religion in India*. London: Routledge, 2012.
Cousins, L.S. 'On the Vibhajjavādins: The Mahiṃsāsaka, Dhammaguttaka, Kassapiya and Tambapaṇṇiya Branches of the Ancient Theriyas', *Buddhist Studies Review* 18, no. 2 (2001): 131–82.
Cousins, L.S. 'Abhidhamma Studies I: Jotipāla and the *Abhidhamma Anuṭīkā*', *Thai International Journal of Buddhist Studies* 2 (2011): 1–36.
Cousins, L.S. 'The Teachings of the Abhayagiri School', in *How Theravāda is Theravāda? Exploring Buddhist Identities*, edited by Peter Skilling, Jason A. Carbine, Claudio Cicuzza and Santi Pakdeekham, 67–127. Chiang Mai: Silkworm Books, 2012.

Cousins, L.S. 'Abhidhamma Studies II: Sanskrit *Abhidharma* Literature of the Mahāvihāravāsins', *Thai International Journal of Buddhist Studies* 4 (2013): 1–62.

Cousins, Lance S. 'Sanskrit Abhidharma Literature of the Mahāvihāravāsins', in *Text, History, and Philosophy: Abhidharma across Buddhist Scholastic Traditions*, edited by Bart Dessein and Weijen Teng, 169–222. Leiden: Brill, 2016.

Cox, Whitney. 'Saffron in the Rasam', in *South Asian Texts in History: Critical Engagements with Sheldon Pollock*, edited by Yigal Bronner, Whitney Cox and Lawrence McCrea, 177–201. Ann Arbor, MI: Association for Asian Studies, 2011.

Cox, Whitney. 'Bhoja's Alternate Universe', *Journal of the Royal Asiatic Society* 22, no. 1 (2012): 57–72.

Cox, Whitney. *Politics, Kingship, and Poetry in Medieval South India: Moonset on Sunrise Mountain*. Cambridge: Cambridge University Press, 2016.

Cox, Whitney. *Modes of Philology in Medieval South India*. Leiden: Brill, 2017.

Crosby, Kate. 'History versus Modern Myth: The Abhayagirivihāra, the *Vimuttimagga* and *Yogāvacara* Meditation', *Journal of Indian Philosophy* 27, no. 6 (1999): 503–50.

Crosby, Kate. 'Tantric Theravāda: A Bibliographic Essay on the Writings of François Bizot and Others on the Yogāvacara Tradition', *Contemporary Buddhism* 1, no. 2 (2000): 141–98.

Crosby, Kate. 'The Origin of Pāli as a Language Name in Medieval Theravāda Literature', *Journal of the Centre for Buddhist Studies, Sri Lanka* 2 (2004): 70–116.

Crosby, Kate. 'Sāriputta's Three Works on the *Samantapāsādikā*', *Journal of the Pali Text Society* 28 (2006): 49–59.

Crosby, Kate. 'Changing the Landscape of Theravada Studies', *Contemporary Buddhism* 9, no. 1 (2008a): 1–6.

Crosby, Kate. 'Kamma, Social Collapse or Geophysics? Interpretations of Suffering among Sri Lankan Buddhists in the Immediate Aftermath of the 2004 Asian Tsunami', *Contemporary Buddhism* 9, no. 1 (2008b): 53–76.

Crosby, Kate. *Traditional Theravada Meditation and Its Modern-Era Suppression*. Hong Kong: Buddha Dharma Centre of Hong Kong, 2013.

Crosby, Kate. *Theravada Buddhism: Continuity, Diversity, and Identity*. Chichester: Wiley-Blackwell, 2014.

Crosby, Kate and Andrew Skilton. 'A Note on the Date of Mahākassapa, Author of the Mohavicchedanī', *Bulletin d'études indiennes* 17/18 (1999): 173–9.

Cuneo, Daniele. 'Unfuzzying the Fuzzy: The Distinction between *Rasa*s and *Bhāva*s in Bharata and Abhinavagupta', in *Puṣpikā: Tracing Ancient India, through Texts and Traditions: Contributions to Current Research in Indology, Volume 1*, edited by Nina Mirnig, Péter-Dániel Szántó and Michael Williams, 49–75. Oxford: Oxbow Books, 2013.

Dasgupta, Nalini Nath. 'The Bengali Commentators on the Amara-Koṣa', *Indian Culture* 2 (1935): 261–9.

Davidson, Ronald M. *Indian Esoteric Buddhism: A Social History of the Tantric Movement*. New York: Columbia University Press, 2002.

Davidson, Ronald M. *Tibetan Renaissance: Tantric Buddhism in the Rebirth of Tibetan Culture*. New York: Columbia University Press, 2005.

Davidson, Ronald M. 'Studies in Dhāraṇī Literature I: Revisiting the Meaning of the Term *Dhāraṇī*', *Journal of Indian Philosophy* 37, no. 2 (2009): 97–147.

Davis, Christopher Edward. 'Early Buddhist Monasteries in Sri Lanka: A Landscape Approach'. PhD thesis, Durham University, 2013.

Davis, Christopher Edward. 'Patterns of Patronage: A Reanalysis of the Contents and Distribution of Inscriptions in Sri Lanka', in *Buddha Rashmi: Vesak Volume: Essays in Buddhism and Buddhist Monastic Archaeology*, edited by Prishanta Gunawardhana, Robin Coningham and Krishnan Nampoothiri, 53–66. Colombo: Sri Lanka Central Cultural Fund, Ministry of Education, 2017.

Davis, Richard H. 'Indian Art Objects as Loot', *Journal of Asian Studies* 52, no. 1 (1993): 22–48.

De Casparis, J.G. 'New Evidence on Cultural Relations between Java and Ceylon in Ancient Times', *Artibus Asiae* 24, no. 3/4 (1961): 241–8.

Deeg, Max. 'Abhayagiri-vihāra – Geschichte und "Geschichte" eines ceylonesischen Klosters', in *Mauss, Buddhismus, Devianz: Festschrift für Heinz Mürmel zum 65. Geburtstag*, edited by Thomas Hase, Johannes Graul, Katharina Neef and Judith Zimmermann, 135–51. Marburg: Diagonal-Verlag, 2009.

Deeg, Max. 'Sthavira, Thera and "*Sthaviravāda" in Chinese Buddhist Sources', in *How Theravāda is Theravāda? Exploring Buddhist Identities*, edited by Peter Skilling, Jason A. Carbine, Claudio Cicuzza and Santi Pakdeekham, 129–63. Chiang Mai: Silkworm Books, 2012.

Deegalle, Mahinda. 'Buddhist Preaching and Sinhala Religious Rhetoric: Medieval Buddhist Methods to Popularize Theravāda', *Numen* 44, no. 2 (1997): 180–210.

Deegalle, Mahinda. *Popularizing Buddhism: Preaching as Performance in Sri Lanka*. Albany: State University of New York Press, 2006.

DeLanda, Manuel. 'Deleuzian Social Ontology and Assemblage Theory', in *Deleuze and the Social*, edited by Martin Fuglsang and Bent Meier Sørensen, 250–66. Edinburgh: Edinburgh University Press, 2006.

De La Vallée Poussin, L. *Bouddhisme, études et matériaux: Théorie des douze causes*. Ghent: Librairie scientifique E. Van Goethem, 1913.

Deleuze, Gilles. 'Desert Islands', in *Desert Islands and Other Texts, 1953–1974*, edited by David Lapoujade and translated by Michael Taormina, 9–14. Los Angeles: Semiotext(e), 2004.

Deleuze, Gilles and Félix Guattari. *What is Philosophy?*, translated by Hugh Tomlinson and Graham Burchell. New York: Columbia University Press, 1994.

Deokar, Mahesh A. *Technical Terms and Techniques of the Pali and the Sanskrit Grammars*. Varanasi: Central Institute of Higher Tibetan Studies, 2008.

Deokar, Mahesh A. 'The *Cāndravyākaraṇapañjikā*: An Important Tool for the Study of the *Moggallānavuttivivaraṇapañcikā*: A Case Study Based on a Cambridge Fragment of the *Cāndravyākaraṇapañjikā* with Special Reference to CV 2.2.1 and MV 3.11', in *Indic Manuscript Cultures through the Ages: Material, Textual, and Historical Investigations*, edited by Vincenzo Vergiani, Daniele Cuneo and Camillo Alessio Formigatti, 695–726. Berlin: De Gruyter, 2017.

Deshpande, Madhav M. 'Who Inspired Pāṇini? Reconstructing the Hindu and Buddhist Counter-Claims', *Journal of the American Oriental Society* 117, no. 3 (1997): 444–65.

De Silva, Chandra Richard. *Sri Lanka: A History*. 2nd ed. Delhi: Vikas Publishing House, 1997.

De Silva, K.M. *A History of Sri Lanka*. Delhi: Oxford University Press, 1981.

De Simini, Florinda. *Of Gods and Books: Ritual and Knowledge Transmission in the Manuscript Cultures of Premodern India*. Berlin: De Gruyter, 2016.

Dessein, Bart. 'Lists as Dynamic Devices in Early Buddhist Doctrine and Textual Tradition', *Antiquorum Philosophia* 7 (2013): 29–48.

Dhammapala, Gatare. *A Comparative Study of Sinhala Literature: Polonnaru Period*. Colombo: Godage International Publishers, 2003.

Dhammaratana, Bhikkhu T. 'La littérature bouddhique des *Ṭīkās* et la *Vimativinodanī*', in *Dharmadūta: Mélanges offerts au Vénérable Thích Huyên-Vi à l'occasion de son soixante-dixième anniversaire*, edited by Bhikkhu T. Dhammaratana and Bhikkhu Pāsādika, 57–82. Paris: Éditions You-Feng, 1997.

Dhammavisuddhi, Yatadolawatte. 'The Buddhist Sangha in Ceylon (circa 1200–1400 AD)'. PhD thesis, University of London, 1970.

Dimitrov, Dragomir. *The Bhaikṣukī Manuscript of the Candrālaṃkāra: Study, Script Tables, and Facsimile Edition* (Harvard Oriental Series 72). Cambridge, MA: Department of Sanskrit and Indian Studies, Harvard University, 2010.

Dimitrov, Dragomir. *The Legacy of the Jewel Mind: On the Sanskrit, Pali, and Sinhalese Works by Ratnamati: A Philological Chronicle (Phullalocanavaṃsa)*. Naples: Università degli studi di Napoli "L'Orientale", Dipartimento Asia Africa e Mediterraneo, 2016.

Dimitrov, Dragomir. 'Trials and Tribulations in the Study of the Cult of Maitreya in Theravāda Buddhism', *Journal of Buddhist Studies* 24 (2017): 151–82.

Drewes, David. 'Revisiting the Phrase "*Sa Pṛthivīpradeśaś Caityabhūto Bhavet*" and the Mahāyāna Cult of the Book', *Indo-Iranian Journal* 50, no. 2 (2007): 101–43.

Dumézil, Georges. *L'idéologie tripartie des Indo-Européens*. Brussels: Collection Latomus, 1958.

Dumont, Louis. *Homo Hierarchicus: The Caste System and Its Implications*, translated by Mark Sainsbury, Louis Dumont and Basia Gulati. Rev. ed. Delhi: Oxford University Press, 1999.

Dundas, Paul. 'Jain Attitudes towards the Sanskrit Language', in *Ideology and Status of Sanskrit: Contributions to the History of the Sanskrit Language*, edited by Jan E.M. Houben, 137–56. Leiden: Brill, 1996.

Durkheim, Émile. *The Elementary Forms of the Religious Life*, translated by Joseph Ward Swain. London: George Allen and Unwin, 1964.

Duroiselle, Charles, ed. and trans. *Jinacarita or "The Career of the Conqueror"*. Rangoon: British Burma Press, 1906.

Eltschinger, Vincent. 'From Commentary to Philosophy, or *Lectio* and *Disputatio* in Indian Buddhist Commentarial Literature', in *L'espace du sens: Approches de la philologie indienne = The Space of Meaning: Approaches to Indian Philology*, edited by Silvia D'Intino and Sheldon Pollock, 271–303. Paris: De Boccard, 2018.

Endo, Toshiichi. *Studies in Pāli Commentarial Literature: Sources, Controversies and Insights*. Hong Kong: Centre of Buddhist Studies, University of Hong Kong, 2013.

Faure, Bernard. *The Rhetoric of Immediacy: A Cultural Critique of Chan/Zen Buddhism*. Princeton: Princeton University Press, 1991.

Fiordalis, David V. 'Miracles and Superhuman Powers in South Asian Buddhist Literature'. PhD thesis, University of Michigan, 2008.

Fisher, Elaine M. *Hindu Pluralism: Religion and the Public Sphere in Early Modern South India*. Oakland: University of California Press, 2017.

Franceschini, Marco, trans. *Buddhaghoṣa, Padyacūḍāmaṇi: Il diadema dei versi*. Milan: Edizioni Ariele, 2010.

Franceschini, Marco. 'Buddhaghoṣa's *Padyacūḍāmaṇi*: A Medieval Mahākāvya on the Life of the Buddha', in *Stylistic Devices in Indian Literature and Arts*, edited by Giuliano Boccali and Elena Mucciarelli, 37–45. Milan: Cisalpino, Istituto Editoriale Universitario, 2013.

Franke, R. Otto. *Geschichte und Kritik der einheimischen Pāli-Grammatik und -Lexicographie*. Strasbourg: Trübner, 1902.

Franke, R. Otto. 'Moggallāna's Saddalakkhaṇa und das Cāndra-Vyākaraṇa', *Journal of the Pali Text Society* (1902–3a): 70–95.

Franke, R. Otto. 'Rūpasiddhi, Moggallāna, Mahāvutti, Vutti', *Journal of the Pali Text Society* (1902–3b): 113–25.

Frasch, Tilman. *Pagan: Stadt und Staat*. Stuttgart: Franz Steiner Verlag, 1996.

Frasch, Tilman. 'A Buddhist Network in the Bay of Bengal: Relations between Bodhgayā, Burma and Sri Lanka, c. 300–1300', in *From the Mediterranean to the China Sea: Miscellaneous Notes*, edited by Claude Guillot, Denys Lombard and Roderich Ptak, with the assistance of Richard Teschke, 69–92. Wiesbaden: Harrassowitz, 1998.

Frasch, Tilman. 'The Buddhist Connection: Sinhalese-Burmese Intercourse in the Middle Ages', in *Explorations in the History of South Asia: Essays in Honour of Dietmar Rothermund*, edited by Georg Berkemer, Tilman Frasch, Hermann Kulke and Jürgen Lütt, 85–97. Delhi: Manohar, 2001.

Frasch, Tilman. 'The Theravāda Buddhist Ecumene in the Fifteenth Century: Intellectual Foundations and Material Representations', in *Buddhism across Asia: Networks of Material, Intellectual and Cultural Exchange, Volume 1*, edited by Tansen Sen, 347–67. Singapore: ISEAS Publishing, 2014.

Frasch, Tilman. 'A Pāli Cosmopolis? Sri Lanka and the Theravāda Buddhist Ecumene, c. 500–1500', in *Sri Lanka at the Crossroads of History*, edited by Zoltán Biedermann and Alan Strathern, 66–76. London: UCL Press, 2017.

Frasch, Tilman. 'Kontakte, Konzile, Kontroversen: Begegnungen in der Theravada-Kosmopolis, ca. 1000–1300', in *Religionsbegegnung in der asiatischen Religionsgeschichte: Kritische Reflexionen über ein etabliertes Konzept*, edited by Max Deeg, Oliver Freiberger and Christoph Kleine, 129–52. Göttingen: Vandenhoeck und Ruprecht, 2019.

Frauwallner, Erich. *Studies in Abhidharma Literature and the Origins of Buddhist Philosophical Systems*, translated by Sophie Francis Kidd. Albany: State University of New York Press, 1995.

Gair, James W. and W.S. Karunatillake. *The Sidat Saṅgarā: Text, Translation and Glossary* (American Oriental Series 95). New Haven: American Oriental Society, 2013.

Ganeri, Jonardon. 'Sanskrit Philosophical Commentary', *Journal of the Indian Council of Philosophical Research* 25, no. 1 (2010): 107–27.

Geiger, Wilhelm. 'The Trustworthiness of the Mahāvaṃsa', *Indian Historical Quarterly* 6, no. 2 (1930): 205–28.

Geiger, Wilhelm. *Pāli Literature and Language*, translated by Batakrishna Ghosh. Calcutta: University of Calcutta, 1943.

Geiger, Wilhelm and C. Mabel Rickmers, trans. *Cūḷavaṃsa: Being the More Recent Part of the Mahāvaṃsa*. Delhi: Asian Educational Services, 1998.

Gethin, Rupert. 'The *Mātikās*: Memorization, Mindfulness, and the List', in *In the Mirror of Memory: Reflections on Mindfulness and Remembrance in Indian and Tibetan Buddhism*, edited by Janet Gyatso, 149–72. Albany: State University of New York Press, 1992.

Gethin, Rupert. *The Foundations of Buddhism*. Oxford: Oxford University Press, 1998.

Gethin, R.M.L. *The Buddhist Path to Awakening*. Oxford: Oneworld Publications, 2001.

Gethin, Rupert. 'Was Buddhaghosa a Theravādin? Buddhist Identity in the Pali Commentaries and Chronicles', in *How Theravāda is Theravāda? Exploring Buddhist Identities*, edited by Peter Skilling, Jason A. Carbine, Claudio Cicuzza and Santi Pakdeekham, 1–63. Chiang Mai: Silkworm Books, 2012.

Gethin, Rupert. 'Body, Mind and Sleepiness: On the Abhidharma Understanding of *Styāna* and *Middha*', *Journal of the International College for Postgraduate Buddhist Studies* 21 (2017): 123–61.
Gillet, Valérie. 'The Dark Period: Myth or Reality?', *Indian Economic and Social History Review* 51, no. 3 (2014): 283–302.
Godakumbura, C.E. *Sinhalese Literature*. Colombo: Colombo Apothecaries' Company, 1955.
Gombrich, Richard F. *Theravāda Buddhism: A Social History from Ancient Benares to Modern Colombo*. London: Routledge and Kegan Paul, 1988.
Gornall, A.M. 'Some Remarks on Buddhaghosa's Use of Sanskrit Grammar: Possible Hints of an Unknown Pāṇinian Commentary in Buddhaghosa's Grammatical Arguments', *Journal of the Oxford Centre for Buddhist Studies* 1 (2011): 89–107.
Gornall, Alastair Malcolm. 'Buddhism and Grammar: The Scholarly Cultivation of Pāli in Medieval Laṅkā'. PhD thesis, University of Cambridge, 2013.
Gornall, Alastair. 'How Many Sounds Are in Pāli? Schism, Identity and Ritual in the Theravāda *Saṅgha*', *Journal of Indian Philosophy* 42, no. 5 (2014a): 511–50.
Gornall, Alastair. '*Kāraka*s in *Cāndra* Grammar: An Interpretation from the Pāli Buddhist *Śāstra*s', in *Puṣpikā: Tracing Ancient India, through Texts and Traditions: Contributions to Current Research in Indology, Volume 2*, edited by Giovanni Ciotti, Alastair Gornall and Paolo Visigalli, 87–113. Oxford: Oxbow Books, 2014b.
Gornall, Alastair. 'Ratnamati et ses œuvres', *Bulletin de l'École française d'Extrême-Orient* 103 (2017): 475–91.
Gornall, Alastair and Amal Gunasena, trans. 'A History of the Pali Grammatical Tradition of South and Southeast Asia by Vaskaḍuvē Subhūti (1876), Part 1', *Journal of the Pali Text Society* 33 (2018): 1–53.
Gornall, Alastair and Justin Henry. 'Beautifully Moral: Cosmopolitan Issues in Medieval Pāli Literary Theory', in *Sri Lanka at the Crossroads of History*, edited by Zoltán Biedermann and Alan Strathern, 77–93. London: UCL Press, 2017.
Gornall, Alastair and Aleix Ruiz-Falqués. 'Scholars of Premodern Pali Buddhism', in *Brill's Encyclopedia of Buddhism, Volume 2: Lives*, edited by Richard Bowring, Vincent Eltschinger and Michael Radich, 420–36. Leiden: Brill, 2019.
Graeber, David and Marshall Sahlins. *On Kings*. Chicago: Hau Books, 2017.
Granoff, Phyllis. 'The Ambiguity of Miracles: Buddhist Understandings of Supernatural Power', *East and West* 46, no. 1/2 (1996): 79–96.
Gray, James, ed. and trans. *Jinālaṅkāra; or "Embellishments of Buddha" by Buddharakkhita*. London: Luzac and Company, 1894.
Green, Richard Firth. *Poets and Princepleasers: Literature and the English Court in the Late Middle Ages*. Toronto: University of Toronto Press, 1980.
Griswold, A.B. and Prasert na Nagara. 'The Epigraphy of Mahādharmarājā I of Sukhodaya: Epigraphic and Historical Studies, No. 11, Part II', *Journal of the Siam Society* 61, no. 2 (1973): 91–128.
Gunasingam, S. *Two Inscriptions of Cola Ilankesvara Deva* (Trincomalee Inscriptions Series 1). Peradeniya: University of Sri Lanka, 1974.
Gunawardana, R.A.L.H. 'Buddhist Nikāyas in Mediaeval Ceylon', *Ceylon Journal of Historical and Social Studies* 9 (1966): 55–66.
Gunawardana, R.A.L.H. 'Ceylon and Malaysia: A Study of Professor S. Paranavitana's Research on the Relations between the Two Regions', *University of Ceylon Review* 25, no. 1/2 (1967): 1–64.
Gunawardana, R.A.L.H. 'Irrigation and Hydraulic Society in Early Medieval Ceylon', *Past and Present* 53 (1971): 3–27.
Gunawardana, R.A.L.H. 'The Kinsmen of the Buddha: Myth as Political Charter in the Ancient and Early Medieval Kingdoms of Sri Lanka', *Sri Lanka Journal of the Humanities* 2, no. 1 (1976): 53–62.
Gunawardana, R.A.L.H. *Robe and Plough: Monasticism and Economic Interest in Early Medieval Sri Lanka*. Tucson: University of Arizona Press, 1979.
Gunawardana, R.A.L.H. 'Subtile Silks of Ferreous Firmness: Buddhist Nuns in Ancient and Early Medieval Sri Lanka and Their Role in the Propagation of Buddhism', *Sri Lanka Journal of the Humanities* 14, no. 1/2 (1988): 1–59.
Günther, Herbert. 'Der Mahānāgakula-sandeśa', *Wiener Zeitschrift für die Kunde des Morgenlandes* 49 (1942): 257–81.
Guruge, Ananda W.P. 'Sri Lankan Attitude to the *Rāmāyaṇa*: A Historical Analysis', *Indologica Taurinensia* 19/20 (1993–4): 131–46.
Haberman, David L. *Acting as a Way of Salvation: A Study of Rāgānugā Bhakti Sādhana*. Delhi: Motilal Banarsidass, 2001.

Hallisey, Charles. 'Devotion in the Buddhist Literature of Medieval Sri Lanka'. PhD thesis, University of Chicago, 1988.

Hallisey, Charles. 'Councils as Ideas and Events in the Theravāda', in *The Buddhist Forum, Volume 2: Seminar Papers 1988–90*, edited by Tadeusz Skorupski, 133–48. London: School of Oriental and African Studies, 1991.

Hallisey, Charles. 'Roads Taken and Not Taken in the Study of Theravāda Buddhism', in *Curators of the Buddha: The Study of Buddhism under Colonialism*, edited by Donald S. Lopez Jr., 31–61. Chicago: University of Chicago Press, 1995.

Hallisey, Charles. 'Works and Persons in Sinhala Literary Culture', in *Literary Cultures in History: Reconstructions from South Asia*, edited by Sheldon Pollock, 689–746. Berkeley: University of California Press, 2003.

Hallisey, Charles. 'Auspicious Things', in *Buddhism in Practice: Abridged Edition*, edited by Donald S. Lopez Jr., 296–310. Princeton: Princeton University Press, 2007.

Hallisey, Charles. 'Learning from *Samāsokti* in Sri Lanka', *Rivista degli Studi Orientali* 90, no. 1–4 (2017): 127–44.

Hanneder, J. 'On "The Death of Sanskrit"', *Indo-Iranian Journal* 45, no. 4 (2002): 293–310.

Hazra, Kanai Lal. *History of Theravāda Buddhism in South-East Asia: With Special Reference to India and Ceylon*. Delhi: Munshiram Manoharlal, 1982.

Heim, Maria. *Theories of the Gift in South Asia: Hindu, Buddhist, and Jain Reflections on Dāna*. New York: Routledge, 2004.

Heim, Maria. *The Forerunner of All Things: Buddhaghosa on Mind, Intention, and Agency*. New York: Oxford University Press, 2014.

Heim, Maria. *Voice of the Buddha: Buddhaghosa on the Immeasurable Words*. New York: Oxford University Press, 2018.

Henry, Justin Wesley. 'Distant Shores of Dharma: Historical Imagination in Sri Lanka from the Late Medieval Period'. PhD thesis, University of Chicago, 2017.

Herath, Dharmaratna. *The Tooth Relic and the Crown*. Colombo: Gunaratne Offset, 1994.

Hiltebeitel, Alf. 'Aśvaghoṣa's *Buddhacarita*: The First Known Close and Critical Reading of the Brahmanical Sanskrit Epics', *Journal of Indian Philosophy* 34, no. 3 (2006): 229–86.

Hocart, A.M. *Caste: A Comparative Study*. New York: Russell and Russell, 1968.

Hocart, A.M. *Kings and Councillors: An Essay in the Comparative Anatomy of Human Society*. Chicago: University of Chicago Press, 1970.

Hocart, A.M. *The Temple of the Tooth in Kandy* (Memoirs of the Archaeological Survey of Ceylon 4). Delhi: Asian Educational Services, 1996.

Holt, John C. 'Pilgrimage and the Structure of Sinhalese Buddhism', *Journal of the International Association of Buddhist Studies* 5, no. 2 (1982): 23–40.

Holt, John Clifford. *Buddha in the Crown: Avalokiteśvara in the Buddhist Traditions of Sri Lanka*. New York: Oxford University Press, 1991.

Ilangasinha, H.B.M. *Buddhism in Medieval Sri Lanka*. Delhi: Sri Satguru Publications, 1992.

Inden, Ronald. 'Hierarchies of Kings in Early Medieval India', *Contributions to Indian Sociology* 15, no. 1/2 (1981): 99–125.

Inden, Ronald. *Imagining India*. Bloomington: Indiana University Press, 2000.

Indrapala, K. 'Book Review – *Ceylon and Malaysia*, by S. Paranavitana (1966)', *Journal of the Ceylon Branch of the Royal Asiatic Society* 11 (1967): 101–6.

Indrapala, K. 'The Origin of the Tamil Vanni Chieftaincies of Ceylon', *Ceylon Journal of the Humanities* 1, no. 2 (1970): 111–40.

Indrapala, K. 'An Inscription of the Time of Rajaraja Cola I from Padaviya', *Epigraphia Tamilica* 1, no. 1 (1971a): 32–6.

Indrapala, K. 'South Indian Mercantile Communities in Ceylon, circa 950–1250', *Ceylon Journal of Historical and Social Studies* 1, no. 2 (1971b): 101–13.

Indrapala, K., ed. *The Collapse of the Rajarata Civilization in Ceylon and the Drift to the South-West: A Symposium*. Peradeniya: University of Ceylon, 1971c.

Indrapala, K. 'An Inscription of the Tenth Year of Cōḷa Laṅkeśvara Deva from Kantalai, Sri Lanka', in *Senarat Paranavitana Commemoration Volume*, edited by Leelananda Prematilleke, Karthigesu Indrapala and J.E. van Lohuizen-de Leeuw, 81–97. Leiden: Brill, 1978.

Ingalls, Daniel H.H., trans. *An Anthology of Sanskrit Court Poetry: Vidyākara's Subhāṣitaratnakoṣa* (Harvard Oriental Series 44). Cambridge, MA: Harvard University Press, 1965.

Ingalls, Daniel H.H., Jeffrey Moussaieff Masson and M.V. Patwardhan, trans. *The Dhvanyāloka of Ānandavardhana, with the Locana of Abhinavagupta* (Harvard Oriental Series 49). Cambridge, MA: Harvard University Press, 1990.

Irvine, Martin. *The Making of Textual Culture: "Grammatica" and Literary Theory, 350–1100*. Cambridge: Cambridge University Press, 1994.

Jaini, Padmanabh S., ed. *Subodhālaṅkāra: Porāṇa-Ṭīkā (Mahāsāmi-Ṭīkā), by Saṅgharakkhita Mahāsāmi; Abhinava-Ṭīkā (Nissaya) (anonymous)*. Oxford: Pali Text Society, 2000.

Jaini, Padmanabh S. 'The Vaibhāṣika Theory of Words and Meanings', in *Collected Papers on Buddhist Studies*, 201–18. Delhi: Motilal Banarsidass, 2001.

Jayatilaka, D.B., ed. *Siṃhala Sāhitya Lipi*. Maharagama: Saman Press, 1956.

Jayawardhana, Somapala. *Handbook of Pali Literature*. Colombo: Karunaratne and Sons, 1994.

Jayawickrama, N.A., trans. *The Inception of Discipline and the Vinaya Nidāna: Being a Translation and Edition of the Bāhiranidāna of Buddhaghosa's Samantapāsādikā, the Vinaya Commentary*. London: Pali Text Society, 1986.

Jespersen, Otto. *A Modern English Grammar on Historical Principles, Part 3: Syntax, Volume 2*. London: George Allen and Unwin, 1965.

Joshi, S.D. and J.A.F. Roodbergen, eds. and trans. *Patañjali's Vyākaraṇa-Mahābhāṣya: Kārakāhnika (P.1.4.23–1.4.55)*. Poona: University of Poona, 1975.

Kahrs, E.G. 'Exploring the *Saddanīti*', *Journal of the Pali Text Society* 17 (1992): 1–212.

Kahrs, Eivind. *Indian Semantic Analysis: The Nirvacana Tradition*. Cambridge: Cambridge University Press, 1998.

Kapferer, Bruce. *The Feast of the Sorcerer: Practices of Consciousness and Power*. Chicago: University of Chicago Press, 1997.

Karunadasa, Y. *Buddhist Analysis of Matter*. Colombo: Department of Cultural Affairs, 1967.

Karunadasa, Y. *The Dhamma Theory: Philosophical Cornerstone of the Abhidhamma*. Kandy: Buddhist Publication Society, 1996.

Karunadasa, Y. *The Theravāda Abhidhamma: Its Inquiry into the Nature of Conditioned Reality*. Hong Kong: Centre of Buddhist Studies, University of Hong Kong, 2010.

Katre, Sumitra M., ed. and trans. *Aṣṭādhyāyī of Pāṇini, in Roman Transliteration by Sumitra M. Katre*. Austin: University of Texas Press, 1987.

Keyes, Charles F. 'Merit-Transference in the Kammic Theory of Popular Theravāda Buddhism', in *Karma: An Anthropological Inquiry*, edited by Charles F. Keyes and E. Valentine Daniel, 261–86. Berkeley: University of California Press, 1983.

Keyes, Charles F. *The Golden Peninsula: Culture and Adaptation in Mainland Southeast Asia*. Honolulu: University of Hawai'i Press, 1995.

Khantipālo, Bhikkhu, ed. and trans. *Bag of Bones: A Miscellany on the Body*. Kandy: Buddhist Publication Society, 1980.

Kieffer-Pülz, Petra. *Die Sīmā: Vorschriften zur Regelung der buddhistischen Gemeindegrenze in älteren buddhistischen Texten* (Monographien zur indischen Archäologie, Kunst und Philologie 8). Berlin: Dietrich Reimer, 1992.

Kieffer-Pülz, Petra. 'Ceremonial Boundaries in the Buddhist Monastic Tradition in Sri Lanka', in *Wilhelm Geiger and the Study of the History and Culture of Sri Lanka*, edited by Ulrich Everding and Asanga Tilakaratne, 43–90. Colombo: Goethe Institute and Postgraduate Institute of Pali and Buddhist Studies, 1999a.

Kieffer-Pülz, Petra. 'Vācissara's *Sīmālaṅkārasaṅgaha* and the Disagreement between Coḷiyas and Sīhaḷas', *Buddhist Studies (Bukkyō Kenkyū)* 28 (1999b): 11–18.

Kieffer-Pülz, Petra. 'Die Klassifizierung des Alkoholverbots in der buddhistischen Rechtsliteratur der Theravādin', in *Im Dickicht der Gebote: Studien zur Dialektik von Norm und Praxis in der Buddhismusgeschichte Asiens*, edited by Peter Schalk, Max Deeg, Oliver Freiberger, Christoph Kleine and Astrid van Nahl, 153–223. Uppsala: Uppsala Universitet, 2005.

Kieffer-Pülz, Petra. *Verlorene Gaṇṭhipadas zum buddhistischen Ordensrecht: Untersuchungen zu den in der Vajirabuddhiṭīkā zitierten Kommentaren Dhammasiris und Vajirabuddhis*, Teil 1 (Veröffentlichungen der Indologischen Kommission 1). Wiesbaden: Harrassowitz Verlag, 2013.

Kieffer-Pülz, Petra. 'Book Review – *The Ornament of Lay Followers: Ānanda's Upāsakajanālaṅkāra*, translated by Giulio Agostini (2015)', *Bulletin of the School of Oriental and African Studies* 78, no. 3 (2015a): 632–3.

Kieffer-Pülz, Petra. 'Quotatives Indicating Quotations in Pāli Commentarial Literature, I *Iti/ti* and Quotatives with *Vuttaṃ*', *Journal of Indian Philosophy* 43, no. 4/5 (2015b): 427–52.

Kieffer-Pülz, Petra. 'Vinaya Commentarial Literature in Pali', in *Brill's Encyclopedia of Buddhism, Volume 1: Literature and Languages*, edited by Jonathan A. Silk, Oskar von Hinüber and Vincent Eltschinger, 430–41. Leiden: Brill, 2015c.

Kieffer-Pülz, Petra. 'Translocal Debates and Legal Hermeneutics: Early Pāli Vinaya Texts in the Adjudication of Sīmā Procedures, c. 1200–1900 CE', *Buddhism, Law and Society* 2 (2016–17): 103–58.

Kieffer-Pülz, Petra. 'Book Review – *Aṅguttaranikāya-Purāṇaṭīkā Catutthā Līnatthapakāsinī*, edited by Primoz Pecenko (2012)', *Orientalistische Literaturzeitung* 112, no. 4/5 (2017a): 422–6.

Kieffer-Pülz, Petra. 'Saṅgharakkhita Mahāsāmi's Oeuvre Based on Intertextual Links in His Texts', *Annual Report of the International Research Institute for Advanced Buddhology at Soka University* 20 (2017b): 23–55.

Kieffer-Pülz, Petra. 'The Relation of the *Saccasaṅkhepaṭīkā* Called *Sāratthasālinī* to the *Vinayavinicchayaṭīkā* Called *Vinayasāratthasandīpanī*', *Buddhist Studies Review* 35, no. 1/2 (2018): 189–223.

Kieffer-Pülz, Petra. 'A Manual of the Adornment of the Monastic Boundary: Vācissara's *Sīmālaṅkārasaṅgaha*; Edition and Annotated Translation', in *Sīmās: Foundations of Buddhist Religion*, edited by Jason A. Carbine and Erik Davis, 417–573. Honolulu: University of Hawai'i Press, 2020.

Kieffer-Pülz, Petra and Anne Peters. 'The Vinayasaṅkhepatthakathā: An Unknown Vinaya Handbook?', in *Buddhist and Indian Studies in Honour of Professor Sodo Mori*, 117–27. Hamamatsu: Kokusai Bukkyōto Kyōkai, 2002.

Kielhorn, F. 'The Mungir Copper-Plate Grant of Devapaladeva', *Indian Antiquary* 21 (1892): 253–8.

Kiparsky, P. and J.F. Staal. 'Syntactic and Semantic Relations in Pāṇini', *Foundations of Language* 5, no. 1 (1969): 83–117.

Kiribamune, Sirima. 'Some Reflections on Professor Paranavitana's Contribution to History', *Ceylon Journal of the Humanities* 1, no. 1 (1970): 76–92.

Kiribamune, Sirima. 'The Royal Consecration in Medieval Sri Lanka: The Problem of Vikramabāhu I and Gajabāhu II', *Sri Lanka Journal of South Asian Studies* 1, no. 1 (1976): 12–32.

Kitsudo, Masahiro. *Pāli Texts Printed in Sri Lanka in Sinhalese Characters with Supplementary Information on Related Texts*. Bristol: Pali Text Society, 2015.

Kloetzli, Randy. *Buddhist Cosmology: From Single World System to Pure Land: Science and Theology in the Images of Motion and Light*. Delhi: Motilal Banarsidass, 1983.

Krishan, Y. 'The Origin and Development of the Bodhisattva Doctrine', *East and West* 34, no. 1–3 (1984): 199–232.

Kulasuriya, Ananda S. 'Regional Independence and Élite Change in the Politics of 14th-Century Sri Lanka', *Journal of the Royal Asiatic Society* 108, no. 2 (1976): 136–55.

Kulkarni, V.M. 'Abhinavagupta on the Alaukika Nature of Rasa', in *Some Aspects of the Rasa Theory*, edited by V.M. Kulkarni, 28–42. Delhi: B.L. Institute of Indology, 1986.

Kulke, Hermann. 'King Anaṅgabhīma III, the Veritable Founder of the Gajapati Kingship and of the Jagannātha Trinity at Puri', *Journal of the Royal Asiatic Society* 113, no. 1 (1981): 26–39.

Ladwig, Patrice. 'Millennialism, Charisma and Utopia: Revolutionary Potentialities in Pre-modern Lao and Thai Theravāda Buddhism', *Politics, Religion and Ideology* 15, no. 2 (2014): 308–29.

Lammerts, D. Christian. *Buddhist Law in Burma: A History of Dhammasattha Texts and Jurisprudence, 1250–1850*. Honolulu: University of Hawai'i Press, 2018.

Law, Bimala Churn, trans. *The Debates Commentary (Kathāvatthuppakaraṇa-aṭṭhakathā)*. London: Pali Text Society, 1940.

Law, Bimala Churn. *Some Jaina Canonical Sūtras*. Bombay: Royal Asiatic Society, 1949.

Law, Bimala Churn. *A History of Pāli Literature*. Varanasi: Indica Books, 2000.

Ledi, Sayādaw Mahāthera. *The Manual of Insight: Vipassanā Dīpanī*, translated by U. Ñāṇa Mahāthera. Kandy: Buddhist Publication Society, 2007.

Le Goff, Jacques. *The Medieval Imagination*, translated by Arthur Goldhammer. Chicago: University of Chicago Press, 1988.

Levman, Bryan. 'Sakāya niruttiyā revisited', *Bulletin des études indiennes* 26/27 (2008–9): 33–51.

Lieberman, Victor B. 'A Note on Burmese Religious Landholdings', *Journal of Asian Studies* 40, no. 4 (1981): 745–6.

Lieberman, Victor. *Strange Parallels: Southeast Asia in Global Context, c. 800–1830, Volume 1: Integration on the Mainland*. Cambridge: Cambridge University Press, 2003.

Lieberman, Victor. *Strange Parallels: Southeast Asia in Global Context, c. 800–1830, Volume 2: Mainland Mirrors: Europe, Japan, China, South Asia, and the Islands*. Cambridge: Cambridge University Press, 2009.

Lingat, Robert. *Royautés bouddhiques: Aśoka et la fonction royale à Ceylan*, edited by Gérard Fussman and Eric Meyer. Paris: Éditions de l'École des hautes études en sciences sociales, 1989.
Liyanagamage, Amaradasa. *The Decline of Polonnaruwa and the Rise of Dambadeniya, circa 1180–1270 AD*. Colombo: Department of Cultural Affairs, 1968.
Liyanagamage, Amaradasa. 'A Forgotten Aspect of the Relations between the Sinhalese and the Tamils: The *Upāsakajanālaṅkāra*: A Re-Examination of Its Date and Authorship and Its Significance in the History of South India and Sri Lanka', in *Society, State and Religion in Premodern Sri Lanka*, 15–72. Kelaniya: University of Kelaniya, 2001a.
Liyanagamage, Amaradasa. 'The Influence of Caste on the Buddhist Saṅgha in Ancient and Early Medieval Sri Lanka', in *Society, State and Religion in Premodern Sri Lanka*, 169–216. Kelaniya: University of Kelaniya, 2001b.
Liyanaratne, Jinadasa. 'La Jinabodhāvalī de Devarakkhita Jayabāhu Dhammakitti: Édition du texte pāli et traduction française', *Bulletin de l'École française d'Extrême-Orient* 72 (1983): 49–80.
Lopez Jr., Donald S. 'On the Interpretation of the Mahāyāna Sūtras', in *Buddhist Hermeneutics*, edited by Donald S. Lopez Jr., 47–70. Delhi: Motilal Banarsidass, 1993.
Ludowyk-Gyömröi, Edith. 'Note on the Interpretation of Pasīdati', *University of Ceylon Review* 1 (1943): 74–82.
Malalasekera, G.P. *Dictionary of Pāli Proper Names, Volume 2: N–H*. London: John Murray, 1938.
Malalasekera, G.P. *The Pāli Literature of Ceylon*. Kandy: Buddhist Publication Society, 1994.
Malalgoda, Kitsiri. 'Millennialism in Relation to Buddhism', *Comparative Studies in Society and History* 12, no. 4 (1970): 424–41.
Matsumura, Junko. 'Remarks on the Rasavāhinī and the Related Literature', *Journal of the Pali Text Society* 25 (1999): 155–72.
Matsumura, Junko. 'The *Sumedhakathā* in Pāli Literature and Its Relation to the Northern Buddhist Textual Tradition', *Journal of the International College for Postgraduate Buddhist Studies* 14 (2010): 101–33.
Maung Tin, Pe and G.H. Luce, trans. *The Glass Palace Chronicle of the Kings of Burma*. London: Oxford University Press, 1923.
McCrea, Lawrence J. *The Teleology of Poetics in Medieval Kashmir* (Harvard Oriental Series 71). Cambridge, MA: Department of Sanskrit and Indian Studies, Harvard University, 2008.
McCrea, Lawrence. 'In the World of Men and beyond It: Thoughts on Sheldon Pollock's *The Language of the Gods in the World of Men*', *Comparative Studies of South Asia, Africa and the Middle East* 33, no. 1 (2013): 117–24.
McCrea, Lawrence. '"Resonance" and Its Reverberations: Two Cultures in Indian Epistemology of Aesthetic Meaning', in *The Bloomsbury Research Handbook of Indian Aesthetics and the Philosophy of Art*, edited by Arindam Chakrabarti, 25–41. London: Bloomsbury Academic, 2016.
McDaniel, Justin Thomas. *Gathering Leaves and Lifting Words: Histories of Buddhist Monastic Education in Laos and Thailand*. Seattle: University of Washington Press, 2008.
McDermott, James P. 'The *Kathāvatthu Niyāma* Debates', *Journal of the International Association of Buddhist Studies* 12, no. 1 (1989): 139–46.
Meddegama, Udaya, trans. *Anāgatavaṃsa Desanā: The Sermon of the Chronicle-To-Be*. Delhi: Motilal Banarsidass, 1993.
Meddegama, Udaya, trans. 'Dambadeni Asna', in *The Sri Lanka Reader: History, Culture, Politics*, edited by John Clifford Holt, 101–6. Durham, NC: Duke University Press, 2011.
Meegama, Sujatha Arundathi. 'South Indian or Sri Lankan? The Hindu Temples of Polonnaruva, Sri Lanka', *Artibus Asiae* 70, no. 1 (2010): 25–45.
Mingous, Lise, ed. and trans. 'Thérapeute, exorciste et hôte: Trois facettes des activités d'un moine bouddhiste dans le Pāḷimuttaka-vinaya-vinicchaya-saṅgaha; Édition critique, traduction et étude du troisième chapitre'. Master's dissertation. Paris: École Pratique des Hautes Études, 2019.
Monius, Anne E. *Imagining a Place for Buddhism: Literary Culture and Religious Community in Tamil-Speaking South India*. New York: Oxford University Press, 2001.
Mudiyansē, Nandasēna. *Mahayana Monuments in Ceylon*. Colombo: M.D. Gunasena, 1967.
Mukherjee, Prabhat. 'Vīrasiṃha, a Forgotten Buddhist Scholar of Orissa', *Proceedings of the Indian History Congress* 3 (1939): 780–5.
Mukherjee, Prabhat. *The History of Medieval Vaishnavism in Orissa*. Calcutta: R. Chatterjee, 1940.
Mukherjee, P. 'The Influence of Vaishnavism in Medieval Orissa', *Proceedings of the Indian History Congress* 12 (1949): 291–5.

Mus, Paul. 'Études indiennes et indochinoises II: Le Buddha paré: Son origine indienne: Çākyamuni dans le Mahāyānisme moyen', *Bulletin de l'École française d'Extrême-Orient* 28, no. 1/2 (1928): 153–278.

Mus, Paul. 'Preface', in *Buddhist Backgrounds of the Burmese Revolution*, by E. Sarkisyanz, vii–xxii. The Hague: Martinus Nijhoff, 1965.

Ñāṇamoli, Bhikkhu and Bhikkhu Bodhi, trans. *The Middle Length Discourses of the Buddha: A New Translation of the Majjhima Nikāya*. Boston: Wisdom Publications, 1995.

Ñāṇānanda, Bhikkhu K., ed. and trans. *Towards a Better World (Lōväḍa Saṅgarāva): A Sinhalese Poem of the 15th Century by Venerable Vīdāgama Maitreya Mahāthera*. Colombo: Dhamma Publications Trust, 2000.

Nance, Richard F. *Speaking for Buddhas: Scriptural Commentary in Indian Buddhism*. New York: Columbia University Press, 2012.

Nattier, Jan. *Once Upon a Future Time: Studies in a Buddhist Prophecy of Decline*. Berkeley: Asian Humanities Press, 1991.

Neri, Chiara. 'The Case of the *Sārasaṅgaha*: Reflections on the Reuse of Texts in Medieval Sinhalese Pāli Literature', *Journal of Indian Philosophy* 43, no. 4/5 (2015): 335–88.

Neugebauer, O. 'The Study of Wretched Subjects', *Isis* 42, no. 2 (1951): 111.

Neumann, K.E., ed. and trans. *Des Sārasaṅgaho, eines Kompendiums buddhistischer Anschauungen, erstes Kapitel*. Leipzig: Max Spohr, 1891.

Nicholas, C.W. 'Historical Topography of Ancient and Medieval Ceylon', *Journal of the Ceylon Branch of the Royal Asiatic Society*, n.s., 6, Special Number (1963): 1–232.

Nicholson, Andrew J. *Unifying Hinduism: Philosophy and Identity in Indian Intellectual History*. New York: Columbia University Press, 2014.

Nilakanta Sastri, K.A. *The Cōlas, Volume 1: To the Accession of Kulottunga I*. Madras: University of Madras, 1935.

Nilakanta Sastri, K.A. *A History of South India from Prehistoric Times to the Fall of Vijayanagar*. 2nd ed. Madras: Oxford University Press, 1958.

Nilakanta Sastri, K.A. 'Ceylon as a Province of the Coḷa Empire', in *History of Ceylon, Volume 1: From the Earliest Times to 1505, Part 2*, edited by H.C. Ray, 411–15. Colombo: Ceylon University Press, 1960.

Nilakanta Sastri, K.A. 'Ceylon and Sri Vijaya', *Journal of the Ceylon Branch of the Royal Asiatic Society* 8, no. 1 (1962): 125–40.

Nobuaki, N. *Sārasaṅgaha no kenkyū* [A Study of the Sārasaṅgaha]. Kyoto: Heirakuji-shoten, 1998.

Norman, K.R. *Pāli Literature, including the Canonical Literature in Prakrit and Sanskrit of All the Hīnayāna Schools of Buddhism* (A History of Indian Literature 7.2). Wiesbaden: Otto Harrassowitz, 1983.

Norman, K.R. 'Devas and Adhidevas in Buddhism', in *Collected Papers, Volume 2*, 162–71. Oxford: Pali Text Society, 1991.

Norman, K.R. 'Pāli Lexicographical Studies VIII', in *Collected Papers, Volume 4*, 155–63. Oxford: Pali Text Society, 1993.

Norman, K.R. *A Philological Approach to Buddhism: The Bukkyō Dendō Kyōkai Lectures 1994* (The Buddhist Forum 5). London: School of Oriental and African Studies, 1997.

Novetzke, Christian Lee. *The Quotidian Revolution: Vernacularization, Religion, and the Premodern Public Sphere in India*. New York: Columbia University Press, 2016.

Nyanatiloka. *Buddhist Dictionary: Manual of Buddhist Terms and Doctrines*, edited by Nyanaponika. Rev. ed. Kandy: Buddhist Publication Society, 1998.

Nyanatiloka. *Guide through the Abhidhamma Piṭaka: A Synopsis of the Philosophical Collection of the Theravāda Buddhist Canon; Followed by an Essay on Dependent Origination*. Kandy: Buddhist Publication Society, 2008.

Oberlies, Thomas. *Studie zum Cāndravyākaraṇa: Eine kritische Bearbeitung von Candra IV.4.52–148 und V.2*. Stuttgart: Franz Steiner Verlag, 1989.

Obeyesekere, Ranjini, trans. *Yasodharā, the Wife of the Bōdhisattva: The Sinhala Yasodharāvata (The Story of Yasodharā) and the Sinhala Yasodharāpadānaya (The Sacred Biography of Yasodharā)*. Albany: State University of New York Press, 2009.

Ohnuma, Reiko. 'Internal and External Opposition to the Bodhisattva's Gift of His Body', *Journal of Indian Philosophy* 28, no. 1 (2000): 43–75.

Ohnuma, Reiko. *Head, Eyes, Flesh, and Blood: Giving Away the Body in Indian Buddhist Literature*. New York: Columbia University Press, 2007.

Ollett, Andrew. *Language of the Snakes. Prakrit, Sanskrit, and the Language Order of Premodern India.* Oakland: University of California Press, 2017.
Panabokke, Gunaratne. *History of the Buddhist Sangha in India and Sri Lanka*. Colombo: Postgraduate Institute of Pali and Buddhist Studies, University of Kelaniya, 1993.
Pannasara, Dehigaspe. *Sanskrit Literature: Extant among the Sinhalese and the Influence of Sanskrit on Sinhalese*. Colombo: W.D. Hewavitarane Esqr., 1958.
Paranavitana, S. 'The Kāliṅga Dynasty of Ceylon', *Journal of the Greater India Society* 3, no. 1 (1936): 57–64.
Paranavitana, S. 'Civilisation of the Polonnaru Period (Continued): Religion, Literature and Art', in *History of Ceylon, Volume 1: From the Earliest Times to 1505, Part 2*, edited by H.C. Ray, 563–612. Colombo: Ceylon University Press, 1960.
Paranavitana, S. 'The *Dhvanikārikās* in Fifteenth Century Ceylon', *Journal of the American Oriental Society* 94, no. 1 (1974): 131–3.
Parkes, M.B. 'The Influence of the Concepts of Ordinatio and Compilatio on the Development of the Book', in *Scribes, Scripts and Readers: Studies in the Communication, Presentation and Dissemination of Medieval Texts*, 35–70. London: Hambledon Press, 1991.
Patel, Deven M. *Text to Tradition: The Naiṣadhīyacarita and Literary Community in South Asia*. New York: Columbia University Press, 2014.
Pathmanathan, S. 'Feudal Polity in Medieval Ceylon: An Examination of the Chieftaincies of the Vanni', *Ceylon Journal of Historical and Social Studies* new series 2, no. 2 (1972): 118–30.
Pathmanathan, S. 'The Velaikkarar in Medieval South India and Sri Lanka', *Sri Lanka Journal of the Humanities* 2, no. 2 (1976): 120–37.
Pathmanathan, S. *The Kingdom of Jaffna, Part 1 (circa AD 1250–1450)*. Colombo: Arul M. Rajendran, 1978.
Pathmanathan, S. 'Kingship in Sri Lanka, AD 1070–1270: The Dhammic Conception, Divinity of Kingship and the Heroic Ideal', *Sri Lanka Journal of the Humanities* 8, no. 1/2 (1982a): 120–45.
Pathmanathan, S. 'The Cities of Medieval Sri Lanka (AD 1000–1250): Centres of Dynastic Power, Religious Authority and Commercial Activity', *Sri Lanka Journal of Social Sciences* 5, no. 1 (1982b): 11–35.
Pathmanathan, S. 'The Nagaram of the Nanadesis in Sri Lanka circa AD 1000–1300', *Sri Lanka Journal of the Humanities* 10, no. 1/2 (1984): 122–63.
Pathmanathan, S. 'Hinduism in Sri Lanka (circa AD 1000–1250): Indian Influences on the Development of Saivism', *Modern Sri Lanka Studies* 2, no. 1/2 (1987): 52–66.
Pathmanathan, S. 'Vikramabāhu II and Vikrama Salamevan', *Sri Lanka Journal of the Humanities* 19, no. 1/2 (1993): 93–111.
Pathmanathan, S. 'The Tamil Pillar Inscription from Mankanay', *Sri Lanka Journal of the Humanities* 21, no. 1/2 (1995): 31–41.
Pathmanathan, S. 'New Light on the Decline of Polonnaruwa (1196–1215): The Tamil Pillar Inscription from Rankot Vihara', *Proceedings of the Peradeniya University Research Sessions* 9 (2004): 31.
Pecenko, Primoz. 'Sāriputta and His Works', *Journal of the Pali Text Society* 23 (1997): 159–79.
Perera, B.J. 'Some Political Trends in the Late Anuradhapura and Polonnaruwa Period', *Ceylon Historical Journal* 10, no. 1–4 (1960–1): 60–76.
Perera, Lakshman S. 'Proprietary and Tenurial Rights in Ancient Ceylon', *Ceylon Journal of Historical and Social Studies* 2, no. 1 (1959): 1–36.
Peterson, Indira Viswanathan. *Design and Rhetoric in a Sanskrit Court Epic: The Kirātārjunīya of Bhāravi*. Albany: State University of New York Press, 2003.
Phadnis, Urmila. *Religion and Politics in Sri Lanka*. London: C. Hurst, 1976.
Pind, Ole Holten. 'Studies in the Pāli Grammarians I: Buddhaghosa's Reference to Grammar and Grammarians', *Journal of the Pali Text Society* 13 (1989): 33–82.
Pind, Ole Holten. 'Studies in the Pāli Grammarians II.1', *Journal of the Pali Text Society* 14 (1990): 175–218.
Pind, Ole H. 'Pāli Miscellany', in *Bauddhavidyāsudhākaraḥ: Studies in Honour of Heinz Bechert on the Occasion of His 65th Birthday*, edited by Petra Kieffer-Pülz and Jens-Uwe Hartmann, 515–36. Swisttal-Odendorf: Indica et Tibetica Verlag, 1997.
Pind, Ole Holten. 'Pali Grammar and Grammarians from Buddhaghosa to Vajirabuddhi: A Survey', *Journal of the Pali Text Society* 31 (2012): 57–124.
Pingree, David. *Jyotiḥśāstra: Astral and Mathematical Literature*. A History of Indian Literature 6.4. Wiesbaden: Otto Harrassowitz, 1981.

Pollock, Sheldon. 'Deep Orientalism? Notes on Sanskrit and Power beyond the Raj', in *Orientalism and the Postcolonial Predicament: Perspectives on South Asia*, edited by Carol A. Breckenridge and Peter van der Veer, 76–133. Philadelphia: University of Pennsylvania Press, 1993a.

Pollock, Sheldon. 'Rāmāyaṇa and Political Imagination in India', *Journal of Asian Studies* 52, no. 2 (1993b): 261–97.

Pollock, Sheldon. 'The Death of Sanskrit', *Comparative Studies in Society and History* 43, no. 2 (2001a): 392–426.

Pollock, Sheldon. 'The Social Aesthetic and Sanskrit Literary Theory', *Journal of Indian Philosophy* 29, no. 1/2 (2001b): 197–229.

Pollock, Sheldon. 'Sanskrit Literary Culture from the Inside Out', in *Literary Cultures in History: Reconstructions from South Asia*, edited by Sheldon Pollock, 39–130. Berkeley: University of California Press, 2003.

Pollock, Sheldon. 'Ratnaśrījñāna', in *Encyclopaedia of Indian Wisdom: Prof. Satya Vrat Shastri Felicitation Volume*, edited by R.K. Sharma, 637–43. Delhi: Bharatiya Vidya Prakashan, 2005.

Pollock, Sheldon. *The Language of the Gods in the World of Men: Sanskrit, Culture, and Power in Premodern India*. Berkeley: University of California Press, 2006.

Pollock, Sheldon, trans. *"Bouquet of Rasa" and "River of Rasa" by Bhānudatta*. New York: New York University Press, 2009.

Powell, Kellie Marie. 'Rituals and Ruins: Recovering the History of Vajrayāna Buddhism in Sri Lanka'. Master's dissertation, University of California, Berkeley, 2018.

Pranke, Patrick Arthur. 'The "Treatise on the Lineage of Elders" (*Vaṃsadīpanī*): Monastic Reform and the Writing of Buddhist History in Eighteenth-Century Burma'. PhD thesis, University of Michigan, 2004.

Pranke, Patrick. 'On Saints and Wizards: Ideals of Human Perfection and Power in Contemporary Burmese Buddhism', *Journal of the International Association of Buddhist Studies* 33, no. 1/2 (2010–11): 453–88.

Premchit, Sommai and Donald K. Swearer. 'A Translation of *Tamnān Mūlasāsanā Wat Pā Daeng*: The Chronicle of the Founding of Buddhism of the Wat Pā Daeng Tradition', *Journal of the Siam Society* 65, no. 2 (1977): 73–110.

Priestley, Leonard C.D.C. *Pudgalavāda Buddhism: The Reality of the Indeterminate Self* (South Asian Studies Paper 12). Toronto: Centre for South Asian Studies, University of Toronto, 1999.

Pruitt, William. *Étude linguistique de nissaya birmans: Traduction commentée de textes bouddhiques*. Paris: Presses de l'École française d'Extrême-Orient, 1994.

Quirk, Randolph, Sidney Greenbaum, Geoffrey Leech and Jan Svartvik. *A Comprehensive Grammar of the English Language*. London: Longman, 1985.

Rahula, Walpola. *History of Buddhism in Ceylon: The Anuradhapura Period, 3rd Century BC–10th Century AC*. Colombo: M.D. Gunasena, 1956.

Rammandala, M.S. 'A Critical Study of Dharmapradipikava'. PhD thesis, University of London, 1954.

Ratnapāla, Nandasēna. The Katikāvatas: Laws of the Buddhist Order of Ceylon from the 12th Century to the 18th Century (Critically Edited, Translated and Annotated). Munich: Kitzinger, 1971.

Ray, H.C., ed. *History of Ceylon, Volume 1: From the Earliest Times to 1505, Parts 1–2*. Colombo: Ceylon University Press, 1959–60.

Reuter, Timothy. 'The "Imperial Church System" of the Ottonian and Salian Rulers: A Reconsideration', *Journal of Ecclesiastical History* 33, no. 3 (1982): 347–74.

Reynolds, Frank E. 'The Many Lives of Buddha: A Study of Sacred Biography and Theravāda Tradition', in *The Biographical Process: Studies in the History and Psychology of Religion*, edited by Frank E. Reynolds and Donald Capps, 37–61. The Hague: Mouton, 1976.

Reynolds, Frank E. and Charles Hallisey. 'Buddhist Religion, Culture, and Civilization', in *Buddhism and Asian History*, edited by Joseph M. Kitagawa and Mark D. Cummings, 3–28. New York: Macmillan, 1989.

Reynolds, Frank E. 'Rebirth Traditions and the Lineages of Gotama: A Study in Theravāda Buddhology', in *Sacred Biography in the Buddhist Traditions of South and Southeast Asia*, edited by Juliane Schober, 19–39. Honolulu: University of Hawai'i Press, 1997.

Rhys Davids, T.W., trans. Buddhist Birth-Stories (Jataka Tales): The Commentarial Introduction Entitled Nidāna-Kathā, The Story of the Lineage. Revised edition by C.A.F. Rhys Davids. London: George Routledge and Sons, 1925.

Rohanadeera, Mendis. 'Mahāsāmi Sangha Rāja Institution in Sri Lanka: Its Origin, Development, Status, Duties and Functions', *Vidyodaya Journal of Arts, Science, and Letters* 13, no. 1 (1985): 27–43.

Rōhaṇadīra, Mǟndis. *Śrī Laṅkāvē Mahāsāmi Saṅgharāja Parapura: Madhyatana Yugaya, Bu. Va. 1708–2135, Kri. Va. 1165–1592*. Nugēgoḍa: Sīmāsahita Mudraṇa/Prakāśana (Paudgalika), 1996.

Ronkin, Noa. *Early Buddhist Metaphysics: The Making of a Philosophical Tradition*. London: Routledge-Curzon, 2005.

Rosenwein, Barbara H. *Rhinoceros Bound: Cluny in the Tenth Century*. Philadelphia: University of Pennsylvania Press, 1982.

Rotman, Andy. 'The Erotics of Practice: Objects and Agency in Buddhist *Avadāna* Literature', *Journal of the American Academy of Religion* 71, no. 3 (2003): 555–78.

Rotman, Andy. *Thus Have I Seen: Visualizing Faith in Early Indian Buddhism*. New York: Oxford University Press, 2009.

Rowell, Teresina. 'The Background and Early Use of the Buddha-kṣetra Concept: Introduction and Chapter One', *Eastern Buddhist* 6, no. 3 (1934): 199–246.

Ruegg, David Seyfort. *Ordre spirituel et ordre temporel dans la pensée bouddhique de l'Inde et du Tibet: Quatre conférences au Collège de France*. Paris: De Boccard, 1995.

Ruiz-Falqués, A. 'On the Authorship of *Kaccāyana*, the Oldest Pāli Grammar', in *Pariyatti: Studies in Pāli Language and Literature*, edited by Bimalendra Kumar and Ujjwal Kumar, 251–68. Delhi: Aditya Prakashan, 2017a.

Ruiz Falqués, Aleix. 'The Role of Pāli Grammar in Burmese Buddhism', *Journal of Burma Studies* 21, no. 1 (2017b): 1–96.

Sahlins, Marshall. 'The Stranger-King; or Dumézil among the Fijians', *Journal of Pacific History* 16, no. 3 (1981): 107–32.

Samuels, Jeffrey. 'The Bodhisattva Ideal in Theravāda Buddhist Theory and Practice: A Reevaluation of the Bodhisattva-Śrāvaka Opposition', *Philosophy East and West* 47, no. 3 (1997): 399–415.

Sannasgala, P.B. *Sinhala Sāhitya Vaṃsaya*. Colombo: M.D. Gunasena, 1964.

Sarkisyanz, E. *Buddhist Backgrounds of the Burmese Revolution*. The Hague: Martinus Nijhoff, 1965.

Sarton, George. 'Seventy-Sixth Critical Bibliography of the History and Philosophy of Science and of the History of Civilization (to May 1950)', *Isis* 41, no. 3/4 (1950): 328–424.

Sasaki, Genjun H., ed. *Sārasaṅgaha*. Oxford: Pali Text Society, 1992.

Savy, Pierre. 'L'histoire à la découpe', *La vie des idées*, 2 April 2014. Accessed 17 June 2019. http://www.laviedesidees.fr/L-histoire-a-la-decoupe.html.

Schaffer, Simon. *The Information Order of Isaac Newton's Principia Mathematica: The Hans Rausing Lecture 2008* (Salvia Småskrifter 11). Uppsala: Office for History of Science, Uppsala University, 2008.

Schalk, Peter. 'Pallava Policy on Buddhism', in *Buddhism among Tamils in Pre-Colonial Tamiḻakam and Īḻam, Part 1: Prologue: The Pre-Pallava and the Pallava Period*, edited by Peter Schalk and Āḷvāppiḷḷai Vēluppiḷḷai, 378–429. Uppsala: Uppsala Universitet, 2002.

Scharf, Peter M. 'Levels in Pāṇini's *Aṣṭādhyāyī*', in *Sanskrit Computational Linguistics: Third International Symposium, Hyderabad, India, January 15–17, 2009: Proceedings*, edited by Amba Kulkarni and Gérard Huet, 66–77. Berlin: Springer, 2009.

Scharfe, Hartmut. *Grammatical Literature* (A History of Indian Literature 5.2). Wiesbaden: Otto Harrassowitz, 1977.

Scheible, Kristin. 'Priming the Lamp of *Dhamma*: The Buddha's Miracles in the Pāli *Mahāvaṃsa*', *Journal of the International Association of Buddhist Studies* 33, no. 1/2 (2010–11): 435–51.

Scheible, Kristin. *Reading the Mahāvaṃsa: The Literary Aims of a Theravāda Buddhist History*. New York: Columbia University Press, 2016.

Schober, Juliane. *Modern Buddhist Conjunctures in Myanmar: Cultural Narratives, Colonial Legacies, and Civil Society*. Honolulu: University of Hawai'i Press, 2011.

Schoening, Jeffrey Davis. 'The "Śālistamba-Sūtra" and Its Indian Commentaries'. PhD thesis, University of Washington, 1991.

Schopen, Gregory. 'The Phrase "*Sa Pṛthivīpradeśaś Caityabhūto Bhavet*" in the *Vajracchedikā*: Notes on the Cult of the Book in Mahāyāna', *Indo-Iranian Journal* 17, no. 3/4 (1975): 147–81.

Schopen, Gregory. 'The Text on the "Dhāraṇī Stones from Abhayagiriya": A Minor Contribution to the Study of Mahāyāna Literature in Ceylon', *Journal of the International Association of Buddhist Studies* 5, no. 1 (1982): 100–8.

Schopen, Gregory. 'The Buddha as an Owner of Property and Permanent Resident in Medieval Indian Monasteries', *Journal of Indian Philosophy* 18, no. 3 (1990): 181–217.

Schopen, Gregory. 'Burial *Ad Sanctos* and the Physical Presence of the Buddha in Early Indian Buddhism: A Study in the Archaeology of Religions', in *Bones, Stones, and Buddhist Monks: Collected Papers on the Archaeology, Epigraphy, and Texts of Monastic Buddhism in India*, 114–47. Honolulu: University of Hawai'i Press, 1997.

Schopen, Gregory. *Buddhist Monks and Business Matters: Still More Papers on Monastic Buddhism in India*. Honolulu: University of Hawai'i Press, 2004.

Schopen, Gregory. 'The Buddhist "Monastery" and the Indian Garden: Aesthetics, Assimilations, and the Siting of Monastic Establishments', *Journal of the American Oriental Society* 126, no. 4 (2006): 487–505.

Schrijvers, Joke. 'Make Your Son a King: Political Power through Matronage and Motherhood', in *Private Politics: A Multi-Disciplinary Approach to "Big-Man" Systems*, edited by Martin A. van Bakel, Renée R. Hagesteijn and Pieter van de Velde, 13–32. Leiden: Brill, 1986.

Sen, Tansen. *Buddhism, Diplomacy, and Trade: The Realignment of Sino-Indian Relations, 600–1400*. Honolulu: University of Hawai'i Press, 2003.

Senart, E. *Kaccâyana et la littérature grammaticale du Pâli, 1re partie: Grammaire pâlie de Kaccâyana, sûtras et commentaire, publiés avec une traduction et des notes*. Paris: Imprimerie nationale, 1871.

Seneviratne, H.L. 'Religion and Legitimacy of Power in the Kandyan Kingdom', in *Religion and Legitimation of Power in Sri Lanka*, edited by Bardwell L. Smith, 177–87. Chambersburg, PA: Anima Books, 1978a.

Seneviratne, H.L. *Rituals of the Kandyan State*. Cambridge: Cambridge University Press, 1978b.

Seneviratne, Maureen. *Some Women of the Mahavamsa and Cūlavamsa*. Colombo: H.W. Cave and Company, 1969.

Shulman, David. *More Than Real: A History of the Imagination in South India*. Cambridge, MA: Harvard University Press, 2012.

Shulman, Eviatar. 'The Protective Buddha: On the Cosmological Logic of *Paritta*', *Numen* 66 (2019): 207–42.

Silber, Ilana Friedrich. *Virtuosity, Charisma, and Social Order: A Comparative Sociological Study of Monasticism in Theravada Buddhism and Medieval Catholicism*. Cambridge: Cambridge University Press, 1995.

Silk, Jonathan A. 'Further Remarks on the *Yogācāra Bhikṣu*', in *Dharmadūta: Mélanges offerts au Vénérable Thích Huyên-Vi à l'occasion de son soixante-dixième anniversaire*, edited by Bhikkhu T. Dhammaratana and Bhikkhu Pāsādika, 233–50. Paris: Éditions You-Feng, 1997.

Sirisena, W.M. 'The Kalinga Dynasty of Ceylon and the Theory of Its South-East Asian Origin', *Ceylon Journal of Historical and Social Studies* 1, no. 1 (1971): 11–47.

Sirisena, W.M. *Sri Lanka and South-East Asia: Political, Religious and Cultural Relations from AD c. 1000 to c. 1500*. Leiden: Brill, 1978.

Skilling, Peter. 'The Advent of Theravāda Buddhism to Mainland South-East Asia', *Journal of the International Association of Buddhist Studies* 20, no. 1 (1997): 93–107.

Skilling, Peter. 'Vasubandhu and the *Vyākhyāyukti* Literature', *Journal of the International Association of Buddhist Studies* 23, no. 2 (2000): 297–350.

Skilling, Peter. 'Buddhist Sealings in Thailand and Southeast Asia: Iconography, Function, and Ritual Context', in *Interpreting Southeast Asia's Past: Monument, Image and Text: Selected Papers from the 10th International Conference of the European Association of Southeast Asian Archaeologists, Volume 2*, edited by Elisabeth A. Bacus, Ian C. Glover and Peter D. Sharrock, 248–62. Singapore: NUS Press, 2008.

Skilling, Peter. 'Scriptural Authenticity and the Śrāvaka Schools: An Essay towards an Indian Perspective', *Eastern Buddhist* 41, no. 2 (2010): 1–47.

Skilling, Peter. 'King Rāma I and Wat Phra Chetuphon: The Buddha-śāsanā in Early Bangkok', in *How Theravāda is Theravāda? Exploring Buddhist Identities*, edited by Peter Skilling, Jason A. Carbine, Claudio Cicuzza and Santi Pakdeekham, 297–353. Chiang Mai: Silkworm Books, 2012.

Skilling, Peter, Jason A. Carbine, Claudio Cicuzza and Santi Pakdeekham, eds. *How Theravāda is Theravāda? Exploring Buddhist Identities*. Chiang Mai: Silkworm Books, 2012.

Smith, Bardwell L. 'The Polonnaruva Period (ca. 993–1293 AD): A Thematic Bibliographical Essay', in *Religion and Legitimation of Power in Sri Lanka*, edited by Bardwell L. Smith, 119–54. Chambersburg, PA: Anima Books, 1978.

Söhnen-Thieme, Renate. 'On the Concept and Function of *Satya* ("Truth") in Ancient Indian Literature', in *International Conference on Sanskrit and Related Studies, September 23–26, 1993: Proceedings*, edited by Cezary Galewicz, 235–44. Cracow: Enigma Press, 1995.

Southern, R.W. *Medieval Humanism*. New York: Harper and Row, 1970.

Spencer, George W. 'The Politics of Plunder: The Cholas in Eleventh-Century Ceylon', *Journal of Asian Studies* 35, no. 3 (1976): 405–19.

Spiro, Melford E. *Buddhism and Society: A Great Tradition and Its Burmese Vicissitudes*. 2nd ed. Berkeley: University of California Press, 1982.

Śrī Dharmārāma, ed. *Moggallāna Pañchikā Pradīpa: A Treatise on Moggallāna's System of Pali Grammar by Saṅgharāja Srī Rāhula Mahāsthavira*. Colombo: H.C. Cottle, Acting Government Printer, 1896.

Sternbach, Ludwik. *A Descriptive Catalogue of Poets Quoted in Sanskrit Anthologies and Inscriptions, Volume 1: Aṁśudhara–Dhoyi*. Wiesbaden: Otto Harrassowitz, 1978.

Sternbach, Ludwik. *A Descriptive Catalogue of Poets quoted in Sanskrit Anthologies and Inscriptions, Volume 2: Nakula–Hevidhanesora*. Wiesbaden: Otto Harrassowitz, 1980.

Strathern, Alan. *Kingship and Conversion in Sixteenth-Century Sri Lanka: Portuguese Imperialism in a Buddhist Land*. Cambridge: Cambridge University Press, 2007a.

Strathern, Alan. 'Transcendentalist Intransigence: Why Rulers Rejected Monotheism in Early Modern Southeast Asia and Beyond', *Comparative Studies in Society and History* 49, no. 2 (2007b): 358–83.

Strathern, Alan. 'Sri Lanka in the Long Early Modern Period: Its Place in a Comparative Theory of Second Millennium Eurasian History', *Modern Asian Studies* 43, no. 4 (2009): 815–69.

Strathern, Alan. 'The Digestion of the Foreign in Lankan History, c. 500–1818', in *Sri Lanka at the Crossroads of History*, edited by Zoltán Biedermann and Alan Strathern, 216–38. London: UCL Press, 2017.

Strathern, Alan. *Unearthly Powers: Religious and Political Change in World History*. Cambridge: Cambridge University Press, 2019.

Strathern, Alan and Zoltán Biedermann. 'Introduction: Querying the Cosmopolitan in Sri Lankan and Indian Ocean history', in *Sri Lanka at the Crossroads of History*, edited by Zoltán Biedermann and Alan Strathern, 1–18. London: UCL Press, 2017.

Strickland, Keir Magalie. 'The Jungle Tide: "Collapse" in Early Mediaeval Sri Lanka'. PhD thesis, Durham University, 2011.

Strickland, Keir Magalie. *A Time of Change: Questioning the "Collapse" of Anuradhapura, Sri Lanka*. Oxford: Archaeopress, 2017.

Strong, John S. 'A Family Quest: The Buddha, Yaśodharā, and Rāhula in the Mūlasarvāstivāda Vinaya', in *Sacred Biography in the Buddhist Traditions of South and Southeast Asia*, edited by Juliane Schober, 113–28. Honolulu: University of Hawai'i Press, 1997.

Strong, John S. *Relics of the Buddha*. Delhi: Motilal Banarsidass, 2007.

Subhūti, Waskaḍuwē. *Nāmamālā; or A Work on Pāli Grammar*. Colombo: Government Printing Office, 1876.

Sundberg, Jeffrey Roger. 'The Wilderness Monks of the Abhayagirivihāra and the Origins of Sino-Javanese Esoteric Buddhism', *Bijdragen tot de Taal-, Land- en Volkenkunde* 160, no. 1 (2004): 95–123.

Sundberg, Jeffrey. 'The Abhayagirivihāra's *Pāṃśukūlika* Monks in Second Lambakaṇṇa Śrī Laṅkā and Śailendra Java: The Flowering and Fall of a Cardinal Center of Influence in Early Esoteric Buddhism', *Pacific World: Journal of the Institute of Buddhist Studies* 16 (2014): 49–185.

Sundberg, Jeffrey. 'Appreciation of Relics, Stūpas, and Relic Stūpas in Eighth Century Esoteric Buddhism: *Taishō Tripiṭaka* Texts and Archaeological Residues in Guhyā Laṅkā, Part 1', *Indian International Journal of Buddhist Studies* 18 (2017): 173–340.

Sundberg, Jeffrey. 'Appreciation of Relics, Stūpas, and Relic Stūpas in Eighth Century Esoteric Buddhism: *Taishō Tripiṭaka* Texts and Archaeological Residues in Guhyā Laṅkā, Part 2', *Indian International Journal of Buddhist Studies* 19 (2018): 181–458.

Sundberg, Jeffrey and Rolf Giebel. 'The Life of the Tang Court Monk Vajrabodhi as Chronicled by Lü Xiang (呂向): South Indian and Śrī Laṅkān Antecedents to the Arrival of the Buddhist Vajrayāna in Eighth-Century Java and China', *Pacific World: Journal of the Institute of Buddhist Studies* 13 (2011): 129–222.

Sūryakānta, ed. and trans. *Kṣemendra Studies: Together with an English Translation of His Kavikaṇṭhābharaṇa, Aucityavicāracarcā and Suvṛttatilaka*. Poona: Oriental Book Agency, 1954.

Tambiah, S.J. *World Conqueror and World Renouncer: A Study of Buddhism and Polity in Thailand against a Historical Background*. Cambridge: Cambridge University Press, 1976.

Tambiah, Stanley Jeyaraja. *The Buddhist Saints of the Forest and the Cult of Amulets: A Study in Charisma, Hagiography, Sectarianism, and Millennial Buddhism*. Cambridge: Cambridge University Press, 1984.

Tambiah, Stanley Jeyaraja. *Magic, Science, Religion, and the Scope of Rationality*. Cambridge: Cambridge University Press, 1990.

Taylor, Keith. 'The Devolution of Kingship in Twelfth Century Ceylon', in *Explorations in Early Southeast Asian History: The Origins of Southeast Asian Statecraft*, edited by Kenneth R. Hall and John

K. Whitmore, 257–302. Ann Arbor: Center for South and Southeast Asian Studies, University of Michigan, 1976.
Taylor, Keith W. 'The Early Kingdoms', in *The Cambridge History of Southeast Asia, Volume 1: From Early Times to c. 1800*, edited by Nicholas Tarling, 137–82. Cambridge: Cambridge University Press, 1992.
Taylor, William. *Oriental Historical Manuscripts, in the Tamil Language: Translated; with Annotations, Volume 1*. Madras: n.p., 1835.
Taylor, William. *A Catalogue Raisonné of Oriental Manuscripts in the Library of the Government*. Madras: Fort St. George Gazette Press, 1857.
Tellenbach, Gerd. *The Church in Western Europe from the Tenth to the Early Twelfth Century*, translated by Timothy Reuter. Cambridge: Cambridge University Press, 1993.
Tournier, Vincent. *La formation du Mahāvastu et la mise en place des conceptions relatives à la carrière du bodhisattva*. Paris: École française d'Extrême-Orient, 2017.
Trainor, Kevin. '*Pasanna/Pasāda* in the Pāli *Vaṃsa* Literature', *Vidyodaya Journal of Social Sciences* 3 (1989): 185–90.
Trainor, Kevin. *Relics, Ritual, and Representation in Buddhism: Rematerializing the Sri Lankan Theravāda Tradition*. Cambridge: Cambridge University Press, 1997.
Trainor, Kevin. 'Seeing, Feeling, Doing: Ethics and Emotions in South Asian Buddhism', *Journal of the American Academy of Religion* 71, no. 3 (2003): 523–9.
Trautmann, Thomas R. 'Consanguineous Marriage in Pali Literature', *Journal of the American Oriental Society* 93, no. 2 (1973): 158–80.
Turnour, George. 'An Examination of the Pali Buddhistical Annals, No. 3', *Journal of the Asiatic Society of Bengal* 7, no. 80 (1838): 686–701.
Vaidya, P.L. 'Pali and Buddhistic Literature', in *Encyclopedia of Literature, Volume 1*, edited by Joseph T. Shipley, 478–81. New York: Philosophical Library, 1946.
Vanderputten, Steven. *Monastic Reform as Process: Realities and Representations in Medieval Flanders, 900–1100*. Ithaca, NY: Cornell University Press, 2013.
Verellen, Franciscus. '"Evidential Miracles in Support of Taoism": The Inversion of a Buddhist Apologetic Tradition in Late Tang China', *T'oung Pao* 78, no. 4/5 (1992): 217–63.
Vergiani, Vincenzo. 'A Quotation from the *Mahābhāṣyadīpikā* of Bhartṛhari in the *Pratyāhāra* Section of the *Kāśikāvṛtti*', in *Studies in the Kāśikāvṛtti: The Section on Pratyāhāras: Critical Edition, Translation and Other Contributions*, edited by Pascale Haag and Vincenzo Vergiani, 161–89. London: Anthem Press, 2011.
Visigalli, Paolo. 'The Cultural Genesis of Systematic Inquiries into Language in Ancient India'. PhD thesis, University of Cambridge, 2014.
Vogel, Claus. *Indian Lexicography* (A History of Indian Literature 5.4). Wiesbaden: Otto Harrassowitz, 1979.
Von Hinüber, Oskar. 'Eine Karmavācanā-Sammlung aus Gilgit', *Zeitschrift der Deutschen Morgenländischen Gesellschaft* 119, no. 1 (1969): 102–32.
Von Hinüber, Oskar. 'Pāli as an Artificial Language', *Indologica Taurinensia* 10 (1982): 133–40.
Von Hinüber, Oskar. *Sieben Goldblätter einer Pañcaviṃśatisāhasrikā Prajñāpāramitā aus Anurādhapura*. Göttingen: Vandenhoeck und Ruprecht, 1983.
Von Hinüber, O. 'On the History of the Name of the Pāli Language', in *Selected Papers on Pāli Studies*, 76–90. Oxford: Pali Text Society, 1994.
Von Hinüber, Oskar. *A Handbook of Pāli Literature*. Berlin: De Gruyter, 1996.
Von Hinüber, Oskar. 'The Paramatthajotikādīpanī, a Fragment of the Subcommentary to the Paramatthajotikā II on the Suttanipāta', *Journal of the Pali Text Society* 23 (1997): 27–41.
Wallace, Vesna A. 'Authenticating the Tradition through Linguistic Arguments', in *Buddhism and Linguistics: Theory and Philosophy*, edited by Manel Herat, 101–22. Cham: Palgrave Macmillan, 2018.
Walshe, Maurice, trans. *The Long Discourses of the Buddha: A Translation of the Dīgha Nikāya*. Boston: Wisdom Publications, 1995.
Walters, Jonathan S. 'Stūpa, Story, and Empire: Constructions of the Buddha Biography in Early Post-Aśokan India', in *Sacred Biography in the Buddhist Traditions of South and Southeast Asia*, edited by Juliane Schober, 160–92. Honolulu: University of Hawai'i Press, 1997.
Walters, Jonathan S. 'Mahāsena at the Mahāvihāra: On the Interpretation and Politics of History in Pre-Colonial Sri Lanka', in *Invoking the Past: The Uses of History in South Asia*, edited by Daud Ali, 322–66. Delhi: Oxford University Press, 1999.

Walters, Jonathan S. 'Buddhist History: The Sri Lankan Pāli Vaṃsas and Their Commentary', in *Querying the Medieval: Texts and the History of Practices in South Asia*, by Ronald Inden, Jonathan Walters and Daud Ali, 99–164. Oxford: Oxford University Press, 2000.

Walters, Jonathan S. 'Communal Karma and Karmic Community in Theravāda Buddhist History', in *Constituting Communities: Theravāda Buddhism and the Religious Cultures of South and Southeast Asia*, edited by John Clifford Holt, Jacob N. Kinnard and Jonathan S. Walters, 9–39. Albany: State University of New York Press, 2003.

Walters, Jonathan S. 'Flanked by Images of Our Buddha: Community, Law, and Religion in a Premodern Buddhist Context', in *Buddhism and Law: An Introduction*, edited by Rebecca Redwood French and Mark A. Nathan, 135–49. New York: Cambridge University Press, 2014.

Warder, A.K. 'The Concept of a Concept', *Journal of Indian Philosophy* 1, no. 2 (1971): 181–96.

Warder, A.K. 'Some Problems of the Later Pali Literature', *Journal of the Pali Text Society* 9 (1981): 198–207.

Warder, A.K. *Indian Kāvya Literature, Volume 5: The Bold Style (Śaktibhadra to Dhanapāla)*. Delhi: Motilal Banarsidass, 1988.

Weber, Max. *The Religion of India: The Sociology of Hinduism and Buddhism*, edited and translated by Hans H. Gerth and Don Martindale. Glencoe, IL: Free Press, 1958.

Weber, Max. *The Agrarian Sociology of Ancient Civilizations*, translated by R.I. Frank. London: Verso, 2013.

Wickham, Chris. *Medieval Europe*. New Haven: Yale University Press, 2016.

Wickramasinghe, Sirima. 'The Age of Parākramabāhu I'. PhD thesis, University of London, 1958.

Wielińska-Soltwedel, Małgorzata. 'The *Bhāṣāvṛttivivaraṇapañjikā* of Viśvarūpa, the First *Adhyāya* and a Detailed Examination'. PhD thesis, Universität Hamburg, 2006.

Wijayatuṅga, W.M.K. 'Some Aspects of Cola Administration of Ceylon in the Eleventh Century', *University of Ceylon Review* 23, no. 1/2 (1965): 67–82.

Wijeratne, R.P. and Rupert Gethin, trans. *Summary of the Topics of Abhidhamma (Abhidhammatthasaṅgaha) by Anuruddha; Exposition of the Topics of Abhidhamma (Abhidhammatthavibhāvinī), Being a Commentary to Anuruddha's "Summary of the Topics of Abhidhamma", by Sumaṅgala*. Lancaster: Pali Text Society, 2007.

Wijesekera, O.H. de A. 'Pali and Sanskrit in the Polonnaruva Period', in *The Polonnaruva Period*, edited by S.D. Saparamadu, 102–9. Dehiwala: Tisara Prakasakayo, 1973.

Wright, J.C. 'The Pali *Subodhālaṅkāra* and Daṇḍin's *Kāvyādarśa*', *Bulletin of the School of Oriental and African Studies* 65, no. 2 (2002): 323–41.

Wujastyk, Dominik. '*Jambudvīpa*: Apples or Plums?', in *Studies in the History of the Exact Sciences in Honour of David Pingree*, edited by Charles Burnett, Jan P. Hogendijk, Kim Plofker and Michio Yano, 287–301. Leiden: Brill, 2004.

Wynne, Alexander. 'The Historical Authenticity of Early Buddhist Literature: A Critical Evaluation', *Wiener Zeitschrift für die Kunde Südasiens* 49 (2005): 35–70.

Yabuuchi, Satoko. 'The Ideal of the Bodhisattva King in Sri Lanka and the Reform of the Saṅgha', *Journal of Indian and Buddhist Studies* 55, no. 3 (2007): 108–11.

Young, Jonathan A. 'Adornments of Virtue: The Production of Lay Buddhist Virtuosity in the *Upāsakajanālaṅkāra*'. PhD thesis, Cornell University, 2011.

Zachariae, Theodor. *Die Indischen Wörterbücher (Kośa)* (Grundriss der Indo-Arischen Philologie und Altertumskunde, Band 1, Heft 3B), edited by G. Bühler. Strasbourg: Trübner, 1897.

Załęski, Paweł. 'Ideal Types in Max Weber's Sociology of Religion: Some Theoretical Inspirations for a Study of the Religious Field', *Polish Sociological Review* 3, no. 171 (2010): 319–25.

Index

CPSIA information can be obtained
at www.ICGtesting.com
Printed in the USA
BVHW021309200920
589199BV00022B/509

9 781787 355163